Mountain Flowers

BRITISH WILDLIFE COLLECTION 4

Mountain Flowers

Michael Scott

BLOOMSBURY

Dedication

In memory of Sonia J Hackett (1951–1989)

Half title: Dwarf Cornel, a plant of upland peat habitats, *Laurie Campbell*
Previous spread: Moss Campion below the Old Man of Storr, Isle of Skye, *Laurie Campbell*

Bloomsbury Natural History
An imprint of Bloomsbury Publishing Plc

50 Bedford Square
London
WC1B 3DP
UK

1385 Broadway
New York
NY 10018
USA

www.bloomsbury.com

First published 2016

British Library Cataloguing-in-Publication Data
A catalogue record for this book is available from the British Library.

HB: ISBN 978-1-4729-2982-2

2 4 6 8 10 9 7 5 3 1

MIX
Paper from responsible sources
FSC® C008047

Edited and designed by D & N Publishing, Baydon, Wiltshire
Printed and bound in China by C&C Offset Printing Co., Ltd.

Jacket artwork by Carry Akroyd

Contents

Preface

If by some unlikely chance I can persuade but one reader ... to accompany me upon my wanderings and to share my triumphs and disappointments, then indeed shall I have achieved something worth achieving, and have added yet one more to the pleasures that I owe to plants.

This is a book I have long wanted to write, for reasons very similar to those described so eloquently above by John Raven (Raven & Raven, 2012). I am hugely grateful, first and foremost, to Andrew and Anne Branson, the founders of British Wildlife Publishing, who commissioned me to write the book, and to their successors at Bloomsbury Publishing who took on the imprint and saw the book to fruition.

I can trace my interest in mountain flowers back to my time at Aberdeen University. Although my botany degree concentrated mainly on plant physiology, I was lucky enough to enjoy several field courses at Bettyhill in Sutherland, where I first got to know the plants of Britain's arctic fringe. Then an honours-year field trip took me to Obergurgl in the Austrian Alps, where I was enthralled by the beauty of the flora, but intrigued by the contrasts with the Scottish mountain flora that I was beginning to know. Professors Charles Gimingham and Paul Jarvis and Dr Bernard Kenworthy were among my inspirations on these field trips. I also made my first trip to the Arctic in 1987 in expert company, joining a British Ecological Society field meeting at Abisko in the far north of Sweden (and I led my own field trips both there and to the Alps in later years).

But perhaps the greatest influence came in 1981, when I treated myself to a field course on mountain flowers at the Kindrogan Field Centre of the Scottish Field Studies Association (now the Field Studies

OPPOSITE PAGE:
Alpine Saxifrage in the Breadalbane hills, Perthshire.

Grant Roger, my late friend and mentor, in his natural habitat at Morrone Birkwood near Braemar in 1985.

Council) in Perthshire. The course was run by one of the true doyens of Scotland's mountain flora, J Grant Roger. Grant had graduated in botany from Aberdeen in 1944. In 1950, he became one of four staff in Scotland of the newly established Nature Conservancy, responsible for his home patch of north-east Scotland. This allowed him to spend many days in the hills, getting to know the flora of key montane sites and discovering new localities for species like Woolly Willow and Mountain Bladder-fern. Grant was not just expert at identifying mountain plants, he was also full of fascinating tales about the plants' discovery, ecology and folklore – and so Grant is the inspiration for this book, which I could never have contemplated without his insights.

For several years, I helped Grant run the mountain flowers course, then, when age sadly meant that Grant had to retreat from the hills, I continued running the course until 2004. Situated in the hills between Pitlochry and Blairgowrie, Kindrogan was an ideal centre because we could guarantee to see more than half of the British montane species in six busy days in the hills (I have also drawn on Kindrogan courses I attended on ferns, sedges and critical plants in writing this book). The many students on the course over the years, and the students on lecture courses on mountain flowers I ran for the Extramural Department of Edinburgh University, were a huge inspiration – and, ever since, I have wanted to write this book.

One of those students, Sonia Hackett, became my wife, and I shared many wonderful days on the hill with her. She brought her architect's eye to spotting subtle differences in the rocks and vegetation, which greatly aided our explorations. Tragically, she died much too young in a chairlift accident when we were botanising in the Alps, and I dedicate this book to her memory and her inspiration.

In recent years, I have spent less time in the British hills and more time exploring foreign floras, but the Arctic and mountains have always been my main inspiration. As a guest speaker on cruise ships, I have been able to botanise regularly in Iceland, northern Norway, Svalbard and Greenland. I have also drawn on that experience to inform this book, and I thank my second wife Sue for her enthusiasm and expertise on these trips – and for her patience while I have been writing this book.

To make the book as comprehensive as possible, I have delved back through past issues of *British Wildlife* and through the many publications of the Botanical Society of Britain and Ireland (BSBI) and the Botanical Society of Scotland (BSS). I have extracted lots of valuable insights from those and from the many field meetings organised by these two societies that I joined, especially in the Scottish mountains. It goes against all my instincts not to give precise references to validate these records and acknowledge their authors, but so many references would completely overwhelm the book. I have therefore cited only a few key references for readers who want to know more about the sites or the species concerned. Instead, I gratefully acknowledge all the botanists who tirelessly explore the hills and meticulously record their discoveries in the botanical press.

A mountain flowers field course in 1997, with me pontificating at the transplant site for Brown Bog-rush below Ben Vrackie in Perthshire. The 'student', Jim McIntosh, has since gone on to great things as Scottish Officer of the BSBI.

In particular, I have drawn heavily on the amazing insights in the *New Atlas of the British & Irish Flora* (Preston *et al.*, 2002), and I offer a debt of thanks to its editors and species authors, and to the many hundreds of individual botanists whose records made the *Atlas* possible. My hope is that my book will inspire many more to take to the hills and record their findings, so that we can add still further to our knowledge and understanding of Britain's mountain flowers. The wonderful new multivolume *Flora of Great Britain and Ireland* (Sell & Murrell, 1996–2014) has also been invaluable, and I only wish Volume One had been available when I was writing, to update my knowledge on ferns, willows and other key families. Needless to say, any errors of fact and interpretation are entirely mine!

In writing the book, I have troubled many busy people for the latest news about sites and species, and I would like to thank them all for their unfailing patience and helpfulness. In particular, I thank Andy Amphlett, Norman Baldock, William Berry, Ken Butler, John Clarke, Neil Cowie, John Crossley, Lynne Farrell, Lorne Gill, William Gloyer, Clare and Daniel Gordon, Peter Gordon, Alan Halewood, Peter Jepson, Miles King, Liz Lavery, Peter Llewellyn, Alex Longton, David Mardon, Ron McBeath, Pat and Angus Macdonald, Heather McHaffie, Eric Meek, Chris Miles, Adam Nicolson, David Parker, Faith and Sarah Raven, Tim Rich, Fred Rumsey, John Savory, Gill Smart, Ian Strachan, Pete Stroh, Des Thompson, Judith Turner, Kevin Walker and Tim Waters. My copy editor, Hugh Brazier, offered invaluable insights, especially on the changing interpretation of Welsh and Gaelic mountain names by the Ordnance Survey. I am also grateful to all the photographers whose images so greatly enhance the book, and to David Price-Goodfellow at D & N Publishing for his guidance on using these to most striking effect. Special thanks also to Carry Akroyd for turning my rough notes and reference photos into such a beautiful and inspiring cover. Finally, I thank my editor, Katy Roper, for applying her enquiring mind to my musings.

Michael Scott, Lochcarron, January 2016

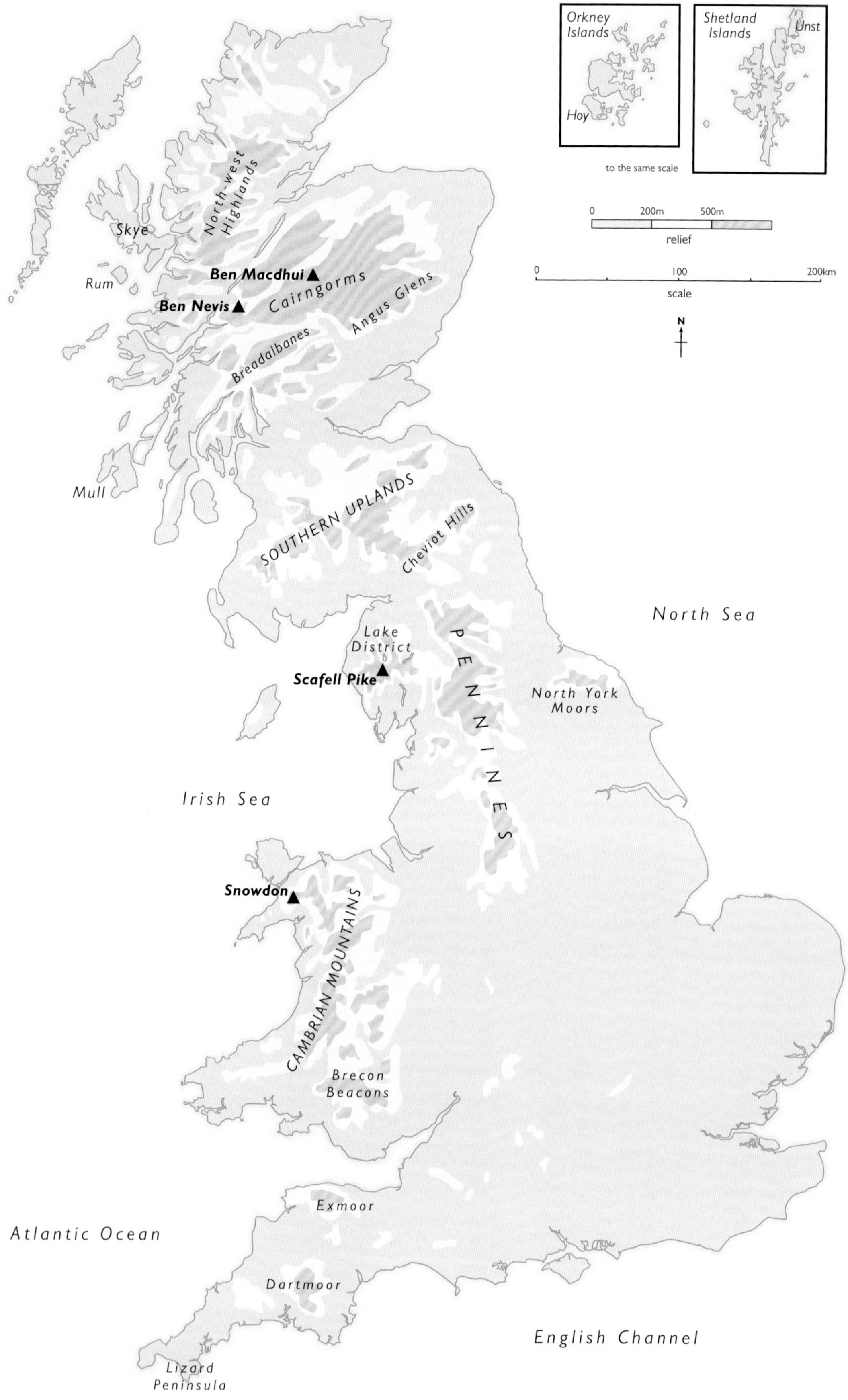
Orkney Islands
Hoy
Shetland Islands
Unst
to the same scale
0
200m
500m
relief
0
100
200km
scale
N
North-west Highlands
Skye
Rum
Ben Macdhui
Cairngorms
Ben Nevis
Angus Glens
Breadalbanes
Mull
SOUTHERN UPLANDS
Cheviot Hills
North Sea
Lake District
Scafell Pike
PENNINES
North York Moors
Irish Sea
Snowdon
CAMBRIAN MOUNTAINS
Brecon Beacons
Exmoor
Atlantic Ocean
Dartmoor
English Channel
Lizard Peninsula

Introduction: the allure of mountain flowers

chapter one

In late May 1980, I set off to climb a rather unremarkable hill, not far from Glenfinnan in the west Highlands of Scotland, with a precious book safely tucked in my rucksack. I was on the quest for one of our rarest mountain flowers, at its only British site. My book told me that the plant here 'occupies a mere acre or so of a rocky crest of hill, at a height of a little over 2,500 feet'. The book also included a black-and-white plate showing a wide view of the species' habitat. In the photo, the waters of a loch are just visible in the middle distance with some rather barren, undulating hills beyond. I had spent many hours poring over this photo, comparing it with Ordnance Survey maps of the area to identify the site. As I climbed, the vista came more and more to match the photograph, until I reached an area of twisted, craggy outcrops that looked very different from the surrounding terrain. And there, to my delight, were plentiful patches of the plant I was seeking, beautifully in flower.

The plant was Diapensia, discovered there, new to Britain, just 29 years previously by Charles Tebbutt, an ornithologist better known for his work on the birds of Huntingdonshire. The precious book that guided me to its home was *Mountain Flowers* by John Raven and Max Walters, in the New Naturalist series (Raven & Walters, 1956). It is still one of my most cherished and well-thumbed books. It is written with great insight and affection, and its scope is as sweeping as the view from the hills it discusses. The 95 pages of its regional section describe the key montane sites in Britain and Ireland and introduce some of the species associated with them. It is written with a mind to conservation, so the sites are rarely named, but instead described by inference. One site in Perthshire, for example, is identified as 'a few miles east

OPPOSITE PAGE: The main mountain areas of Britain.

south-east from [the previously described site], at the head of one of the several burns that feed the [River] Lochay from the south' – a strong clue for a determined mountain botanist, but hopefully enough to deter any unscrupulous collector.

The book has inspired many of my days on the hill. John Raven was a classical scholar and Fellow of King's College, Cambridge, who inherited from his father, Charles, a deep interest in wild flowers. An amateur in a true sense, he was one of the first people to document the discovery of several rare species in Britain in the 1950s. He was also a keen painter of these plants, and I am delighted to be able to publish three of his paintings in this book, thanks to his widow Faith and daughter Sarah.

TOP: My copy of *Mountain Flowers* beside the Diapensia that the book helped me find, in the hills above Glenfinnan in Inverness-shire.

ABOVE: John Raven, the co-author of *Mountain Flowers*, was one of the first botanists to visit Iceland Purslane after it was recognised as a new species to Britain in 1950. He painted it at its site on the Isle of Skye in August 1951.

A 21st-century perspective

That book by Raven and Walters has never been superseded, and I certainly cannot match the breadth of its erudition, but it was published in 1956. In the sixty years since, much has changed. The hills themselves remain essentially the same, but their management has altered markedly, as I will discuss in Chapter 19. Our rarest montane species are now protected by legislation, and most botanists these days use a camera to record their finds, rather than a vasculum to collect samples. The availability of transport and new access legislation means that many more people take regularly to the hills. Above all, our knowledge of the biology of mountain plants has increased exponentially, both as a result of the work of scientists and dedicated volunteers in Britain and through the enhanced exchange of knowledge with botanists in other countries.

In this book, therefore, I want to bring a 21st-century perspective to the understanding of our mountain flora. Rather than seeking to supplant Raven & Walters, I hope I can add to the earlier volume by approaching our mountain flora from a different angle. I want to concentrate as much on the plants themselves as on the sites, outlining the latest understanding of their ecology. Using that approach, I hope to encourage readers onto the hills to explore our montane flora for themselves.

As with all books in this series, the focus is British (and, for reasons of length, I have chosen to exclude Ireland, despite its wonderful botanical sites). However, I will also reflect a little on the ecology of British mountain plants in the Arctic, the mountains of Europe and beyond, where this allows us better to understand their distribution and behaviour in Britain. I have restricted my ambit to flowering plants and ferns, in the hope that later titles in the British Wildlife Collection can do justice to the wonderful mosses, liverworts, lichens and fungi of our mountain environments. Strictly speaking, therefore, this book should be called *Mountain Vascular Plants* – except that title would probably not do wonders for its sales!

A day in the hills

People who go walking amongst the highest summits of Britain are invariably known as 'hillwalkers'. Typically they use the rather deprecating term 'hill' for even the highest mountains. I will follow their lead and use hill and mountain interchangeably in the text.

I can think of few pastimes more satisfying and enjoyable than exploring the hills in search of mountain plants. It combines exercise for the body and the exhilaration of hillwalking with exercise for the mind and the exhilaration of discovery. There is a huge pleasure in planning a trip, poring over maps to select the most rewarding route and identify potentially interesting sites. Books, articles and websites need to be perused for clues on plants to look out for. I hope this book too might guide readers in interesting directions, but I have tried to avoid overly specific details that would spoil the thrill of discovery (and lead to unnecessary pressure on fragile sites). In planning a route, it is important to realistically assess your abilities, because walking in mountains can be much tougher than a map might suggest. It is vital to check the weather forecast and consider alternatives if the forecast is bad.

Once the planning is done, there is the preparation. Cleaning walking boots and packing the rucksack are all part of the hill experience. A good map (and the skill to use it), basic safety gear, and of course waterproofs, are essential in the kit. Mobile phones are useful, but should never be relied on for finding your way or for emergencies,

Some of the kit required for a safe botanising trip in the mountains. Add food to taste!

because signals all too often fail in the mountains. A good field guide is essential for identifying the plants you find. We are spoilt for choice these days, with several excellent guides, but my current favourite is the *Collins Flower Guide* (Streeter *et al.*, 2009) which combines superb illustrations with botanical keys to aid identification. A hand lens is useful to check the finer details sometimes needed to confirm a species' identity.

Then there is the day on the hill itself. The scenery never disappoints, constantly changing as you climb. The hills have many moods. For plant lovers they can be just as rewarding when shrouded in cloud and rain, because the plants are still there to be discovered. Finding these plants gives a welcome respite from the slog of climbing. Carefully exploring the species on a few square metres of species-rich crag or a grassy hill slope no bigger than a garden lawn can be every bit as rewarding as yomping over a whole mountain range.

Mountain botanising is always best done with friends or like-minded people, so that you can share pleasure in the scenery and the excitement of discoveries. My mentor Grant Roger called this the 'companionship of the hill'. I also think it is irresponsible to go into the hills alone. Even experienced hillwalkers can get into trouble, and I know from experience that a simple sprained ankle can become a huge burden on a remote hillside. It is unfair to rely on the skill and dedication of mountain rescue teams if you get into trouble.

Cul Beag, Wester Ross. Mountain scenery and healthy exercise inspire many people to go hillwalking, but mountain botanists have the added thrill of never knowing what intriguing plants they might discover.

On the trail of mountain flowers

There is, of course, the immediate question of how to define a mountain flower, which I will return to in the next chapter. The table at the end of that chapter (pp.30–35) lists 152 montane and submontane species that will be the central focus for the rest of the book. Each species will be the subject of a brief profile (indented in the text), usually where we first meet it on our journey; a few particularly intriguing plants are given an extended profile, as we will see shortly. If a visitor from foreign parts wanted to get to know all these species, he or she would be best advised to start in the south and get to know the relatively few montane species there, before progressing gradually northwards, with more new species likely to be discovered at each northward step. So that is the approach I have followed in this book. I have arranged the text as a journey, beginning at sites in the south of Britain that have only a few of the commoner montane species, then progressing northwards, meeting more species and some real rarities with each successive chapter.

Diapensia growing 1,220m up on Mount Washington in New Hampshire, USA, in a habitat very different from its sole British locality.

In practice, of course, most British readers will start at the mountain area most accessible to them, then explore outwards from here. But, very broadly, the first few chapters introduce the commoner species that are likely to be met, relatively easily, on most British mountains. The rarer species are only likely to be discovered, with rather greater effort, in areas described in later chapters where the mountains are generally higher and the climate tends to be more arctic.

Three-star enigmas

As it happens, Diapensia is the perfect example of the interest I want to explore in this book. The next time I saw the species, four years later, it was flowering prolifically close to the summit of Mount Washington, 1,916m above sea level in the mountains of New England. I have since found it in flower in arctic Sweden and in Greenland, and searched for it (so far without success) in Iceland. That perspective has helped me understand far more about the ecology of the species, but it leaves me all the more intrigued by one question: why does the species only grow abundantly in Britain on that one, rather unremarkable, windswept 'rocky crest' near Glenfinnan?

Mysteries of this sort will be a particular focus of this book, and there are plenty more of them. Why, for example, is Alpine Rock-cress found only in a single corrie in Scotland, when it grows almost as a weed in disturbed ground in the Alps and Arctic? Why (and how) is Iceland Purslane dispersed all the way from Iceland to Tierra del Fuego, yet in Britain it only grows on gravelly slopes on the Isles of Skye and Mull?

The three-star concept for the mountain enigmas in later chapters was inspired by the rarity scoring in my well-used copy of the 1956 *Collins Pocket Guide to Wild Flowers*.

The distribution of these plants seems to defy simple geographical explanation. They are all extremely localised in their British distribution, yet often widespread in the rest of their European alpine or arctic ranges. I call them 'three-star mountain enigmas'. They are three-star plants in the sense of the venerable but still valuable *Collins Pocket Guide to Wild Flowers* (McClintock & Fitter, 1956) – 'real rarities, growing in only a few places, and usually rare even there'.

These three-star enigmas are the botanist's equivalent of the birder's 'crippler'. I checked birding slang on birdforum.net, and this defines a 'crippler' as 'an extremely good tick ... not just for you, but for any birder, even the most jaded of veterans ... which leaves you emotionally crippled by its beauty/size/whatever, as well as its extreme rarity'. I love that description, which I think perfectly fits my three-star plants. They are not easy to find. Each one probably requires a special 'pilgrimage' to visit, but that makes it all the more satisfying when you find them. They include some of the most beautiful mountain plants (Alpine Sowthistle, Yellow Oxytropis and Alpine Forget-me-not are among my favourites), but all of them, in their way, shine like jewels in the uncompromising habitats in which they survive.

For me, the real fascination is trying to understand why these plants are so rare. We visit their sites not just to see and admire the plants, but to try to understand what is so special about the place that allows them to survive there. Sometimes there are particular features of their habitat that explain why they grow at one particular site, but often it is much more difficult to explain why they don't grow at other sites which appear equally suitable. Each of these three-star enigmas will merit an extended profile in a separate box, usually when we first meet them on our botanical exploration northwards. For some of these species, I hope to shed insight, based on the latest scientific researches of dedicated mountain botanists; for others, I can only pose questions, in the hope of inspiring someone to find an answer.

Intrigue and insight

In exploring these hills, we are following a distinguished tradition. There is a long list of early botanists, who explored Britain's remote mountains at a time when the limited transport infrastructure made every trip a major expedition. John Ray was amongst the first botanists to explore Snowdonia and the Lake District in the second half of the 17th century, discovering Alpine Bartsia, for example, in Westmorland. Edward Lhuyd (born Edward Lloyd) explored the mountains of Wales late in the same century, discovering Snowdon Lily, which long celebrated his memory in its scientific name of *Lloydia* (although sadly that name has now been dropped to fit the latest taxonomic understanding). In the Scottish mountains, Robert Sibbald, the first professor of botany at Edinburgh University, was amongst the pioneers (and thankfully Sibbaldia is still named in his honour). The Reverend John Lightfoot carried out extraordinary explorations in the mid-18th century of what were then still very remote corners of the kingdom, and he was followed by the likes of James Dickson and George Don (to whom I will return).

I have eschewed a chapter on the work of these men (and, in that generation, they were all men), because the history of the botanical exploration of Britain's mountains is well documented elsewhere (see for example Marren, 1999), but the work they did, and the discoveries they made, were truly remarkable, and we owe them all a great debt. I will try to acknowledge a few of the doughty individuals who have been exploring the hills in more recent years, because that long tradition continues.

To make the text as inclusive as possible (and to make best use of space), I have used common English names for species throughout, quoting scientific names only where they add particular insight. The scientific names of the mountain species are given in the table at the end of Chapter 2 and in their individual profiles, while those of the lowland species mentioned in the text are listed on pages 399–401. However, I would urge anyone seriously interested in our flora to learn to love these scientific names, which aid communication and provide an insight into the relationships between species.

I have had to use some technical terms in this book; some key ecological terms are defined on page 56, but I would refer readers to any plant field guide for an explanation of botanical terms. Similarly, I have had to use some geographical terms for mountain features, but most hillwalkers will know these anyway and I have tried to keep them to a minimum. I do not have the space to go into the fascinating geology of the mountain sites I cover. Instead I consider geology only in the most superficial sense of how the rocks affect the soil, as discussed in Chapter 3. I prefer to use the Welsh and Gaelic names for our mountains, because these are a rich element of our British culture. As a Scot, I also make no apology for using a few Scottish terms in the Scottish chapters; there are, after all, no streams in Scotland, only burns, and only one natural water body in Scotland is a lake (the Lake of Menteith) while the rest are lochs.

I write this book as an enthusiast for mountain plants and their environment, rather than as a dedicated field botanist. In doing so, I hope to share my enthusiasm for these resilient survivors in some of the most extreme environments of Britain. If I have one overarching ambition, it is to try to capture the imagination of the many hillwalkers who set off to 'bag' their Munros and Corbetts (distinct Scottish peaks whose summits exceed 3,000 or lie between 2,500 and 3,000 feet respectively, although these heights sound rather less inspiring at 914m and 762m) and their equivalents in Wales and England. If I can persuade a few of these hillwalkers to slow their relentless pace, to look around them as they climb, to venture off the beaten path and explore an interesting-looking crag or delve into the watery runnels that seep from the tops – in other words, to enjoy *seeing* a hill, rather than just conquering it – then this book will have been truly worthwhile.

Near the site of Norwegian Mugwort on Cul Mor ('the big back') in Wester Ross, looking towards Stac Pollaidh ('the stack of the pool'). Like Welsh names, Gaelic names are an important part of our culture.

What are mountain flowers?

chapter two

The summit plateau of the Cairngorm Mountains in Scotland, lying at an altitude of around 1,100m, is a vast expanse of bare rock and open granite gravel. Few plants survive here. Woolly Fringe-moss is one of the commoner plants, but amongst it can be found compact cushions of a select band of vascular plants, hugging low to the ground to escape the often bitter winds. One of these produces cushions of narrow, leathery leaves. In dry weather these become crisp and crunch underfoot; in autumn, they turn a deep orange-brown colour. The plant is easier to identify in July and August, when it produces globular clusters of pink flowers, perhaps 2cm in diameter, although these quickly wither and turn brown. You could hardly find a more punishingly montane environment, and this plant is clearly a mountain survivor. Yet the same species flowers much more prolifically a metre or two above sea level all around the coast of Britain, because this plant is Thrift or Sea Pink.

Ben Lawers in Perthshire is a mountain especially known for its rich montane flora. Beneath its most famous line of crags, there is an area of large, tumbled boulders of the area's characteristic mica-schist rock (see Chapter 13). In the damp shade of these boulders, one of the most delicate and elusive plants is Moschatel, much more typically a plant of deciduous woodlands and shaded hedge banks, mainly in southern Britain. Here it reaches its highest elevation, 1,065m above sea level, in another uncompromisingly montane environment. But does that qualify it as a mountain flower?

This occurrence of typically lowland species in the mountain environment is familiar to anyone botanising in the Scottish mountains. A thousand metres up on Ben Lawers, the commonest species include

OPPOSITE PAGE: Alpine Lady's-mantle, here growing below the Old Man of Storr on the Isle of Skye, is almost exclusively montane throughout its range.

Although we sometimes call it Sea Pink, Thrift is a common mountain plant. Here it is flowering 60km from the sea and 470m above sea level in Perthshire.

BELOW: Moschatel, a typical woodland plant, also grows 850m up on Ben Lawers in Perthshire, where it finds the rich soils and shady conditions it needs in the shelter of boulders.

Common Bent and Sheep's Fescue, common plants of grassy places at all altitudes across Britain. Also growing here, quite commonly, are Heath Bedstraw, Common Sorrel and Marsh Violet, species which are widespread on acid soils throughout Britain. There are also incontrovertibly montane species at that elevation, but they are generally more restricted in their occurrence.

That juxtaposition of lowland and upland species reflects a special quality of Britain's mountains, when compared to those of Europe. In the context of the Alps, for example, our highest peak of 1,343m would be regarded as no more than a foothill. This relatively low altitude, combined with the mild and humid oceanic climate of Britain, results in large expanses on many of our mountains being botanically dull, compared to the rich plant treasures of the high Alps. Upland grassland, with a small variety of near-ubiquitous species, dominates the slopes, and the truly montane species are confined to a few limited areas of extreme exposure and soil conditions, as discussed further in Chapter 4. Yet the elusiveness of these plant-rich sites greatly adds to the excitement of exploring Britain's mountain flora, and is one of the features that make it special in a world context.

High-livers

In one sense, all these plants are montane: they all are adapted to survive the particular environmental conditions they experience in Britain's mountains. However, if we exclude those species that also occur in lowland situations, is it possible to define a range of species which are exclusively montane in Britain?

The answer depends on our definition of a mountain. The dictionary definition of a 'high, steep hill' is not especially helpful. The normal ecological definition is that a mountain extends above the treeline, so that its upper slopes and crags are naturally treeless (although, as discussed in Chapter 4, the timberline might offer a more useful boundary than the treeline). As we will see in that chapter, the natural treeline in Britain is around 600–650m at present, although this varies with location and has undoubtedly varied over time. There is a distinctive set of plants which are primarily found above this altitude, and these essentially are the 'mountain flowers' to which this book is devoted. However, some of these occur, very locally, at sites which do not meet the normal definition of a mountain – on Dartmoor, for example, where the maximum altitude is only 621m. In fact, for the purposes of this book, I will define mountains as places where mountain flowers occur, rather than vice versa, even if that risks becoming a circular argument!

Lowland highlanders

One species that neatly illustrates the difficulty of defining mountain flowers, rather appropriately, is Mountain Avens. It is found at altitudes up to 1,035m on Ben Avon in the Cairngorms. It also grows 700m up on Helvellyn in the Lake District, and at 530m on the mountain rocks of Glyder Fawr, above Llyn Idwal in north Wales. But I have sat beside a lovely patch of Mountain Avens, no more than 10m above sea level on limestone rocks at Camas Malag on the Isle of Skye and watched Red throated Divers displaying on the tidal waters of Loch Slapin beyond. Its associates there include lowland species like Ramsons and Common Valerian. Nearby also is Roseroot, another species with a

Mountain Avens (inset), despite its name, grows just 10m above sea level on the windswept shore of Loch Slapin on the Isle of Skye.

montane and coastal distribution, and Stone Bramble which is much more typically montane.

The explanation of this intriguing mix of species lies in the special features of the British climate. As a result of our exposed position towards the north-west of Europe, we have areas where climate and exposure lead to an influence that is more arctic than montane. Indeed, if you draw a line on a map from Mont Blanc (4,807m), the highest point in western Europe, to the point at which the Arctic Circle bisects the east coast of Greenland (where arctic plants grow at sea level), the line runs directly past our highest peak on Ben Nevis. This neatly (if somewhat simplistically) emphasises our midway point ecologically between the Alps and the Arctic. Of course, it is not a simple straight-line projection, or Ben Nevis would have to be twice its height. However, it is probably pushing this simplistic model too far to suggest that this below-the-line

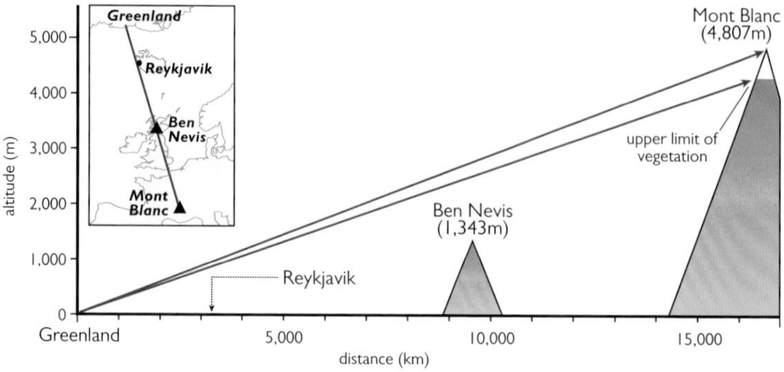

A simplified profile diagram showing the ecological place of Ben Nevis midway between the Alps and the Arctic (see text for explanation), with (inset) a map of the profile illustrated.

position helps explain the comparative impoverishment of Britain's mountain flora compared to the Arctic or the Alps!

Mountain specialists

The best way to define which British plants are truly montane is to take into account their ecology in the wider context of Europe and beyond. It means that we concentrate our attention on those plants which are broadly arctic and alpine in their distribution. Derek Ratcliffe used this approach to select a range of montane and submontane species, which he listed in his *Nature Conservation Review* (1977). Few scientists were more qualified to make this selection than Ratcliffe, who knew the British mountains supremely well from his studies of the montane flora and of the Peregrine Falcon. I have adapted his lists in compiling my selection of 152 montane and submontane plants (pp.30–35), excluding a few species from Ratcliffe's lists and adding a few more to best fit the scope of this book. In one or two cases, the plants listed by Ratcliffe are now generally regarded as subspecies, but they are sufficiently distinctive ecologically to merit inclusion in this book.

Broadly speaking, the 118 montane plants in this table are the ones most likely to be restricted denizens of remote, high-altitude sites in Britain, although some of the 34 submontane species, which are generally found rather lower on the mountains, are so specialised in their ecological requirements that they too are restricted and uncommon. The rest of this book will focus primarily on these 152 species and subspecies. I do not have space to go into detail on the more widespread species which also form an important component of montane plant communities, although I consider these briefly in the next chapter.

European associations

As shown in the table on pages 30–35, Ratcliffe defines each species according to its range in Europe (and beyond). The majority of the species are truly arctic-alpine (abbreviated in the table to AA), which is to say they are found in arctic and subarctic regions but also at relatively high altitudes in the mountains of central Europe. Twenty-three species are found in arctic and subarctic regions only, but not in the mountains of central Europe (AS), while just eight species are plants of the European mountains which have found their way to Britain but do not reach further north into the Arctic, so they are defined as purely alpine (A).

Seeing British mountain plants elsewhere in the world adds insight into their ecology here. Alpine Gentian is shy to flower at its two British sites (see Chapter 11), but is flowering extravagantly in this roadside verge in Narsarsuaq in Greenland.

The remainder, mainly submontane plants, belong to two groupings defined in an important earlier paper (Matthews, 1937). Continental northern (CN) species (of which 11 are listed) are 'species whose main area of distribution in Europe is central and northern, decreasing or becoming montane southwards'. Northern montane (NM) plants (26 species) are 'species of northern Europe generally absent from the low-lying plains but reappearing in montane or subalpine situations in central or southern Europe'. Two species or subspecies may be endemic, meaning they are found in the British mountains and nowhere else in the world (B).

There is an important conclusion to draw from this consideration of the European distribution of our mountain plants. Although the British mountains may be regarded as an impoverished outpost of the continental European mountains, plants meet on the British mountains which do not grow together anywhere else in the world. That is an important feature of British mountains, and it is part of the special fascination of our montane flora.

Limits of distribution

The list of mountain plants shows data on the highest and lowest altitudes at which the species have been recorded in Britain, based on Pearman & Corner (2004) but with records updated to 2015 on the bsbi.org.uk website. This is a provisional list. The authors state that 'there is much more work to be done to establish the true altitudinal limits of plants in Britain', and I would encourage readers to report on the website any records which they find outside the stated ranges of the species.

From this list of altitudinal limits, it is interesting to draw out those species that are high-altitude record-holders (see table), found above the extreme of 1,300m topped by only two of our peaks, Ben Nevis and Ben Macdui, by 44m and 9m respectively.

High-altitude record holders

Fir Clubmoss (M)	Moss Campion (M)	Stiff Sedge (M)
Parsley Fern (N)	Bilberry* (M)	Mat-grass* (M)
Alpine Saxifrage (M)	Dwarf Cudweed (M)	Viviparous Fescue (N)
Starry Saxifrage (N)	Three-leaved Rush (M)	Alpine Hair-grass (N)
Sibbaldia (N)	Curved Wood-rush (M)	Wavy Hair-grass* (M)
Dwarf Willow (N)	Spiked Wood-rush (M)	

Species found above 1,300m on Ben Nevis (N) and Ben Macdui (M). Species marked * are not exclusively montane.

Three of these record-holders are not montane species but are widespread plants of upland grasslands. Satisfyingly, the apparent altitude record holder is Starry Saxifrage, a delicate but attractive species recorded just 4m below the summit of Ben Nevis.

Site richness

Another use of Ratcliffe's lists is the one for which they were originally compiled. Ratcliffe (1977) set out to establish a scientifically robust mechanism for identifying the nature conservation sites of highest biological importance in Great Britain. The list of montane plants was therefore used to produce a species 'score' for our main mountain sites. This showed that the area of Caenlochan Glen and Glen Clova in Angus was the richest site, with 79 montane and submontane species. The Cairngorms came second, with 77 species, but over an area more than six times as large and including areas with base-rich schist rocks as well as the more typical granite of the main mountain massif. The area of Ben Lawers and Meall nan Tarmachan in Perthshire came third, with 75 species. However, because this covers a smaller area than the top two, I have always suspected that it must be the part of Britain with the highest density of montane species, and therefore the most rewards for botanists within a limited area.

As I was preparing this book, it occurred to me that all the information for testing my suspicion about plant densities was available in the remarkable electronic databases developed by the BSBI. I am very grateful to Andy Amphlett, the botanical recorder for Banffshire and a 'whizz' with data, for carrying out the analysis I wanted for this book. He brought together the distribution maps for all 152 species listed on pages 30–35, to show the total numbers of these species in each of the hectads used for botanical recording (corresponding to the 10km × 10km squares on Ordnance Survey maps). The result is shown in the figure overleaf.

The Angus mountains, from Glen Clova west to these crags of Caenlochan Glen, have the richest range of montane and submontane plants in the whole of Britain.

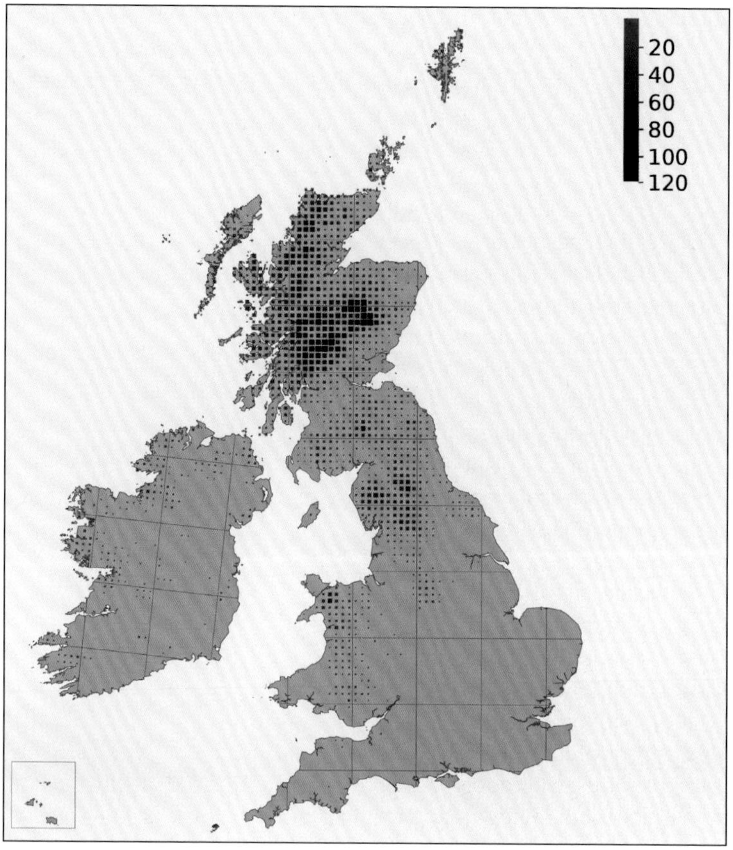

The number of montane species recorded in each 10km grid square across Britain. Only squares with a minimum of five species are shown. Reproduced courtesy of the Botanical Society of Britain and Ireland.

Because a few submontane species occasionally turn up in lowland areas, there are a few strange results, especially around Scottish coasts. However, the map neatly highlights all the upland areas I have selected to cover in later chapters. Snowdonia clearly has the biggest range of species in Wales, shown by the larger squares. The Pennines and Lake District are the richest sites in England, with the hectad that includes Cronkley Fell in Upper Teesdale having the darkest colour, with 63 species. In Scotland, the north-west Highlands has a high diversity of montane species, and Rum stands out amongst the islands for its richness. The map shows that the richest areas of all, in terms of species numbers, lie in a band from the Cairngorms south to the glens of Angus, then west along the Breadalbane hills to Argyll. And it also proves what I always suspected: the square with the highest total of montane plants (103 species) is the one around Ben Lawers, closely followed by one that includes the Cairnwell and Glas Maol in Angus, with 101 species. We will return to all these wonderful, plant-rich areas in later chapters.

List of British mountain vascular plants

The table which follows draws heavily on Ratcliffe (1977). It includes virtually all the species listed as typically montane in Table 27 of that book, highlighted in mauve. It also includes a range of submontane species from Table 28, but I have excluded those that I do no regard as true mountain plants. I have added a small number of other mountain species that I particularly wanted to discuss in the book, bringing the overall total to 152 species. The final **Page** column lists the page on which each of these species is profiled in this book.

I have updated the nomenclature and taxonomic order to Stace (2010) and have largely followed his English names, but, where an earlier scientific name is used in Ratcliffe, I have also included this. Species marked § have full legal protection in the UK. *** after the common name of a plant means it is one of the 'three-star mountain enigmas' which are given extended treatment in the text (see Chapter 1). The column headed **Ecol** shows the broad soil requirements for the species. This and the column headed **Euro. dist.** (European distribution) are drawn directly from Ratcliffe (1977), and there is an explanation of the codes below.

The **Alt. range** column shows the lowest and highest recorded altitudes of the species in Britain, based on data in Pearman & Corner (2004), with published records updated to 2015. For some species, this only quotes the upper known altitudinal limit, in which case the symbol < is used (although this does not imply that the species occurs at all elevations below this maximum). In a few cases, the lowest elevation is quoted as 'sl' = sea level. The **N/S** column highlights those species which have the northernmost (N) or southernmost (S) extremes of their presumed native European range in Britain, based on Preston (2007).

Key to broad ecological requirements (Ecol. column)

- A Acidic: soil pH less than 4.8, with less than 30mg of exchangeable calcium per 100g
- M Medium basic: soil pH 4.8–6.0, with 30–300mg of exchangeable calcium per 100g
- C Calcareous: soil pH more than 6.0, with more than 300mg of exchangeable calcium per 100g
- S Special: soils in which a mineral other than calcium is prominent, or with an unusual balance of minerals

Key to European distribution

- AA Arctic-alpine
- AS Arctic-subarctic
- A Alpine
- NM Northern montane
- CN Continental montane
- C Continental
- B British endemic

Derek Ratcliffe, the distinguished natural historian and scientist whose lists of montane and submontane plants form the basis for the species selection in this book.

Species	Recommended English name	Ecol.	Alt. range	Euro. dist.	N/S	Page
LYCOPODIACEAE (Clubmoss family)						
Huperzia selago (= *Lycopodium selago*)	FIR CLUBMOSS	A	5–1305m	NM		79
Lycopodium annotinum	INTERRUPTED CLUBMOSS	A	5–1145m	NM		220
Diphasiastrum alpinum (= *Lycopodium alpinum*)	ALPINE CLUBMOSS	A	<1220m	NM		100
Diphasiastrum complanatum ssp. *issleri*	ISSLER'S CLUBMOSS	A	<960m	AA		314
SELAGINELLACEAE (Lesser Clubmoss family)						
Selaginella selaginoides	LESSER CLUBMOSS	M/C	<1170m	AA		108
PTERIDACEAE (Ribbon Fern family)						
Cryptogramma crispa	PARSLEY FERN	A	50–1330m	NM		84
ASPLENIACEAE (Spleenwort family)						
Asplenium viride	GREEN SPLEENWORT	C	<988m	AA		86
Asplenium septentrionale	FORKED SPLEENWORT	A	<1060m	NM		210
WOODSIACEAE (Lady-fern family)						
Athyrium distentifolium (= *A. alpestre*)	ALPINE LADY-FERN	A/M	455–1220m	AA		235
Gymnocarpium robertianum (= *Thelypteris robertiana*)	LIMESTONE FERN	C	<585m	NM		130
Cystopteris montana	MOUNTAIN BLADDER-FERN	C	490–1125m	AA		279
Woodsia ilvensis §	OBLONG WOODSIA ***	M	355–700m	NM		200
Woodsia alpina §	ALPINE WOODSIA	C	430–975m	AA		249
DRYOPTERIDACEAE (Buckler-fern family)						
Polystichum lonchitis	HOLLY FERN	M/C	180–1065m	AA		131
Dryopteris oreades (= *D. abbreviata*)	MOUNTAIN MALE-FERN	A	100–850m	NM	N	147
Dryopteris submontana (= *D. villarii*)	RIGID BUCKLER-FERN	C	<465m	A		139
CUPRESSACEAE (Juniper family)						
Juniperis communis ssp. *nana*	DWARF JUNIPER	A/M	<850m (ssp)	NM		358
RANUNCULACEAE (Buttercup family)						
Trollius europaeus	GLOBEFLOWER	M/C	<1090m	NM		101
Thalictrum alpinum	ALPINE MEADOW-RUE	M/C	<1209m	AA		102
SAXIFRAGACEAE (Saxifrage family)						
Saxifraga hirculus §	MARSH SAXIFRAGE ***	M/C	170–750m	AA		168
Saxifraga nivalis	ALPINE SAXIFRAGE	M/C	325–1300m	AA		102
Saxifraga stellaris	STARRY SAXIFRAGE	A/M/C	<1340m	AA		103
Saxifraga oppositifolia	PURPLE SAXIFRAGE	M/C	<1211m	AA		87

Species	Recommended English name	Ecol.	Alt. range	Euro. dist.	N/S	Page
Saxifraga aizoides	YELLOW MOUNTAIN SAXIFRAGE (YELLOW SAXIFRAGE)	M/C	sl–1175m	AA		184
Saxifraga rivularis	HIGHLAND SAXIFRAGE	A/M	795–1240m	AS	S	305
Saxifraga cernua §	DROOPING SAXIFRAGE	C	830–1138m	AA		288
Saxifraga hypnoides	MOSSY SAXIFRAGE	M/C	10–1210m	NM	S	88
Saxifraga cespitosa §	TUFTED SAXIFRAGE ***	C	520–1180m	AS	S	109
CRASSULACEAE (Stonecrop family)						
Sedum rosea	ROSEROOT	M/C	<1166m	AA		89
Sedum villosum	HAIRY STONECROP	M	50–1138m	CN		171
FABACEAE (Pea family)						
Astragalus alpinus	ALPINE MILK-VETCH	C	650–770m	AA		267
Oxytropis halleri	PURPLE OXYTROPIS	M/C	<760m	A	N	267
Oxytropis campestris	YELLOW OXYTROPIS ***	C	75–640m	AA		247
Vicia orobus	WOOD BITTER-VETCH	A/M	560m	NM		206
POLYGALACEAE (Milkwort family)						
Polygala amarella (= *P. amara*)	DWARF MILKWORT (BITTER MILKWORT)	C	<530m	CN		157
ROSACEAE (Rose family)						
Dryas octopetala	MOUNTAIN AVENS	C	sl–1035m	AA		112
Rubus chamaemorus	CLOUDBERRY	A	90–1160m	AS		188
Rubus arcticus	ARCTIC BRAMBLE (non-native?)	A	?	AS		261
Rubus saxatilis	STONE BRAMBLE	M/C	<975m	NM		138
Potentilla fruticosa	SHRUBBY CINQUEFOIL	M/C	<700m	NM		147
Potentilla rupestris §	ROCK CINQUEFOIL ***	M	90–150m	NM		362
Potentilla crantzii	ALPINE CINQUEFOIL	M/C	70–1065m	AA		132
Sibbaldia procumbens	SIBBALDIA	A/M/C	210–1310m	AA		228
Alchemilla alpina	ALPINE LADY'S-MANTLE	A/M/C	<1270m	AA		183
BETULACEAE (Birch family)						
Betula nana	DWARF BIRCH	A	150–860m	AA		154
SALICEAE (Willow family)						
Salix lapponum	DOWNY WILLOW	M/C	210–1125m	AA		198
Salix lanata	WOOLLY WILLOW	M/C	610–1035m	AS	S	253
Salix arbuscula	MOUNTAIN WILLOW	M/C	125–870m	AA	S	261
Salix myrsinites	WHORTLE-LEAVED WILLOW	M/C	180–1000m	AA	S	254
Salix herbacea	DWARF WILLOW (LEAST WILLOW)	A/M	sl–1310m	AA		89
Salix reticulata	NET-LEAVED WILLOW (RETICULATE WILLOW)	C	520–1125m	AA		236

Species	Recommended English name	Ecol.	Alt. range	Euro. dist.	N/S	Page
VIOLACEAE (Violet family)						
Viola rupestris	TEESDALE VIOLET ***	C	<600m	NM		150
Viola lutea	MOUNTAIN PANSY	M	<1050m	A	N	123
GERANIACEAE (Cranesbill family)						
Geranium sylvaticum	WOOD CRANESBILL	M/C	<1005m	CN		133
ONAGRACEAE (Willowherb family)						
Epilobium anagallidifolium	ALPINE WILLOWHERB	A/M	155–1190m	AA		192
Epilobium alsinifolium	CHICKWEED WILLOWHERB	M	120–1140m	AA		192
BRASSICACEAE (Cabbage family)						
Arabidopsis petraea (= *Cardaminopsis petraea*)	NORTHERN ROCK-CRESS	A/M	sl–1220m	AA		279
Arabis alpina §	ALPINE ROCK-CRESS ***	–	820–850m	AA		338
Draba norvegica	ROCK WHITLOW-GRASS	M/C	310–1202m	AS		271
Draba incana	HOARY WHITLOW-GRASS	M/C	<1157m	AA		122
Noccaea caerulescens (= *Thlaspi alpestre*)	ALPINE PENNY-CRESS	C/S	4–940m	A		121
Cochlearia pyrenaica (ssp. *alpina*) (= *C. officinalis* ssp. *alpina*)	ALPINE SCURVY-GRASS	A/M/C	135–960m	AA		104
POLYGONACEAE (Knotweed family)						
Persicaria vivipara (= *Polygonum viviparum*)	ALPINE BISTORT	M/C	sl–1210m	AA		158
Koenigia islandica	ICELAND PURSLANE ***	M	314–693m	AS	S	342
Oxyria digyna	MOUNTAIN SORREL	M/C	sl–1240m	AA		104
CARYOPHYLLACEAE (Pink family)						
Arenaria norvegica ssp. *norvegica* §	ARCTIC SANDWORT ***	C/S	15–650m	AS	S	350
Arenaria norvegica ssp. *anglica* §	ENGLISH SANDWORT ***	C	295–410m	B		350
Minuartia verna	SPRING SANDWORT	C/S	<875m	AA		121
Minuartia rubella	MOUNTAIN SANDWORT	C	120–1180m	AS	S	221
Minuartia stricta §	TEESDALE SANDWORT (BOG SANDWORT) ***	C	490–510m	AA		152
Minuartia sedoides (= *Cherleria sedoides*)	MOSSY CYPHEL	A/M/C	165–1213m	A	N	272
Cerastium cerastoides	STARWORT MOUSE-EAR	A/M	335–1240m	AA		307
Cerastium alpinum	ALPINE MOUSE-EAR	M/C	300–1214m	AA		236
Cerastium nigrescens (= *C. arcticum*)	ARCTIC MOUSE-EAR	A/M/C	570–1240m	AS	S	305
Cerastium nigrescens var. *nigrescens* (= *C. nigrescens*)	SHETLAND MOUSE-EAR ***	S	–	AS		374
Sagina nivalis (= *S. intermedia*)	SNOW PEARLWORT	M	640–1190m	AS	S	289
Sagina saginoides	ALPINE PEARLWORT	M/C	460–1213m	AA		289

Species	Recommended English name	Ecol.	Alt. range	Euro. dist.	N/S	Page
Sagina x normaniana (= *S. normaniana*)	SCOTTISH PEARLWORT	M/C	<950m	AA		289
Silene acaulis	MOSS CAMPION	A/M/C	sl–1305m	AA		116
Silene viscaria (= *Lychnis viscaria*)	STICKY CATCHFLY (RED GERMAN CATCHFLY)	S	sl–475m	CN		209
Silene suecica (= *Lychnis alpina*) §	ALPINE CATCHFLY ***	S	600–870m	AA		178
CORNACEAE (Dogwood family)						
Cornus suecica (= *Chamaepericlymenum suecicum*)	DWARF CORNEL	A	135–915m	AS		190
POLEMONIACEAE (Jacob's-ladder family)						
Polemonium caeruleum	JACOB'S-LADDER	C	190–?	NM		127
PRIMULACEAE (Primrose family)						
Primula farinosa	BIRD'S-EYE PRIMROSE	M/C	<570m	NM		132
Trientalis europaea	CHICKWEED WINTERGREEN	A	<1100m	NM		205
DIAPENSIACEAE (Diapensia family)						
Diapensia lapponica §	DIAPENSIA ***	A	<780m	AS	S	333
ERICACEAE (Heather family)						
Arctostaphylos uva-ursi	BEARBERRY	A/M/C	sl–760m	AA		185
Arctostaphylos alpinus (= *Arctous alpinus*)	ARCTIC BEARBERRY	A	100–1100m	AA		327
Empetrum nigrum (ssp. *nigrum*)	CROWBERRY	A	<760m+	AA		82
Empetrum nigrum (ssp. *hermaphroditum*) (= *E. hermaphroditum*)	MOUNTAIN CROWBERRY	A/M/C	sl–1130m	AA		113
Phyllodoce caerulea §	BLUE HEATH ***	A	660–800m	AA		317
Kalmia procumbens (= *Loiseleuria procumbens*)	TRAILING AZALEA (MOUNTAIN AZALEA)	A	240–1195m	AA		221
Andromeda polifolia	BOG ROSEMARY	A	<735m	CN		123
Vaccinium microcarpum	SMALL CRANBERRY	A	sl–850m	NM		312
Vaccinium vitis-idaea	COWBERRY (CRANBERRY Scot.)	A/M	30–1095m	AA		83
Vaccinium uliginosum	BOG BILBERRY (BOG WHORTLEBERRY)	A/M/C	8–1130m	AA		191
Pyrola media	INTERMEDIATE WINTERGREEN	A/M	<550m	CN		222
Orthilia secunda	SERRATED WINTERGREEN	A/M/C	30–730m	CN		223
RUBIACEAE (Bedstraw family)						
Galium boreale	NORTHERN BEDSTRAW	M/C	<1065m	CN		90
GENTIANACEAE (Gentian family)						
Gentiana verna §	SPRING GENTIAN	C	370–730m	A		159
Gentiana nivalis §	ALPINE GENTIAN (SNOW GENTIAN)	C	730–1095m	AA		237

Species	Recommended English name	Ecol.	Alt. range	Euro. dist.	N/S	Page
BORAGINACEAE (Borage family)						
Myosotis stolonifera (= *M. brevifolia*)	PALE FORGET-ME-NOT	M	130–820m	B		172
Myosotis alpestris	ALPINE FORGET-ME-NOT ***	C	685–1180m	AA	N	286
VERONICACEAE (Speedwell family)						
Veronica alpina	ALPINE SPEEDWELL	M/C	710–1190m	AA		223
Veronica fruticans	ROCK SPEEDWELL	C	540–1100m	AA		238
LAMIACEAE (Dead-nettle family)						
Ajuga pyramidalis	PYRAMIDAL BUGLE	A/M	15–650m	NM		359
OROBANCHACEAE (Broomrape family)						
Bartsia alpina	ALPINE BARTSIA	M/C	245–950m	AA		146
ASTERACEAE (Daisy family)						
Saussurea alpina	ALPINE SAW-WORT	A/M/C	sl–1207m	AA		224
Cirsium heterophyllum	MELANCHOLY THISTLE	M/C	<760m	CN		134
Cicerbita alpina §	ALPINE SOWTHISTLE (ALPINE BLUE-SOWTHISTLE) ***	M	530–1090m	AA		232
Antennaria dioica	MOUNTAIN EVERLASTING	A/M/C	<907m	NM		159
Gnaphalium norvegicum	HIGHLAND CUDWEED	A/M	600–980m	AA		239
Gnaphalium supinum	DWARF CUDWEED	A	<1305m	AA		224
Erigeron borealis §	BOREAL FLEABANE (ALPINE FLEABANE)	C	640–1100m	AS	S	240
Artemisia norvegica	NORWEGIAN MUGWORT ***	A/M	700–907m	AS	S	357
Homogyne alpina §	PURPLE COLTSFOOT ***	C	600m	A	N	250
APIACEAE (Carrot family)						
Meum athamanticum	SPIGNEL	A/M	<610m	CN	N	213
TOFIELDIACEAE (Scottish Asphodel family)						
Tofieldia pusilla	SCOTTISH ASPHODEL	M/C	40–975m	AA		160
LILIACEAE (Lily family)						
Gagea serotina (= *Lloydia serotina*) §	SNOWDON LILY ***	C	550–760m	AA		98
ORCHIDACEAE (Orchid family)						
Neottia cordata (= *Listera cordata*)	LESSER TWAYBLADE	A	<1065m	NM		193
JUNCACEAE (Rush family)						
Juncus alpinoarticulatus (= *J. alpino-articulatus*)	ALPINE RUSH	M/C	128–880m	NM		161
Juncus biglumis	TWO-FLOWERED RUSH	M/C	370–1137m	AA		272
Juncus triglumis	THREE-FLOWERED RUSH	M/C	60–1175m	AA		161
Juncus castaneus	CHESTNUT RUSH	M/C	610–990m	AA		281

Species	Recommended English name	Ecol.	Alt. range	Euro. dist.	N/S	Page
Juncus trifidus	THREE-LEAVED RUSH	A/M	240–1305m	AA		225
Luzula arcuata	CURVED WOOD-RUSH	A	760–1305m	AS	S	307
Luzula spicata	SPIKED WOOD-RUSH	A/M	275–1305m	AA		225
CYPERACEAE (Sedge family)						
Schoenus ferrugineus	BROWN BOG-RUSH ***	M	200–360m	CN		263
Kobresia simpliciuscula	FALSE SEDGE	C	360–1065m	AA		282
Carex lachenalii	HARE'S-FOOT SEDGE	A	950–1150m	AA		308
Carex x grahamii (= *C. stenolepis*)	MOUNTAIN BLADDER-SEDGE	M	–	?		254
Carex saxatilis	RUSSET SEDGE	A/M/C	460–1164m	AS		273
Carex capillaris	HAIR SEDGE	C	10–1150m	AA		162
Carex vaginata	SHEATHED SEDGE	M/C	380–1150m	AA		207
Carex atrofusca	SCORCHED ALPINE-SEDGE	C	680–1000m	AA		291
Carex rariflora	MOUNTAIN BOG-SEDGE	A	790–1125m	AS	S	229
Carex atrata	BLACK ALPINE-SEDGE	M/C	550–1095m	AA		241
Carex norvegica	CLOSE-HEADED ALPINE-SEDGE	M/C	700–975m	AA		255
Carex bigelowii	STIFF SEDGE	A/M	15–1305m	AA		113
Carex microglochin	BRISTLE SEDGE	M/C	610–975m	AA		292
Carex pauciflora	FEW-FLOWERED SEDGE	A	<650m	NM		186
Carex rupestris	ROCK SEDGE	C	sl–935m	AA		226
POACEAE (Grass family)						
Festuca vivipara	VIVIPAROUS FESCUE (GRASS)	A/M	<1335m	AA	S	91
Poa flexuosa	WAVY MEADOW-GRASS	A	760–1120m	AS		257
Poa glauca (= *P. balfourii*)	GLAUCOUS MEADOW-GRASS	M/C	300–1110m	AA		242
Poa alpina	ALPINE MEADOW-GRASS	M/C	430–1240m	AA		242
Sesleria caerulea (= *S. albicans*)	BLUE MOOR-GRASS	C	sl–1005m	A		163
Deschampsia cespitosa ssp. *alpina* (= *D. alpina*)	ALPINE HAIR-GRASS	A/M	395–1234m	AS		243
Alopecurus magellanicus (= *A. alpinus*)	ALPINE FOXTAIL	A/M	600–1220m	AS		173
Phleum alpinum	ALPINE CAT'S-TAIL	M/C	610–1220m	AA		228
Melica nutans	MOUNTAIN MELICK (GRASS)	M/C	<820m	NM		124
Elymus caninus (var. *donianus*) (= *Agropyron donianum*)	DON'S COUCH (DON'S TWITCH)	C	–	AS		352

Origins and survival of our mountain flora

chapter three

Some of the plants that grow in British mountains are very far removed from their nearest sites elsewhere in Europe. It is a long way, for example, from Snowdonia to the next nearest site of Snowdon Lily in the Alps, or from Upper Teesdale to the Pyrenees in the case of Shrubby Cinquefoil. This leads to two intriguing questions. First, how did these plants find their way to their isolated locations in the British mountains? And second, having found their way to these locations, what has allowed them to survive there? The second question will be the focus for much of the rest of the book, as I profile the plants and the sites where they grow. However, to understand their present occurrence, we also need to answer the first question about their origins, and, to do that, we need to explore the ecological history of our island.

The grip of the ice

Geological evidence suggests that approximately 2.6 million years ago, in the geological epoch called the Pliocene (see table overleaf), the northern hemisphere entered a period of extreme cold, perhaps triggered by changes in the circulation patterns of ocean currents. The Arctic ice-cap began to form and extensive ice-sheets extended southwards. South of the ice, tundra-type vegetation stretched southwards to the Mediterranean Sea, with large glaciers in the mountains. As the ice advanced, sea levels fell and concentrations of carbon dioxide in the atmosphere reduced. Evidence of this is captured in the geological record, helping us to understand these changes.

OPPOSITE PAGE: Dwarf Cornel, Cloudberry, Bog Bilberry and Crowberry are some of the 'peat alpines' that grow on deep peat banks in Britain.

A guide to the terminology used to describe the time periods of geological events and the ages of rocks. Some controversy remains about the precise dating of boundaries between time periods. mya, million years ago; BP, years before present.

A geological perspective on time

Eon	Precambrian	4,560–543 mya
Eon	Phanerozoic	543 mya – present day
Era	Palaeozoic	543–252 mya
Period	Cambrian	543–490 mya
	Ordovician	490–443 mya
	Silurian	443–418 mya
	Devonian	418–354 mya
	Carboniferous	354–290 mya
	Permian	290–252 mya
Era	Mesozoic	252–65 mya
Period	Triassic	252–199.5 mya
	Jurassic	199.5–142 mya
	Cretaceous	142–65 mya
Era	Cenozoic	65 mya – present day
Period	Tertiary	65–1.8 mya
Epoch	Palaeocene	65–54.8 mya
	Eocene	54.8–33.5 mya
	Oligocene	33.5–24 mya
	Miocene	24–5 mya
	Pliocene	5.0–1.8 mya
Period	Quaternary	1.8 mya – present day
Epoch	Pleistocene	1.8 mya – c.11,500 BP
	Holocene	11,500 BP – present day

Conditions did not remain stable during the predominantly cold period which followed. There were numerous fluctuations in the climate. Short interglacial periods, with temperatures similar to those of today, briefly broke the grip of the ice. Over the last million years, the extent of the ice-sheets has oscillated at intervals of around 100,000 years, with a gradual build-up of ice, followed by a rapid thaw and a short interglacial period before the ice began to grow once more. This periodicity may relate at least partly to the shape of the Earth's orbit around the Sun. The most recent period of glaciation began around 110,000 years ago, and at its peak, around 28,000 years ago, ice covered Britain north of a line from south Wales to north Yorkshire (see map opposite). With so much water locked up in ice, sea levels were lower and there was a land bridge between the ice-free south of Britain and the European mainland.

This most recent phase of the Ice Age in Europe is generally known as the Weichselian period. Geological and fossil records from this period are plentiful, but tend to be disjointed and sometimes contradictory. However, based on geological and other records, the period is sometimes divided into the Early Weichselian (70,000–50,000 BP), the Middle Weichselian (50,000–15,000 BP) when the ice

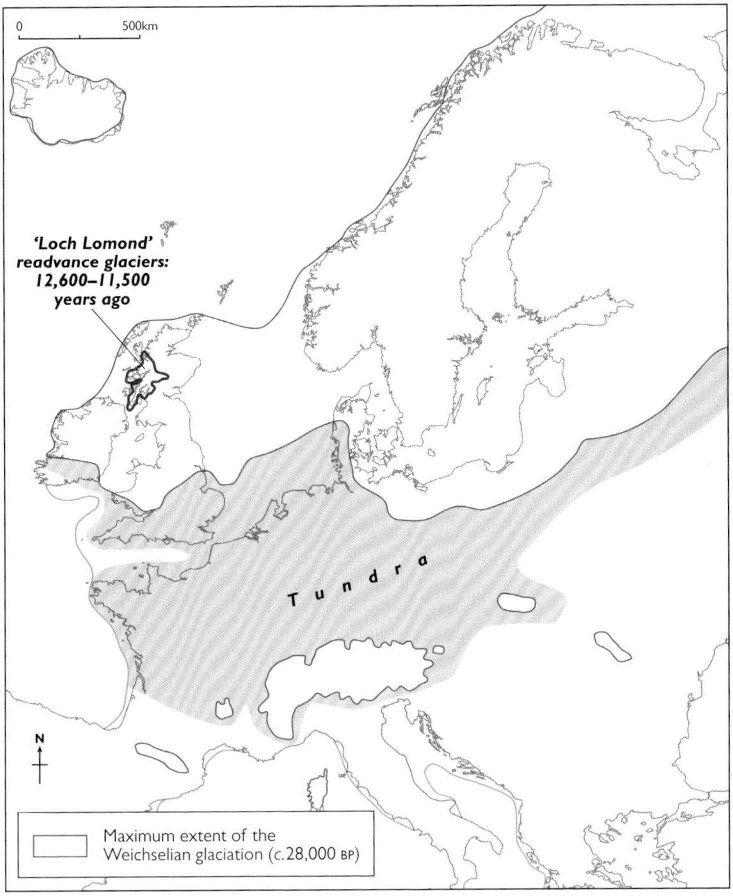

The maximum extent of the ice-sheet over Britain about 28,000 years ago.

was at its greatest extent, and the Late Weichselian (15,000–10,000 BP) when the ice was in retreat.

The warming world

Fifteen thousand years ago, the climate was warming and most of England and eastern Scotland had become free of ice. Sometime around 12,000 years ago, cold temperatures returned for around 600 years. The glaciers briefly advanced once more, covering the West Highlands from Wester Ross to Loch Lomond, with ice-caps in the mountains of the central Highlands. Then around 11,500 years ago the climate warmed very rapidly over just a few decades, the ice disappeared, and the glacial period was finally at an end. This marks the start of the Holocene or modern epoch, when many of the biggest influences on the environment were from human rather than natural factors.

The rocks and 'primitive soils' around modern-day glaciers – as here at Langjökull in Iceland – give an idea of how Britain must have appeared as the Ice Age glaciers retreated.

As an aside, it is worth noting that when I was at university in the early 1970s we were told that we were currently living in a warm interglacial period that was overdue to end and that, perhaps within a few decades or certainly centuries, we should expect to see the ice expand once more. It was therefore wrong to talk about the 'end of the Ice Age' 15,000 years ago. Strictly speaking, we should refer to 'the end of the most recent glacial advance of the present Ice Age'. However, I may revert to the technically incorrect but widely used and shorter phrase elsewhere in the book, because it is at least intelligible! It is a measure of just how seriously humans are impacting on the climate with our emissions of greenhouse gases that concern about a return to the Ice Age is now discounted, and the predictions instead are of rapidly rising global temperatures.

Piecing together the past

We can produce a detailed picture of how the vegetation of Britain changed over this period, thanks to a variety of natural archives. You only need to look in your garden to see the constant rain of dead leaves, seeds and other plant material that accumulates there from the surrounding vegetation. Microscopic pollen is also plentiful in the atmosphere, as any hay-fever sufferer knows. Normally, these plant materials quickly decay and disappear, but in certain circumstances they are locked up and preserved, and it is this archive of preserved remains which records the changing vegetation.

Where meltwater streams flowed across the open tundra as the glaciers retreated, or where lakes formed, this rain of plant material fell on their banks and was quickly frozen. More gravel, sand and silt was deposited on top of this material at the next thaw, and this moist blanket sealed off the plant remains from the air above. Without oxygen from the atmosphere, the organisms of decay could not do their work and so the material was preserved. By excavating these sediments, we can reveal a perfectly preserved record of the vegetation that once grew nearby. As the plant material is carbon-rich, we can use radiocarbon dating to estimate when it was deposited, and, by studying different depths through the sediments, we can build a picture of how the vegetation changed over time.

Another archive of the past depends on bog-mosses (*Sphagnum* species). These plants grow in wet hollows, and even over relatively flat areas in cooler regions where the input from rainfall exceeds around 130cm per year. Bog-mosses act like sponges, absorbing water more rapidly than they release it. As old moss plants die, new ones grow upwards through their remains, forming spongy hummocks. At the base of these waterlogged hummocks there is very little oxygen, and this, combined with the cool temperatures, slows the work of the bacteria that cause decay. The partial breakdown of the bog-mosses releases humic acids, and the acidic conditions then further impede decay. The partially decayed remains of the bog-mosses accumulate as peat, forming peat bogs that may be many metres deep. Anything that falls into this acid peat is literally 'pickled', just as we pickle onions to preserve them. This process functions so effectively that 2,000-year-old human bodies have been excavated from peat in such a perfect state of preservation that it was possible to identify the last meals they had eaten.

Macroscopic plant material falling in the peat is equally well preserved: leaves, flowers, fruits and sometimes even complete tree trunks can be excavated from ancient times when the vegetation was rather different from that of today. Microscopic remains tell us even more. Plant pollen grains are tough and resistant, with a resilient outer coat that protects the genetic material within. Individual pollen grains can be extracted from different levels down through the peat archive, and their age can be estimated by radiocarbon dating of the peat.

Most pollen grains can be identified to their species, or at least to their genus, from their shape and the sculpting of their outer case. The evidence in the peat has to be interpreted with caution: different plants produce different amounts of pollen, and the distance over which this is dispersed is also very variable. Pollen from forest trees, for example, tends to disperse much further than pollen from grasses and sedges. Nevertheless, careful analysis of the pollen record in the peat allows us to build up a clear picture of changes in the local vegetation over time.

A microscope view of the distinctive pollen grains of Dwarf Birch, extracted from a peat deposit.

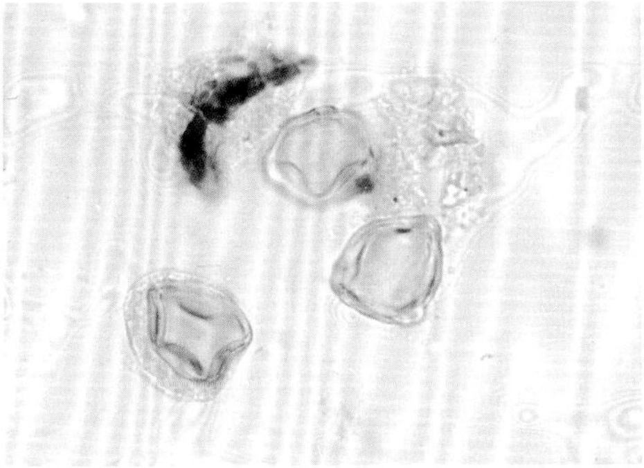

The British tundra

The analysis of macroscopic remains from meltwater sediments and the pollen from peat bogs gives a picture of the tundra that prevailed in southern Britain at the height of the Weichselian period, when the rest of Britain was encased in ice, and it shows what changes occurred in areas further north as the ice began to retreat. Perhaps the best-known evidence is from glacial deposits in the river terraces of the Lea Valley, north of London. These consist of rafts of organic material preserved in coarse gravel. Their appearance suggests they were frozen solid when they were embedded, and radiocarbon dating shows that they date from around 28,000 BP in the Middle Weichselian (Godwin, 1956), when the ice-sheet was at its most extensive.

Analysis of these macroscopic remains offers a clear picture of the flora that grew in the area at the height of the Ice Age (Reid, 1949). Most of these plants are what we would now regard as arctic-alpine species (in a broad sense), and, as we saw in Chapter 2, these are also the species which form the basis of our modern mountain flora. Material identified from the sediments of the Lea Valley included, for example, the leaves, fruit and seeds of Dwarf Willow and the nut-like fruits of Black Alpine-sedge. Other remains in the sediments came from Mountain Avens, Purple Saxifrage, Mossy Cyphel, Moss Campion, Alpine Catchfly, Alpine Cinquefoil and what was possibly Bird's-eye Primrose. Interestingly, at least two species were tentatively identified which are no longer found in Britain: Arctic Buttercup *Ranunculus hyperboreus* and Snowy Cinquefoil *Potentilla nivea*, species found today in Scandinavia and the mountains of central Europe.

Fruits of Arctic Buttercup have been found in the glacial deposits of the Lea Valley, near London, although the nearest site for the species now is in Scandinavia.

Overall we can conclude that a flora broadly similar to the modern tundra prevailed in southern England 28,000 years ago. There were also plants that we would now identify as ruderals or 'weeds', suggesting that the ground was very disturbed and open, probably through flooding and the action of frost. Material studied at other British sites presents a similar picture. Fruits and seeds in gravelly soil layers from the Late Glacial period on Bodmin Moor in Cornwall, for example, included Dwarf Birch, Dwarf Willow, Alpine Meadow-rue and possibly Tufted Saxifrage.

After the ice

As other sites began to emerge from the retreating ice at the end of the Weichselian period, we can follow the plants that invaded the newly exposed land by extracting their remains from local sediments and peat. These records show that many of the plants which had survived in southern England migrated northwards into the newly exposed gravels left behind by the glaciers.

In Caernarfonshire, for example, plant macrofossils were extracted from lake sediments at Nant Ffrancon on the edge of Snowdonia (Rhind & Jones, 2003). These show that the first flowering plants to colonise after the ice retreated were Tufted Saxifrage and a pearlwort. Dwarf Willow soon followed, along with Dwarf Birch, Starry Saxifrage, Moss Campion and Trailing Azalea. One site nearby produced a record of Iceland Purslane, today a rare species found on only two Scottish islands (see pp.342–343).

An even more compelling picture emerges from Whitlow Mosses near Selkirk in the Scottish Borders (Webb & Moore, 1982). Here macrofossils and pollen deposits from 13,000–10,000 BP give a clear picture of the different habitats that were forming as the climate warmed. There was an open scrub of Downy Birch and Juniper. Areas of base-rich, short turf were home to Fir and Alpine Clubmoss, Mountain Avens and species that were tentatively identified from their remains as Yellow Oxytropis, Alpine Bartsia and Spring Gentian.

Plant fossils found in lake sediments in Nant Ffrancon in Snowdonia give clues to the species that grew there as the glaciers retreated, 15,000 years ago.

Other species here were clearly associated with disturbed rocky soil, sands and gravels, including Moss Campion and Purple Saxifrage. Also recorded were Mountain Sandwort and possibly Norwegian Mugwort, two rare montane species that today are only found far from the Borders. Very few of these plants survive in the Borders today.

Survivors or invaders?

That brings us back to the question of why our mountain flowers grow in the places where we know them today. One long-standing suggestion was that our richest montane sites somehow remained clear of the glaciation and provided a refuge for arctic-alpine plants – a theory called *per-glacial survival*. In modern glaciers, rocky outcrops called nunataks are observed standing proud of the ice, and the suggestion was that something similar happened around Upper Teesdale in County Durham or Ben Lawers in Perthshire, for example, explaining the wealth of arctic-alpine species found at these sites today.

However, this seems unlikely. Evidence suggests that the ice-sheet was up to 2,500m thick – almost twice the height of Ben Nevis. The ice might have been thinner near its southernmost edge, but even so conditions on any exposed rocks free of the ice must have been exceptionally severe and unlikely to support many plants.

The other theory was that, as the ice retreated, the species that we know were growing in the British tundra followed the ice northwards and upwards. In the mountains, they found the conditions they needed, and that has allowed them to survive there ever since. This theory of *post-glacial succession* seems more likely and is now generally accepted as the explanation for our mountain flora.

Genetic studies suggest that, after the last Ice Age, Mossy Cyphel invaded the Scottish mountains and the Alps from a common source in the tundra that then covered southern Europe.

This is supported by recent genetic studies. For example, Valtueña *et al.* (2015) compared the DNA of Mossy Cyphel plants in Scotland with samples from the Alps and Pyrenees. They found no significant genetic differences between Scottish plants and those in the European mountains, suggesting that the populations had not been isolated for any great length of time. They concluded that Mossy Cyphel was widespread in areas of tundra in southern Europe at the height of the last Ice Age, and had then moved northwards to the Scottish hills and upwards into its current localities high in the mountains of continental Europe as the ice retreated.

Ice Age survivors

But this simple model of post-glacial succession may not be the complete picture. One species that somewhat confounds the model is not a montane plant, although it was an important component of the post-glacial forests that once covered an estimated 70 per cent of Scotland: Scots Pine. Scientists have found differences in the biochemistry of these trees, based on chemicals called terpenes which help defend the trees against insect and fungal attack. The quantities and composition of these terpenes in pine trees vary across the Scotland, probably in response to differences in the climate, allowing genetically distinctive populations to be identified.

By analysing these differences, seven 'biochemical regions' have been recognised. Pines in each region share broadly similar chemical characteristics, and the differences between the regions are mostly slight. However, the biochemical region centred on Kinlochewe in the north-west Highlands is significantly distinct from the other six regions. The trees there tend to have more of the terpenes, perhaps to better protect them against fungal attack in such a damp climate. Pollen records from peat bogs show that pines have grown in this area for at least 8,500 years. However, the chemical distinctiveness of the pines suggests that they have a separate origin from those elsewhere in Scotland. One possibility is that they are descended from trees which survived through the Ice Age in some remote location in Ireland or off the Scottish coast, whereas the pines in other parts of Scotland were invaders that moved in from the south as the ice retreated.

The biochemistry of Scots Pine trees around Kinlochewe in Wester Ross suggests that they might have had a different origin from those elsewhere in Scotland.

Scots Pine is not alone in suggesting that both per-glacial survival and post-glacial succession might have played a part in establishing our modern flora. For example, genetic differences between Snowdon Lilies in Wales and those in the Alps have led to suggestions that the Welsh population might have clung on somewhere in the region during the Ice Age, rather than invading from the south later.

There is also some evidence from Norway that plants were able to survive the peak of the last glaciation on nunataks. At this time, Andøya, the northernmost of the Lofoten islands, lay very close to the westernmost edge of the Scandinavian ice-sheet. Sediments obtained from lakes near the island's northern tip include pollen grains and plant seeds dating from the height of the glaciation, suggesting that a few small areas, probably on the west faces of mountains, remained ice-free and provided a refuge for a few hardy plants (Mørkved & Nilssen, 1993).

It is possible that similar conditions might have prevailed in the Outer Hebrides or far north-west of Scotland. Although most of our montane plants probably did invade from the southern tundra at the end of the last glaciation, perhaps some were able to survive in ice-free refuges around north-western Europe and reinvade from there.

The retreat of the arctic-alpines

As we have seen, the last glacial period ended around 11,500 years ago. The next question is what happened to these plants of the southern tundra as the ice retreated. Ever since then, warmer conditions have prevailed, although there have been fluctuations in the climate which impacted on plant distribution. Essentially these fluctuations can be divided into five phases or *palaeoecological periods*, as shown below.

Changes in the British climate over the last 10,000 years

Palaeoecological period	Timescale	Conditions in Britain
Pre-Boreal	10,000–9,000 BP	Began with subarctic conditions but characterised by rapidly rising temperatures
Boreal	9,000–7,500 BP	Climate as warm as the present day, but drier and more continental; trees covered the largest extent of the British Isles during this period
Atlantic	7,500–5,000 BP	Climatic optimum, a little warmer than today but wetter and more oceanic
Sub-Boreal	5,000–2,500 BP	Climate became drier; initially warmer than today but started to cool towards end of period
Sub-Atlantic	2,500 BP – present	Climate became cooler and wetter

As the climate warmed in the Pre-Boreal, characteristic lowland species invaded from the south and across land bridges from Europe to the east. These soon outcompeted the more specialist arctic-alpines. The Boreal period saw trees spread rapidly across the land, and forest swamped the remaining tundra plants. The increasing temperatures led to a rise in sea level. Sometime towards the end of the Boreal, the sea broke through between the southern North Sea and the Straits of Dover and Britain became an island. Subsequently plants could only invade Britain by long-range seed dispersal or with the aid of human activities.

With sea currents now sweeping all around the British island, oceanicity and rainfall increased in the Atlantic period. This led to the spread of bogs, which smothered the gravelly glacial soils in which the arctic-alpines had flourished. Very quickly, the plants of the tundra were pushed back to limited areas in the mountains that mimicked the post-glacial conditions in which they had flourished, and the species became essentially montane or submontane as we know them today.

The story in the peat

These changes in our vegetation and climate are all captured in the peat archive, as the pollen diagram below illustrates. The diagram is adapted from an original drawing by Dr Judith Turner in Clapham (1978), based on her work in Turner *et al.* (1973), which looked at material extracted from peat deposits on Widdybank Fell in Upper Teesdale before it was flooded to create the Cow Green Reservoir (see Chapter 8). It is a good example of the vegetational changes that

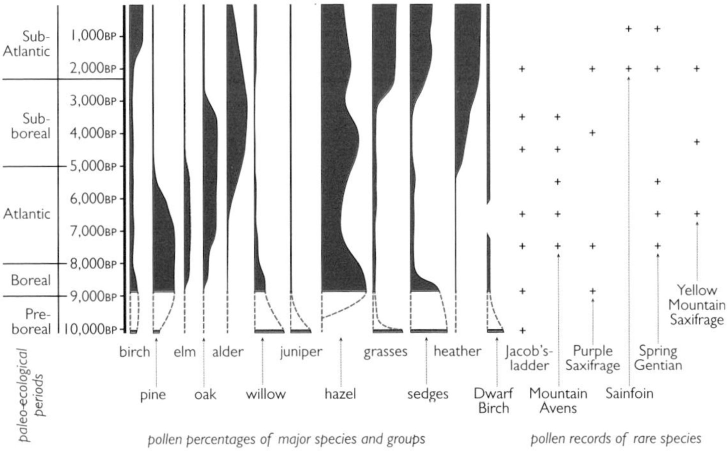

a Yellow Mountain Saxifrage
b Jacob's-ladder
c Purple Saxifrage
d Spring Gentian

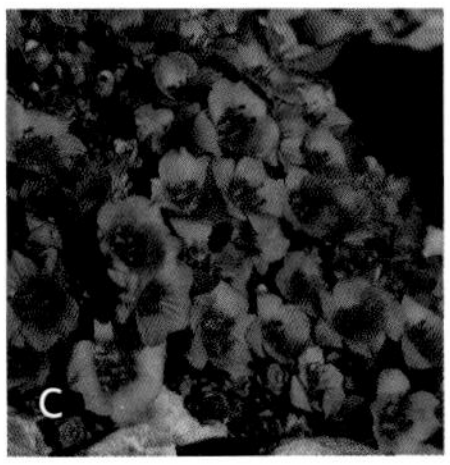

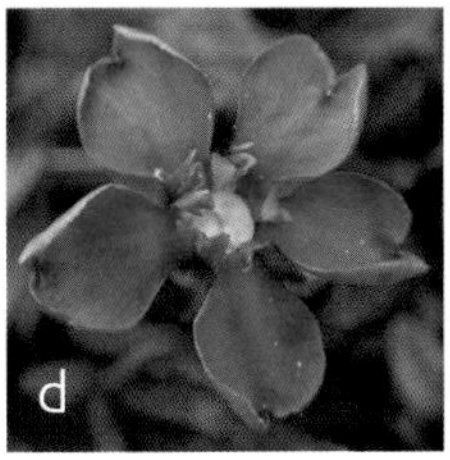

LEFT: Pollen diagram from Widdybank Fell in Upper Teesdale, showing the typical pattern of vegetational change across Britain during the last 10,000 years. Adapted from Clapham (1978).

happened all over Britain during the last 10,000 years, although I have chosen this pollen diagram in particular because it also hints at why Upper Teesdale is special today, as we will see in Chapter 8.

At the foot of the diagram, in the Pre-Boreal period between 10,000 and 9,000 BP, the prevalence of grasses and sedges shows that tundra vegetation prevailed, although this was already in decline. Dwarf Birch, Juniper and low-growing arctic willows flourished locally, but the scarcity of tree pollen suggests that full-sized trees grew only at lower altitudes. The levels of Scots Pine, elm and especially Hazel pollen increase into the Boreal period around 9,000 BP when, elsewhere in Britain, tree cover was at its maximum. At the altitude of Widdybank Fell, however, oak did not fully establish until after 8,000 BP, as the climatic optimum of the Atlantic approached. By then, average temperatures were about 2°C higher than they are today. However, these trees never formed dense forests in Upper Teesdale; there was enough space between them for a wide variety of herbs, grasses, sedges and rushes to continue growing, and that is critical to the survival of the flora we see in the area today.

From about 6,000 BP the rise of Alder in the pollen profile shows that the climate was becoming wetter and more oceanic, and it was probably this which led to the virtual disappearance of Pine by 5,000 BP at the start of the Sub-Boreal. The increase in Heather pollen thereafter suggests that conditions were becoming more open and

The Teesdale difference

Although in many ways the pollen profile illustrated on the preceding page is typical of the vegetational changes that happened across Britain over the last 10,000 years, there is one important difference in Upper Teesdale which helps explain why the area is so important botanically today. Pollen of Dwarf Birch is found at all levels through the peat archive, suggesting that tundra-like communities survived somewhere on the fells right through this period, probably on the high plateaux and a few remaining areas of exposed limestone. This is confirmed by the occurrence of pollen from relatively rare arctic-alpines throughout the peat column, most noticeably from Mountain Avens and Spring Gentian. Interestingly, three of the species recorded in the peat profile have died out from Teesdale in relatively recent times, Jacob's-ladder within the last 150 years and Sainfoin (right) and Purple Saxifrage rather earlier, probably as a result of the spread of grassland and blanket bog.

Pollen records show that Sainfoin grew in Upper Teesdale a few centuries ago, but it was probably lost as a result of grazing pressure.

the climate was cooling. Elm also disappeared from the pollen record about the same time, perhaps because of disease.

After about 3,000 BP, peat began to accumulate more rapidly and the bogs began to spread. This led to waterlogging of some woodland so that old trees died and young seedlings were unable to establish. As a result, oak declines greatly in the pollen record, and birch and willow make something of a comeback. The reappearance of grasses and sedges could be interpreted as a return towards tundra-like conditions, but more probably was caused by the opening up of the land by humans for farming. It was not until about 1,000 years ago that woodland disappeared almost completely from the dales, to be replaced by grassland and blanket bog. Radiocarbon dating in one bog on Widdybank Fell shows that this happened as recently as 540–700 years ago. It seems likely that this was due to the introduction of sheep grazing, which interfered with the growth and establishment of tree seedlings. Similar patterns would be reflected in pollen records all round Britain.

Factors for survival

The relict tundra flora that flourished south of, and immediately after, the ice was therefore progressively swamped by the invasion of ranker-growing southern and lowland species, and especially by the closure of the forest canopy. It retreated to a few sites in the mountains, and some sites at lower altitudes in the far north of Britain.

But what allowed the tundra species to survive at these sites? The short answer is that they needed to find conditions similar to those which allowed them to flourish in the tundra. That encompasses a range of factors that we need to consider in more detail if we are to understand the ecology of the montane sites that will feature in the rest of this book. Let us look at each of these factors in turn.

Temperature

Temperature is the most obvious factor controlling the distribution of arctic-alpine species: by definition, these are plants adapted to survive in cold climates. However, it is more complex than that. Few montane species actually require low temperatures. Some need a period of deep freeze before their seeds will germinate, and others need time at low winter temperatures to initiate or accelerate the flowering process, but most arctic-alpines will grow perfectly well in a lowland garden.

A few arctic-alpines seem impossible to maintain in the garden. One such, appropriately, is Glacier Buttercup *Ranunculus glacialis*, a plant that grows higher in the Alps and further north in the Arctic than most others; dedicated gardeners can only cultivate it successfully in open gravel, like the glaciers left behind, and with constant irrigation and aeration of its roots. Other species, such as the snowbells of the Alps, suffer root-rot in relatively mild, wet winters in gardens without the protection of a blanket of snow. However, many arctic-alpines flourish in temperate gardens, so long as gardeners provide one essential service: regular weeding. Otherwise, these precious plants are quickly swamped by ranker-growing lowland species.

The main impact of temperature seems to be on the plants' growing season. As a very rough generalisation, the growing season for northern and upland plants has been estimated as the period of the year during which the daily average temperature exceeds 5°C. At lower temperatures, many of the chemical processes within plant cells shut down and growth stops. For a few species, the growing season is better defined by the period of the year that is frost-free. These plants seem to be susceptible to night frosts, which can occasionally occur in spring and autumn even when the average temperature over the whole day exceeds 5°C.

In the most extreme mountain situations and in much of the Arctic, this growing season can be as brief as mid-June to early September. Arctic-alpines have evolved to invest all their energy into establishing rapidly in a landscape opened up by the glaciers, flowering quickly and setting seed before the snows return. They are adapted to cope with these truncated growing seasons, and so can flourish. Lowland plants, on the other hand, are adapted to a more prolonged and leisurely growing season. They cannot grow where the season is too short. As a result, arctic-alpines are able to survive in these high-altitude or high-latitude situations without competition from lowland plants.

Glacier Buttercup grows well in the Tromsø Botanic Garden in arctic Norway, but needs special measures to be grown successfully in the milder, damper climate of Britain.

Although the growing season is short in the Arctic, there is some compensation. In southern mountains such as the Alps, temperatures can rise quite high during the brief summer, which accelerates the growth of the arctic-alpines. Temperatures never rise as high in the Arctic, but instead plants have the advantage in midsummer of 24 hours of daylight in which they can photosynthesise. This difference between arctic and alpine regions may be one reason why some of the species listed on pages 30–35 are confined to alpine regions and do not occur in the Arctic, and others are arctic species which do not grow in the southern mountains.

Precipitation

Precipitation has a role to play. The gravelly substrate left behind by glaciers is free-draining, so arctic-alpines are generally poorly adapted to damp conditions (that is why some of them suffer from winter root-rot in gardens). If rainfall is above about 130cm per year, blanket bogs tend to establish over flat areas and in damp hollows in the uplands. Bog peat buries the underlying rocks, producing conditions very different from the gravelly tundra to which most arctic-alpines are adapted. The pollen archive in the peat often records the disappearance of arctic-alpine species in the vicinity as the bogs became established. However, a small group of plants are adapted to growing in mountain bogs, including Cloudberry, Dwarf Cornel, Bog Bilberry and some of the sedges. These plants are often known as peat alpines.

On steep slopes, high rainfall is not an issue. It rapidly drains away and the erosion it causes often creates new, open habitats in which montane or arctic-alpine species can flourish.

Snow

In combination, precipitation and low temperatures produce snow, and snow-lie is another important feature in mountains. Wind exacerbates this, blowing snow off exposed tops and ridges and dumping it on sheltered slopes where it accumulates and lies well after the snow has melted elsewhere. At these locations, the growing season is not defined by temperature but by the short period between the last snow melting (which leaves a damp, open substrate perfect for germination and rapid growth) and the next snowfall returning. Some mountain plants are particularly associated with snow hollows where the growing season is restricted in this way, including Sibbaldia and Alpine Lady-fern.

Snow also provides a warming winter blanket. Beneath accumulated snow, the soil temperature usually stays significantly above freezing. A

The climate of Ben Nevis

A photograph from around 1890 shows the weather observatory that operated near the summit of Ben Nevis from 1884 to 1903.

For understandable reasons, there are few weather stations on mountaintops. Normally we have to make assumptions on how altitude affects weather in order to extrapolate climatic conditions on the high tops from data recorded at lower-altitude weather stations. One notable exception is Ben Nevis, thanks to a weather observatory that was established near the 1,344m summit of the mountain in 1884 by the Scottish Meteorological Society and manned full-time by observers who lived in the building. It closed in 1904, due to inadequate government funding.

As the table below shows, the prevailing temperatures over this period were low; indeed the annual mean temperature was –0.3°C. July is the only month in which the daily mean temperature (roughly equivalent to the daily average) exceeds

Average monthly temperatures (°C) at the Ben Nevis Observatory, 1884–1903.

Month	Average daily min	Average daily max	Daily mean temperature
Jan	–6.3	–2.5	–4.4
Feb	–6.4	–2.8	–4.6
Mar	–6.3	–2.6	–4.5
Apr	–4.3	–0.5	–2.4
May	–1.6	+2.5	+0.5
Jun	+2.2	+6.5	+4.4
Jul	+3.1	+7.1	+5.1
Aug	+2.8	+6.4	+4.6
Sep	+1.4	+5.3	+3.4
Oct	–2.1	+1.4	–0.4
Nov	–3.5	+0.1	–1.7
Dec	–5.5	–2.0	–3.8

The climate of Ben Nevis *continued*

the critical 5°C above which plants can grow, although June and August temperatures are close to this. We can therefore estimate that the growing season at the summit might be as short as eight weeks from mid-June to mid-August. Only a few hardy arctic and alpine species are able to complete their annual lifecycle in such a short period, hence the dearth of vegetation around the top of the Ben.

Data from the observatory show an average annual precipitation over the period of just over 400cm (that is 4m!), with rain typically falling on 220 days per year. A notable feature was the very high frequency of hill fog at the summit, which reduces the light levels plants need for photosynthesis. In November to January this occurred almost 80 per cent of the time, and even in May and June the summit was shrouded in cloud for 55 per cent of the time. Freezing winter fog, gathering as a rime on plant leaves, is undoubtedly another limiting factor on plant growth around the summit. Strong winds also depress plant growth, especially when the 'chill factor' of cold winds kills growing buds, although observatory records show that the winds on Ben Nevis were less severe than the altitude might suggest.

surprising number of arctic-alpines rely on this winter protection and are quickly killed if they are exposed to frost on open slopes. As we will see in later chapters, only a few species, such as Trailing Azalea and Dwarf Willow, are able to withstand the extremely low temperatures that can prevail on windswept summits and ridges where the snow is stripped off by winter winds.

Exposure

Wind has another effect: the wind-chill factor with which any hillwalker is familiar. Exposure to winds significantly shortens the growing season at many sites, even where the ambient temperature is theoretically high enough for growth. That is why many arctic-alpines grow as low cushions, streamlined for protection against the winds. Wind also leads to desiccation, so many of these plants have thick, leathery leaves to reduce water loss.

Exposure to wind also brings benefits for arctic-alpines. Windy conditions exclude competing lowland species and stop trees from growing. Where woodland becomes established, arctic-alpines are shaded out and outcompeted by woodland plants. Leaf litter from the trees produces a richer, deeper soil in which montane species can no longer flourish.

Substrate

While all these climatic factors contribute to the survival of arctic-alpines, the nature of the soil is also important. We can understand this best if we regard montane species as 'glacier followers'. The constant sliding forwards, then melting backwards, of glaciers grinds up the rocks beneath them, creating a drift of fine gravel. This is piled up at the feet and margins of the glaciers in heaps called moraines. When first exposed, these newly formed gravels are rich in minerals, but these are progressively dissolved and washed away (leached) by the rain. However, erosion and frost-heave (caused by the expansion and contraction of water in the soil as it freezes and melts) constantly stir up the gravel, maintaining open, unstable conditions and bringing minerals back to the surface. These glacial soils tend to be rich in the minerals that plants need for growth, such as calcium and magnesium. We refer to such soils as basic, which strictly means that they are alkaline with a pH measurement of more than 7.0.

At first, these gravels lack any organic nutrients. Only rain-fed lichens and mosses are able to grow on the new gravels, but their death and decay begins to add a little humus to the substrate, creating what is called a primitive soil. This process of decay adds nutrients to the soil, especially nitrogen, phosphorus and potassium, and this makes the soil more fertile for plant growth. Many arctic-alpines are adapted to establish in the primitive soils left behind by the glaciers, which are basic but not especially fertile. They need conditions which mimic these soils if they are to survive in the mountains. The widest range of montane plants is therefore found where there are friable (crumbly), mineral-rich rocks that are subject to rapid erosion by frost and exposure – replicating the conditions in the immediate environs of a melting glacier.

Calcium is especially important for plant growth, and so a high proportion of arctic-alpines are calcicoles (meaning they thrive in calcium-rich soils). Some are calcifuges, meaning they do not grow well on soils rich in calcium, but these are often adapted to soils rich in other minerals such as potassium and magnesium. The main component of calcium-rich (calcareous) soils is usually calcium carbonate or lime. Calcicoles are therefore often referred to colloquially as 'lime-loving' species and calcifuges as 'lime-hating' species.

Many of the minerals in soils are at least slowly soluble. In the high rainfall typical of upland habitats, dissolved minerals are rapidly leached into deeper soil beyond the reach of plant roots. Calcicolous arctic-alpines in these habitats need a regular resupply of these minerals, usually provided by further erosion from cliffs above. That often restricts their range to a limited area immediately below the cliffs. Some arctic-alpines, such as Alpine Scurvy-grass, Starry Saxifrage and Yellow Mountain Saxifrage, typically grow close to springs and flushes in which the water is enriched with minerals dissolved from the rocks beneath.

Rock and soils

In one sense, the type of rock is irrelevant to vascular plants. Their roots cannot extract from the rocks the minerals they need for growth. Plants rely on water from rainfall dissolving soluble minerals from the rocks and releasing them into the soil in a form which the roots can absorb. A few plants are able to insert their roots into natural cracks in softer rocks, further opening the crack as the roots expand, but they still need water to release the minerals from the rock. The chemical action by which water dissolves minerals happens where the water is in contact with the rock surface. Small rock fragments have a larger surface area, compared to their volume, so minerals are released more abundantly when rocks are broken down into fine gravel. That is why the soil formed in the gravel close to glaciers or beneath crumbly cliffs tends to be richer in available minerals.

Heavy folding weakens this schist rock below Ben Lawers so that it crumbles readily and produces mineral-rich soils.

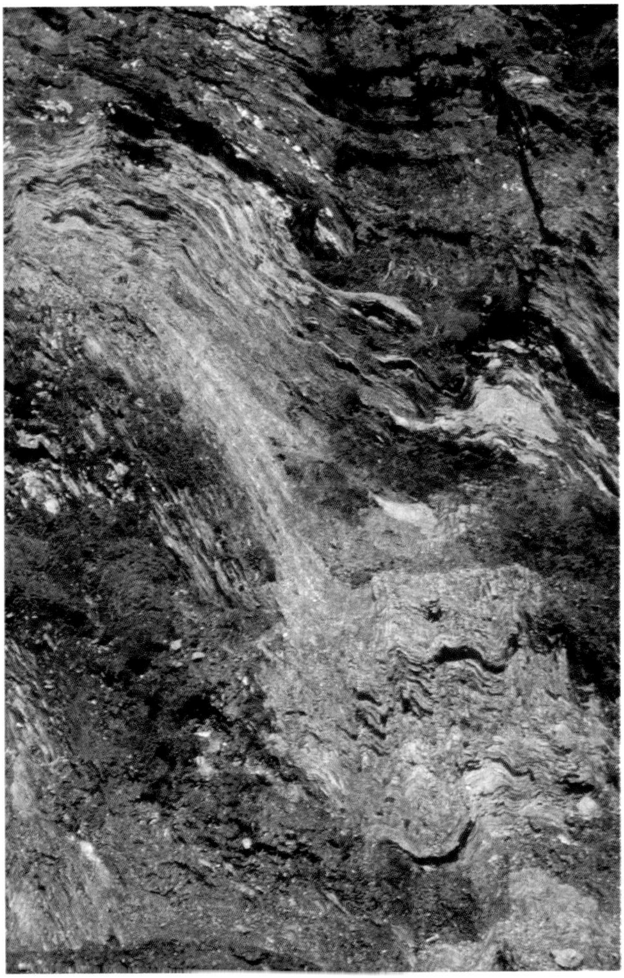

As any geologist will tell you, all rocks are packed with minerals. However igneous rocks such as granite, which came directly from the Earth's core, and metamorphic rocks such as slates and gneiss, which were changed and compacted by temperature and pressure in the Earth's crust, tend to be harder and lock up their minerals more tightly. As a result, very few minerals can be dissolved out of them, even where they are crushed into gravel. The soil associated with these rocks is therefore mineral-poor and usually acid.

Many sedimentary rocks were formed from muds and sands that accumulated on the seabed. These muds and sands were often rich in calcium and other minerals. Although sedimentary rocks were compressed by the weight of sediments accumulating above them, they are generally softer than igneous or metamorphic rocks. They may have been laid down in distinct bands, with lines of weakness between them – like the chocolate layers in a wafer biscuit. If they were folded by Earth movements, this further weakens them (try bending a wafer!). These rocks therefore tend to be more friable, crumbling readily into fine gravels from which minerals are more easily dissolved by water. Banded sedimentary rocks therefore often produce more mineral-rich, basic soils.

Geologists will have winced at that horribly simplified botanist's explanation of what goes on in soils. But it roughly explains why the widest range of arctic-alpine species are found associated with friable sedimentary rocks, and why there are rather fewer species in the more acid soils associated with hard igneous and metamorphic rocks. In the geographical tour around Britain which follows in Chapters 5 to 17, I will often mention specific rock types associated with the different mountain blocks. These are important to geologists and geographers, because the nature of the rock has a huge impact on the landscape. The precise identity of the rock is less important botanically. Essentially all that matters is the extent to which these rocks release minerals into the soil. I will therefore not go into huge detail about different rock types in the subsequent chapters, and will primarily discuss the nature of the soils they produce.

Some ecological terms used in the text

Acid	Term used, in a broad sense, to describe a soil that is low in the minerals that plants need for growth such as calcium and magnesium, usually with a pH acidity measurement of less than about 6.6. This would not feel acid to the touch!
Basic	Term used to describe rocks with high concentrations of calcium, silica, iron and/or magnesium, and the soils derived from them, typically with a pH greater than 7. A gardener would describe such soils as 'rich' because they are generally good for plant growth.
Calcareous	Containing calcium carbonate (referring to rocks or soils).
Calcicole (adj. **calcicolous**)	A 'lime-loving' species adapted to growing on basic soils rich in calcium carbonate.
Calcifuge	A 'lime-hating' species that does not grow in soils rich in calcium.
Exclosure	An area fenced off to exclude grazing animals.
Fellfield	Arctic expanse of rocks and gravel interspersed with occasional patches of vegetation.
Flush	A patch of gently sloping, wet ground through which water runs diffusely, rather than in channels; the water may carry minerals which enrich the soil.
Friable	Crumbling easily, releasing minerals into the soil.
Krummholz	Low, twisted trees growing in a shrubby form above the timberline but below the treeline.
Peat alpine	Montane species associated with peaty, acid soils.
Timberline	The altitude on a hill above which trees cannot grow straight and tall enough to be an economic crop.
Treeline	The altitude on a hill, varying with latitude, aspect and exposure, above which trees are unable to grow.

For botanical terms, please refer to any field guide on plants.

Solifluction

Another process which enriches the soil and opens up new habitats on mountain slopes is solifluction. In winter, moisture in the soil freezes solid. Because ice is less dense than water, the soil expands in this process, disrupting the topsoil. As temperatures rise in the spring, the warmth of the sun melts the surface of this frozen mass first, forming a treacly, semi-liquid layer of wet soil. On any slopes steeper than about 45 degrees, this top layer will begin to slither downhill over the still solid ice beneath. If the slope is vegetated, rafts of vegetation will begin to move on this liquid conveyor belt, forming what are called solifluction terraces.

The process of solifluction has created the narrow terraces on this hillside below the Cairnwell in Aberdeenshire. Sheep follow these natural terraces with their tracks and have opened up the bare erosion scar across the slope.

Sometimes whole lumps of vegetation will break loose and tumble downhill, further stirring up the slope as they do. This movement creates new areas of open soil into which the typical glacial pioneer species can quickly move. The alternate freezing and thawing churns the soil and brings stones back to the surface, so these exposed soils can look stony, even though the soil may be more than a metre deep. This process reverses leaching within the solifluction zone, and maintains mineral-rich conditions at the surface in which the lime-loving arctic-alpines can flourish.

It was the combination of all these factors just discussed which created the ecological niches that allowed the arctic-alpines to find a home and survive in the mountains. Today, as we will see in Chapters 5 to 17, we find the richest diversity of montane species in sites in which some or all of these ecological factors combine to greatest effect. In searching out mountain flowers, we are generally looking for sites with extreme climates and unstable, mineral-rich soils that most closely match the conditions immediately after the glaciers retreated.

Opportunity, chance and the 'chequerboard theory'

There is one other consideration that is important in understanding the modern montane flora of Britain. The richest habitats we are

Blue Heath in a wood near Dalarna in southern Sweden. Finding British plants elsewhere in the world can often raise intriguing questions about their occurrence in Britain.

considering are often extremely localised and widely dispersed. They are also highly sensitive to short-term change. Even in the Arctic, there can be brief periods of time that are inimical to arctic-alpines: a succession of cold years when the snow does not melt and plants do not have a chance to germinate and flower, or a series of summers that are too hot and dry for plants to survive. Most arctic-alpines have long-lived seeds to cope with such eventualities. The extreme is shown by Arctic Lupins; some of their seeds were excavated from soils in Canada that had been frozen into permafrost 10,000 years ago, and a small proportion of them were still able to germinate.

Nevertheless, in small areas of arctic habitat reliant on a particular combination of climatic conditions, many of our British montane species are surviving 'on the edge'. They can all too easily be eliminated by chance (or what scientists call *stochastic events*). I think this element of serendipity is more important than we realise in explaining the occurrence – and especially the absence – of species in the British mountains.

The best analogy I can offer is what I call the 'chequerboard theory'. Imagine a board for Chinese chequers, completely filled with playing pieces. If you were to remove these chequers one by one on a truly random basis, you could never predict which would be the last chequer left on the board. By that token, there is no reason why that chequer was the last to survive; it is purely a matter of chance. In the same way, as the climate warmed after the last Ice Age, I think many arctic-alpines retreated to a few sites that provided the conditions they needed for survival. In these small sites, the entire population of plants could easily be killed by landslips, late snow-lie, droughts or hungry herbivores. If this happened repeatedly over several seasons, the seedbank in the soil would quickly become exhausted and the species would die out.

Over the 10,000 years or so in which these plants have had to survive in their mountain refuges, there is a high chance of such events occurring, wiping out their remaining sites one by one. Eventually that could leave just a single site, before it too was destroyed and the species became extinct. There would be no particular reason why that site was the last to survive; just like the last chequer on the board, it was purely a result of chance. I think that element of chance might well apply to some montane species that are now confined to just a single locality in Britain. We may be witnessing the last stages of the slow extirpation of these species since the Ice Age.

A sceptical note on summer isotherms

I have deliberately omitted mentioning one factor that is sometimes quoted to explain the distribution of montane plants, because I am highly sceptical about its usefulness. In 1970, the British specialist in fossil plants Ann Conolly and a Norwegian ecologist called Eilif Dahl published an article in which they related the distribution of British montane species to maximum summer temperatures (Conolly & Dahl, 1970). The maps they used, based on an earlier paper by Dahl, are still sometimes cited in explaining the distribution of montane species. It was an extremely valuable piece of work in its time, but I believe its conclusions need to be treated with caution.

So, for example, the map opposite is based on their work and shows that all the records for Dwarf Willow in northern Scotland are in areas where the maximum summer temperature does not exceed 23°C (and can therefore be contained within a line showing what is called the 23°C *isotherm*). In the same way, those in southern Scotland lie within the 24°C isotherm and those in northern England and Wales within the 25°C isotherm. This is based purely on statistical correlations. Such correlations are only as useful as the lessons they offer, which I believe are very limited in this case. For example, there is no explanation why Dwarf Willows in Wales should be able to cope

Summer temperatures alone probably do not explain the occurrence of Dwarf Willow in the British mountains.

with higher temperatures than their Scottish equivalents, or indeed why the same species in Scandinavia is contained instead within the 26°C isotherm.

Closer investigation shows that the data they used are actually no more than approximations, and simply record the highest temperatures recorded at a series of weather stations, without any reference to whether that temperature was a short-lived peak or part of a longer hot spell. Any gardener will know that many plants can survive a few hours of hot weather but not a prolonged heatwave. It is also important to note that Dahl's original paper related to distribution of these species in the lowlands, and sought to explain why some plants like Dwarf Willow and Glacier Buttercup are difficult to maintain in cultivation. His paper did not claim that maximum temperatures are the direct cause of the absence of species outside the isotherm, and he emphasised that his work should not be misinterpreted to imply that the species in question die when they are exposed to higher temperatures than the particular isotherm embraces.

It is very probably true that some montane species cannot stand exposure to high temperatures, especially for prolonged periods. However, even in these cases, drought stress may be as important as temperature. In many other cases, I believe the maximum summer temperature isotherms are a proxy for a whole range of climatic factors, such as those I have described in the sections above. I am afraid, therefore, that I do not find isotherms terribly useful in explaining the often perplexing distribution of montane species. They will not feature much in the chapters which follow.

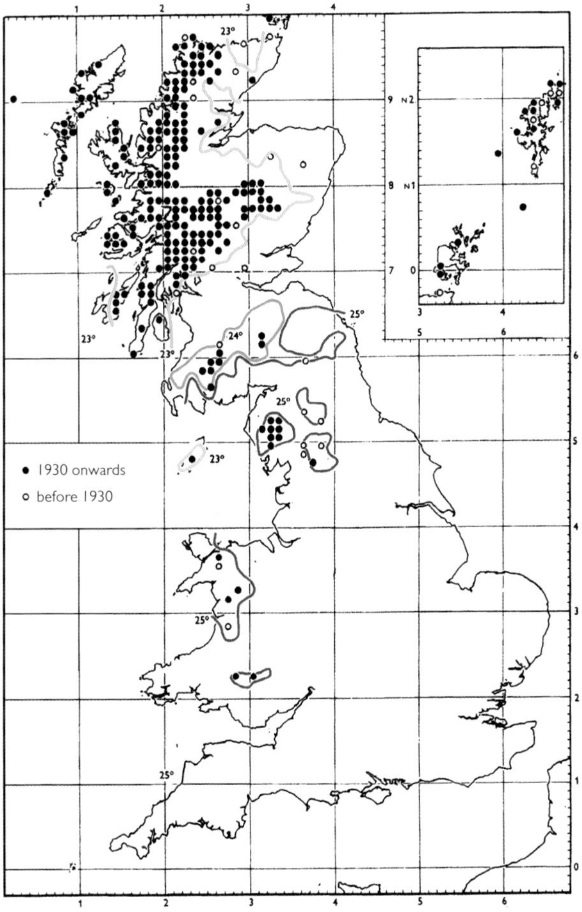

The distribution of Dwarf Willow compared to the maximum summer temperature in areas where it grows (isotherms). Adapted from Beerling (1998) using distribution data from the BSBI.

Opportunism on the riverbank

I have suggested that invasion by lowland plants is one of the main factors controlling where arctic-alpine species can (or rather cannot) survive. Evidence of this comes from unlikely places, much further down the courses of rivers that originate in mountains. For example, at Ballinluig near Pitlochry in Perthshire, there is an area where the River Tay regularly bursts its banks, especially in springtime when snow melts rapidly in the mountains that feed the river.

These floods strip the vegetation off a series of islands in the river channel and open up an expanse of bare gravel. Often the first plants to establish in these gravels after the floods pass are arctic-alpines whose seeds have been washed down in the river from the mountains.

Shingle banks downstream from mountains, like these beside the River Feshie in Inverness-shire, are worth checking for montane plants growing from seeds or fragments washed down from above.

On visits to these gravel islands in June, I have found montane species including Alpine Cinquefoil, Mountain Pansy, Alpine Bistort and Northern Bedstraw, as well as lowland species that we might typically regard as weeds. The adaptations of the arctic-alpines allow them to establish quickly, and they have flowered and set seed long before lowland species can develop around them and swamp them. The higher summer temperature did not seem to cause them any problems. I have no idea whether they would have survived the next winter, but, before then, the next flood will have washed them away and opened up the habitat once more. The gravel banks of other fast-flowing mountain rivers, such as the Feshie, the Spey and the Dee, are also worth checking for montane species washed down from the hills.

Zones of life

chapter four

As any hillwalker knows, the mountain environment changes with altitude. A sunny day in the valley may give way to cloud and bitter winds on the mountaintop. Those climatic changes also have a conspicuous impact on the vegetation. A mountain walk might begin in the shelter of a forest, then proceed onto open, heather moorland. Climbing higher, the Heather will become shorter and eventually disappear and other species will take its place. On the high top, the wind will be chill and probably a good deal stronger than experienced down below. We might want to seek shelter behind the summit cairn, just as the few plants of the windswept summit find their shelter behind boulders.

In this chapter, I want to look further at these altitudinal changes up the mountainside. The old formula was that mountain temperatures drop by 1°F for every 300 feet of ascent: in modern measurements, that roughly translates as 1°C for every 150m of ascent. All other things being equal, therefore, it might be 9°C colder at the summit of Ben Nevis than on the seashore of Loch Linnhe below. That is compounded by the effects of exposure, wind chill and the other climatic factors discussed in Chapter 3. That has a profound effect on the vegetation, which varies with altitude in response to these changing environmental conditions. These changes occur as a continuous gradation but can be represented as a series of altitudinal zones up mountain slopes.

OPPOSITE PAGE: Treeline woodland in the north of Norway shows how the mountains of Scotland might once have looked, with forest grading naturally with altitude into a zone of montane scrub, with montane heath above.

Forests in the mountains

If we could go back to the Boreal period, we would see a very different landscape around our mountains. The valleys would mostly be filled with forest. In places this would be dense, but there would be open

A lone tree stands as an evocative memorial to the forests that once covered our hillsides before humans intervened.

areas where the soils were thinner, where river flooding caused erosion, and where peat bogs formed in areas of impeded drainage.

In southern Britain, these forests were predominantly of Sessile Oak, often mixed with other broadleaved species, such as elms, Hazel and Hawthorn. The ground flora included familiar species like Wood Sorrel, Common Dog-violet, Wood Anemone and Primrose. In limestone areas, Ash would be the dominant species, perhaps mixed with Field Maple in the south and Rowan further north. Here Dog's Mercury was a characteristic understorey plant, and upland ashwoods in northern Britain were also the home for montane species such as Wood Cranesbill, Melancholy Thistle and Globeflower.

In central and eastern Scotland north of the Highland Boundary Fault, Scots Pine was the dominant tree species, usually intermixed with Downy Birch. On the west coast this was replaced by dripping wet, bryophyte-rich 'temperate rainforests' of Sessile Oak, usually intermixed with Hazel and Rowan. The Old Caledonian Pinewoods of Scotland probably never formed dense forests, because there were always open rocky, heathery and grassy areas where trees could not establish or where the death of an old pine left an open glade in which pine seedlings established only slowly. Heather was the most important understorey species here, along with Bilberry, Cowberry, Crowberry, Common Cow-wheat and carpets of beautiful mosses. Here and there, Lesser Twayblade would lurk under the Heather and Twinflower would scramble over mossy boulders.

A few Junipers and Rowan trees grew in open areas amongst the pines, and willows and birches occurred, particularly along streambanks. On thin soils and exposed valley-sides, Juniper might have been the dominant species, forming scrub like that we still see in some limestone areas in northern England or open 'Juniper savannah'. Heath Bedstraw, Wood Anemone and Harebells grew with the Juniper, perhaps along with Heath Fragrant-orchids where the soil was a little richer. Montane species like Lesser Twayblade, Intermediate and Serrated Wintergreen and the unrelated Chickweed Wintergreen grew amongst the Juniper. On a few particularly exposed, usually north-facing, slopes Downy Birch formed woodlands where Scots Pine could not survive, perhaps with some Juniper amongst the trees.

Reaching the treeline

The forests of the valleys then swept up the mountainside, with breaks along streamsides or where there were crags, boulder scree slopes and landslips. Occasional storms probably opened up whole swathes of woodland. As the forests continued up the mountainside, the trees would become progressively shorter and more scattered as climate and exposure made it more difficult for seedlings to establish and for trees to flourish. Eventually the trees would peter out completely at what we call the treeline. This is something of a misnomer: it was never a simple line. Trees could continue much higher in sheltered gullies on the hillside than on exposed ridges. They did not suddenly stop at some clearly delineated altitude, but gradually faded out up the mountainside.

Two terms are commonly confused here. The timberline is a forester's concept for the maximum altitude at which trees can grow straight and tall enough to produce an economic timber crop. That more or less corresponds to the point above which trees no longer form a forest community. It is thought that the natural upper limit of forest in Britain – the timberline – is about 500–600m, although this varies with species, latitude and prevailing winds.

However, individual trees can grow at considerably higher altitudes than this, perhaps in the shelter of a crag or in the form of low-growing, twisted shrubs (what German ecologists call *krummholz*, meaning 'twisted wood'). These *krummholz* trees rarely produce fruits and seeds at the prevailing temperatures, and they never gain much height because their vertical growing shoots are killed by exposure to the freezing winds or broken by winter snows. However, their own shelter allows their side branches to reach out horizontally for a considerable distance away from the prevailing winds.

Very broadly, it is estimated that trees stop growing and reproducing when the mean temperature of the warmest month drops below 10°C, and that is what defines the treeline. Sessile Oak, for example, is not recorded above 475m in England. In the Cairngorms, some tree species such as Scots Pine can continue to grow in a *krummholz* form to altitudes around 650–700m. This drops to just 300m in the exposed conditions of north-west Sutherland and scarcely reaches above sea level on Orkney and Shetland. Even above the treeline, individual trees can cling on to survival: the BSBI altitudinal database records Downy Birch growing to altitudes of 540m and Rowan to 870m both on Helvellyn and in Perthshire. Remarkably, Scots Pine is recorded to 1,160m on Cairn Lochan in the Cairngorms.

Farewell the forest

Today, of course, most of this native mountain woodland has vanished. Clearance of the forests on hill slopes began 3,900 years ago and continued almost to the present day. With the trees gone, remnants of the forest understorey were left behind as the prevailing vegetation. On hills in southern Britain, this is mainly grassland with some of the woodland herbs: Common Dog-violet and Heath Bedstraw are amongst the commonest on hill slopes. In northern Britain, the low-growing heath species of the forest floor, including Heather and Bilberry, were left behind as what is called dwarf-shrub heath, with expanses of peatland vegetation in the wetter regions.

From around 500 years ago (but mainly since the late 18th century) extensive grazing by sheep was introduced. Together with burning to produce a 'spring flush' of new growth for the sheep, this rapidly reduced the dwarf-shrub heath to species-poor acid grassland. Many areas were ploughed, fertilised and reseeded to enhance the carrying capacity for sheep (and deer) and this greatly altered the natural vegetation. Bogs in the wetter areas were drained to produce safer grazing for sheep and cattle. At the same time some areas of dwarf-shrub heath were retained in the north of England and Scotland as Heather moors for Red Grouse, which are shot for sport. These moors are traditionally managed by a patchwork pattern of burning to produce young Heather as grouse food while retaining taller patches where the grouse can breed. This pattern of burning for sheep grazing and grouse shooting (generically called muirburn) is a major factor depressing floral diversity in the uplands. Remote upland areas where it is impractical to keep sheep are maintained as hill range for Red Deer which are also shot for sport, and I will consider further the considerable impact that deer have on the vegetation in Chapter 19.

Because of these impacts, the mountain landscapes that we know today, which attract so many hillwalkers and tourists and which grace so many guidebooks and calendars, are denuded remnants of the original vegetation and pale shadows of their natural potential. They are 'cultural landscapes' shaped by over two centuries of human activities. We will return shortly to the plants of these impoverished slopes.

However, while heavy grazing undoubtedly represses many of these species, the removal of cattle grazing from many upland areas in the

Heather moorland, like this in the Lammermuir Hills, is a beautiful feature in the uplands of northern England and Scotland, but it is no more natural than an oilseed rape field, maintained by regular burning to support grouse shooting.

face of economic pressures is leading to another problem: the rapid spread of Bracken. Grazing animals generally avoid eating Bracken, which has carcinogenic properties. In the past, cattle trampling helped to knock back the young croziers of this tough fern as they emerged, but sheep are too light, and Red Deer wander too widely, to have this beneficial impact. The resulting spread of Bracken is significantly changing the landscape and flora of many hill districts.

Plantation forests

The First World War did trigger some action to return forest to the uplands, but mainly with fast-growing, non-native conifers. Initially these plantings were 'timber farms' designed to secure a strategic timber crop in case of future wars. Only within the last thirty years or so has the focus of management turned more to the amenity and conservation value of these forests. Some forests are being restructured to a more natural form and, in Scotland, the Forestry Commission is leading an effort to revitalise and restore remnant pinewoods and to create what are branded as 'new native pinewoods'. Land managers are also taking some measures to encourage and restore the shrubs and herbs that once grew on the pinewood floor. As a result, some of these plantation forests now have a more natural appearance, with a flora to match. A number of montane species can be found within the forests of Glenmore and Rothiemurchus in the Cairngorms, for example.

Wee trees above the timberline

As the mountain forests were cleared, the vegetation which previously lay just above this forest zone disappeared even more rapidly, until it became probably Britain's rarest natural habitat. It is only when you go to the mountains of Scandinavia or central Europe that you realise what we are missing in the British hills: the band of vegetation called montane scrub – the 'wee trees above the timberline'.

I have written extensively about this 'Cinderella' habitat (Scott, 2000), but, in the context of this book, it is important to emphasise that this was probably the main habitat for eight species of montane willow, most of which have now become rare or scarce species because of the destruction of montane scrub. Dwarf Birch and mountain forms of Juniper also grew in this scrub, along with species like Wood Cranesbill and Globeflower. Montane scrub was probably the main

Members of the Montane Scrub Action Group inspect the *krummholz* pine trees that form one of the few natural areas of montane scrub left in Britain, above 500m on Creag Fhiaclach in the Cairngorms.

habitat for Alpine Sowthistle, now confined to just a few Scottish crags as we will see in Chapter 11.

Today tiny remnants of montane scrub provide a glimpse of this lost habitat. Perhaps the most famous is on a steep, rocky, north-west-facing slope at Creag Fhiaclach in the Cairngorms. The timberline for Scots Pine here is at about 500m, but pine continues growing to 648m, forming the best natural pine treeline in Britain. The pines here are intermixed with a few Juniper bushes. They grow no more than 2m tall, with gnarled and twisted trunks and widely spreading, contorted branches. Despite their short stature, counts of tree rings in cores taken from their trunks show them to be 100–250 years old. At Coire Sharroch, an offshoot of Coire Fee in Angus, a very different kind of montane scrub grows on relatively base-rich rock at 750–800m, dominated by Woolly and Downy Willow. We will return to this remarkable site in Chapter 11.

Interest in these sites led government agencies and non-governmental organisations in Scotland to form the Montane Scrub Action Group, with the aim of promoting the conservation and restoration of montane scrub. The group, which I had the privilege of chairing from 1997 to 2004, has encouraged or supported a number of projects, most notably by the National Trust for Scotland in exclosures that we will meet in Chapter 13 on the slopes of Meall nan Tarmachan in Perthshire, and by organisations such as Highland Birchwoods and Trees for Life elsewhere in Scotland. Forestry Commission Scotland now offers grant support for the restoration of treeline woodland as part of larger forestry projects in the Scottish mountains, and is itself working to expand montane willow scrub on its land in the Merrick–Kells hills of Kirkcudbrightshire.

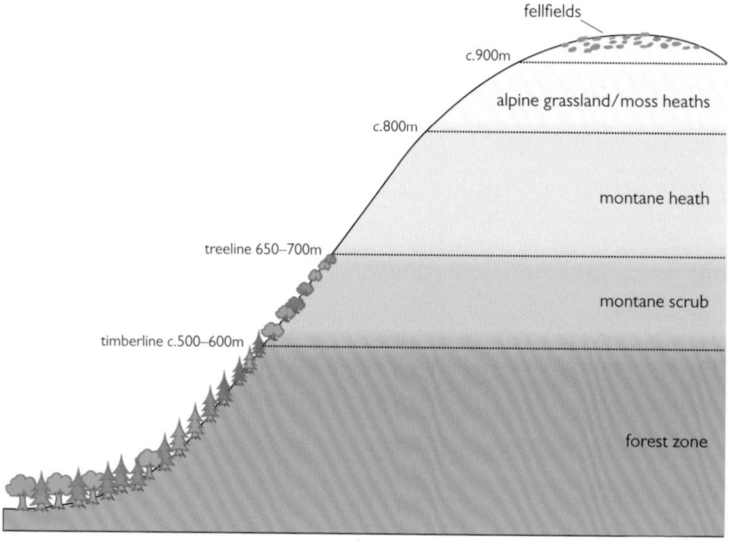

Highly stylised diagram of zonation on a Scottish mountain. Altitudes stated apply roughly to the central Highlands of Scotland.

Perhaps the most ambitious restoration project is being undertaken by the Royal Society for the Protection of Birds (RSPB) on its reserve at Abernethy in the Cairngorms National Park. The plan is to extend the existing pine forest there across open moorland from which the trees were removed long ago, sweeping up the mountain slopes to the natural limit for pines. This would create the largest contiguous area of native woodland in Britain and the only place to show the full natural zonation from pine forest on lower ground to the mountaintop fellfields. This would undoubtedly benefit the flora of the area, as well as birdlife, and I look forward to watching the project begin to develop (even if it may take 200–300 years before its vision is fully realised).

Above the trees

Above the treeline, this natural zonation would have continued, as represented in the diagram above (although I can say with confidence that in reality no such mountain ever existed!). Montane scrub would have graded gradually into more dwarfed vegetation dominated by montane heath species. This montane heath zone has been less impacted by human activities and still persists on our mountain slopes today. On the richer but slightly lower hills of England and Wales, the main species in this zone is Bilberry, along with Cowberry and some Crowberry. On more acidic hills further north, Heather is the dominant species on the middle slopes, but it suffers from exposure and grows in a dwarfed, prostrate form. It grows here with Bilberry and Bell Heather and, in wetter areas, with Cross-leaved Heath. At higher altitudes, these species die out, and Cowberry and Crowberry become dominant. Montane heath is also influenced by temperature and exposure, so it begins above about 700m in the Cairngorms, but at 550m in Sutherland and 300m in the hills of Shetland.

On more exposed slopes and at higher altitudes, even the heath species die out, to be replaced by a zone of alpine grasslands, moss and lichen heaths. A wider variety of arctic-alpines can be found in these alpine grasslands and moss heaths, especially where boulder scree slopes or steep crags provide shelter from the weather and grazing animals. Higher still, these give way to rocky fellfields and stone deserts on the highest tops. Fellfields are open, rocky areas of frost-shattered stone and gravel, interspersed with a sparse vegetation typically of Fir Clubmoss, Dwarf Willow, Stiff Sedge, Three-leaved Rush, Dwarf Cudweed, Trailing Azalea and Woolly Fringe-moss. These fellfields occur above about 900m in the central Highlands, but from as low as 450m on Ronas Hill in Shetland.

The composition of these high-altitude communities varies across Britain, and is best reviewed in the context of the geographical chapters which follow. However, even these upper zones have been impacted to some extent by the processes discussed earlier – by the hill sheep which graze here in summer, by the unnaturally high populations of Red Deer that are sustained by sport shooting, by muirburn and by the long-distance transportation of pollution from our power stations and factories.

A view from the fellfield high on the plateau of the Cairngorms, looking down to the alpine grassland and montane heath zones around Loch Avon.

Flora of the cultural landscapes

The cultural landscapes wrought by human activities across vast areas of our uplands may still have a wild and rugged aspect, beloved of hillwalkers, but for the botanist they are often depressingly dull. It is often necessary to make a long hike over unrewarding areas of species-poor acid grassland or heavily managed dwarf-shrub heath, created and shaped by human activities, in order to reach the precious small enclaves in which our richest mountain flora clings to survival. However, it is essential to get to know the commoner species of these depauperate hillsides in order to appreciate the more special plants of the mountain refuges.

The flora of managed heather moors includes some of the species that once grew on the floor of pinewoods, including Tormentil, Common Dog-violet, Heath Bedstraw and Germander Speedwell. Red and Sheep's Fescue, Common Bent and Sweet Vernal-grass grow in more open areas. Some moors are almost pure Heather with a little Wavy Hair-grass, but in parts of the Pennines Bilberry is a conspicuous feature, forming a dominant, bright green band, called 'bilberry edge', at the top of steep Millstone Grit escarpments.

Species growing amongst the Heather include Bell Heather, Cowberry and Crowberry on northern hill moors. Tormentil and Heath Bedstraw are again common. Green-ribbed Sedge is a conspicuous species which survives the trampling along rocky hill paths, and Hard Fern may appear in the shelter of rocks or streambanks. In wetter areas, Deergrass is common, with Bog Asphodel and Common Cottongrass as associates. Round-leaved Sundew and Common Butterwort supplement the poor moorland soil by trapping insects and absorbing their nutrients. Bog-myrtle grows in some wetter areas or forms banks by mountain streams.

Amongst hard granites, sandstones and grits, Sheep's Fescue, Common Bent and Mat-grass are the commonest grasses, often associated with Sheep's Sorrel. On slightly richer soils, Sweet Vernal-grass joins the previous grasses. Here you might also find Yorkshire Fog, Field Wood-rush, Bird's-foot Trefoil, Selfheal and Yarrow. Lady's Bedstraw grows in slightly deeper soil beds, and Wild Thyme and Harebell point to more base-rich conditions. Smooth Lady's-mantle is fairly common here; although it is essentially a lowland species, it is recorded at altitudes up to 1,210m on Ben Lawers, the highest mountain in Perthshire. Alpine Lady's-mantle begins to appear in this grassland above about 600m.

Lowland species can persist to remarkably high elevations in our mountains. As an example to emphasise this point, Ben Lawers is best known for its rich montane flora. However, in an hour or two exploring its summit area above 900m, you are just as likely to come across Mat-grass, Brown Bent, Wavy Hair-grass and Sheep's Fescue, Dioecious Sedge, Common Sedge, Common Mouse-ear, Marsh Violet, Common Dog-violet, Wild Thyme, Common Sorrel, Heath Bedstraw and Harebell. I have even found Wood Sorrel growing just 54m below the summit. The list on pages 399–401 gives the scientific names of all these lowland species, and shows the highest elevations at which they have been recorded.

Although the foregoing is by no means a comprehensive list of lowland species which invade the mountain environment, I hope it provides a background against which to set the more specialised montane and submontane species that are the focus of the next 13 chapters.

COMPARE AND CONTRAST: although climate and geology play their part, humans have had a huge impact on this magnificent, rugged but depauperate landscape, looking over the Mamore hills towards Ben Nevis from Glen Coe (above) ...

... In contrast, this landscape above Geiranger in Norway (below) shows high-altitude mountain woodland in the foreground with extensive semi-natural forest clothing the mountainsides and rising towards a natural treeline.

Southern outliers

chapter five

For anyone based in southern Britain, the most accessible starting points to begin exploring the flora of our mountains would be Dartmoor in Devon or the fine hills of the Brecon Beacons across the Severn in south Wales. Both are substantially higher than the surrounding land, and the resulting exposure results in a relatively severe climate. As a result they are home to many montane species that become commoner further north, plus a few specialities of their own.

The Lizard Peninsula, at the southernmost point of the British mainland, seems very much less obviously montane. This area of dramatic coastal cliffs and rolling heathlands is one of the classic sites of British botany, with many nationally rare heathland species (Byfield, 1991), but it rises to no more than 115m above sea level. Yet if we define a mountain as a site where any of the montane plants listed on pages 30–35 can be found, then the Lizard qualifies on the basis of two species. Considering why they occur here has the benefit of immediately testing the theories about the origins and survival of our mountain flora discussed in Chapter 3. It also offers a neat synergy with the endpoint of our botanical tour amongst the equally dramatic scenery and similar rock outcrops on Unst at the far north of Shetland in Chapter 17.

OPPOSITE PAGE: Fir Clubmoss growing on the hills of the Isle of Harris in the Outer Hebrides, in a more typically montane habitat than at its southernmost British locality on the Lizard.

The Lizard Peninsula

Geologically, the southern half of the Lizard is a complex mix of metamorphic and igneous rocks, but botanically the most important rock here is serpentine. This is a rare rock nationally, and where it

The Lizard Peninsula in Cornwall is best known botanically for its coastal and heathland plants, but, rather surprisingly, it is also home to two species from our montane list.

occurs in exposed locations, in the hills of Angus or on Shetland for example, it is often associated with an intriguing mountain flora. It is described as ultrabasic, because it contains very low levels of silica and calcium but high levels of magnesium and iron in particular. The low calcium levels mean it does not suit calcium-demanding species (true calcicoles) but the soil is basic enough for other calcicolous species to flourish. Conversely, many calcifuge species, more usually associated with acid soils, can grow on these basic but low-calcium soils.

The high levels of heavy metals in serpentine soils, especially magnesium, chromium and nickel, are toxic to many plant species. The soils are also low in many of the nutrients that plants need for growth, and often form no more than a shallow skin over the rock beneath. However, these conditions are not so different from the primitive soils around glaciers in which many arctic-alpines have evolved to grow.

The other critical factor here is climate. The Lizard has relatively mild winters and cool summers, but the headland is exposed to the full force of the Atlantic gales as deep depressions pass close to the British Isles. The frequency and strength of these depressions is greatest in winter, when gusts of up to 91 knots (169km/hour) have been recorded, and gales occur on around 30 days a year. This depresses temperatures and batters and desiccates any species that are not adapted to a windswept existence. Most importantly, the combination of soil and

Spring Sandwort on the serpentine soils of the Lizard in Cornwall.

exposure serves to exclude the blanket of woodland that exterminated the post-glacial flora elsewhere in southern England, and explains why two of our montane species can grow here.

The first of these, Spring Sandwort, is relatively plentiful on the serpentines on the western side of the peninsula. On an all-too-brief day visit there in May 1979 I found the sandwort, without too much difficulty, above Kynance Cove. It was growing with Spring Squill, Sea Campion and Sea Plantain, which are typical maritime species. It occurs much more regularly on the toxic soils of lead-mine spoil heaps in northern Britain, but the form on the Lizard tends to be smaller, with more blue-green leaves and bristly hairs. Beyond the Lizard, its next nearest site is in Somerset, where it grows in old lead workings in the Mendip Hills.

The other montane species here is Fir Clubmoss. It has a slightly different habitat. Parts of the Lizard are covered in a blanket of loess, a fine soil that was carried in on the wind. This is derived from granite, so it is poor in the minerals needed for plant growth. Fir Clubmoss is particularly associated with mounds of loess which are subject to waterlogging in winter and drought in summer. Although the soil here is acidic, as opposed to the ultrabasic soil on which the sandwort flourishes, the soil conditions and exposure again serve to exclude trees and other swamping vegetation. This has allowed this post-glacial survivor to hang on since the time when all of southern England was covered in arctic vegetation at the end of the last advance of the Ice Age.

We will return to Spring Sandwort in Chapter 7 in its more typical habitat on lead-mine spoil heaps further north, but this seems the appropriate place to introduce the other montane inhabitant of the Lizard.

Fir Clubmoss *Huperzia selago*

Fir Clubmoss (see photo p.76) features first on our list of British montane vascular plants because it is a relative of ferns that is regarded as one of the most primitive of our vascular plants. It is rather pleasing therefore that it also features first in our botanical tour. The common name is descriptive, and it always reminds me of the rather inadequate models of fir trees that are sold to accompany toy railways. It has stubby, stiff, upright branches which are forked once or twice and quite densely clothed in narrow, lance-shaped leaves.

Fir Clubmoss has a rather neat mechanism for dispersal. In the upper part of its stem it produces small, leafy, flattened bulbils (small buds) that project a little way beyond the leaves. As the plant dries out in late summer, these become taut. When an animal grazes the plant, or even brushes against it, the spring-loaded bulbils ping off (a great trick I used to enjoy showing students). This propels the bulbils some distance from the parent plant, and the wind may carry them further. If they land on open ground, they readily root and begin to grow. Because this mechanism is non-sexual, it results in genetically identical clones of the parent plant. The species can also reproduce sexually, with spores released from yellow, sausage-shaped pouches called sporangia at the bases of its upper leaves in late summer, but these are probably less important for its dispersal in Britain.

Its occurrence on the Lizard is not entirely surprising because, elsewhere in its range, Fir Clubmoss is one of the montane species that sometimes comes down from the high tops to grow on moorland at lower altitudes. This is a plant of acidic, nutrient-poor, sandy or peaty soils, generally in upland areas. It is relatively common across all the mountain areas discussed in this book, at altitudes up to 1,310m on Ben Nevis. It is most characteristic of bare, open windswept mountaintops and shoulders, but it also grows on rocky mountain ledges, as well as in upland grassland, heathland and blanket bog, with a few records virtually down to sea level. It was formerly found in a scattering of lowland sites in the west and north of England, but was lost from there by the 1930s as a result of agricultural 'improvement', drainage and muirburn. Outside Britain, it is a plant of the Arctic, and of mountains in Europe, the Himalayas and eastern North America.

Dartmoor

When I helped run field courses for young people on Dartmoor in the late 1970s, I never thought of myself as heading for the mountains. Yet when I think back to some of the biting winds and sleet showers we encountered, even in July, I realise that Dartmoor shares several characteristics with higher mountains further north.

Dartmoor is a big, rugged, dome-shaped mass of granite rock that rises to 621m at High Willhays. Significantly, it is the only British mountain block that lay south of the great ice-sheet that covered most of Britain during the last advance of the Ice Age, and its climate 15,000 years ago would have been as severe as that experienced by coastal regions of Greenland and Svalbard today. Water which penetrated narrow cracks in the granite froze and expanded in winter, prizing apart the rock to form the massive blocks we see today as tors – the dramatic towers of bare rock that crown many of the hilltops around the edge of Dartmoor – and creating the jumble of rocks called *clitter* that tumbles beneath them.

At this period, an arctic-alpine flora would have ruled on Dartmoor, just as we saw in Chapter 3 elsewhere in southern Britain. At Hawks Tor on nearby Bodmin Moor, for example, leaves and/or fruits of Dwarf Birch, Dwarf Willow, Alpine Meadow-rue and possibly Tufted Saxifrage have been found in gravelly soil buried in the late glacial period, showing that these species once grew on these Devon heights. As the climate warmed after the last advance of the Ice Age, the rainfall of Dartmoor rapidly increased. Peat began to spread, and today blanket bog smothers most of the rock above 450m, creating the rather bleak expanses of open moorland that are such a feature of Dartmoor.

Even although it mostly lies below 600m, Dartmoor is the highest land in the area and so is exposed to the worst of the Atlantic gales. This depresses temperatures and means that Princetown, 452m up

Dartmoor has many wild and rugged corners, such as Tavy Cleave where the River Tavy cuts through a dramatic steep-sided gorge. This is a site for Fir Clubmoss.

on the moor, has an average minimum temperature in February of just 0.8°C and an average July maximum of 17.7°C. Annual rainfall is 1,974mm, which accelerates the formation of blanket bog. Between 1961 and 1990, the Met Office recorded an annual average of 20 days of falling snow on the moor, although snow lay for significantly longer. In combination, those climatic conditions exclude swamping tree growth and leave the top of Dartmoor as a naturally open habitat.

The top of Dartmoor today resembles the lower slopes of many of Britain's mountains discussed in Chapter 4, and even the highest parts are no more than submontane. From our montane list, Cowberry grows at just two sites and Crowberry at only a few scattered sites on the north moor. Fir Clubmoss is thinly distributed on north-facing ledges on the tors and in several of Dartmoor's well-grazed valley mires. Forked Spleenwort, a submontane species that we will meet in Chapter 10, grows on the eastern edge of Dartmoor.

In August 1979, I set off to find another montane fern on Dartmoor at its southernmost British site. A botanical friend had given me a rough location for Parsley Fern near Princetown, and we drove down a minor road to a site in the middle of Dartmoor. There, we found a couple of clumps of the fern growing on a drystone granite wall. Nick Baldock of the Dartmoor National Park Authority tells me that two plants were still growing at this site recently.

Dartmoor, then, is very much on the edge of the range of montane and submontane species, but that makes it even more relevant to consider the ecology of the species that grow here.

Crowberry may get its name from its crow-black berries – or perhaps because its berries are so bitter that only a crow would eat them!

Crowberry *Empetrum nigrum*

Both Crowberry and Cowberry are submontane species of upland moors, but Crowberry is the commoner of the two on Dartmoor, growing at a few high-level sites. It is a low-growing, mat-forming shrub with rather shiny, deep-green, narrow leaves clustered around its stem. Its inconspicuous, short-lived, pale pinkish flowers are barely 2mm in diameter and develop into berries which are green at first but ripen to crow-black. True Crowberry in subspecies *nigrum* is dioecious, meaning it produces male and female flowers on different plants (only female plants therefore produce berries). High-altitude specimens with male and female flowers on the same plant belong to a separate subspecies, *hermaphroditum*, which we will return to in the next chapter.

Crowberry is a species of well-drained acid soils on moorlands and mountains, mainly in the west and north. It also grows on blanket bogs that have dried out through erosion or burning. In southern England, it is confined to high levels on Dartmoor and Exmoor, but it is widespread in the uplands of Wales and northern England and in suitable habitats almost throughout Scotland. It also grows almost down to sea level at exposed sites in Scotland, for example near Bettyhill in Sutherland. Indeed, as a coastal plant, it features in a plant community described by ecologists as 'decalcified fixed dunes with *Empetrum nigrum*' which marks a late stage in the progressive succession over time of undisturbed sand dunes towards woodland. Good examples of this far-from-montane community occur at Sands of Forvie in Aberdeenshire and Morrich More in Cromarty.

Beyond Britain, Crowberry is circumpolar in its distribution, extending from the mountains of Europe to the northern tip of Scandinavia, Siberia, Japan and North America south to California. It is also found in the lowlands of the Netherlands and Denmark. Bell & Tallis (1973) suggest that it is confined to cooler regions because low temperatures are needed to break the dormancy of its seeds. However, it cannot survive severe winter temperatures without the insulating effect of snow-cover, which is why it is absent from windswept mountaintops. Because many records do not distinguish between the two subspecies, it is unclear what upper altitude is reached by subspecies *nigrum*, but I suspect it rarely occurs above 760m.

Cowberry produces small bell-shaped flowers in drooping clusters, followed by glossy red berries in late summer.

Cowberry *Vaccinium vitis-idaea*

Like the previous species, Cowberry is a low-growing shrub, usually no more than 30cm tall. Its oval, leathery, evergreen leaves are characteristically dotted with small glands on their undersurface. It has small, white or pale pink flowers that develop in late summer into acidic red berries. Although the species has just two sites at the southern edge of its range on Dartmoor, it is a little commoner on the Brecon Beacons and then is found in most other upland areas as far north as Shetland. It grows on peaty heaths and moors, the drier parts of blanket bogs, in the understorey of pine and birch woods, and on well-drained slopes, ledges and screes in the mountains, at altitudes up to 1,095m in the Breadalbane hills of Perthshire. Its tough leaves are frost-tolerant and relatively unpalatable to sheep (Ritchie, 1956). Because it spreads by extensive horizontal rhizomes, it seems to be able to recover relatively quickly from muirburn.

Outwith Britain, it ranges from Iceland and the Faroes across northern Europe and Asia to Korea and Japan, as well as the mountains of central Europe, with separate subspecies in North America and Greenland. In Scotland it is often, rather confusingly, known as 'Cranberry', a name that elsewhere is applied to a related species found creeping through peat bogs.

Parsley Fern *Cryptogramma crispa*

When I found Parsley Fern growing on that wall in Dartmoor it was early August, so it was well developed and showed both its vegetative fronds – which are quite reminiscent of parsley leaves, as its name suggests – and its narrower, more upright fertile fronds, clustered with brown spores on their undersides. It is typically a species of boulder fields and fairly stable screes of acid rocks. It is nowhere common, but fortunately its bright green patches make it easy to spot from quite some distance. North of Dartmoor, it is found throughout the mountain regions of Britain, including a single site on Exmoor, always on acid substrates, but it is relatively rare in the north of Scotland and absent from Orkney and Shetland. It has disappeared from many parts of the Pennines, and may have declined elsewhere because of grazing. However, as I saw on Dartmoor, it is an adaptable plant which can readily colonise walls and bridges of local stone, roadside banks and the ruins of old buildings.

The Parsley Fern that I photographed on a drystone granite wall near Princetown in Dartmoor in August 1979; apparently it still survives at the same site all these years later.

It seems to grow most luxuriantly in fern beds that are protected under a prolonged blanket of winter snow. It is recorded at altitudes up to 1,300m on Ben Nevis, but as low as 50m on the Isle of Rum. Beyond Britain, it grows in the mountains of central Europe, Iceland, the Faroes, parts of western Scandinavia and eastern Siberia, but it is absent from the high Arctic.

Brecon Beacons

Crossing the Severn into south Wales, we reach the Brecon Beacons. These fine, green, rolling hills, interrupted here and there by dramatic crags, are indisputably mountainous in character, with a flora to match. They represent a ridge of Old Red Sandstone rock rising to a summit of 886m at Pen-y-Fan. The slopes of that hill are a similar mix to Dartmoor of upland grassland, heather moorland and bog, but the narrow summit ridge provides the southernmost site for Dwarf Willow – or it once did; Preston *et al.* (2002) show only pre-1986 records in the Brecon Beacons. To the west of the main ridge, Craig Cerrig-gleisiad is a dramatic, ice-carved escarpment, rising from 460m to a summit at 628m, with tall cliffs and stony scree slopes. Although lower than Pen-y-Fan and beneath the theoretical treeline, at around 640m here, its ungrazed rocks and ledges support a rich montane flora, which adds Green Spleenwort, Roseroot, Purple Saxifrage, Mossy Saxifrage and Northern Bedstraw to the species we have already met.

Crags like these beneath the 886m summit of Pen-y-Fan, the highest point in the Brecon Beacons, are home to several montane species.

A little way south-east of here, Craig y Cilau, overlooking Crickhowell and the Usk valley, is one of the biggest exposures of upland limestone in south Wales. I often dragged my poor in-laws there when visiting them in the 1980s, and found Mountain Melick quite commonly on the slopes, Limestone Fern amongst limestone screes, and Mossy Saxifrage in mossy runnels. The occurrence of Fairy Flax shows how lime-rich the soil is, but Crowberry grows where the soil is more acid on the Waun Ddu raised mire. Viviparous Fescue and Green Spleenwort are other montane species recorded here.

Moving west, the Old Red Sandstone crags above Llyn y Fan Fawr at the western edge of Fforest Fawr are another rich montane site. The route in from the east made for a pleasant family walk, giving me the excuse for a couple of visits there to find Mossy Saxifrage on ledges dripping with water, Green Spleenwort and abundant Roseroot. In flushes below the crags, Marsh Marigold grows in its small montane form, with stems that creep over the damp, mossy soil and root at their nodes. This miniature version usually has just a single flower less than 3cm in diameter. It is sometimes called subspecies *minor* of Marsh Marigold, although Stace (2010) reduces it to variety *radicans*. I think it is probably an ecological form produced in response to the cool climate and short growing season.

The crags above Llyn y Fan Fach to the west of here are even richer, with Stone Bramble, Dwarf Willow and Northern Bedstraw, and Cowberry on more open slopes. Further west still, there are some fine examples of limestone pavement – flat-topped exposures of bare limestone rock intercut with shady crevices, described more fully in Chapter 7. Crevices in the limestone pavement at Carreg Yr Ogof add Mountain Everlasting and Limestone Fern to our montane tally, along with Fir Clubmoss, Green Spleenwort and Mossy Saxifrage.

South of this, Craig-y-Llyn near Hirwaun has Parsley Fern, Fir Clubmoss Roseroot and Cowberry. Stone Bramble, Mossy Saxifrage and Serrated Wintergreen were known here in the past, but are apparently now lost. Several of these species merit further attention before continuing on our journey to the more dramatic mountains of north Wales.

Green Spleenwort *Asplenium viride*

It is no real surprise that Green Spleenwort should be the first true fern that we meet on our mountain journey northwards, at its southernmost site in the Brecon Beacons, because it is not one of the most strongly montane plants. It is recorded to no higher than 988m in the Breadalbane hills of Perthshire and comes down almost to sea level in the far north-west. It is a neat little fern, with tufts of fronds that have delicate green stalks and rounded green, lightly toothed lobes. It is typically a plant of damp, shady ledges and moist crevices, always amongst base-rich rocks. Very occasionally it grows on man-made habitats, such as the mortar of walls, and as a rare colonist of old metal mine workings.

Green Spleenwort has a green leaf stalk (more correctly called a rachis in ferns), distinguishing it from the rather similar Maidenhair Spleenwort, which has blackish stalks.

Globally, Green Spleenwort is a typical arctic-alpine. It is found from southern Greenland and Iceland to the mountains of southern Europe east as far as Turkey, and in the mountains of northern Asia and North America, always in base-rich habitats.

Purple Saxifrage *Saxifraga oppositifolia*

Purple Saxifrage is one of the most attractive of montane plants. It flowers early in the year in March or April, producing its showy clusters of pink-purple flowers as soon as the snows have melted. By the time most botanists go hillwalking, its beautiful displays are well past, although a few battered flowers may last into August. However, with experience, its loose mats of creeping stems are fairly easy to recognise. They look a bit like Thyme, but their leaves are more blue-green and their stems are red.

The species is found in base-rich and stony ground in only the richest montane sites, so that its distribution map shows a scattering of dots in the Brecon Beacons and Snowdonia, the Pennines, Lake District and Southern Uplands. It is a little more widespread in the Scottish Highlands, where it is recorded to 1,211m on Ben Lawers. It also grows on mountains on several Scottish islands, including Hoy in Orkney, North Roe in Shetland, the mountains of Rum, and Trotternish on Skye. In the north-west, it comes down almost to sea level, for example on the sea-cliffs of Lewis and Cape Wrath. It even grows in the clifftop pastures of Hirta, in the wonderful archipelago of St Kilda to the west of the Western Isles.

Beyond here, it is found right across arctic Europe, Asia and America, in the high mountains of central Europe and central Asia, and in the mountains of North America. In Greenland, it grows in the most northerly terrestrial plant community in the world at 83°N in Peary Land, suggesting a remarkable degree of frost-resistance. By hugging low to the ground, Purple Saxifrage maximises the heat available from the early-spring sun, and its cup-shaped flowers may trap heat to speed the maturation of its seeds.

Purple Saxifrage produces mats of long, creeping, leafy stems covered with showy clusters of pink-purple flowers in early spring.

Mossy Saxifrage *Saxifraga hypnoides*

The dripping ledges where Mossy Saxifrage grows in the Brecon Beacons are very much its typical habitat. It is a plant of streamsides, mossy runnels and wet grassland in mountains, spreading onto damp screes and cliffs. It is commoner in base-rich areas, but also grows in more acid sites. Its leggy, upright flowering stems stand to 20cm tall, topped by a loose cluster of one to five very open, showy, white flowers.

Mossy Saxifrage grows at one site south of the Brecon Beacons, in the Cheddar Gorge in Somerset, where it is rare and difficult to find. There are other odd records for it in southern England and west Wales, but these are thought to be escapes from cultivation. North of here, it is found in the higher mountains of Wales, the Peak District, north Pennines and Lakes, through the Border hills and in the central and western Highlands, including Skye and Rum. It is much rarer in the east Highlands and absent from the Outer Hebrides and Northern Isles. In the north of England, it is known by the alternative name of Dovedale Moss, after a popular Peak District beauty spot where the species grows.

It is recorded at altitudes up to 1,210m in Perthshire, with a lowest record at 10m above sea level on a north-facing slope beneath cliffs on the south shore of the Moray Firth in Banffshire, where it grows with Purple Saxifrage and Roseroot. Beyond Britain,

The leafy shoots of Mossy Saxifrage look quite moss-like, but, unlike mosses, it spreads by long runners into the surrounding vegetation.

its distribution is somewhat unclear, because it belongs to a group of very similar 'mossy' saxifrages whose taxonomy is difficult and confused. However, it seems to be confined to the Faroes, Iceland, and restricted areas in western Norway, Belgium and France. By that token, Mossy Saxifrage may well be rarer globally than relatives such as Highland and Tufted Saxifrage, which we regard as conservation priorities in Britain.

Roseroot *Sedum rosea*

Roseroot is a submontane species that reaches its southernmost British site in the Brecon Beacons. It is a handsome plant, with sturdy stems up to 30cm tall which are surrounded by succulent, overlapping, rather greyish-green leaves that curl upwards like praying hands. From May to early July, its stems are topped by dome-shaped clusters with many small greenish-yellow flowers. These ripen on female plants into swollen, reddish fruiting capsules that are easily mistaken for flowers.

Roseroot occurs in most of the mountain areas we will be visiting in later chapters (although not in the Peak District). It grows most typically in the mountains in a rock crevice, amongst boulder scree or on an open, mossy rock ledge. It is found at altitudes up to 1,166m in Perthshire, usually in base-rich soil. It also has a second, discontinuous range on sea-cliffs, especially near seabird colonies, on the coasts of Wales and northern Britain, including the Western and Northern Isles. It is also a traditional cottage-garden plant, so it can turn up elsewhere as a garden escape. Grazing animals may be one of the main controls on its distribution; sheep love it, and I suspect Red Deer do too. It is found throughout arctic Europe, Asia, Greenland and North America and in many of the mountains of these continents, south in Europe to the Pyrenees and Italian Alps.

The attractive flowery heads of Roseroot can be found on cliff ledges and crevices, or sheltered amongst boulders – as here in the Northern Corries of Cairn Gorm.

Dwarf Willow *Salix herbacea*

In lots of ways, I think of Dwarf (or Least) Willow as an associate of Fir Clubmoss, in broadly similar habitats – on rocky, windswept ridges and summits or in mossy hollows where snow lies late. It is easily overlooked because its shrubby stems stay mostly underground, so just its glossy, rounded, strongly veined leaves, each no more than 2cm long, appear above ground. Just occasionally, behind the shelter of a boulder, it can appear as a mini-bonsai tree, perhaps to a glorious height of 10cm. Its short, stubby catkins (see photo on p.60) appear at the same time as its leaves in June and early July, with male and female flowers on separate plants. The swollen, reddish capsules on female plants split around August to release seeds that are dispersed in the wind on long, woolly hairs.

It is unusual to find Dwarf Willow below 600m, although it does come down to near sea level in Shetland and Sutherland, and it is found at altitudes up to 1,310m on Ben Nevis. North of the Brecon Beacons, it occurs in a few spots in north Wales and the Yorkshire Dales, including Ingleborough and Pen-y-ghent, the north Pennines, the Lake District, and the Dumfries and Galloway hills. It is much more widespread in the north and west Highlands and the Northern and Western Isles. Elsewhere, it has a wide circumpolar distribution in Europe, Asia and North America, and in mountains of southern Europe.

Northern Bedstraw's strongly veined dark green leaves form whorls of four around its sturdy, upright stems.

Northern Bedstraw *Galium boreale*

This white-flowered bedstraw is a relatively scarce plant of mountain rocks in the Brecon Beacons and Snowdonia. It is commoner further north in the limestone scars of Teesdale and the northern Pennines and base-rich rocks in the Lake District, but in all these areas it tends to be restricted to ledges and crevices beyond the reach of grazing sheep. It is also found more widely throughout the Southern Uplands, Scottish Highlands and Inner Hebrides, but not on the Outer Hebrides or Northern Isles.

It prefers base-rich substrates and damp or slightly shaded conditions amongst rocks or on mountain ledges. It is recorded to 885m on Helvellyn and 1,065m in the Breadalbane hills, but also comes down virtually to sea level in stabilised sand dunes in the far north-west. More widely, it has a boreal and continental montane distribution, from northern Europe south to the Italian Alps and the Caucasus, as well as Asia, Greenland and northern North

America. Beware that Heath Bedstraw is also common in mountain areas and ascends even higher, to 1,220m on Ben Nevis, but it is a much more delicate, rather sprawling plant.

Viviparous Fescue *Festuca vivipara*

Grasses are not always easy plants to identify, not least because of the complex terminology used for their different parts. However, this widespread upland grass is easier to recognise than most. It has tufts of fine leaves at the base of shoots which stand around 10–20cm tall. In place of tiny flowers at the tip of the stem, it has green bulbils which sprout into new plantlets while still attached to the stem. These plantlets can be knocked or blown off the parent plant and develop into new, independent plants. This is clearly an adaptation to the short growing season and extreme exposure of its mountain and arctic habitats. Other grasses occasionally produce plantlets in the same way, but this species is always 'viviparous' (meaning that it carries live young).

Viviparous Fescue is at the southernmost limit of its world range in the Brecon Beacons. North of here, it is widespread in Snowdonia, the Lake District, the Southern Uplands and throughout the Highlands and Islands, and beyond there in arctic regions and north-east Europe. It is a plant of grassy and rocky places in the uplands, on both basic and acid soils. It ascends to 1,215m on Ben Macdui in the Cairngorms but descends virtually to sea level in north-west Scotland. It is a tough plant, one of the few species that can thrive in the thin, rocky soil of windswept mountaintops, alongside species like Three-leaved Rush and Spiked Wood-rush. It also grows in open, upland woods, on streambanks and in the drier parts of bogs.

The little plantlets sprouting at the top of the stems of Viviparous Fescue give the grass head a characteristic leafy, fan-shaped appearance.

The mountain heart of Wales

chapter six

Snowdonia is the first truly spectacular mountain area on our journey northwards, with rugged peaks, dramatic crags and verdant, steep-sided valleys. It is appropriate therefore that the Welsh name for the area, Eryri, probably means 'the mountain land'. Snowdonia has a proud history of botanical exploration and a diverse range of montane species, including several tantalising rarities and one species that is found nowhere else in Britain. It is not a landscape coloured by spectacular flowers. You have to work hard to find its most special plants, but that makes finding them even more rewarding. Nearby, Cadair Idris also hosts a good range of montane plants and adds to the interest of the region.

Snowdonia (*Eryri*)

Geologically, Snowdonia is built from a complex mixture of igneous and sedimentary rocks. Large areas of acidic rocks including slates, grits, rhyolite and granite host a very restricted flora, and most of the landscape is species-poor acid grassland, further denuded by a long tradition of sheep grazing. The richest flora clings onto limited outcrops of lime-rich rocks, which geologists recognise as dolerites and pumice tuffs, on crags beyond the reach of sheep. Even here, the historic depredations of plant collectors have impacted on plant populations. Erosion caused by the huge numbers of visitors who come to enjoy the spectacular scenery has not helped, although the Snowdonia National Park Authority has made great progress in upgrading the paths so they can better cope with this pressure.

Only around 70km^2 of land here lies above the 2,000-foot (610m) contour – an area about a tenth the size of Anglesey – although there

OPPOSITE PAGE: The view down to Llyn Idwal and the floor of Cwm Idwal from deep within Twll Du, when I was botanising there in 1983.

Snowdon: a view towards the summit from the top of the Pyg Track, with Glaslyn below.

are 16 tops above 3,000 feet (914m). The close proximity to the sea produces an oceanic climate, and the Snowdon summit is one of the wettest places in Britain, with an estimated annual rainfall of around 5m. Although not excessively cold, frost and ice are frequent at high altitudes, especially during periods of easterly wind. Snow rarely falls on more than 40 days a year between December and March, and lies for maybe 70 days in total, although accumulated snow can last in a few gullies until early summer.

The whole landscape of Snowdonia was shaped and sculpted by glaciers, and these cut two great valleys through the massif. The Pass of Llanberis separates Snowdon from the Glyder Mountains to the east, then the Nant Ffrancon Pass divides these from the Carneddau further east still. Each of these blocks shares a common flora, but there are subtle differences too. Today, some of the rarest plants which survive in Snowdonia have been lost from Snowdon itself, although there is always a chance that they hang on in the seedbank or perhaps on some little-visited rock ledge.

Snowdon (*Yr Wyddfa*)

At 1,086m, Snowdon is the highest British mountain south of the Scottish Highlands. Strictly speaking, the Welsh name Yr Wyddfa (which is thought to mean 'The Tumulus', although the derivation is obscure) refers only to the summit region, which consists of a series of narrow ridges spreading out like a misshapen, five-legged starfish, with vertiginous slopes on either side. The main walking routes pick their way up these slopes, then follow the ridge tops, which makes for spectacular scenery and rewarding walking.

Walking up Snowdon on the Watkin Path, we always used to stop near Cwm Llan to admire the spectacular displays of Parsley Fern that grew on the spoil heap from an old slate mine.

In the 1970s, I helped run adventure holidays here for children. Ascending the mountain really was an adventure for them and they were often overawed by the rugged landscape – a response which I think we too readily repress as adults. On these holidays we climbed Snowdon mainly by the Watkin Path from Pont Bethania to the south, but I have also slogged up the spectacular Pyg Track from Pen-y-Pass. I saw relatively little mountain flora along these routes, because the slopes are heavily sheep-grazed, the vegetation near the paths is badly eroded and the rocks are mainly acid. The best bit on the Watkin Path is the former slate quarry in Cwm Llan. Parsley Fern grows abundantly on the slate spoil heaps and on the walls of the old quarry workers' barracks. Small plants of Starry Saxifrage grow on damp, shady patches on the walls, as well as higher up where the path reaches the shoulder between Bwlch Ciliau and Bwlch y Saethau.

The summit area around Snowdon is so eroded, and the soil so acid, that frankly it is dull botanically. There is plenty of Woolly Fringe-moss, a few rather scruffy plants of Dwarf Willow and occasional tufts of Stiff Sedge, Alpine Clubmoss and Fir Clubmoss, and I believe one patch of Dwarf Juniper, but little else.

To see more of the Snowdon flora, you need to allow plenty of time to scramble up to the crags, seeking out the lime-rich rock outcrops that sheep cannot reach. The steep slopes of Clogwyn Du'r Arddu are the richest for their montane flora, but the north- and east-facing crags of Cwm Glas and the slopes of Crib Goch are also worth exploring, although none of these slopes reveal their plants easily. Here you will find patches of Purple and Mossy Saxifrage, perhaps with Starry Saxifrage in damp scree, cushions of Moss Campion, tufts of Green Spleenwort, the white flowers of Spring Sandwort and Alpine Scurvy-grass, and the more robust-looking Mountain Sorrel and Roseroot, along perhaps with the bright yellow spheres of Globeflower.

Some of the most special Snowdon plants grow on the inaccessible crags of Clogwyn Du'r Arddu, where the soil is enriched by a band of fossil-bearing limestone rock.

Search amongst the damp grass and you may find the glossy leaves and inconspicuous, wind-pollinated flowers of Alpine Meadow-rue. Alpine Saw-wort is also recorded, although less commonly, and I believe Holly Fern still survives on Clogwyn y Garnedd. Another rarity around Snowdon is Alpine Bistort, at its only Welsh, and southernmost British, site. It was found on Cwm Glas Mawr, above Llanberis Pass, by Edward Lhuyd in the 1690s, then lost until it was rediscovered in 1947 by the botanist Evan Roberts. The species is also known from Cwm Idwal, although I have never found it there. One plant that is perplexingly rare in Snowdonia, although quite frequent in similar-looking acidic hillsides across mid-Wales, is Mountain Pansy – which we will return to in the next chapter.

Snowdon specialities

Two of Snowdon's rarest plants merit special mention here. The first is Irish Saxifrage *Saxifraga rosacea*, which was first reported in the area on the rocks of Cwm Idwal in 1796, but was also found on Snowdon at a height of about 850m. The herbarium of the Croydon Natural History and Scientific Society has a specimen collected in the region of Llyn Du'r Arddu in 1918, although the label hints at some disagreements as to whether this was truly Irish Saxifrage or the commoner Mossy Saxifrage. Rather improbably, it was flowering in early March. However the species has not been seen in Snowdonia since 1978, so that today within the British Isles it is only known from western Ireland. (The Manchester Museum herbarium has a specimen collected by

The knife-edged stony ridge of Crib Goch (the 'red ridge') looking westwards towards the summit of Snowdon, the background peak just left of centre.

George Don from Glen Dole – presumably Glen Doll in Angus which we will meet in Chapter 11 – but it has never been refound there and is now thought to be an error from a mixed collection.)

The problem is that Irish Saxifrage belongs to the Mossy Saxifrage group, the species of which are often difficult to separate because they are so highly variable in their growth form, leaf-shape and the size and shape of their petals, sometimes even within one patch of plants. Because of these identification challenges, it is possible that Irish Saxifrage may still grow unrecognised elsewhere in Britain. The key distinction to watch out for is that Mossy Saxifrage always has a long bristle-like point to its leaf, whereas the end of the leaf of Irish Saxifrage is more broadly angled, with no more than a short bristle. Irish Saxifrage is also recorded from Iceland and the Faroes, and on mountains from Germany to Poland.

The most charismatic of all Snowdon plants was discovered in the 1690s and described as *bulbosa alpina juncifolia* ('bulbous alpine plant with rush leaves') by Edward Lhuyd, the Welsh botanist, linguist and antiquary. He was born in Shropshire, the son of Edward Lloyd, but adopted the Welsh form Lhuyd (or Lhwyd). He recorded the plant 'on the highest rocks of Snowdon' and on the 'Trigyfylchau Rocks' (a name referring to the three adjoining gullies) above Cwm Idwal. Until very recently, this plant was named *Lloydia serotina* in his honour, but we know it more commonly as Snowdon Lily. It is recorded in Britain only from the Snowdon and Glyder massifs, and, because of this restricted range, it qualifies as the first of our three-star mountain enigmas (see Chapter 1).

★★★ Snowdon Lily *Gagea serotina*

Snowdon's most special mountain plant is a delicate lily, no taller than 15cm, with narrow, grass-like leaves and solitary or occasionally paired flowers. These are 10–15mm across, with four rather waxy, dark-veined white petals. It flowers in May or June and the leaves wither soon after, to regrow from the underground bulb next year. It always seemed appropriate that it was named *Lloydia serotina* after one of the area's first botanical explorers, Edward Lhuyd. Sadly, recent studies of its molecular chemistry have shown it to be so closely related to the stars-of-Bethlehem that it should be united with them as *Gagea serotina*.

Our name of Snowdon Lily is highly parochial, because the species is also found at a scattering of mountain sites from the Alps to the Himalayas, Japan and western China, Arctic Russia (but not the European Arctic) and the mountains of western North America from Alaska to New Mexico (where it is known as Common Alp-lily). Given that geographic range, the alternative name of Mountain Spiderwort seems rather more appropriate. In the Alps, I have found it, beautifully in flower, in open gravel close to the glacier that still hangs in the Rotmoostal, high above Obergurgl in Austria.

Beyond its shady home in Cwm Idwal, it is known from five other sites in a 13km belt from Snowdon to the Carneddau, on north- and east-facing corries at altitudes of 640–730m, sometimes embedded in cushions of Moss Campion. It is mainly confined to shady, inaccessible ledges and narrow rock fissures, partly as a result of the wholesale destruction of the Victorian era (Marren, 1999). In those days, wealthy collectors would pay substantial sums for rooted specimens of the Snowdon rarities. Guides made a living by leading plant connoisseurs to the choicest specimens, armed with long hooked poles to pluck them from their lofty perches. Unscrupulous collectors were known to strip every last specimen from sites to deny their competitors.

As a result, the already reclusive Snowdon Lily became desperately rare. One site recently had only six plants, although the largest may hold as many as 2,000. A few criminals may still be

INSET: The delicate flowers of Snowdon Lily are white with reddish veins. They are pollinated by flies, but rarely seem to set seed in Britain.

Snowdon Lily, growing on a hidden ledge on the steep slopes of Clogwyn Coch, below Snowdon. The photos are from the invaluable plant identification website at www.ukwildflowers.com.

prepared to break the law by collecting this protected species, but the worst destruction now comes from sheep, which strip any plant within their reach. Plants are not easy to spot, with just a tuft of grass-like leaves, so just possibly other populations survive undetected on ledges elsewhere in Snowdonia.

If all that is not bad enough, the surviving sites of Snowdon Lily are largely on routes favoured by rock and ice climbers in winter, such as the route called 'Travesty' on Clogwyn Du (BMC, 2010). If they climb purely on ice, the lilies should be safe, but if they are tempted to climb when the rock ledges are ice-free, the plant would be hugely susceptible to damage. To its credit, the British Mountaineering Council recognises these threats and is publicising them to its members.

When not in flower, the narrow, twisted, rush-like leaves of Snowdon Lily make it a difficult plant to spot.

The most intriguing question is why Snowdon Lily clings on in Snowdonia but not on other British mountains, given its large international range. Unusually amongst our mountain enigmas, we seem to have a rather satisfying answer for this species.

The starting point is recent studies which showed that the plants in Wales are more different from their relatives in the Alps than can be explained by 12,000 years of genetic drift since the end of the last Ice Age (Rhind & Jones, 2003). That suggests that the Welsh plants did not invade from continental Europe after the ice retreated, but had been living in the area for rather longer. We need to remember that the Ice Age was not an unremitting, unwavering event. There were warm periods when the ice melted back, followed by colder periods when it advanced once more. As the last period of the Ice Age drew to a close, it seems plausible that some of the peaks of north Wales began to project through the ice. Snowdon Lily was then able to make the short hop to there from the tundra south of the ice, and it clung on to these ice-free outcrops until the climate warmed and the ice departed.

Then, very quickly, the lily became isolated at a few sites that had the altitude, exposure and soil type it requires, and probably died out from many more. Today in Wales it rarely forms ripe seed and relies almost entirely on vegetative spread by bulbs. Assuming this was always the case, it would have no way of invading new habitats further north after the Ice Age, and was left stranded in the Welsh mountains. It has clung on ever since, probably slowly declining in suboptimal habitat. In the higher mountains of Europe, where glaciers still prevail, it may still regularly set seed, allowing it to spread and flourish. Given its sensitivity in Wales, climate change could soon become a major threat to the species. For now, its relict population appears stable, so long as the sheep, the ice climbers and unscrupulous collectors are kept at bay.

One other great Snowdon rarity, Tufted Saxifrage, is best considered at the next stop on our journey, but before we move on, we should first consider some of the commoner arctic-alpines that we have encountered on Snowdon itself.

Alpine Clubmoss *Diphasiastrum alpinum*

Like Fir Clubmoss, which we met in Chapter 5, Alpine Clubmoss frequently grows near the summit of mountains, but the two species look quite dissimilar and prefer different habitats. The creeping stems of Alpine Clubmoss are densely covered in blue-green leaves. Upright stems branch off from these and form even-topped clusters, with a cylindrical 'cone' at the tip of each upright branch. This produces the plant's reproductive spores. Some of the creeping stems reach out to find new habitats, budding off fan-shaped clusters of stubby stems that can break off and form new plants. In my experience, these almost always seem to run downhill, and I joke that it will one day become a lowland plant.

Whereas Fir Clubmoss inhabits windswept summits, Alpine Clubmoss prefers short grassy or heathy areas just below the summit. It typically grows on well-drained, rather stony slopes, but sometimes amongst quite dense vegetation that is clipped short by the wind or grazing animals. Although it is rare at the south of its range in the Brecon Beacons, Alpine Clubmoss is common, but fairly localised, in all the other montane areas from Snowdonia northwards, reaching 1,220m on Ben Macdui in the Cairngorms. Beyond Britain, it is found throughout the Arctic and in high mountains from the Pyrenees to Japan and Quebec.

Alpine Clubmoss: creeping stems and blue-green leaves help distinguish it from other clubmosses.

Globeflower *Trollius europaeus*

Globeflower qualifies as montane from its appearance on mountain ledges, but it also turns up far from mountains. Indeed, at its southernmost sites in the Brecon Beacons, it mainly grows in unimproved grassland and wet meadows. It is a delightful plant that we happily grow in our garden back home. Its stems stand up to 60cm tall, topped in summer by rich yellow flowers whose petal-like sepals wrap together into an all-enclosing globe. Its leaves are palmate (meaning they have usually five spreading lobes, originating from a single point). They look confusingly like the leaves of Wood Cranesbill, with which this species sometimes grows. The flowers attract various small insects, which must crawl between the overlapping golden, glossy sepals to pollinate the flower.

I think of Globeflower primarily as a plant of upland meadows, such as the lovely nature reserve near Malham appropriately called Globeflower Wood that we will meet in the next chapter. As George Peterken eloquently showed in his book on *Meadows* in this series (2013), upland meadows are disappearing across Britain as they are drained, ploughed and drenched in fertiliser by intensive farming. Today few upland meadows with Globeflower survive, but the species is commoner on mountain rock ledges or sheltered crevices, beyond the reach of large herbivores, or on the sides of a rushing mountain stream in all the mountain areas we will visit in later chapters, usually on base-rich soils.

Globeflower is recorded up to 1,090m on Beinn a' Bhuird in the Cairngorms, but comes close to sea level on cliffs in the far north-west. It is common on Mull, Rum and Skye, but does not reach the Outer

Globeflower, beyond its remaining meadow habitats, is a showy component of the tall-herb community on mountain rock ledges with a deep, damp soil, beyond the reach of grazing animals.

Hebrides or Northern Isles. Outside Britain, it is common in all the European mountains in damp meadows and clearings in mountain woods. It also grows in similar grasslands and hillsides in Scandinavia, to well north of the Arctic Circle, but does not reach Svalbard or Iceland.

Alpine Meadow-rue *Thalictrum alpinum*

Alpine Meadow-rue is a difficult plant to spot because its glossy, lobed leaves are easily lost amongst surrounding vegetation. In midsummer, its wiry, unbranched flower stems grow no more than 15cm tall (usually less). Its tiny flowers have pale purple, petal-like perianth segments around 3mm long, and slightly longer stamens topped by yellow anthers. These are near-invisible because, being wind-pollinated, they have no need to attract insects.

There is something almost ethereal about Alpine Meadow-rue. With short, wiry stems and tiny, wind-pollinated flowers, it is difficult to spot – and difficult to photograph – in its damp mountain habitats.

It typically grows at the edges of stony streams and flushes, amongst open hill grassland and on damp rock ledges, from around sea level in the north of Scotland to 1,190m in the Perthshire hills. North of Snowdonia, it is found only in the Lake District and the northern Pennines, quite sparsely in the Dumfries and Galloway hills, then widely in the Highlands, especially in the wetter west, north to Orkney and Shetland. Beyond here, it is found throughout the arctic and alpine areas of Europe, Asia and North America.

Beware confusion with Lesser Meadow-rue, which has branching inflorescences, is usually taller than 15cm, and has larger and more multilobed leaves. It also grows on cliff ledges and scree in Wales (reaching 855m on Snowdon) and in the hills of northern England, but not in the Scottish mountains.

Alpine Saxifrage *Saxifraga nivalis*

This short but sturdy white-flowered saxifrage grows most characteristically on mossy ledges or crevices on bluffs of base-rich rock that are so narrow that very little else can establish there. The rocks are usually shady, damp but not dripping wet, and often north- or east-facing.

It is recorded from Clogwyn y Garnedd and Clogwyn Du'r Arddu on the sides of Snowdon, and there are also a few plants on the rock face of Cwm Idwal. In the Lake District it is known only from High Cup Nick and from the east side of Helvellyn at around 855m. In the Southern Uplands only one small colony may survive on a mossy rock at Black Hope in the Moffat hills. It is a more widespread, although scarce, at scattered sites through the Scottish Highlands, where it has a rather western tendency, probably because of the risk of drought in drier eastern areas.

Amongst the Scottish islands, it is found on Skye, where it is rare at sites on the Trotternish ridge and even rarer on damp rock ledges high in the corries of the Cuillin hills. I have seen it on Fionchra on Rum, and there is an intriguing old record from a gully below Beinn Mhor on South Uist. It is recorded from altitudes of 356m at Quiraing on the Isle of Skye to 1,300m in the Cairngorms. It often seems reluctant to fully open its rather scruffy-looking flowers, but it does set seed readily at its Highland sites. Seed is rarely if ever recorded at its Cumbrian sites, suggesting that it may be struggling to survive there. It is found all round the arctic and subarctic regions of Europe, Asia, Greenland and eastern North America, and in Europe as far south as northern Germany.

ABOVE: Alpine Saxifrage grows most typically on damp, mossy, base-rich rock ledges, as here in the Breadalbane hills of Perthshire.
BELOW: The ovaries of Starry Saxifrage at the centre of the white flowers are yellowish when the flowers first open, but turn red after the fruits are fertilised.

Starry Saxifrage *Saxifraga stellaris*

Starry Saxifrage is a charming plant of damp rock ledges, streamsides, flushes and damp, stony, usually rather acidic ground throughout the British mountains, from here in Snowdonia northwards to Hoy on Orkney. It spreads by stolons (creeping stems) that extend over the damp soil, producing neat rosettes of oval leaves with very slightly serrated edges. Its delicate flowers have five narrow white petals, each with two yellow spots towards their base, contrasting nicely with the pinkish anthers. It is recorded at a higher altitude than any other British plant at 1,340m on Ben Nevis, but does not occur in the lower hills of the Peak District or Yorkshire Dales. Outside Britain, it is widespread from arctic Russia to Greenland and Labrador and through the European mountains, south to Corsica.

Scurvy-grasses in upland areas are tricky to tell apart. This one on a lead-mine spoil heap in the Yorkshire Dales National Park has fleshy enough leaves to be subspecies *alpina*, but plants in similar habitats are usually assigned to subspecies *pyrenaica*.

Alpine Scurvy-grass *Cochlearia pyrenaica* subspecies *alpina*

Alpine Scurvy-grass is another conspicuous plant of mountain streamlets, flushes and wet rock ledges, recorded at altitudes up to 1,240m on Ben Nevis. It has small, white, four-petalled flowers and open rosettes of glossy kidney-shaped leaves. The leaves are relatively fleshy, which may help protect the plant from frosts, but nowhere near as fleshy as those of scurvy-grasses growing at coastal sites.

Alpine Scurvy-grass is sufficiently distinctive that Sell & Murrell (2014) still regard it as a full species, *Cochlearia alpina*, although the argument has always been whether this is a true species or just a form developed in response to exposed mountain habitats. The problem is that it belongs to an aggregate of three very similar and closely related scurvy-grasses which tend to grade one into another, but the current consensus is that the mountain plant is a subspecies of Pyrenean Scurvy-grass *C. pyrenaica*. Whenever we find a scurvy-grass growing on damp montane cliffs, wet mountain gullies, mossy flushes and springsides we can safely call it Alpine Scurvy-grass. The confusion in identity makes the species' world range unclear, but similar plants are known in the mountains of central and western Europe.

Mountain Sorrel *Oxyria digyna*

Mountain Sorrel is related to the common docks that occur as familiar weeds in gardens. It has dock-like flowering and fruiting heads, but is best recognised by its rather fleshy kidney-shaped leaves. These do taste acid, as 'sorrel' would suggest, although I don't especially recommend them.

It typically grows – as it does here in Snowdonia – on ungrazed rock ledges, in wet, shady gullies, on scree slopes and beside streams. It is found in the mountains of Wales and the Lake District, at a few sites in the Southern Uplands, then throughout the Scottish Highlands at altitudes up to 1,240m on Ben Nevis. It grows as far north as Shetland, where it is found almost at sea level beside Ronas Voe. Climbing any mountain, it is worth checking gravel on the banks of streams, because rooted plants of the sorrel are easily washed off their crags by rainstorms or melting snow and become established, at least briefly, on streambanks at lower altitude. Elsewhere it is found in similar habitats throughout the Arctic and the mountains of north temperate regions.

Mountain Sorrel is a conspicuous feature of many mountain crags and scree slopes, with its fleshy, kidney-shaped leaves and dock-like fruiting heads.

Glyder Fawr and Cwm Idwal

Moving eastwards, the central block of mountains between the Llanberis and Nant Ffrancon passes is dominated by Glyder Fawr (999m). Although a little lower than Snowdon itself, this area has rather more outcropping calcareous rock and so is even richer botanically. The crags below Tryfan and at Clogwyn Du are worth exploring, but the most famous, and probably the best, of all the Snowdonia sites is the magnificent, sweeping, glacial-cut corrie of Cwm Idwal. This is approached by a relatively easy path from Llyn Ogwen, passing Llyn Idwal on the way.

Edward Lhuyd knew Cwm Idwal, and amongst his discoveries there was Oblong Woodsia. Thomas Johnson, a 17th-century apothecary who was interested in the herbal uses of wild plants, also explored the area and recorded several of its most special plants. His first visit in August 1639 was on a day when thick cloud shrouded the tops. That fits the reputation of Cwm Idwal, which amusingly is recorded in three different volumes of the New Naturalist series: Bruce Campbell's visit was in 'some of the most atrocious summer weather in which natural history field-work could be attempted' (North *et al.*, 1949); John Raven ventured into Cwm Idwal when it was 'not only ... raining in torrents, but there was a full gale blowing as well' (Raven & Walters, 1956); and William Condry described being there in fog and rain when 'if I'd been alone, I daresay I would have turned back, discouraged by the water seeping coldly down my neck' (Condry, 1981).

That weather is partly a key to the site's importance. The north-east facing cliffs of the corrie get weather severe enough to exclude many, but not all, lowland species (Moschatel and Coltsfoot, for example, grow quite commonly on the crags). Even more critical, though, are the rocks exposed on these dramatic cliffs: they belong to what geologists call the Bedded Pyroclastic Series, effectively the ashes of explosive volcanic eruptions, and these are quite strongly calcareous. The rather crumbly lime-rich rock, the constantly dripping water and the relative shade of the northerly exposure combine to support spectacular 'hanging gardens' of vegetation, most notably in a dark cleft in the cliffs known as Twll Du ('black hole'), which marks the bottom of a great rock fold called the Snowdon Syncline. In English this cleft is known as

What is a corrie?

Coire Fee in Angus (see Chapter 11) is a classic glacial corrie, with a dramatic amphitheatre of ice-cut crags. The stream below it has to meander to find a route between terminal moraines left behind by the glacier.

If you stood on the stage of the Albert Hall in London looking up to the tiered semicircle of balconies above, you could almost be looking into a corrie. That name is anglicised from the pronunciation of the Gaelic word *coire*. In Wales, it would be a *cwm*, while a geologist would call it a *cirque* (from the French). A corrie is a semicircular basin cut into a mountain valley by a glacier that once hung there. The slow movement of the glacier excavated the surrounding rock into its amphitheatre shape, and stones embedded in the moving ice gouged out a concave base to the corrie, which is frequently filled with a small mountain lake or tarn.

Often the glacier left behind heaps of stone debris, called moraines, at the entrance of the corrie. The walls towards the top of the corrie tend to be the steepest and most exposed, so that only a few highly adapted plants can establish there. A crest of snow often hangs high up on the corrie wall; this is called a cornice, after the decorative moulding installed between house walls and ceilings. Snow cornices may cause dangerous avalanches as they melt.

the Devil's Kitchen, perhaps because of the plumes of mist that sometimes emerge from it.

I was luckier than the New Naturalists when I spent a couple of pleasant days exploring there in July 1983, and quickly rattled off a pretty impressive list of montane species. In large boulder scree below Twll Du I found Fir and Alpine Clubmoss, Parsley Fern, Green Spleenwort, and the seedheads of Roseroot and Spring Sandwort. The distinctive blue-green leaves of Purple Saxifrage I noted only on large boulders, perhaps beyond the reach of sheep. Starry and Mossy Saxifrage grew beside streams, along with Mountain Sorrel and Alpine Scurvy-grass. I failed to find Alpine Saxifrage, which grows on just a few boulders here, but I did come across plants of Lesser Clubmoss, growing here almost at the south of its British range.

Twll Du – the 'Devil's Kitchen' – is the deep dark crevice visible here, high on the cliffs of Cwm Idwal, with a tumble of boulder scree below.

Many of these plants should be commoner now than when I visited. Since 1998, sheep grazing has been removed from Cwm Idwal in a ground-breaking agreement between the National Trust, which owns the site, the Countryside Council for Wales (now Natural Resources Wales) and the tenant farmer. Mossy Saxifrage is one of the species that has benefited, and by 2013 I was pleased to read that 'in places it now tumbles down over the rocks and grassy slopes, changing the whole feeling of the normally sombre Welsh hillside with a bright display of delicate white flower heads' (Jones & Radford, 2014). I only wish that initiative could be replicated at more sites.

Penetrating into the shady dampness of Twll Du on my visit, I found a lush flora which included most of the species already described, along with some magnificent tall specimens of Common Valerian and Goldenrod in its shorter mountain form. Another distinctive local member of the tall-herb community of these cliffs, and others around Snowdonia, is Welsh Poppy. Although it has become widely established across Britain as a garden escape, it is thought to be native on these shaded cliff ledges and in damp, rocky woodlands in Wales and Devon, with Cwm Idwal probably its highest-altitude site at 640m.

As I explored the west side of Twll Du, I happened across a tantalising trampled path towards one craggy outcrop. No sheep would have been tempted here, so the only explanation was botanical, and, sure enough, on a ledge at path-end I found some shrivelled, spidery leaves that were most probably Snowdon Lily (although I would not have spotted these, were it not for the suspicious path trampled by botanists' feet).

Lesser Clubmoss always looks to me like a starved version of Fir Clubmoss, with more slender, attenuated stems, densely covered in lance-shaped leaves.

Lesser Clubmoss *Selaginella selaginoides*

Lesser Clubmoss is such a feature of damp mountain grassland that it surely should count as montane. Its prostrate stems creep amongst mosses and damp grassland for no more than about 15cm. From these, it grows a few upright stems, about 3–6cm tall, which somewhat resemble the stems of Fir Clubmoss, but are more slender and densely covered in small, finely toothed, lance-shaped leaves. These stems are topped by a leafy cone region covered in specialised leaves called sporophylls. Each of these has a swollen pocket at its base which produces the spores by which the clubmoss spreads.

These swollen pockets come in two kinds. The creamy-yellow ones are called microsporangia, because they release many dust-like microspores, and the shining white ones are megasporangia, which each release four megaspores, large enough to be just visible to the human eye. As the megasporangia mature and dry in summer, tension builds up within their walls. Eventually they split explosively, and the megaspores are catapulted up to 2m from the parent plant, helping the species to spread through suitable habitats. As a back-up strategy, the fine microspores are dispersed widely in the wind.

Lesser Clubmoss was once found in boggy lowland sites, but it has largely been eliminated there by drainage and habitat destruction. Today it is mainly found in damp, base-rich upland sites in Snowdonia, the Pennines and Lake District, the Southern Uplands and throughout the Scottish Highlands and Islands at altitudes up to 1,170m in the Breadalbane hills. In the north and west it comes down to near sea level in wet areas amongst coastal dunes. Outside Britain, it is found in arctic regions of Europe, Asia and North America, with outlying populations in the Pyrenees and Alps and a single site on El Hierro in the Canary Islands.

Cwm Idwal puzzles

Two puzzles intrigued me from my visit to Cwm Idwal. Why is there no Alpine Lady's-mantle or Yellow Mountain Saxifrage here, when

Cwm Idwal is clearly a hotspot for montane plants and these two are such reliable components of similar sites further north? I still have no real explanation, other than the botanical serendipity discussed in Chapter 3.

Then there was the mystery of my favourite montane plant. I knew Mountain Avens was recorded here and wanted to pay my respects. I prided myself in having an eye for its habitat, which I can best describe as 'soft crags' – broken outcrops of rock that is often paler and has lots of green, grassy ledges. I scanned the great sweep of Cwm Idwal, selected the perfect crags and headed towards them. On the crags, I added Moss Campion to my plant list, and Chickweed Willowherb grew in a mossy stream below the crags, but I could not find Mountain Avens.

I have since tracked a six-figure grid reference for its site, which is actually on the other side of Llyn Idwal within a kilometre of where I stood. It grows there with Purple Saxifrage and Moss Campion. However, this site had not struck me as suitable. Either my instincts were faulty, or the species behaves rather differently here at its southernmost site on mainland Britain. Its other site in Snowdonia is beyond Nant Ffrancon on one small limestone outcrop in the Carneddau, where it was first discovered in 1935.

I did not spend long enough in Cwm Idwal to find one of its greatest rarities, Oblong Woodsia, which I believe grows on just a single rock there. Fortunately, it still clings on in Snowdonia, with 16 clumps recorded at three sites in 2010. I also failed to discover Alpine Woodsia, Holly Fern, Alpine Mouse-ear or Tufted Saxifrage – which just survives in the corrie at the south of its British range and has been the subject of a major conservation effort. Its distribution is so restricted that it qualifies as another of our three-star mountain enigmas.

★★★ Tufted Saxifrage *Saxifraga cespitosa*

As the ice retreated at the end of the last advance of the Ice Age, Tufted Saxifrage was one of the first flowering plants to colonise the rich gravels left behind by the glaciers in Nant Ffrancon, as shown by fossil seeds extracted from the sediments of a former lake there (see p.43). As the climate warmed, the saxifrage was forced higher up into the surrounding mountains, where it has clung on to the present day in small enclaves of friable, calcareous rocks.

It is a plant I am always thrilled to discover in the Arctic, where it is a tough little survivor with a closely tufted cushion of three-lobed leaves, covered in stubbly hairs. Despite the short growing season, it always seems remarkably flowery there, forming dense clusters of shining white flowers, etched with green veins, on short stems that rarely exceed 6cm tall. It is quite

A fine, flowery arctic specimen of Tufted Saxifrage, growing on ash from the Eldfell volcano on Heimaey in the Westmann Islands of Iceland.

a common plant across a wide arctic and subarctic range, from Alaska to arctic Asia and in the mountains of North America. I have seen it on gravelly hillsides in Svalbard, on shady rock faces close to the sea in Greenland, and beside a river gorge in arctic Sweden, on cliffs that I suspect are shrouded in winter ice. On Heimaey in the Westmann Islands of Iceland, I have found it commonly colonising the lava fields of the Eldfell volcano that erupted in 1973, where the toxicity of the volcanic ash creates the open conditions it requires.

Sadly, I have never seen this plant in Britain, where it is a much more elusive – and exclusive – species. Beyond Cwm Idwal, where it grows in moss cushions on three large boulders, it has been recorded since 1980 on only seven Scottish mountains, each of which requires a major expedition to visit. At most of these sites its population is tiny. In the Cairngorms, it now only grows high on the walls of a corrie below Ben Avon, where it was discovered, new to Britain, by James Robertson in 1771. Getting there requires a demanding 30km round walk, so it is rarely visited, but at least four plants survived there in 2008. It seems to have disappeared since 1980 from previous sites on Ben a' Bhuird and Ben Macdui. On Ben Nevis, it grows on sheer rock faces at altitudes up to 1,180m, and a recent survey by botanists using ropes to climb to its craggy heights has shown it to be rather commoner there than was realised, as we will see in Chapter 15. Its two other sites are in the Grey Corries, east of Ben Nevis, and on Liathach in Wester Ross. In 2014 a new site was added to this list, when a few plants were discovered on the Trotternish ridge on Skye, and I hope I will have finally made a pilgrimage to see it there by the time this book is published. Other claimed sites are generally attributed to misidentifications of Mossy Saxifrage, in the same closely related group.

One of the best colonies of Tufted Saxifrage grows on Liathach in Wester Ross – a site to which we will return in Chapter 16.

Cwm Idwal (where it was discovered in 1778) is not only its southernmost British site, but as far south as it grows anywhere in Europe or Asia (although it reaches further south in North America). This southern situation may explain its parlous state in Snowdonia. Nineteenth-century collectors decimated its population, but subsequently the climate and grazing sheep have been its major threats. By 1976, there were just two small clumps left, and one of those died during that year's long hot summer.

Three introduced plants on one of the restocking sites in Cwm Idwal (top), photographed in June 1979, a year after they were planted, and (above) a typical, tiny plant that had re-established by 2012 on a mossy cushion where four plants still grew in 1976.

Then a rescue mission was launched by botanist David Parker. Seeds from the remaining plants were collected and propagated at the University of Liverpool Botanic Gardens. In May 1978, 325 young plants from there were transplanted to Cwm Idwal with the help of the reserve warden. However, this determined effort only served to confirm the problems for the species there. Just 31 plants were still growing there three years after their reintroduction, and by 2014 only a single plant survived from the restocking project. Given these problems, there are currently no plans for further reintroductions. However, the native plants have proved more resilient than expected. In 1994, plants reappeared at the site that was feared lost in 1976, from seed that must have remained buried in the moss cushions for almost 20 years. In 2014, 13 plants still grew at its two native sites.

It is thought that dry summers and mild, wet winters are the main problem for the species in Wales (Kay & Deacon, 2010). That certainly corresponds with my experience growing it in our garden in Wester Ross. Initially, it establishes and grows well, but then the little tussocks die from the centre, I suspect because winter damp rots the roots. Given the projections for future climate change, I fear that the outlook for the Welsh plants, which are genetically distinct from those in Scotland, is bleak, and the future looks pretty insecure also for the Scottish plants. However, I think that Britain would be infinitely the poorer if we let this tough little survivor from the Ice Age disappear from our islands.

Mountain Avens *Dryas octopetala*

Although I failed to find Mountain Avens in Cwm Idwal, this nevertheless seems the right place to introduce one of the most distinctive and attractive of mountain flowers. It has glossy green, slightly lobed leaves, which are silvery on the underside, and large, white flowers with eight petals (although I have found occasional flowers with nine or even ten petals). It grows in some of the richest arctic-alpine sites in Britain, from its southernmost location here in Cwm Idwal to the north coast of Scotland (with rare records even on Hoy in Orkney). It is found from close to sea level on Skye and in Sutherland to 1,035m on Ben Avon in the Cairngorms. It is always found in lime-rich soils, typically in situations that are slightly unstable because of the friability of the rocks or the impact of solifluction. In England, it is known in Littondale in the Yorkshire Dales, with an old record from the Cross Fell area in Upper Teesdale, and at one site each in the Helvellyn and Scafell ranges in the Lake District. It is scattered in mica schist and limestone sites in Scotland, including the Inner Hebrides. At a few sites in the far north, as we will see in Chapter 17, blown shell sand provides the calcium and creates the instability that it needs.

The scientific name of Mountain Avens is an evocative description: *Dryas* after the dryads, or oak fairies, from the rather oak-like appearance of its crinkle-cut leaves, *octopetala* because its large, showy white flowers have eight petals.

Elsewhere it is more or less circumpolar in arctic and subarctic regions, and grows quite commonly in the mountains of central Europe from the Pyrenees to the Balkans, through southern Asia, and from Alaska to the Rocky Mountains of North America.

Carneddau

Moving eastwards again, the hills north and east of the Nant Ffrancon pass are dominated by Carnedd Llewelyn (1,062m) and Carnedd Dafydd (1,043m). These are amongst the least visited hills in Snowdonia, because the only approach is by a long walk in, usually from Bethesda or Tal-y-Bont, south of Conwy. The crags above Llyn Dulyn (the Black Lake) are the most visited by botanists and have many of the common Snowdon species including Parsley Fern, Green Spleenwort, Globeflower, Roseroot and Starry Saxifrage. Alpine Scurvy-grass and Chickweed Willowherb grow beside streams and in mossy runnels, and Mossy Saxifrage is abundant in some of the screes. Alpine Mouse-ear has its only Welsh station below Carnedd Llewelyn.

Ysgolion Duon, the north-facing crag below Carnedd Dafydd, was described by 18th-century naturalist Thomas Pennant as 'the most horrid precipice that thought can conceive'. Perhaps it is best left to the climbing fraternity, who know it as the Black Ladders, but its inaccessible ledges are home to several of the species we met earlier this chapter, including Globeflower, Alpine Meadow-rue and Mountain Sorrel, along with Moss Campion, which we will meet shortly. The Carneddau summits are worth visiting for their scenery. They also have the best examples in Snowdonia of the typical windswept Woolly Fringe-moss community of mountaintops, with Fir and Alpine Clubmoss, Stiff Sedge, Mountain Crowberry and small patches of Dwarf Willow. Hair Sedge is known on Creigiau Gleision, overlooking the Llyn Cowlyd Reservoir. Two of these species merit consideration before we leave Snowdonia.

Stiff Sedge *Carex bigelowii*

Sedges are easy to ignore and can be off-putting to the non-botanist, but they are important components of montane vegetation, and fortunately most montane sedges are quite distinctive. That is particularly true of Stiff Sedge, which is most characteristic of lichen heaths and acid grassland on windswept summit ridges, as here in the Carneddau. It grows most robustly in the shelter of stable boulder scree or in hollows where snow lies late. Its stiff, arching leaves are rather bluey-green but turn reddish-brown as they dry. Its rigid stems are strongly quadrangular in section and topped by a single elliptical male inflorescence and two or three rather broader female inflorescences (although I refer readers to technical field guides to explain these subtleties of sedge biology).

Stiff Sedge is scarce in Wales, but rather commoner in the north Pennines, Lake District and Southern Uplands and in the right habitats throughout the Highlands, north as far as Shetland. It is found from close to sea level on windy Shetland to 1,305m on Ben Macdui in the Cairngorms. Elsewhere it is circumpolar and grows in mountains south to the Urals and Japan.

On a few windswept mountain shoulders, Stiff Sedge forms a turf, as here. Crunching across this when the leaves are dry in late summer is like walking through Corn Flakes!

Mountain Crowberry *Empetrum nigrum* subspecies *hermaphroditum*

I featured this in the table of montane plants because it was regarded as a separate species

The mountain subspecies of Crowberry has stubby, boat-shaped leaves with rounded edges. This is not always an easy distinction to make; the altitude at which the plant is growing is generally a better guide.

at the time Derek Ratcliffe drew up his lists. It also has a very different biology from the more widespread Crowberry subspecies *nigrum* that we met in the last chapter. This helps it survive high in the mountains. Subspecies *hermaphroditum* replaces subspecies *nigrum* at altitudes above around 600m, although the ranges of the two overlap. The more lowland subspecies produces separate male and female plants. However, having only half of plants able to produce berries is a luxury that can be ill afforded in the mountains, so the mountain subspecies is hermaphrodite, as its scientific name suggests. That means that all its plants produce tiny flowers which have both an ovary and pollen-producing stamens, so all of them can produce berries if successfully wind-pollinated. Field guides list other distinctions between the two forms: in general, subspecies *nigrum* has shoots that scramble and root along the ground and leaves with parallel margins, whereas *hermaphroditum* has stems that are more erect and shorter leaves with rounded edges, but these distinctions are tricky without flowers or fruits to check.

Mountain Crowberry is found very locally at high altitudes in Snowdonia, the Lake District and the Southern Uplands, where subspecies *nigrum* is commoner. It is more widespread throughout the Scottish Highlands and islands to altitudes of at least 1,130m. Its global distribution is unclear, because of confusion between the two subspecies, but it certainly occurs in Greenland, Iceland, Scandinavia and the Alps.

The hills of mid-Wales

Several hills to the south of Snowdonia share some, at least, of the species we have met there. For example, the Berwyn Mountains (Y Berwyn), south-west of Llangollen, are worth exploration. They rise to 827m at Moel Sych, and their sheep-grazed blanket mire is one of very few Welsh sites for Cloudberry, which reaches its southernmost British site on the hills east of Lake Vyrnwy. At Craig Breiddin, overlooking the River Severn north-east of Welshpool, Edward Lhuyd discovered Rock Cinquefoil, a species that we will not meet again on our travels until much further north in Chapter 16. Quarrying for roadstone at the site reduced its population to just six plants, but a subsequent attempt to reinforce the population with transplants met with little success. Sticky Catchfly is also recorded on these crags, as well as the western subspecies *hybrida* of Spiked Speedwell, a plant of base-rich lowland rocks and cliffs.

West of here, at Ystumtuen near Devil's Bridge, I photographed a very fine specimen of Fir Clubmoss way back in 1978, growing in a shady gorge that could not have been more than 250m above sea level. Parsley Fern also grows nearby. South of Machynlleth, Starry Saxifrage is fairly common on the ridge of Pumlumon Fawr, which rises to 752m. Fir Clubmoss and Viviparous Fescue grow on the cliffs here, with Alpine Clubmoss and Dwarf Willow on the windswept summit ridge and Stiff Sedge at its southernmost British site.

Cadair Idris

Cadair Idris, north of Machynlleth near the southern boundary of the Snowdonia National Park, is a much more satisfying walk than many of the Snowdon routes, nicely varied, visually dramatic, less busy and with a summit unspoilt by development. It is also a site with a long history of exploration. In 1658, the pioneering botanist John Ray climbed the hill and found Globeflower, Alpine Clubmoss and Lesser Clubmoss. A few years later, Edward Lhuyd added Roseroot and Mountain Sorrel to the list, the latter at its southernmost British site. Alpine Meadow-rue was also recorded here, but is thought to have been an introduction. Moss Campion, Alpine Scurvy-grass, Alpine Saw-wort, Hair Sedge and Oblong Woodsia are also recorded here at their southernmost British sites, although the woodsia seems long-gone.

The usual ascent is from near Minffordd, up into the fine corrie of Cwm Cau, with vertiginous cliffs soaring to 300m and a dark brooding lake at its base. The path then climbs past some lime-rich outcrops where Green Spleenwort, Mossy Saxifrage, Starry Saxifrage and Roseroot are found, onto a dramatic ridge, overlooking the corrie lake below, with occasional patches of Parsley Fern. The summit itself, called Penygadair (893m), offers spectacular views but I have found only Fir Clubmoss, Stiff Sedge and wind-blasted plants of Thrift in its vicinity. Mountain Crowberry nearby is yet another southernmost record. Lime-rich rocks on the north face of the mountain support an interesting flora, including Purple Saxifrage, although it is rare and very localised. One curious record on the hill is Spignel, which we will meet again in Chapter 10 in hill meadows further north. Because it was grown as a garden and pot herb for its aniseed-flavoured leaves, there must be a suspicion that it was introduced here. Forked Spleenwort is also recorded on acidic rocks at a somewhat lower altitude.

Moss Campion *Silene acaulis*

This cushion-forming, mossy plant looks especially attractive when adorned with delicate pink flowers in midsummer (see photo on p.2). This flowering is timed for when the weather is most likely to encourage the pollinating butterflies, bees and other insects that are attracted by its sweet scent. North of Cadair Idris, it is only known from a few sites in Snowdonia, between 335m in the Pass of Llanberis and

A view of Cadair Idris in considerably better weather than when I visited, with Llyn Cau in the foreground and the steep crags of Cwm Cau to the left.

1,054m on Snowdon itself. It is found in the Lake District but not the Southern Uplands. In the Highlands, it has a western tendency, but is surprisingly widespread on Shetland, virtually down to sea level.

Although it looks delicate, it is a tough, frost-resistant plant, found at altitudes of up to 1,305m on Ben Macdui in the Cairngorms. It grows on rock ledges and crevices, amongst small scree that is relatively stable, and in the gravel of mountaintops, usually on basic soils. At high altitudes it can also turn up on non-basic rocks such as quartzite and sandstone. Its neat cushions of moss-like leaves hug close to the ground, so that the wind whips over them. Elsewhere, it grows in the high mountains of central and western Europe and North America, and throughout arctic regions.

Peaks and dales

chapter seven

The Peak District, at the southern end of the Pennines, is an area of great scenic value, with extensive moorland heights interrupted by lush, green valleys (dales), rising to a summit of 636m at Kinder Scout. More than 16 million people live within an hour's drive from here, and the rich variety of scenery attracts tens of thousands of visitors every year. That accessibility makes it an excellent place to begin exploring many of the commoner montane species. Further north in the Pennines, the limestone of the Yorkshire Dales around Malham has a rich flora to match the gaunt and dramatic scenery. In combination, these two areas will introduce many more new species on our northward journey.

The Peak District

The Peak District became Britain's first National Park in December 1950, covering 1,438km^2 (about the size of Greater London). Geologically, it represents a broad dome of Carboniferous limestone, topped by bands of shale and Millstone Grit. In places erosion has stripped off the grit and shale to reveal the limestone below. The area where limestone outcrops near the surface, mainly in the centre and south of the park, is known as the White Peak, in contrast to the Dark Peak where a cap of Millstone Grit remains at the surface, giving rise to broad swathes of moorland.

The area has a relatively high rainfall (around 1m per year) but the climate is not particularly extreme. For example, Buxton, at 289m, has an average July maximum of 18.9°C and a February minimum of 0.2°C, with an average 59 days of air frost per year. Much of the land here is used for sheep and cattle grazing, and heather is burnt

OPPOSITE PAGE: Mountain Pansy is a relatively common species in rich upland grassland in the Peak District and mid-Wales, but it occurs here more typically in the yellow form shown on page 124.

Over a million people a year visit the limestone valley of Dovedale, owned by the National Trust. Jacob's-ladder is one of the species recorded there.

over large areas to support grouse shooting, which further restricts the limited montane flora.

Flora of the Peaks

The dominant vegetation on the Millstone Grit is upland acid grassland, grading above about 500m into moorland of Heather, Bilberry and Cowberry. Crowberry is unusually plentiful on Kinder Scout, and in places good quantities of Cloudberry are established on the deeper peat. Bog Rosemary is recorded from a couple of wetter sites. There is also a record for Bearberry near the source of the River Derwent. However, Kinder Scout, in particular, has large areas of bare peat hag, where grazing, burning and past industrial pollution have killed off the vegetation cover, leading to erosion.

Where the Carboniferous limestone is exposed, the flora is rather different. Mountain Pansy, Mountain Everlasting and Mountain Melick grow in the grassland, with Green Spleenwort in shady cracks and fissures. Limestone Fern and occasionally Stone Bramble grow in the scree slopes beneath the outcrops. Jacob's-ladder occurs on some rockier outcrops, more commonly on the White Peak than anywhere else in Britain, with an estimated 40,000 plants at 17 localities in 1990.

In 2008–2009 there were 47 'active' quarries in the park, but botanically the main interest lies in areas that were formerly mined for lead. The lead-mine spoil heaps, locally called 'rakes', support a range of metal-loving plants, of which Spring Sandwort is most notable, but also including Alpine Penny-cress and Hoary Whitlow-grass. This therefore seems the appropriate place to introduce these three species, and three more that have been mentioned above.

Spring Sandwort *Minuartia verna*

Spring Sandwort forms loose, mossy cushions with fragile, leafy flowering shoots to 15cm tall, topped throughout the summer by a few white flowers on branching stalks. It is found in short grassland, limestone pavements and scree slopes throughout the Carboniferous limestone districts of the Pennines. It also grows, much less commonly, on base-rich volcanic rocks on the Lizard in Cornwall (see photo on p.79), in the Mendip Hills and in Snowdonia. Typically it grows below 600m, but is recorded to 875m on Snowdon. Open habitats are preferred, which may explain its particular association with spoil heaps from mines, where high concentrations of lead and other metals in the soil exclude competing vegetation.

In Scotland it is a rare plant with a very scattered distribution that defies easy summary. It is known from basic scree on one coastal cliff in Kirkcudbrightshire and from serpentine rock in the Scottish Wildlife Trust's Grey Hill Grasslands reserve near Girvan in Ayrshire. I know it on a steep volcanic hill near St Abb's Head in Berwickshire, and from crags below Arthur's Seat in Edinburgh (see Chapter 10). It is also recorded from the Ochil Hills, on a hill near Ben Lomond and on another overlooking Glen Lochay in Perthshire, and on serpentine rocks in the Ladder Hills of Banffshire. Such a disparate distribution suggests that it has the potential to turn up elsewhere. It is also found throughout upland areas of southern Europe into North Africa, and in Siberia, but not in northern Europe.

Alpine Penny-cress *Noccaea caerulescens*

Mine wastes, spoil heaps and metalliferous river gravels are the typical habitat of Alpine Penny-cress in England and Wales, where it is largely confined to rocks or soils that are naturally or artificially enriched with lead or zinc. It is most widespread in the Pennines, with sites also on Helvellyn in the Lake District, in Snowdonia, at low altitudes on the Lleyn Peninsula and near Aberystwyth in Wales, and in the lead-mining areas of the Mendip Hills. Many of these populations number only a few tens of individuals.

In Scotland, its association with metalliferous rocks is less evident. It was recorded near the same serpentine site in Ayrshire as the previous species but has not been confirmed there since 1990. Its distribution then jumps to base-rich rocks and screes in Angus, where it is recorded at altitudes up to 940m. In Perthshire, it is known on calcareous rocks at the head of Glen Lochay and near Kinloch Rannoch, and it is also found on the basalt of Fionchra on the Isle of Rum. In Europe, it is widespread from the Pyrenees east to Slovakia. It also grows in the mountains of temperate North and South America and through northern Asia.

The spatula-shaped leaves of Alpine Penny-cress form a rosette at the base of a slender, leafy stem, topped by a cluster of white or pale lilac flowers.

Hoary Whitlow-grass *Draba incana*

The third of our trio on the lead-mine rakes of the Peak District is much less strongly associated with metalliferous habitats. Hoary Whitlow-grass grows upwards from a cabbage-like rosette of leaves which, like its stem leaves, are grey-hairy (hence 'hoary'). Its stems are surprisingly variable in height; usually they are not much more than 10cm tall, but on sheltered, mountain rock ledges I have occasionally found them three or four times that height. Its characteristically twisted fruiting pods distinguish it from the much rarer Rock Whitlow-grass (see Chapter 12), which is a more delicate plant with leafless stems and untwisted pods.

Hoary Whitlow-grass: its small white flowers develop into long, narrow fruits which are characteristically twisted up their length.

Hoary Whitlow-grass grows on limestone rock ledges, screes and pavements, and spreads from there onto dry grassland on thin, base-rich soils. It grows down to sea level in a few sand dunes in the north, but is more typically montane, recorded at altitudes up to 1,157m in Perthshire. The Peak District and Snowdonia are its southernmost British sites; it is then quite widespread in the northern Pennines and Lake District. In Scotland, it often grows on base-rich igneous and mica-schist rocks, but has a slightly puzzling distribution. It is absent from the Southern Uplands, fairly widespread in the southern Highlands, largely absent from the central core of the Highlands, but then widespread again in the northern Highlands, with sites also in the Inner and Outer Hebrides, Orkney and Shetland. Globally, it is found in the mountains of central Europe and central Asia, in arctic and subarctic Europe and in Greenland.

Bog Rosemary *Andromeda polifolia*

Bog Rosemary is a straggling dwarf shrub, with lance-shaped leaves and nodding pink bell-like flowers. It often grows, as here, on bog-moss.

This pink-flowered, straggling, low-growing shrub is commonest in lowland raised bogs in the wetter west of the country, but it also occurs in upland peats in Wales, northern England and the Southern Uplands, at altitudes up to 530m in the north Pennines. Its range has declined considerably as a result of peat extraction and the drainage of peat bogs. It can survive in drained bog vegetation, but suffers from the disturbance of peat extraction and the resulting competition from species that move onto the newly dried surfaces (Jacquemart, 1998). It is still quite frequent in undrained upland peat bogs where waterlogged, undisturbed surfaces make access difficult.

It appears not to tolerate cold, especially during the growing season. That may explain why it is scarcely recorded north of Flanders Moss and other bogs in the central Forth Valley of Scotland. In 1979, it was discovered on Mount Keen, close to the Angus–Aberdeenshire border at the head of Glen Esk, well north of any other records for the species and at its highest British altitude (735m), but that record needs confirmation. It has not been seen since the 1990s at another outlying site in raised bogs on the Isle of Mull. However, these records suggest it might survive in other isolated sites, because its creeping stems are easily overlooked when not in flower. It is also found throughout northern Europe and in the mountains of central Europe, Asia, Greenland and northern North America.

Mountain Pansy *Viola lutea*

The large, flat-faced flowers of Mountain Pansy are reminiscent of Garden Pansies – and every bit as showy. They are usually yellow at lowland and southern sites, as in the Peak District and Malhamdale. In more upland and northern sites, they are more typically blue-violet or red-violet, although always with a yellow patch at the base of the lower

petal. This colour distinction may be irrelevant to pollinating bees, which are attracted by ultraviolet light reflected off the flowers. Mountain Pansy is a plant of hill grasslands and damp mountain rock ledges, usually close to calcareous rocks but where there is enough leaching to produce conditions that are not strongly base-rich (it seems to avoid both very basic and very acidic soils). It can cope with relatively high metal content in soils, around metal spoil heaps, for example (Balme, 1954).

It is widespread, but quite localised, throughout the Peak District, Pennines, Lake District, Southern Uplands, and the southern and eastern Highlands. It is recorded from 200m in Derbyshire to 1,050m in the Breadalbane hills. It is also quite common on acid hillsides in mid-Wales but surprisingly rare in the higher mountains of south and north Wales. Its southernmost British site is in rough upland grassland on Exmoor, where it flowers only sporadically. There are very few records in the north-west Highlands and none on the islands. It seems to be in significant decline in the far north and may now be extinct in Sutherland, perhaps because of increased grazing. This might also reflect an early impact of climate change, because maximum summer temperatures are thought to be a limiting factor in the distribution of the species, especially here at the northernmost limits of its global range. Outside of Britain, it is only found from Belgium south to Austria, with a separate subspecies in Hungary and the Balkans.

Mountain Pansy: in northern and upland sites, this species usually has blue-violet flowers like those shown on page 118, but in more lowland and southern sites they are more often yellow, justifying the scientific name *lutea* meaning yellow.

Mountain Melick is a striking grass with a head of large oval flowerheads at the tip of its stem. These droop in a single row like Christmas-tree lights.

Mountain Melick *Melica nutans*

The limestone grassland of the White Peak seems as good a place as any to introduce this delicate grass, recognisable by its drooping, one-sided head of grass flower spikelets. It is a widespread species on base-rich soils in all the upland areas of Britain from the Brecon Beacons northwards. It scarcely even qualifies as submontane, growing quite commonly around the edges of deciduous woods

and in shady scrub, even in lowland sites like the Bedford Purlieus, a mixed broadleaved woodland west of Peterborough which lies barely 50m above sea level. However, it does also grow on mountain rock ledges, at altitudes of up to 820m in Glen Isla in Angus, and in crevices in limestone pavements. It is largely absent from the islands, but does occur in Mull and on the limestones of Skye. It is also found in similar habitats around Europe, eastwards to Japan.

Malhamdale

Moving north in the Pennines, we reach the Yorkshire Dales. I got to know the Craven area, north of Settle, in the late 1970s when I helped run adventure holidays for children, based near Malham. I have returned since to further explore the spectacular, almost skeletal landscapes, where the soil often seems to be no more than a thin skin over the Great Scar Limestone from the Carboniferous era. Crags outcrop everywhere, with extensive areas of limestone pavement (the Yorkshire Dales are said to account for more than half of the limestone pavements in Britain). Rushing streams disappear underground into spectacular caves, leaving what is called a karst landscape of dramatic dry valleys etched by floods of the past.

The flora of the limestones is rich and diverse, and in a few days botanising in the area you could find a good number of species on our montane list. It is a big block of relatively high land, and, although its maximum altitude is just 538m, it is very exposed, with quite a severe climate (the monthly mean temperature at Malham in January is only 2°C, with a July mean of 13°C). That is critical to the survival of a mountain flora in the area.

Throughout the Yorkshire Dales, the skeleton of limestone rocks seems to lie just a little way beneath the thin skin of vegetation, as here above Ingleton.

The most famous local landmark is Malham Cove, a dramatic curved amphitheatre of almost white limestone, 80m high and over 300m wide. At the end of the last Ice Age a huge waterfall tumbled over the edge here, fed by glacial meltwaters, and this cut back the sheer rock face. Today, a much smaller and more sedate stream flows out of Malham Tarn to the north, but this now disappears underground into 'water sinks' about 1.5km above the Cove, leaving a dramatic dry valley beneath. Malham Beck emerges from the foot of the cove, but this is actually a different stream which crosses the original stream underground in a complex of largely unexplored caverns.

The Pennine Way follows Malham Beck to the Cove, then climbs a set of irregular stone steps up its western edge. Another, lesser path crosses beneath the Cove itself. One of the most special plants to grow here is Jacob's-ladder, first reported in a letter to the great botanist John Ray in 1670 which described it 'on both sides of the [Malham Beck] spring in great tufts'. Ray himself later saw it 'in a wood on the left of the water as you go to the cove from Malham' – although both the wood and the plant have now gone from here, and Jacob's-ladder now grows only on the right-hand slopes of the Cove. As well as typical purple flowers, some of the plants here have white flowers with a slightly smaller corolla, an occurrence that was noted in Ray's 1670 description.

As snow melted at the end of the Ice Age, a massive river tumbled over the limestone at Malham Cove, eroding the rock amphitheatre that is such an iconic landmark of the area.

The walls of the Cove are mostly bare, although I have found Rue-leaved Saxifrage and Wall Whitlow-grass below the crag. Alpine Penny-cress also grows here, but is difficult to find. The Cove is topped by a large limestone pavement, which is worth exploring although there are better pavements in the dry valley north of the Cove.

Jacob's-ladder *Polemonium caeruleum*

A familiar plant in gardens, Jacob's-ladder grows to around 50–70cm tall, with ladder-like leaves and big, showy, bell-shaped flowers. Most garden plants have pale purplish-blue flowers with yellow anthers and pollen. Escaped garden plants are widespread in the lowlands along hedgerows, on riverbanks and near habitation. Wild plants are rather different, with more open, deeper purple-blue flowers (or occasionally white, as at Malham) and orange anthers and pollen.

As a native plant, Jacob's-ladder is mainly confined to areas of Carboniferous limestone, typically at altitudes of 190–580m. It grows there on cool, moist, north-facing slopes, usually where higher hills nearby influence the local microclimate (Pigott, 1958). The largest population is in the White Peak of the Peak District, with a smaller group of sites in the Craven limestones, and a couple of riverside sites in the Cheviot Hills of Northumberland. Pollen records show that it was much more widespread in England and Wales as the last advance of the Ice Age was drawing to a close. There are even two Scottish fossil records from Dumfriesshire and Aberdeenshire. It would seem the changing climate then drove it back to the spots where it survives today. Elsewhere it is a plant of northern and central Europe, Siberia and North America amongst alpine rocks and in mountain meadows, but also in the tall-herb community of birch forests in Scandinavia.

Jacob's-ladder growing wild in Lathkill Dale, one of the finest limestone dales in the Peak District, near Bakewell in Derbyshire.

Limestone pavements and scars

Limestone pavements occur where past glaciers have stripped the limestone down to its flat bedding planes. Rain by its nature is slightly

The limestone pavement at Scar Close in the Yorkshire Dales, with two typical limestone pavement plants, Bloody Cranesbill and Common Rock-rose.

acidic, so it readily eats its way into stress fractures in the rock, opening them up as deep cracks called grykes. The table-like tops, called clints, are rapid-draining and exposed, so they support no more than thin soil or remain as bare rock. Soil accumulates in the depth of the grykes, which are damp and shady and provide a refuge for woodland plants including Dog's Mercury, Wood Anemone and Ramsons. Rarer species in the grykes include Baneberry, Angular Solomon's-seal and two ferns from our montane list, Rigid Buckler-fern and Holly Fern. Another submontane species, Limestone Fern, seems to prefer shallower, sunlit grykes and also grows amongst limestone crags and scree slopes.

Continuing up to the dry valley above Malham Cove, there are drifts of Mountain Pansy in places, always in the yellow southern/lowland form, and there are nice patches of the lime-loving Common Rock-rose. An even more dramatic walk climbs past the Janet's Foss waterfall, with curtains of mosses encased in tufa (precipitated limestone). The walk then follows Gordale Scar northwards. I always found this valley richer botanically than the one directly above Malham, with even better limestone pavements. Typical limestone grasses here include Crested Hair-grass and another species from our montane list, Blue Moor-grass. Marshy areas beside Gordale Beck and grassy north-facing slopes nearby are the best places locally to find another delightful submontane species, Bird's-eye Primrose, often growing with Grass of Parnassus. Lesser Clubmoss grows on the slopes here, and Bloody Cranesbill is common on the limestone scars. Hair Sedge was discovered on the limestone scars to the west of the valley in 1878 and refound in 1939, but it is an elusive plant.

Other Malhamdale sites

To the west of Malham, Pikedaw Hill lies along the Mid-Craven Fault line. Its vegetation is sharply defined between limestone species on the northern side of the fault and acid grassland on the other. There are also old shafts and spoil heaps from mine workings on the slopes, where I have found Alpine Penny-cress growing with Common Whitlow-grass. Mossy springs nearby are another site for Bird's-eye Primrose. Spring Sandwort and Hoary Whitlow-grass are recorded from mine workings elsewhere in the area.

Globeflower Wood near Malham, looking at its best in June 1978. I have not been back for many years, but hope it still looks as good.

Another site worth a brief roadside stop is the small Yorkshire Wildlife Trust reserve called Globeflower Wood, which lies in a fork between two roads about 1.5km west of Malham Tarn. It covers just 0.08ha (about a fifth of an acre) where a triangle of limestone walls encloses an ungrazed, damp meadow fringed by various small willows. The meadow is flushed with base-rich water draining off the surrounding limestone, and in early summer it produces wonderful displays of Globeflowers, Wood Cranesbill and Melancholy Thistle. These survived because the meadow was left ungrazed by the farmer, who then passed it to the Trust to ensure its future protection.

However, my favourite botanising spot in the area is the craggy, north-west-facing slopes on the far bank of Cowside Beck, as viewed from the minor road south-west of Arncliffe. Here there is an abundance of Mountain Avens, Limestone Fern and Bird's-eye Primrose. A few plants of Mossy Saxifrage grow amongst the scree, with, surprisingly, some small specimens of Goldilocks Buttercup, more typically a woodland species. Other montane plants recorded in the Malham–Arncliffe area include Green Spleenwort, Alpine Cinquefoil and Mountain Everlasting. Dwarf Milkwort just hangs on in the area, but is much commoner further north in Upper Teesdale, where we

Mountain Avens – the white flowers in the grass in the foreground – is just as common on the steep terraced slope below the road to Arncliffe as on the limestone crags at the other side of Cowside Beck.

will meet it again. Alpine Bartsia, Hair Sedge, Cloudberry and Bog Rosemary are amongst the species recorded in bogs around Malham Tarn (closed to the public) and at Great Close Mire.

Six more of the area's plants merit special consideration before we explore further into the Yorkshire Dales.

Limestone Fern *Gymnocarpium robertianum*

This delicate fern superficially resembles the much commoner Oak Fern, which grows in deep, damp soil banks in woodlands but also finds its way onto mountain rocks and screes, mainly in acid soils. Limestone Fern, however, has more robust stipes (stems), and its fronds are a dull greyish green, compared to the bright green of Oak Fern, which has a more neatly triangular shape.

As its name suggests, Limestone Fern is mostly confined to calcium-rich substrates on the ledges and crevices of limestone cliffs, in the scree beneath these cliffs and in the grykes of limestone pavements. Its headquarters are in the Cotswolds, the Peak District and here in the Yorkshire Dales. It is mainly found at low altitudes, between 75m and 300m, although it is recorded up to 585m at Carreg yr Ogof in the Brecon Beacons. It occasionally becomes established on the mortar of walls and culverts in lowland areas. It seems to prefer warm, sunny, dry habitats, and the mealy surface of its leaves may protect it by reflecting bright sunlight.

Limestone Fern growing on the crags overlooking Cowside Beck.

That preference for warmer sites probably explains its virtual absence from Scotland, where it is recorded at just two sites. It has been known since the 1960s in two small crevices in the limestone pavement near Schiehallion in Perthshire, although it may now be extinct there. It still survives, in some quantity, on a single ledge below the limestone crag south of Inchnadamph Hotel in Sutherland. Outside Britain, it is found in limestone habitats from northern Scandinavia to Spain and the Caucasus, and in the mountains of Asia and North America.

Holly Fern *Polystichum lonchitis*

This tough, evergreen fern lives up to its common name, with glossy, leathery, dark green leaf lobes (pinnules) that look remarkably like Holly leaves. It is most typically found half-shaded in fissures at the base of mountain cliffs or in the shade of large boulders on stabilised screes, always where the rocks are to some extent lime-rich. It also grows on shady, damp rock ledges and in the grykes of limestone pavements. It is a poor competitor, which may explain why it grows where the shade is too deep for other species to establish. It is slow-growing but long-lived, and this made it susceptible in the past to over-collection, which is the main reason it is now very rare in Snowdonia.

There are a few small populations of Holly Fern in the northern Pennines and Lake District in grykes and on cliffs at moderate elevations. It is surprisingly rare in the Southern Uplands, where it was previously only known from inaccessible crags in the Moffat hills of Dumfriesshire but was recently discovered just across the border into Peeblesshire at a couple of sites near Tweedsmuir. It is much more widespread in the central, western and north-western Highlands, including the Isle of Skye and Hoy in Orkney. It is unusual to find it below about 600m, although it is recorded at 180m below the limestone cliff at Inchnadamph in Sutherland and up to 1,065m in the Breadalbanes. It is widespread in arctic and mountain regions of Asia, Europe, Greenland and North America.

A typical site for Holly Fern (with a coin for scale), hidden in the deep shade between large boulders, below a base-rich cliff in the Breadalbane hills of Perthshire.

Alpine Cinquefoil

Potentilla crantzii

The bright yellow flowers of Alpine Cinquefoil are an unexpectedly showy sight in its harsh mountain habitats. The plant looks very similar to Spring Cinquefoil in lowland chalk and limestone grasslands, but lacks the creeping, rooting, mat-forming stems of the latter species. That distinction is not always clear-cut, but fortunately the two species have quite different habitats and rarely overlap in range.

The bright yellow flowers of Alpine Cinquefoil are the size of a 50p piece, usually with an orange spot where the petals overlap at the centre of the flower.

Alpine Cinquefoil is found scattered through the Pennines and Lake District, with a few sites also in Snowdonia, but it is always very localised in these upland habitats, preferring closely grazed, lime-rich grassland and dry, basic rock faces and ledges. It is rather more widespread in the southern and central Highlands, with a few sites also in the north-west Highlands, from 250m in Assynt in Sutherland to 1,065m in the Breadalbane hills, where it is at its commonest. It is also known from the Suardal limestone on the Isle of Skye. It is found through arctic and subarctic Europe, the high mountains of southern Europe and Asia Minor.

Bird's-eye Primrose *Primula farinosa*

This beautiful, delicate, pink-flowered primrose is one of the main attractions of the Craven limestones, even for non-botanists. It stands up to 20cm tall, although often much shorter, topped by a candelabra-like head of flowers. It is now entirely confined in Britain to northern England, typically between 200m and 400m, although it is recorded from near sea level in west Lancashire to 570m on Jeffrey Pot in Wensleydale. It is found most typically on moist, usually spring-fed, grassy or peaty flushes on basic soils, where it can be locally abundant. It also grows on steep banks beside streams and rivers where erosion and slippage opens up the vegetation. It has a few remaining sites in unimproved, closely grazed, damp pastures, but many of these have been lost as a result of drainage, fertilisation or re-sowing.

It is another glacial relict species that was much more widespread at the end of the last Ice Age, and it appears still to be retreating, largely as a result of human activities. It has disappeared from the Magnesian limestone of Durham and from the Pentland Hills, south of Edinburgh, as agriculture there was intensified. Its European distribution is somewhat unclear owing to taxonomic confusion with similar species, but it seems to occur across most of Europe, mainly in mountains. In Scandinavia, it is a lowland plant confined to southern Sweden and the shores of the Baltic, replaced in the mountains by Northern Primrose *Primula scandinavica* (a close relative of Scots Primrose). It is also found across Asia, but North American plants are now assigned to a separate species.

The scientific name of Bird's-eye Primrose refers to the mealy white covering on its rosette leaves (*farinosa* comes from the Latin for ground corn). Its common name refers to the yellow eye-spot in the centre of its flower.

Wood Cranesbill *Geranium sylvaticum*

A showy cranesbill with pinkish-purple to magenta flowers, this is very much a northern species, not found south of around Leeds, except for a few remaining native sites in upland woods and mountain ledges in Wales. From Upper Teesdale northwards, it progressively replaces the rather similar but more blue-flowered Meadow Cranesbill as the common species in old-style hay meadows, and the latter plant is largely absent from the Highlands (although even it reaches altitudes of 845m on Great Dun Fell in the north Pennines). Within that range, Wood Cranesbill is quite common in woods, hay meadows and even roadside verges at relatively low altitudes. It qualifies as submontane because it also grows commonly in the tall-herb communities of mountain cliffs and beside mountain streams and gullies in northern Britain, at altitudes up to 1,005m in Perthshire. It is rare and largely coastal in the far north of Scotland, and absent from the islands except for Mull and possibly Islay (although it occurs elsewhere as a garden escape).

In Scandinavia it is common plant of northern and upland woodlands, but in Britain there are few similar native woods in which it can escape heavy grazing. It is declining across its range as meadows

Melancholy Thistle and Wood Cranesbill often grow together in traditional agricultural meadows, as here near Muker in Swaledale in the Yorkshire Dales.

are increasingly fertilised and managed for silage rather than hay crops. In Europe, it is fairly widespread from Iceland and arctic Russia southwards, but only in mountains in the south of its range.

Melancholy Thistle *Cirsium heterophyllum*

This handsome thistle follows naturally from the previous species, with which it often grows. Globeflower is another typical associate, as in the wood near Malham described above. It can be over a metre tall, with a swollen, purple flowerhead that reminds me of an old-fashioned studio microphone. Its lance-shaped leaves are toothed round the edge or sometimes slightly lobed, and their undersides are covered in a white felt of cottony hairs, but the plant is not at all spiny. Perhaps its solitary flowerheads look melancholy where a single plant grows on a mountain rock ledge, fancifully suggesting to the old herbalists that it would be a powerful herb to 'expel superfluous melancholy' from the human body. However, where I have seen massed meadows of it – in lower Glen Shee in Perthshire, for example – it has always seemed to me to be a highly sociable and affable sort of plant!

Melancholy Thistle is perhaps most at home in damp woodland margins and streambanks, but this has also allowed it to colonise upland hay meadows from north Wales and Derbyshire northwards. It is less frequent than Wood Cranesbill and Globeflower in the tall-herb communities of mountain cliffs, although it is recorded to 760m in the Breadalbane hills of Perthshire. Because of its association with hay meadows, its seeds may have been moved around the country with harvested crops. It is certainly regarded as an introduction to Orkney and Shetland, and its distribution in northern England suggests that it followed cattle drove roads there from southern Scotland. Like the previous species, it is declining as hay fields give way to earlier-harvested silage crops. Outside Britain, it is a relatively common plant across northern Europe, east to Siberia, and in the mountains of central Europe.

The Three Peaks

The same Great Scar Limestone seen at Malham also provides the foundation for the tourist landmarks of the Three Peaks in the Yorkshire Dales – Ingleborough, Pen-y-ghent and Whernside – but these hills are topped by a hard crown of Millstone Grit. This has slowed the rate of erosion and allowed the Three Peaks to stand proud at heights of 723m, 694m and 703m respectively.

The pasture at Sulber is typical of the limestone scenery around the Three Peaks, with Pen-y-ghent in the background. It hosts one of the largest populations of the endemic English Sandwort (inset).

The lower slopes of Ingleborough, in particular, offer another fine example of the limestone landscape known as karst, with extensive limestone scars, crags and screes, large areas of limestone pavement that are even richer than those around Malham, sink-holes where streams disappear underground, potholes and enormous underground caverns. An area of 1,014ha north and east of the summit is protected as the Ingleborough National Nature Reserve (NNR) by Natural England, which offers several way-marked walks around the reserve; the quarry walk from Ribblehead railway station is a good place to see Bird's-eye Primrose.

The limestone pavement at Scar Close near Chapel-le-Dale, north of the summit, is particularly rich because grazing animals are fenced out to stop them stumbling into deep grykes. That allows meadow plants to flourish on the thin soil atop the clints, including Globeflower, Melancholy Thistle, Lily-of-the-Valley and Bloody Cranesbill. Baneberry is again common in the grykes. Other montane and submontane species recorded here include Spring Sandwort, Alpine Cinquefoil, Stone Bramble, Hairy Stonecrop, Northern Bedstraw and Bird's-eye Primrose. Partly for safety reasons, a permit is required from Natural England to visit this part of the NNR.

On the lower slopes of Ingleborough, Holly Fern, Rigid Buckler-fern and Limestone Fern are recorded in grykes and on clints. Hairy Stonecrop grows sporadically over the slopes, as does Teesdale Violet, although nothing like as commonly as in Teesdale, where we will meet it in the next chapter. Stiff Sedge is recorded above about 610m, and there are records of Dwarf Willow on windswept crags. However, the richest flora is on ledges and gullies in the crags of what is called the 'Main Limestone' at about 640m. Here there are luxuriant stands of Yellow Mountain, Purple and Mossy Saxifrages, Roseroot, Spring Sandwort, Hoary Whitlow-grass and Alpine Meadow-grass. Alpine Saw-wort prefers the Millstone Grit outcrops.

The eastern slopes of Ingleborough, and a small area of nearby Fountains Fell, are the only known localities for the delicate, white-flowered English Sandwort. This endemic subspecies of the more widespread Arctic Sandwort (Chapter 16) is confined to just 21 populations here, most typically where thin peaty soil overlies the limestone outcrops. Between 2000 and 2013 the total number of individual plants – the entire world population of this endangered subspecies – ranged between 300 and 800.

The crags of Pen-y-ghent have one of the best displays of Purple Saxifrage anywhere in Britain.

Enthusiasts for the 'microspecies' of lady's-mantle can find several rare examples around Ingleborough, including the plant known as Least Lady's-mantle *Alchemilla minima*. This very local endemic, first described in 1949, grows in short turf near the summit of Ingleborough and on one other nearby fell. Ingleborough also holds important populations of at least eight nationally rare or threatened hawkweeds. I will return to these so-called 'critical plants' in Chapter 18. Pen-y-ghent shares many of the Ingleborough species, but Whernside is botanically the least interesting of the Three Peaks because it lacks the limestone scars and cliffs.

Outlying sites

Other species from our mountain plant list occur in a variety of other upland habitats locally. For example, bogs at Austwick, south of Ingleborough, and Helwith Bridge to its east, were sites for Bog Rosemary. Further east, the wood at Grassington hosts Wood Cranesbill, Melancholy Thistle, Stone Bramble and Mountain Melick.

West of Whernside, the limestone pavements at Hutton Roof are one of the best sites to find Rigid Buckler-fern. Other montane species in the pavements include Green Spleenwort, Limestone Fern, Spring Sandwort, Stone Bramble and Mountain Melick. In places, Blue Moor-grass is a common grassland component, Melancholy Thistle is found amongst open scrub and Holly Fern is recorded on Farleton Fell. Gait Barrows, south-west of Beetham, has areas of limestone pavement with more Rigid Buckler-fern, Northern Bedstraw and Blue Moor-grass. Continuing westwards, Arnside Knott, which rises to a mere

159m, is a rather anomalous site for Teesdale Violet. It also has small quantities of Spring Sandwort and Mountain Everlasting.

Moving northwards, some of the species already mentioned also occur in the north Yorkshire Dales, although there is slightly less diversity here. Both Alpine Penny-cress and Spring Sandwort grow in old lead-mine workings around Swaledale and Wensleydale, with Hoary Whitlow-grass on some of the limestone scars. Great Shunner Fell at the head of Swaledale is home to three scarce species that we will meet later: Marsh Saxifrage, Sheathed Sedge and Alpine Foxtail. The peaty moorland between Stainmoor and Bowes Moor is another home for Marsh Saxifrage as well as Bog Rosemary. However, most botanists will be tempted to continue a little further north to the botanical gem of Upper Teesdale, described in the next chapter. Before we move on, two more species call for our attention.

Stone Bramble *Rubus saxatilis*

Stone Bramble is best described as a rather scraggy-looking bramble. It is never terribly common or conspicuous, partly because of its creeping, rather than patch-forming, growth form. Its straggly stems may or may not have a few prickles. Its rather tatty, off-white flowers ripen into red fruits with one to six drupelets (the individual 'baubles' of a Bramble fruit). These are rather bitter but are eaten by a few mountain birds and perhaps Mountain Hares, which spread the seeds.

Yet, for all that, Stone Bramble is a plant I always delight in finding, because it is a true survivor in challenging habitats. I have seen it looking thoroughly montane on cliffs high in the Scottish mountains (it is

Stone Bramble flowers always look faded and tatty, with narrow, off-white petals.

recorded to 975m in the Breadalbane hills), but in limestone pavements and woods like that at Grassington it frequently coexists with distinctly lowland species. It spreads by far-creeping stolons through base-rich soils on crags and in ravines, limestone pavements and rocky woods, and is found in suitable upland areas from Exmoor and the Brecon Beacons north to Shetland. Elsewhere, it is quite widespread from Iceland, Scandinavia and arctic Russia to the Pyrenees, in northern Asia, and as a rare plant in Greenland.

Rigid Buckler-fern *Dryopteris submontana*

The limestone of the Pennines is the core of the British distribution of this fern, which grows in upright clumps of grey-green feather-like fronds. Although these are noticeably stiff and rigid, the plant seems to need protection from high winds to produce its spores. As a result, an estimated 80 per cent of the British population grows in the grykes of limestone pavements, with sites also in crevices in limestone scars or in the shelter of block scree beneath limestone cliffs. It is probably more common in the grykes on the south-west side of Ingleborough than anywhere else in Britain. It is also abundant in the limestones at Gait Barrows and Hutton Roof, where there are said to be thousands of plants. At Silverdale nearby, it grows almost at sea level, but it climbs to 465m on Highfolds Scar, north of Malham Tarn.

Beyond this core, there is a scattering of outlying sites where it is rare and difficult to find. There are old records for the species on calcareous rocks on Cadair Idris in north Wales and Cwm Glas below Snowdon (Gilbert, 1970). It still grows in small quantities in the Darren Fawr nature reserve on the southern edge of the Brecon Beacons and on the limestone of Mynydd Eglwyseg, north of Llangollen. In 1974, it was discovered in Derbyshire on two railway cuttings in limestone rock (raising intriguing questions as to how it got there). Outside Britain, the species is confined to the mountainous regions of the northern Mediterranean and Algeria. Its northernmost Pennine site on Hilton Fell is probably therefore also its northernmost locality in the world.

The upright clumps of Rigid Buckler-fern are shaped like shuttlecocks, and are said to smell of balsam when crushed. It is commonest in limestone pavements like this.

Upper Teesdale and the north Pennines

chapter eight

With this chapter, we reach one of the true botanical hotspots of the British Isles, a place that is also of international importance for its unique grouping of arctic and alpine species, often at the extremes of their world range. The fells at the head of the River Tees in Upper Teesdale have been a magnet for botanists since their riches were first recognised in the late 18th century, particularly by John Binks, a miner who regularly escaped to the fells for the benefit of his health and first found many of the area's special plants. When I became enthused by mountain flowers, Upper Teesdale was the obvious choice for one of my earliest pilgrimages outside the Scottish hills, in June 1977. I have returned regularly to Teesdale ever since to further explore the dramatic landscape and the intriguing assemblage of plants that grow there.

The fells around Upper Teesdale form the largest contiguous area of land above 500m in England. Their exposure leads to a severe climate which makes life a constant struggle for the local farmers, even although the land is relatively fertile thanks to the underlying limestone rock. As I will try to show in this chapter, the combination of tough climate, rich soil and low-intensity agriculture explains the botanical riches of the area. There is plenty of interest also in the fells north of Teesdale, although, as we will see, it took an agricultural crisis before botanists fully recognised their importance.

OPPOSITE PAGE: The overall purple colour of Alpine Bartsia makes clumps of the plant easy to spot from some distance away in damp pastures or on mountain rock ledges.

An extreme climate

Upper Teesdale lies in the middle of one of the narrowest parts of Britain, so that it is only 70–80km from the Irish Sea to the west and

The waterfall at Cauldron Snout is one of the iconic landmarks of Upper Teesdale, where the River Tees tumbles over a ledge of hard Whin Sill rock below Widdybank Fell.

60–70km from the North Sea to the east. The sea therefore has a strong moderating influence, but this is counteracted by the altitude, which rises to 893m at Cross Fell in the north-west corner of the area. The area is sheltered in the lee of the Lake District hills with respect to moisture-carrying winds, so it has a lower rainfall than the Lakes. However, on many days of the year, clouds form over the escarpment of the north Pennines, depressing solar radiation and temperatures.

From 1931 to 1980 meteorological records were kept at the Moor House research centre, lying towards the west of the area at 556m, and an automatic weather station was put in place there from 1991. These data (from 1931 to 1979) show that the mean monthly temperature does not rise higher than 12°C in the warmest month of July, and drops to about –1°C in February (Holden & Adamson, 2002). Air frosts occurred on around 133 days annually, and snow lay on the ground for 69 days per year (rising to 106 days a year on the top of Cross Fell). All this helps exclude lowland species and selects for a flora adapted to alpine and arctic environments.

However, this unusually long-term dataset also shows potentially worrying changes. Mean January and February temperatures rose by around 1.5°C between 1931–1979 and the 1990s, although summer temperatures were largely unchanged. Over a similar period, the number of days of ground frost dropped by 32 days and the days with snow cover by 19 days. This may partially explain recently noted changes in the flora, to which we will return shortly.

As discussed in Chapter 3, one of the main impacts of mountain climates on plants is through their growing season, which broadly equates to the length of time when mean daily temperatures exceed 5°C. On this basis, it has been calculated that the typical growing season at 450m in Teesdale is from 18 April to 23 October, reducing still further at 670m to between 4 May and 16 October (Clapham, 1978). Plants of arctic and alpine environments, adapted to short growing seasons, are best suited to cope with these conditions.

Relicts on the sugar limestone

Upper Teesdale lies on the same band of limestone rocks as the Peak District and Yorkshire Dales, uplifted here as a broad dome to rather higher elevations. There are three bands of limestone, interspersed with shales and thin coal seams. The Middle Limestone group forms the bedrock underlying most of the region. Above it, rocks of the Upper Limestone group outcrop in the higher fells to the west of the region, while beneath it the Lower Limestone group has been intruded by the hard, grey igneous rock of the Great Whin Sill.

Where the Great Whin Sill pushed its way into the Lower Limestone band on Widdybank and Cronkley Fells at the end of the Carboniferous period, it baked the limestone above and below it into a coarsely crystalline marble. This weathers readily into a fine granular material known from its consistency and colour as 'sugar limestone'. The friable rock and the resulting, relatively unstable red-brown soils support the richest of the Teesdale plant assemblages.

Widdybank Fell: an exposure of the coarsely crystalline limestone rock weathering to produce the fine granular material called 'sugar limestone'.

The River Tees flows through the area, rising as a series of springs on the gently sloping eastern flanks of Cross Fell. It continues along the western slopes of Widdybank Fell through a valley that formerly had several deep deposits of peat, and tumbles over the Whin Sill intrusion at the Cauldron Snout waterfall. It then passes through the narrow, steep-sided valley between Widdybank and Cronkley Fells, before plunging 22m over the Whin Sill at the High Force waterfall.

When, in 1966, plans were announced to flood the peat-filled valley west of Widdybank Fell to form the Cow Green Reservoir (see pp.148–9), urgent efforts were made to study the pollen preserved at different depths in the peat deposits that were about to be flooded. As a result, we know a great deal about the vegetational history of the area. As I outlined in Chapter 3, the pollen archive in the peat shows that the late-glacial vegetation was replaced only slowly by woodlands, but critically these never formed a closed canopy on the fells, and some areas of open limestone remained. Pollen grains from many of the rare species that grow in the area today were found at multiple depths through the peat, showing that these plants have persisted here continuously since the glaciers retreated. It is that relict flora that makes Upper Teesdale so important.

Teesdale meadows and pastures

For many years, Dr Margaret Bradshaw, formerly of the Extramural Department at Durham University, has been the doyenne and champion of the Teesdale flora. She has always been generous in sharing her knowledge with aspiring botanists, and in late July 1981 I had the privilege of joining her for a week crawling in the rain over Widdybank Pasture, trying to meticulously record every species present along transects (narrow strips) through the vegetation. What I remember was the extraordinary diversity in such a small area, typically with 20 or more species in any square metre. In fact, a single field in Upper Teesdale can easily contain 120 species of vascular plant.

Some members of the group I joined in July 1981, hard at work meticulously recording the diversity of the vegetation on Widdybank Pasture.

According to my partial notes from the time, there were at least nine species of sedges in the area we surveyed, including Hair Sedge from our montane list. Bird's-eye Primrose and Alpine Bartsia were quite common in our survey area, along with the leaves of Northern Bedstraw, rosettes of Spring Gentian, seedheads of Scottish Asphodel and delicate tufts of Least Clubmoss. We found isolated patches of Hairy Stonecrop and Yellow Mountain Saxifrage, here virtually at the south of its British range, and I became quite expert at recognising Alpine Rush and Blue Moor-grass. There were several lowland species in the mix too, including large numbers of tiny Frog Orchids, Grass of Parnassus and Heath Fragrant-orchids.

I remember some of the nearby meadows being yellow with Globeflowers, replacing the Marsh Marigolds that flower abundantly earlier in the year. In some of the damper meadows Melancholy Thistle grew alongside Meadowsweet and Marsh Valerian. The characteristic plant of the riversides here is Shrubby Cinquefoil, scattered along both banks of the Tees but especially abundant below High Force. Other montane species find at least a foothold on riverside gravels and silts, where flooding maintains an open habitat in which they can thrive.

Riverside banks and crags

One of the richest riverside sites is Cetry Bank. It lies just off the Pennine Way, below Widdybank Pasture on the north bank of a great sweep of the River Tees. Seepage and springs keep the calcareous boulder clay nicely wet. On my several visits to this site, I found plenty of Alpine Bartsia, Bird's-eye Primrose, Spring Gentian, Alpine Bistort and Starry Saxifrage. Mountain Pansy grows in grassland above the bank, and Scottish Asphodel, Hair Sedge and Alpine Rush are also found on the slopes.

Further up the river, the Whin Sill outcrops below Cauldron Snout as cliffs and large boulder scree which feature a more acid-loving flora. The rocks here, called Falcon Clints, are especially good for ferns and their allies, including Parsley Fern, Holly Fern, Mountain Male-fern, Green Spleenwort and Fir Clubmoss. I have found

Two Teesdale specialities, Spring Gentian and Bird's-eye Primrose, growing on Cetry Bank beside the Tees in 1983.

Oblong Woodsia: a well-established and healthy plant in the population reintroduced to the species' former rocky habitat on Falcon Clints and Cronkley Scar.

a few leaves of Bearberry on the rocks near Cauldron Snout, along with Crowberry and Cowberry. Mossy Saxifrage and Bird's-eye Primrose also occur on the Clints, along with occasional Juniper plants.

Oblong Woodsia was recorded on Falcon Clints and on Cronkley Scar until as recently as 1950, when the last specimens were lost, at least partly as a result of indiscriminate collecting by plant hunters. In 1999–2000, 63 and 50 plants of the species were reintroduced to two locations in the vicinity of their former sites, as part of a project that I will return to in Chapter 10. As there were no surviving local plants, plants of Scottish, Welsh and Lake District origins were used to maximise genetic diversity and optimise the likelihood of the plants regenerating. Heather McHaffie, who helped mastermind the project, tells me that by 2012 there were 12 surviving plants at the first site and 29 at the second, after slow attrition in the preceding years. Some of the plants looked big and healthy – the best had an impressive 175 fronds – but there was no sign of offspring appearing at either site, suggesting that the future for the species there still hangs on a knife-edge.

The main botanical attraction of the region lies in the sugar limestone grassland on the higher fells, but three species call for our attention before we reach there.

Alpine Bartsia *Bartsia alpina*

To my mind, the steep, grassy slopes along the banks of the Tees are the real heartland of Alpine Bartsia in Britain (see photo p.140). 'Purpleness' is its overriding characteristic. It has rather hairy, unbranched stems which stand up to 25cm tall (but often half that). From June to August it produces tubular, dull purple, two-lipped flowers, typical of the figwort family. The leafy bracts beneath these flowers also turn purple, and sometimes the whole plant is suffused with that colour, so it looks dark and brooding.

The species grows as a hemi-parasite, meaning its roots tap into those of sedges, grasses and other plants to steal some nutrients (Taylor & Rumsey, 2003), although it still makes its own food by photosynthesis. As well as Upper Teesdale, a few plants survive in Great Close Mire near Malham, a small population in pastures near Orton in Westmorland and rather more at Crosby Gill, an SSSI east of Shap Summit on the M6 motorway. It also grows on basic rock ledges towards the western end of the Breadalbane hills in Perthshire and Argyll, typically at altitudes between 600m and 800m but up to 950m on Beinn Heasgarnich. It is disappearing from many pasture sites because of overgrazing, trampling by cattle and drainage. It occupies very similar habitats elsewhere in its range from arctic Europe south to the Pyrenees, Alps and Bulgarian mountains. It is also found in Greenland and northern Canada.

Shrubby Cinquefoil *Potentilla fruticosa*

This plant is still more of a Teesdale speciality. Even non-botanists make a pilgrimage to sites like High Force to see its densely branched bushes, which grow to a height of around 50cm (occasionally more), covered with silky, five- or seven-fingered leaves and showy golden-yellow flowers. It is widely grown in gardens and in civic amenity plantings (although many of these are cultivars of Asian origin, with white or orange petals). The native plant is confined to a 16km stretch along both banks of the Tees, intermittently from Falcon Clints downstream to Middleton, and three sites in the Lake District, which we will meet in the next chapter. Elsewhere in Europe, the species is found only at a few sites in the Pyrenees and Alpes Maritimes and around the Baltic (Elkington & Woodell, 1963).

Shrubby Cinquefoil seems to be intolerant of shade, and it never invades surrounding woodland in Teesdale. The spread of woodland at the climatic optimum, some 8,000 years ago, may have eliminated it from other parts of Teesdale, so it survives today only where regular river flooding prevents trees from establishing. Its characteristic ridged fruits have been found in glacial sediments at sites in Cambridgeshire and the Lea Valley in Essex. These date from shortly after the end of the last Ice Age, around 15,000–20,000 years ago, although oddly its remains have not been identified from any of the post-glacial deposits studied in Upper Teesdale.

Bushes of Shrubby Cinquefoil growing on the banks of the River Tees downstream from the High Force waterfall.

Mountain Male-fern *Dryopteris oreades*

The boulder scree below Cauldron Snout is typical habitat for this medium-sized, clump-forming

fern. It is fairly widespread through the mountains of north Wales, then rather more scattered through the north Pennines, Lake District, Southern Uplands and central and western Highlands, usually on relatively acidic rocks. It is also found in the more mountainous of the Hebridean islands, and at 180m on Ward Hill on Rousay, Orkney at what is probably its northernmost site in the world.

Male-ferns are not an easy group of plants to identify. With experience, Mountain Male-fern is recognisable by its stiff, strongly upright, lance-shaped and rather crinkly fronds.

It typically grows on well-drained rock ledges, in the upper, more unstable zone of scree slopes and in gullies, at moderate elevations from 100m on the Isle of Rum to 850m in the Cuillin hills of Skye. It seems very susceptible to grazing, without which it would be more widespread on mountain slopes. Elsewhere, it is mainly a plant of the mountains of western Europe, from northern Germany south to Spain and east to Turkey.

The battle for Cow Green

Widdybank Fell, on the north-eastern side of the Tees in County Durham, is the most famous and richest botanical site in Upper Teesdale. It also has an important place in the history of plant conservation.

In 1948, the BSBI (which, back then, stood for Botanical Society of the British Isles), set up a committee to deal with threats to the British flora, and one of their early campaigns was for the establishment of a National Nature Reserve (NNR) in Upper Teesdale. In 1963, the Nature Conservancy agreed, and established an NNR covering 2,630ha on the Yorkshire side of the Tees, including Cronkley Fell (in 1999, this was amalgamated with land at Moor House into a larger, but discontinuous, NNR). However, the Durham side, including Widdybank Fell, was excluded from the NNR. In 1965, the Tees Valley and Cleveland Water Board proposed the construction of a large dammed reservoir at Cow Green, adjacent to Widdybank Fell, to provide water for industrial developments nearer the river mouth. The BSBI objected, but its case was not helped by the decision to exclude the area from the NNR. For the first time, the BSBI realised that it had to be more than a scientific body studying the British flora, and raised £25,000 from a public appeal to fight the dam proposal, which had been laid before Parliament in a Private Bill.

The access road built when the Cow Green Reservoir was constructed now offers visitors the opportunity to see many of the most interesting plants of the Teesdale flora without causing damage to the fragile fell.

Ultimately the campaign failed, the peat-filled valley of Cow Green was flooded, and several important plant communities were lost. However, a number of concessions were made and Widdybank Fell was left largely intact. The chemical company ICI, one of the main beneficiaries from the reservoir, contributed £100,000 towards research in the area, and the awakening of botanical conservation put in train a series of developments which ultimately led in 1989 to the creation of Plantlife as a wild plant conservation charity to campaign alongside the more scientific work of the BSBI.

Widdybank Fell today

These days, the metalled road built for constructing the Cow Green dam provides a convenient nature trail, allowing many of the plants of the fell to be conveniently seen without risk of erosion to the fragile vegetation. The trail begins from the Cow Green car park, with spectacular views across the reservoir to Cross Fell and Great Dun Fell. At various points, the track passes outcrops of thin-soiled sugar limestone, the richest of which are fenced off to exclude grazing animals. Here there are masses of Spring Gentians – a real Teesdale gem, flowering best in May – as well as Alpine Bistort and low-growing Moonwort ferns. Limestone sand, blown into these exclosures from where the reservoir is cutting into its banks, helps support Teesdale Violet – a species whose rarity makes it another of our three-star enigmas. The vegetation here is desperately fragile, and visitors are urged to keep to the metalled track so the plants can continue to flourish for others to enjoy. A permit is needed to enter the exclosures (but is scarcely needed, as you can see all the plants well from the roadside).

★★★ Teesdale Violet *Viola rupestris*

Teesdale is the core site for this species in Britain, meriting its rather parochial common name – elsewhere in Europe it is known as Rock or Sand Violet. It is not an easy plant to tell from the much more widespread Common Dog-violet. Although its flowers are a paler blue-violet, this distinction is not definitive and open flowers are often difficult to find because the majority of plants shed their pollen within closed, bud-like flowers. In Teesdale Violet the leaf-stalk is typically covered in a dense fuzz of short hairs, whereas the Common species is usually hairless. However the leaf-stalk of Teesdale Violet can be hairless and that of Common Dog-violet sometimes has a few hairs – and this potential confusion is further compounded by the occasional appearance of hybrids between the two species. Rich & Jermy (1998) and Roberts (2013) offer guidance on the characters needed for definitive identification.

Although around ten per cent of its population was lost with the flooding of Cow Green, Wigginton (1999) estimated that 10,000 plants still grow on the sugar limestone on Widdybank Fell. It was first discovered there, new to Britain, by the botanist James Backhouse in 1862. In 1960 it was found at two sites in Westmorland: on Long Fell and at Arnside Knott (although this site was actually recognised from a herbarium specimen collected in 1927 but misidentified as Common Dog-violet). At the latter site, it has declined dramatically since its discovery because insufficient grazing has led to it being smothered by a dense growth of Blue Moor-grass.

The finders of the Westmorland sites suggested that the species might survive at other sites, and highlighted the Craven limestones as an area worth searching. Sure enough, in 1976 a small population was discovered beside a track in Ribblesdale, and around 50 other colonies have since been found, centred on Ingleborough and nearby limestones. It grows here amongst an open clitter of small stones or on gentle slopes of fine scree. Many of these colonies are very small, but there are said to be over 1,000 plants in one of these sites. Other sites may still await discovery within this core range.

Beyond these English sites, Teesdale Violet is found from eastern Siberia to northern and central Europe, reaching west to the Pyrenees and south-east France. It even grows in coastal sand dunes in the Netherlands. A separate subspecies is widespread in Scandinavia. In the Alps, it is relatively uncommon on dry, stony slopes between 600m and 2,500m, and it probably survives on the Craven and Teesdale limestones because these are the only British sites that provide similar habitats and a sufficiently severe climate to exclude competing lowland vegetation. The Arnside Knott site at a mere 150m appears somewhat anomalous, but it grows there in a patch of just 20m^2 on top of an unstable limestone cliff battered by winds that whip across Morecambe Bay.

The blue-violet flowers of Teesdale Violet are usually a paler blue than the flowers of Common Dog-violet, but the two species are not easy to tell apart.

One of the mineral-rich rocky streams, called 'sikes', which emerge from the limestone rock and run across Widdybank Fell, one of the most important botanical areas in Upper Teesdale.

The path now crosses the first of several rocky streams, locally known as 'sikes', full of mineral-rich water that has emerged from springs in the limestone. These are rich in mosses and liverworts, and are a good place to see Bird's-eye Primrose. A little further on, the path passes the spoil heap from a barytes mine that was worked here until the 1950s, and this offers a home to Hoary Whitlow-grass, Spring Sandwort, Three-leaved Rush and Blue Moor-grass. Just beyond, the grass around the weather station is a good place to spot Spring Gentian (I have counted over 300 plants in the turf here) and tiny plants of Hair Sedge.

Continuing onwards, the path crosses the most distinctive of the streams, called Red Sike. In the damper grassland near the sike, you can spot Scottish Asphodel, Three-flowered Rush, Alpine Rush and another Teesdale speciality, Dwarf Milkwort. Broad-leaved Cottongrass grows in a base-rich flush nearby. Elsewhere in the grassland, you might spot the leaves of Mountain Everlasting, Sea Plantain and Alpine Cinquefoil, and the dull-purple flowers of Autumn Gentian. From here, the track continues towards the Cow Green dam, beyond which a rough path leads over rocks to the top of Cauldron Snout waterfall – a dramatic endpoint to one of the finest botanical walks in Britain.

The trail is an excellent way to see virtually all the Teesdale plants without risking their survival. Only one rarity is likely to elude you without a permit to leave the track, and that is the Teesdale Sandwort. This rare species is a little more reclusive in its habits, and definitely qualifies as a three-star mountain enigma.

★★★ TEESDALE SANDWORT *Minuartia stricta*

On my first visit to Widdybank Fell in June 1977, I was lucky enough to be accompanied by the NNR warden at the time, Ian Findlay. He granted me privileged access to see one of the area's great rarities, Teesdale or Bog Sandwort. To approach it, he insisted I should walk up the middle of a sike in full flood, then kneel in the water to photograph a single accessible plant on the bank. It was pouring with rain at the time, and the flowers were not even open, but it was still satisfying to photograph the species at its only British home.

In truth, the plant would not have been worth getting soaked for were it not for its extreme rarity. In June and July its thread-like flowering stems are topped by inconspicuous white flowers which are short-lived and seem reluctant to open. They resemble those of the similarly unimpressive Mountain Sandwort (Chapter 11). In fact, the two can only be safely distinguished on the basis of minor technical differences between the length of the sepals and the distance between the flowers and nearest leaf.

The discovery on Widdybank Fell was made in 1844 by a group of botanists including James Backhouse. Over 170 years later, this is still its only known British site. It grows in open gravelly and stony flushes beside two sikes that run across the sugar limestone of Widdybank Fell, typically around the base of mossy hummocks. Surveys in the 1980s and 1990s found between 280 and 374 plants, making it one of Britain's rarest plants. Sadly it seems to be getting rarer: Stroh *et al.* (2014) quote the most recent count as just 133 plants and classify the species as endangered.

Beyond this single British locality, it is a plant of arctic and subarctic Europe, Greenland and arctic North America. It was formerly recorded in south-west Germany and in the French and Swiss Jura mountains but is probably now extinct in these areas, and it has never been recorded in the Alps.

Not exactly an impressive plant: Teesdale Sandwort has tufts of narrow, moss-like leaves, thread-like flowering stems which stand 5–10cm tall, and inconspicuous white flowers.

Fossil records suggest it was more widespread in Britain in the immediate post-glacial period, probably associated with late snow beds. So why is Widdybank Fell its only surviving British site? Perhaps the clue comes from the habitat where I found it in the Abisko National Park in arctic Sweden. It grows there within a vertical scar where avalanches regularly descend from the mountain above, clearing a strip through the surrounding birch woodland and leaving an open stony chute in which the sandwort can flourish without competition. In summer this constantly runs with ice-cold water from melting snow on the base-rich slopes above.

Teesdale Sandwort appears to be so slender and delicate that it cannot compete with other plants, and relies on other factors, like those avalanches, to maintain an open habitat. It seems to require continuous moisture and the sort of primitive, base-rich soils that were left behind by retreating glaciers after the last Ice Age. In most limestone areas, water disappears underground, leaving a well-drained surface susceptible to summer drought. However, the sikes of Teesdale run over the intrusion of Whin Sill. Water cannot penetrate this hard rock, so the streams flood across a wide area. That water is enriched with calcium from the outcrops of sugar limestone it has passed. On the banks of the sikes, therefore, Teesdale Sandwort can find the damp, calcareous conditions it requires, while exposure on Widdybank Fell and the thin soil maintain an open community. The cool climate may also play a part, because studies in Scandinavia suggest it prefers mean summer temperatures no higher than 23°C. I can think of no other limestone area in Britain with quite this combination of features, allowing the sandwort to survive at what is now probably its southernmost site in the world.

So-called 'Teesdale' Sandwort a long way from Teesdale, in the Abisko National Park in arctic Sweden. It was growing in a stony area in the middle of birch woodland, kept open by regular avalanches that descended in winter from the mountain above.

Many of the peat-filled hollows on Widdybank Fell were lost with the flooding of Cow Green, but several areas of peat survived. These bogs are dominated by Heather and Harestail Cottongrass, with Bog-mosses and other typical bog species. There is an old record, dating from 1722, of Dwarf Birch 'near Birkdale' on one such bog. The pollen record shows that the species had grown in the area throughout the last 10,000 years, but it was assumed to have died out until 1965 when a small group was refound, very possibly on the same bog. It is not surprising that this small colony had eluded discovery, because the tallest plant was a mere 15cm high. Intriguingly, semi-fossilised leaves of Dwarf Birch were excavated from peat close to the colony, at a depth of 90–105cm. The survival of such a small colony, at the species' southernmost British site, is precarious, and concerns have often been expressed about its long-term survival, although it was still thriving in 2014.

Dwarf Birch *Betula nana*

Dwarf Birch is a mini-tree which rarely exceeds 30cm in height, but it can grow up to a metre tall in ideal, ungrazed conditions. It has red stems and neatly rounded, bright green, deciduous leaves. The rounded teeth of these leaves and its characteristic small fruits are easily recognisable amongst fossil plant remains preserved in peat, and it also has distinctive pollen grains which look like the head of Mickey Mouse with two swollen ears (see p.41). Such remains show that it was abundant and widespread across Britain in the immediate post-glacial period, but since then it has suffered from steady attrition as a result of changing climate, burning, grazing and afforestation of its former peatland habitats. The paper dedicated to it in the invaluable *Biological Flora* series (De Groot *et al.*, 1997) suggests that it is confined in Britain today to sites where the mean annual maximum temperature is less than 21°C and where February temperatures reliably dip below freezing – reminiscent of the long, cold winters and short, cool summers it experiences in the

Dwarf Birch survives in small numbers on a bog beside Widdybank Fell. This plant was photographed in 2014, beneath a cage to protect it from grazing animals.

rest of its range in the subarctic tundra and taiga. Its exposed site on Widdybank Fell narrowly meets those conditions, but climate change undoubtedly threatens its future there.

Today, suitable conditions for Dwarf Birch prevail mainly in the wet upland heaths and blanket bogs of the Scottish Highlands, so it is widespread, but rarely common, throughout that area, from Rannoch Moor in Perthshire/Argyll to Ben Loyal in Sutherland, at altitudes between 120m in Sutherland and 860m above Glen Cannich in Inverness-shire. Within this range, there are often only scattered small plants that are easily overlooked, but in a few places ankle-high forests spread across many hectares. In England, a record from Darwen Moor in south Lancashire is assumed to be an introduction. North of Widdybank Fell, a small patch is thought to be native at an inaccessible site on Emblehope Moor in the Kielder Forest. More recently, it has also been found in the Wark Forest, about 30km south of there, and in the Spadeadam military area in Cumbria at the unusually low altitude of 220m.

Cronkley Fell

The other great honeypot for botanists and casual walkers in Upper Teesdale is Cronkley Fell, on the southern (Yorkshire) side of the Tees. The usual approach is from the Hanging Shaws car park on the Teesdale road, following a short but steep track down to the river, joining the Pennine Way across Cronkley Bridge, then climbing up

Cronkley Scar, the northern face of Cronkley Fell, seen from the Pennine Way east of the Cow Green Reservoir.

onto the fell. This route passes the largest area of Juniper in England, which sadly now looks very degraded. Meadows on the path have lots of Globeflower and Mountain Pansy in both its yellow and purple forms.

The route then takes a right turn onto a broader 'green trod' that climbs steadily onto the fell itself. Here the flora can be seen most dramatically in a series of exclosures beside the track (the three that I knew have since been increased to seven, so my recollections here may be slightly out of date). The first exclosure had many plants of Bird's-eye Primrose, Alpine Bistort, Spring Sandwort, Hoary Whitlow-grass, Hair Sedge, Blue Moor-grass and, in some years, abundant, low-growing Moonwort ferns. There are nice plants of both Common Rock-rose and the smaller-flowered Hoary Rock-rose, whose leaves are noticeably white-felted on the underside. The latter is a rare and very local plant of short, open grassland on Carboniferous limestones at sites like the Gower peninsula in south Wales and the Great Orme in north Wales. It is predominantly a lowland species, and the plants that grow 535m up on Cronkley Fell are recognised as a separate and endemic subspecies *levigatum*.

Inside the exclosure, I have been shown the leaves of Horseshoe Vetch in one open patch of ground. This is another very local, lowland species of sunny chalk and limestone grassland that here reaches its northernmost site in Britain. Apparently, it has not been recorded in flower here since 1930.

One of the exclosures on the Cronkley Fell limestone grassland, which is designed to protect the plants from grazing animals.

The exclosures are all subtly different in their plant communities and species composition, but almost all their variety can be seen by circumnavigating the fence-line (a permit is required to enter the exclosures). Along with further Hoary Rock-rose, another exclosure has superb displays of Spring Gentian in late May. Mountain Avens only appeared in one of the exclosures I knew, where there were also a few plants of Dark-red Helleborine, another species of grassy limestone slopes and ledges, Hoary Rock-rose and delicate little plants of Hair Sedge. I have also found Alpine Meadow-rue and Green Spleenwort in this exclosure, along, rather surprisingly, with Cloudberry – which is normally a species of acid peat. Many of these species also appear, less abundantly, on the sugar limestone grassland outside the exclosures.

As you would expect from two such celebrated botanical sites, a number of the plants of Widdybank and Cronkley Fells are ones that we have not previously met on our journey, several of them at or near their southernmost sites. These merit further description before we continue northwards.

Hoary Rock-rose is a rare plant also found at two lowland limestone sites in Wales. The plants on Cronkley Fell are recognised as subspecies *levigatum*, which grows nowhere else in the world.

Dwarf Milkwort *Polygala amarella*

Dwarf Milkwort is an endangered species which is probably easier to find on Widdybank Fell than anywhere else in Britain. This neat, tufted little plant is easily overlooked, as it rarely grows more than 10cm tall. Its tiny flowers, around 5mm long, are most commonly pink in Teesdale, although there are small groups of blue-flowered plants on both Widdybank and Cronkley Fells. In 2011–2013, it was estimated that just 876 plants survive at 16 sites in Britain (all in England), and Widdybank holds one of the largest populations, with 100 plants counted there in 1994. It is an extreme calcicole, found in short, open grassland overlying calcareous rocks, usually on well-drained sites. As well as Teesdale, where it is recorded up to 530m on Cronkley Fell, it is also known from limestone near Orton in Cumbria, and from the Malham area, where it grows in a rather different situation on tussocks in calcareous mires, raised above the wetter surroundings.

Surprisingly, the same species is also recognised in the chalk grassland of the North Downs in Kent, where it is known as Kentish Milkwort and typically has blue or greyish-white flowers. Plants there were once considered to be a separate species on the basis of minor morphological differences, but they are generally now regarded as different races or varieties of one very variable species. This taxonomic

confusion leads to some uncertainty over its European range, although the species seems to be fairly widespread in grassland habitats in southern Scandinavia, the Pyrenees and the Alps. Sadly, it is declining in Britain, largely as a result of increased grazing. Because plants only live for around 3–6 years, they are quickly eliminated from a site if their flowers and fruits are grazed off over several successive years. It may also be susceptible to summer drought in Kent.

Dwarf Milkwort is usually pink-flowered in Upper Teesdale, but these plants on the limestone of Orton Fell in Cumbria are the more typical blue colour. Plants in Kent are often a greyish-white.

Alpine Bistort *Persicaria vivipara*

Alpine Bistort is a distinctive plant in the turf of mountain pastures. Its unbranched stems usually stand only 10–20cm tall. Swollen red bulbils, like miniature radishes, appear in the angle of leaves near the top of the stem. These can break off and sprout into new plants, but, because this involves no genetic exchange, they are identical to the parent. Its stems are topped by a cluster of pinky-white flowers. These are normally pollinated by flies or small bees, although they can self-fertilise if necessary. These two options for propagation help the species survive in the mountain environment; in poor summers, when there are few insects active, the bulbils ensure that at least some new plants will appear.

I always think of Alpine Bistort as a valuable indicator of 'good' montane sites: wherever you find it, you can be pretty sure of other interesting species nearby. However, it is not found south of the mid-Pennines in England and is a great rarity at its only Welsh locality in Snowdonia (Chapter 6). As well as the northern Pennines, it is found in the Lake District, the Southern Uplands of Scotland, then pretty well throughout the Highlands and Islands in the right habitats. It most typically grows on base-rich soils but spreads onto more acidic soils. It is most abundant in mountain pastures, but you can also find it on damp cliff

Alpine Bistort has long-stalked leaves at the base of its stem and stalkless leaves up its stem. The stem is topped by an inflorescence of white flowers, with a cluster of red bulbils beneath.

ledges, in amongst stable scree slopes and in the damp grassland beside mountains springs and flushes. It is recorded to 1,210m in Perthshire but descends almost to sea level in the north of Scotland. It is also a common species in arctic and northern Europe, Asia and America, and in the high mountains of these continents.

The beautiful displays of Spring Gentians in one of the exclosures on Cronkley Fell matches any I have seen of the species, even in the core of its world range in the Alps.

Spring Gentian *Gentiana verna*

These stunning gentians are as attractive as any garden variety. The dramatic, deep-blue flowers have a corolla tube up to 25mm long, and the flower lobes spread to 30mm across (whereas those of the much smaller Alpine Gentian, as we will see in Chapter 11, are a third of that diameter).

In Britain, the species is mostly confined to this area of the north Pennines at altitudes between 350m and 730m on Little Fell in Westmorland. It is also recorded on Mickle Fell in Westmorland, and Bellbeaver Rigg and near Yad Moss in Cumberland (Elkington, 1963). Its total range is just 18km from north to south and 15km east to west, although it is locally frequent within that range. In some years as many as of 4,000 rosettes have been counted in its main Cronkley exclosure. However, this considerably overestimates the number of plants, because they spread by an extensive system of creeping stolons within the turf, each of which ends in a leaf rosette. The species is also found in the Burren in Ireland, in northern Russia and throughout the mountains of central Europe, with separate subspecies recognised in Asia and in Morocco.

Mountain Everlasting *Antennaria dioica*

This grey-woolly species is quite distinctive in its grassland habitats, with a spreading rosette of leaves that are white with hairs underneath, hairy stems, and pinkish-white, button-like flowerheads. Despite its common name, it is at best a marginally submontane species. It is recorded at altitudes of up to 907m on Seana Bhraigh, to the east of Ullapool in Ross-shire, but I also remember looking for it in 1985 at one of its southernmost sites, at Barnack Hills and Holes near Peterborough. This grassland reserve, famous for its springtime displays of Pasque Flowers, lies less than 50m above sea level. The warden seemed

bemused as to why I should be interested in such an insignificant flower, but with a lot of searching we eventually found three plants, in a patch no more than 5cm by 5cm!

It was formerly found in chalk and limestone grassland in southern England, but has largely vanished from there because of habitat destruction, although a few plants hang on at sites in Cornwall, Wiltshire and the Mendip Hills. It is also known from the Brecon Beacons, but is much more widespread in northern Britain, throughout the Highlands and on many Scottish islands, coming right down to near sea level in sand dunes and the machair grassland of far north-west coasts. It is always found on thin soils, usually basic but sometimes mildly acidic. In the mountains it is most typical of well-drained heathy areas. It is dioecious, meaning it has separate male and female plants. This can be a problem at isolated sites; if its population is reduced there to a few plants that are predominantly or all of one sex, then its chance of producing seed is greatly reduced. Elsewhere the species is widespread in similar habitats in northern and central Europe, Asia and North America.

The hairy stem of Mountain Everlasting is rarely more than 10cm tall. It is topped by a cluster of pinkish-white button-like flowerheads.

Scottish Asphodel *Tofieldia pusilla*

Some of the most attractive mountain flowers are also the most diminutive. Their small size makes them difficult to spot but all the more satisfying to find amongst the sweeping grandeur of mountain landscapes. That certainly applies to Scottish Asphodel. It is like a miniature version of the much commoner Bog Asphodel, rarely standing more than 8cm tall with a basal tuft of iris-like leaves and an elongated triangle of around ten tiny greenish-white flowers.

'Scottish' is an appropriate name for the species in a British context, because, apart from these sites in Upper Teesdale, it is a plant of the southern and western Highlands, absent from the Border hills and absent also from the Scottish islands, except for Skye, where it is rare in the Cuillin hills, and Rum, where it

Scottish Asphodel is an elusive but attractive little plant of open, gravelly, lime-rich flushes, as here on the slopes of the Cairnwell in Perthshire (see Chapter 11).

is slightly commoner. It is usually found in open, gravelly, lime-rich flushes and streamsides that stay permanently wet but are not too waterlogged. It is recorded up to 975m in Perthshire, but almost down to sea level in Sutherland. One oddity of the plant's history is that it was discovered as a species new to science by the great botanist John Ray in 1671 'about two miles from Berwick, by the side of a rivulet'. This would probably place the site in England rather than Scotland, but the plant has never been refound in the area. Outside of Britain, it is widespread in the arctic and subarctic regions of Europe, the Alps and arctic North America.

Alpine Rush is an enthusiast's species! You may need a good field guide to distinguish it from other, very similar relatives.

Alpine Rush *Juncus alpinoarticulatus*

Rushes are often regarded as 'difficult' plants, and, in honesty, I would struggle to tell this species from the very similar Jointed Rush *J. articulatus*. Its spiky stems stand up to 40cm tall, with two or three narrow, up-curving leaves and a tight head of 6–8 dark red flowers that ripen into bluntly oval fruits (although it often fails to set fruit).

Alpine Rush typically creeps through base-rich mountain flushes or gravelly stream beds. It is found at only a few sites in the northern Pennines near Malham, in Upper Teesdale and in the Dumfriesshire hills. Its main distribution is then in the southern Highlands, with occasional outlying records further north. It is recorded at altitudes from 128m on the limestone of Tullach Hill near Pitlochry in Perthshire to 880m near Ben Alder in Inverness-shire. Beyond Britain, it is widespread in northern Europe, Asia and North America, south to the mountains of Spain, Italy and the Balkans.

Three-flowered Rush *Juncus triglumis*

Three-flowered Rush is both commoner and somewhat easier to identify than the previous species. It has a wiry stem, up to 20cm tall in very sheltered situations but typically about a third of that, with a few narrow leaves near the base. It grows in wet, usually relatively base-rich, gravelly flushes and damp, open, rocky places, generally at fairly high altitudes, often with Scottish Asphodel.

It is found in Snowdonia, in the north Pennines and Lakes, then scattered through the Highlands with a rather western tendency,

Three-flowered Rush has a tight little cluster of three oval flowers, all spreading out from the same base at the top of the stem (which distinguishes it from Two-flowered Rush in Chapter 12).

but not in the Border hills. It is recorded at altitudes up to 1,175m in the Breadalbane hills of Perthshire but comes down to lower altitudes in the north. There is an old record at 60m on the Shetland island of Unst, but it was last seen there in 1962 and it died out from Orkney sometime before 1930. Its lowest record now is at 90m beside the Storr Lochs of Skye. It is quite widespread globally in the arctic and mountain regions of Europe and North America and in the Himalayas.

Hair Sedge *Carex capillaris*

Like Stiff Sedge (Chapter 6), this is another sedge that it is much easier to identify than many of its commoner, lowland relatives, at least when it is in flower or fruit. Its slender, wiry stem is about twice as long as its stiff, arched leaves and usually only about 5–15cm tall. The stem is topped by a single oval male spike, and a little cluster of female spikelets that seem too heavy for their hair-like stalks so that they hang downwards.

It is a plant of short, base-rich mountain grassland, open, gravelly areas flushed by base-rich water and damp mountain ledges of limestone or mica schist. It also grows, rather more luxuriantly, in mineral-rich mires, where it can reach heights of 40cm or more. It is very rare in north Wales, local in the north Pennines and absent from the Lakes. In the Southern Uplands it is known only from a small population in the vicinity of Loch Skeen near Moffat. It is quite widespread in suitable habitats in the southern Highlands, reaching altitudes of 1,150m on Ben Lawers, then appears again in the far north, where it comes down almost to sea level, for example in dune grassland beside Dunnet Bay in Caithness. Elsewhere, it grows in the mountains of Scandinavia, southern Europe east to the Caucasus, Iceland, Greenland, Svalbard and northern Asia. It also occurs surprisingly widely in North America, from Canada south to New York State.

In June 1993, I was botanising on a flat grassy plain, enriched by blown shell-sand, just a few metres above sea level on the island of Papa Westray in Orkney, and was surprised to discover Hair Sedge growing there, just a small distance from a patch of Scots Primrose. I did not realise it at the time, but this was a first record for Orkney, about 80km from its nearest site on the Scottish mainland, and remains, I believe, the only record from any of the Scottish islands. It is still thriving there, although the primrose nearby has sadly

If any sedge could be described as cute, it would be Hair Sedge! The top spike is formed by male flowers, and the delicate, nodding clusters consist of female flowers, which here have developed into fruits.

gone, but this chance encounter neatly illustrates that there is still plenty to discover about the distribution of our mountain plants in unexpected places.

The tiny grass florets of Blue Moor-grass are clustered together in a dense, egg-shaped or cylindrical head.

Blue Moor-grass *Sesleria caerulea*

The problem with grasses is in understanding their biology and then having the terminology to describe the distinctions between them. Fortunately, several montane grasses are very distinctive in appearance, including this one. Blue Moor-grass has a rather rush-like form, with a dense tuft of greyish leaves that have a waxy bloom on one side. Its rigid stem can grow to 45cm tall and is topped by an egg-shaped flowerhead (properly called a panicle). This typically is rather bluish or bluish-violet at its base, hence the species' name.

It is a plant of open limestone grassland and heath, limestone scree slopes and hollows in the flat tops of limestone pavements. It has an intriguing distribution in Britain, very much centred on the Carboniferous limestones of the north Pennines and Lake District, and lowland outcrops of Magnesian limestone in Durham and Northumberland, with a small outlying population in the Peak District which was only discovered in 1989. It has a second centre in a very limited area towards the western end of the Breadalbane hills in the southern Highlands, where it grows on mica schist. Old records from the east Grampians are now thought to be mistaken. It is found from nearly sea level around Morecambe Bay to 1,005m in the Breadalbanes. It is also found in two areas of western Ireland, on limestone and serpentine rocks in the mountains of central Europe, and at two localities in Iceland (Dixon, 1982).

The changing nature of Teesdale

Having celebrated the diverse flora of Upper Teesdale, it is sadly necessary to add a note of caution. The methodical recording that Margaret Bradshaw has carried out in the area over many years has alerted her to 'an insidious reduction in the size of the populations of most of the rare plant species, accompanied by a deterioration in the quality of many of the plant communities', which she authoritatively described in *British Wildlife* (Bradshaw, 2012).

A management agreement with the new owner of Widdybank Farm in 1995 led to the number of sheep being significantly reduced. A succession of mild winters then led to a huge increase in the population

of rabbits, which grazed the fell more closely and more intensively than sheep would have done. On Cronkley Fell, Dr Bradshaw estimated there were more rabbits inside the recently enlarged exclosures than outside. When the rabbit population reached plague proportions in 2005, action was taken to drastically limit their population, but since then, with reduced grazing by both rabbits and sheep, the height of the vegetation on Widdybank Fell has increased greatly. Blue Moor-grass and some of the sedges have become dominant, and many of the smaller, rare species have been shaded out. Spring Gentian responded by producing more vegetative shoots but fewer flowers. Bird's-eye Primrose and Teesdale Violet declined greatly, and only a single non-flowering plant of Dwarf Milkwort was left in the Cronkley exclosures in 2010. On Cetry Bank, grazing by Galloway cattle opened up tracks across the steep face, allowing stagnant water to accumulate and leading to slumping of large pieces of turf, which took rare plants with them.

TOP: Cetry Bank, when I photographed it in 1977, was a wonderful, open slope of species-rich grassland, full of Spring Gentians and other species.

ABOVE: By 2013, it had changed beyond recognition. Grazing Galloway cattle had enriched the soil with their dung, producing more rank vegetation. Stagnant water accumulated in puddles created by the cattle's trampling.

Overall, Dr Bradshaw's general impression of the species-rich grassland and dwarf sedge-marsh communities in 2010 was that they were too tall and dense for the rare species to compete successfully. She thinks it will be very difficult now to restore the conditions that the rare species need to thrive. I suspect these sorts of problems are not unique to Upper Teesdale, and we will return to them in Chapter 19. However, we can only log these changes with certainty in Teesdale because of the detailed studies that Dr Bradshaw and her volunteers carried out in the 1970s and 1980s. I am pleased to have played a small part in that work, even if I am saddened by what it is now happening.

Mickle Fell and Moor House

Part of the luxuriant population of Alpine Forget-me-not on Little Fell.

Beyond these most visited areas, two other areas in Upper Teesdale merit special mention. Mickle Fell lies in the south-west corner of the Upper Teesdale section of the National Nature Reserve but is also within the Warcop Military Training Area, which makes its exploration problematic. Access to the fell is only available on a permit system, and is subject to training requirements, fire risk and other factors (visit the website at www.gov.uk/public-access-to-military-areas to find out more).

Mickle Fell has higher north-facing limestone cliffs than other parts of Teesdale, and extensive scree slopes. Its maximum altitude of 790m means that parts of it always remained above the tree-limit (estimated to have reached no higher than 760m in this area since the last glaciation). As a result, it has a rich montane flora including Spring Gentian, Spring Sandwort, Mossy Saxifrage, Alpine Scurvy-grass, Alpine Bistort, Northern Bedstraw and Mountain Pansy. Dwarf Willow was formerly recorded here and on Cross Fell, although it has not been seen recently.

The most interesting denizen of Mickle Fell and the adjacent Little Fell was first discovered there in 1862. Alpine Forget-me-not is a widespread species in the Alps, as its name suggests, but is known in Britain only from here and on Ben Lawers in Perthshire, yet on Little Fell it can be so abundant as to turn the turf blue in places. I will return to that perplexing distribution in Chapter 13.

The area of the National Nature Reserve around Moor House is important scientifically, but lacks the spectacular concentrations of rare species elsewhere in the reserve, particularly as it has no outcrops of sugar limestone. Over most of the area, glacial drift has accumulated over the underlying limestone. Because the drift soil is impervious to water, extensive peat bogs have built up, on which some of the commoner peat alpines like Cloudberry and Crowberry flourish.

Where bare outcrops of limestone rocks (scarps) are exposed, Spring Sandwort and Mossy Saxifrage are common. Roseroot is fairly frequent on limestone ledges, along with Alpine Cat's-tail grass at its only surviving English sites. Mountain springs provide a home for Starry Saxifrage and, much more rarely, for Alpine Foxtail grass. There are many old lead workings whose typical inhabitants include Alpine Penny-cress, Alpine Scurvy-grass and occasionally Alpine Clubmoss. Bird's-eye Primrose is recorded from a single locality and Alpine Forget-me-not is very rare in the limestone grassland. Perhaps most important botanically are the mires, enriched with minerals from the limestone beneath, which provide a habitat for Three-flowered Rush, Hairy Stonecrop and Marsh Saxifrage.

Cross Fell and other outlying fells

Just north-west of the reserve, Cross Fell rises to the highest point of the Pennines at 893m, easily accessible from the Pennine Way which crosses just below. The summit plateau is dominated by Woolly Fringe-moss, with typical species of exposed hilltops such as Stiff Sedge, Fir Clubmoss and Alpine Clubmoss, but Dwarf Willow seems to have disappeared and Bog Bilberry has not been recorded recently in the high-level peatlands.

Outcrops of limestone occur higher on Cross Fell than anywhere else in the Pennines and so provide a home for a good range of montane species, although some are quite scarce. These include Alpine Cinquefoil,

A view towards Cross Fell and Great Dun Fell from Knock Fell, with high altitude limestone grassland in the foreground.

Alpine Bistort, Northern Bedstraw, Holly Fern and small areas of Alpine Forget-me-not. Spring Gentian and Hair Sedge grow in the limestone turf of Bellbeaver Rigg, a lower summit to the east of the main fell.

The fells in this area are heavily sheep-grazed, and their botanical richness was not appreciated until 2001, when a devastating outbreak of foot-and-mouth disease led to the almost complete removal of sheep from the hills. As a result, plants burst into flower in unexpected profusion. Alpine Foxtail grass grows in at least nine colonies beside springs and in grassy flushes over the Cross Fell range. When grazing was removed, 3,800 flowering heads were counted in these colonies, including over 2,000 plants at one site which was described as 'a fantastic sight ... reminiscent of the Greenland tundra' (Rich, 2003). Chickweed Willowherb, which we will return to in the next chapter, filled some streams with its flowers, and Hairy Stonecrop flowered in unprecedented profusion, showing just how much these species were normally repressed by sheep grazing.

The removal of grazing led to the discovery in 2002 of Sheathed Sedge, new to England, at no fewer than 13 separate locations across these high fells from Green Fell, just north-west of Cross Fell, to Mickle Fell and beyond. Perhaps most unexpectedly of all, the lime-rich marshes and flushes high on Cross Fell were suddenly filled with thousands of flowers of Marsh Saxifrage, a species whose distribution and frequency is so puzzling that it qualifies as another of our three-star enigmas.

When sheep were removed, following the outbreak of foot-and-mouth disease in 2001, flowers of Marsh Saxifrage appeared in their thousands on lime-rich marshes and flushes high on the fells.

★★★ Marsh Saxifrage *Saxifraga hirculis*

The conservation importance of this showy yellow-flowered saxifrage was rather overlooked in Britain until our adoption of the EC Habitats Directive, which listed it in Annex II as a species 'whose conservation requires the designation of Special Areas of Conservation' (SACs). It is found in bogs and other wet places quite widely across northern and central Europe, but is a European priority because it is rapidly declining in many parts of its range. It is thought to be extinct in Austria, for example, with just a single site remaining in Switzerland and only three in France. It is still fairly common in Sweden and Finland, and I have found it quite abundantly in Svalbard and Iceland. It is also known from the Caucasus and Himalayas, and across arctic Asia and North America.

Marsh Saxifrage is very reminiscent of, but much rarer than, Yellow Mountain Saxifrage. It grows in open tufts, rather than the loose cushions of the commoner species. It is somewhat taller and usually has just one or two flowers in its inflorescence. It is rather less montane, recorded to only 750m on Mickle Fell. The need for its conservation in Britain is neatly illustrated by the story at its first recorded, and southernmost, English site on Knutsford Moor in Cheshire. It was discovered there sometime before 1720, but by 1842 one authority was warning that it was 'almost destroyed by the rapacity of some individuals who have dug it up for sale in the most remorseless manner' (Lusby & Wright, 1996). Soon after, it was exterminated from the site.

Today, the main stronghold of Marsh Saxifrage in Britain is along a 50km length of the north Pennines between Stainforth and the fells between South Tynedale and Weardale, where there is estimated to be a population in excess of 50,000 plants. Implementation of the Habitats Directive led to designation of the area around Upper Teesdale and Moor House as an SAC for the species. The designation papers for the SAC suggest that ten flushes emerging from the Carboniferous limestones of the Appleby Fells, Cross Fell and Upper Teesdale could conceivably contain over 270,000 plants. This high estimate is fuelled in part by experience after sheep were removed from the fells during the foot-and-mouth outbreak of 2001, when

Marsh Saxifrage has big, showy, bright yellow flowers, the size of a 10p piece, usually dotted with deeper yellow spots.

thousands of flowerheads appeared on slopes where just a few had been seen before.

At Great Shunner Fell, west of Swaledale, the third highest peak in the Yorkshire Dales, it grows in the company of two other elusive species, Alpine Foxtail and Sheathed Sedge, which also seem highly susceptible to grazing pressure. In 2012, it was discovered by local botanist Linda Robinson in calcareous flushes at two sites a little way north-east of there in Swaledale.

Part of the Marsh Saxifrage colony discovered in 2002 in the Munsary Peatlands in Caithness, which might be the biggest population in Britain.

The relationship between grazing and Marsh Saxifrage is complex. It was once found at various sites close to sea level in northern England and Scotland, but all these sites have been lost through drainage, agricultural intensification and forestry. It is now confined to base-rich flushes and mires in upland areas. As a weak, straggly plant, it seems unable to compete with tall vegetation. Robinson (2012) records how the saxifrage was completely overwhelmed by tall herbs within three years of a small exclosure being erected around one patch near Moor House, although it continued to grow in a grazed area outside the fence. She believes it can survive very high grazing pressures, and notes that, where good numbers of sheep are seen gathered around a flush on the fells, there is a good chance that the site will hold Marsh Saxifrage! She warns that the fencing off of whole moors to improve the habitat for Black Grouse presents another threat to the species.

Although grazing significantly depletes the number of flowers and reduces seed output, moderate levels of grazing seem to be beneficial by repressing competition. In 1999, I helped Plantlife negotiate the purchase of 1,238ha of peatland at Munsary in Caithness as a nature reserve, and since then I have had the privilege of chairing the reserve's management group. Our objective has always been to show best practice in land management, and, as part of that, we commissioned a series of detailed surveys by the University of East London (UEL). In 2002, the UEL team led by Dr Richard Lindsay discovered Marsh Saxifrage growing in a flushed area of mineral soil within the reserve. This was a previously unknown site, although the species had been recorded at another site in Caithness prior to 1912. The following August, the local vice-country recorder Ken Butler counted more than 1,000 flowering shoots and around five times that number of non-flowering shoots in a patch no bigger than the average garage. Since then another adventurous botanist, Sandy Payne, has found six more patches in nearby peatlands.

The stems of Marsh Saxifrage can be anything from 4cm to 25cm tall, depending on how heavily their habitat is grazed. The pale green stems are covered in a stubble of reddish hairs.

So why are these populations only now being discovered? The land at Munsary was grazed at relatively low intensity by hill sheep until two years before Plantlife bought it. Our concern in the management group was that past sheep grazing had maintained open conditions in which the species could survive, that the removal of grazing then allowed the plant to 'let loose' and flower in quantity, but that this would not be sustained as ranker vegetation choked out the saxifrage. Sample surveys in subsequent years have shown a decline in flower numbers, and we are monitoring this carefully in case we need to take action to keep its habitat open.

There are old records for Marsh Saxifrage also in wet pastures in the Pentland Hills, south-west of Edinburgh. In August 1980, I went to visit a recently rediscovered site near the source of the Medwin Burn in a triangular no-man's land where the counties of Midlothian, Peebleshire and Lanarkshire meet. The area was surrounded by a broken-down fence, once intended to stop cattle and sheep from blundering into boggy ground, although there were clear signs of recent grazing. Here, in wet grass, I found one small patch of Marsh Saxifrage, with a single malformed flower and one flower bud. Hairy Stonecrop was the only other notable species present, but lots of buttercups made the saxifrage difficult to spot. A little searching found a few more groups of leaves, but, as far as I know, that was (and probably still is) the entire Southern Upland population, as an old record in the Ochil Hills has never been refound.

Its fate in the north-east of Scotland has been only slightly rosier, thanks to its local champion, David Welch. Six colonies were recorded there over previous centuries, but by 1996 only three sites remained at altitudes of around 400m in north Aberdeenshire, with approximately 800 flowering plants between them (Welch, 2006). At another site at Towie in south Aberdeenshire no plants had been seen since 1969, and the remaining sites had almost certainly disappeared because of moorland drainage. In 1996, Scottish Natural Heritage approved David's proposal to reintroduce the species at Towie. Thanks to his work, nine reasonably vigorous transplants were still surviving there in 2005, with 3–5 flowering shoots produced in most years.

I have dedicated so much space to Marsh Saxifrage because I suspect it might still hang on at other hill sites, grazed to invisibility: indeed, a new population was found in 2014 in an area of blanket bog at the north end of the Monadhliath Hills in Inverness-shire. However, it is very clear that careful management will be essential at all of its key sites if we are to ensure its survival in Britain.

To the west of Cross Fell, the grey limestone fells above Appleby have an interesting flora. Long Fell, near Brough, is a recorded site for Teesdale Violet. The deep valley down from Hilton Fell hosts Rigid Buckler-fern and Limestone Fern. The slopes east of this, leading up to Little Fell, have Spring Sandwort, Spring Gentian, Hoary Whitlow-grass and Alpine Forget-me-not in some quantity. Further north, the limestone around High Cup Scars is worth exploring for Roseroot, Alpine Penny-cress and Hoary Whitlow-grass. Alpine Meadow-grass grows on two limestone scars here, and a precious few plants of Alpine Saxifrage grow at one spot on the intrusive Whin Sill, at the species' only Pennine site. Calcareous flushes below the summits of Little Fell and High Cup Nick are the habitat of Alpine Meadow-rue, Three-flowered Rush, Pale Forget-me-not, and the two montane willowherbs, while Alpine Cinquefoil, Northern Bedstraw and Hairy Stonecrop are recorded from limestone near the head of Maize Beck. It seems appropriate therefore to end this chapter with profiles of three more of these montane species.

Hairy Stonecrop *Sedum villosum*

It is always a pleasant surprise to find this delicate plant in its preferred habitat on otherwise unprepossessing hillsides. Its stems, which rarely exceed 10cm in height, branch at the base to produce little offshoots that help it spread through its damp habitat. In late June and July, the stems are topped by a small cluster of pink-purple flowers, and its leaves and stems are often reddish in colour.

Despite its name, Hairy Stonecrop is never conspicuously hairy, although close inspection reveals short, stubbly hairs over its reddish leaves and stems.

Hairy Stonecrop is found characteristically in flat, stony, mossy flushes where seeps of base-rich water enrich otherwise relatively acidic ground, typically in heather moorland or species-poor hill grassland. These localised sites are nowhere common, sometimes transient, and highly susceptible to damage or drainage, yet the species' dispersal is so effective that it regularly turns up in suitable habitats, including shallow ditches and the wet gravel of hill tracks. It is only found from Wensleydale northwards, including Teesdale and Cumbria. It is surprisingly widespread in the Southern Uplands, although, even here, it is in steady decline through drainage and land-use changes.

It is more scattered in the southern Highlands, as far north only as the Cairngorms, where it is rare and declining. There are isolated records on the Morvern Peninsula and on the Isle of Mull. It is recorded from near sea level to 1,138m in Perthshire, but I think of it mostly as a species of middle mountain slopes, between perhaps 250m and 500m. It also occurs in Iceland, Greenland, the Scandinavian mountains, then south to mountains from Spain to Morocco.

Pale Forget-me-not *Myosotis stolonifera*

This delicate forget-me-not has flowers which are a mere 5mm across and such a pale blue as to be almost white. It has short stem leaves, and a dense mat of leafy side shoots characteristically develops in late summer from the angles of its lower leaves.

Pale Forget-me-not is a plant of relatively base-poor springs and pools, flushes and seepage areas. It is commoner on the fells of the north Pennines and Lake District than anywhere else in Britain. It is also found on the North York Moors and a scattering of sites in the Southern Uplands. It is mainly upland, with records from 130m in the Lune Valley up to 820m on Cross Fell. Although it was first collected in 1892 in the Howgill Fells, north of Sedbergh, its significance was not recognised until 1926, when it was named as *M. brevifolia* and considered a potential British endemic. It has since been confirmed as the same species as plants from the

Pale Forget-me-not is a rather elusive plant, but it is abundant in a few sites, like this colony in a bog pool on Yad Moss to the north of Widdybank Fell.

mountains of northern Portugal and Spain, but, even so, that limited range may make it one of our rarest species internationally.

Alpine Foxtail *Alopecurus magellanicus*

Alpine Foxtail is a truly handsome mountain grass, at least when it is in flower or fruit. The bases of its lower leaves form inflated sheaths around its stems, which can reach 40cm tall but usually less. In midsummer, its cylindrical flowerheads look distinctively silky because of the grey hairy floral leaves (called glumes) that tightly enwrap the flowers.

The species was discovered, new to science, on Lochnagar in Aberdeenshire in 1794 by a botanical explorer called Robert Brown. It was unknown outside of the central Highlands (which is still its core range) until 1956 when Derek Ratcliffe discovered it at around 760m in the Moffat hills. Three years later, he and another botanist, Alan Eddy, further extended its range when they found it at a similar altitude on Cross Fell in Cumberland, and a second population was found soon after on the Westmorland slopes of the fell. Both populations were recorded as infrequent, but plants of this species are difficult to recognise wherever grazing animals snip off its distinctive flowerheads. The huge population of the grass revealed in 2001 when grazing had been removed from Cross Fell in response to foot-and-mouth disease was therefore as unexpected as it was exciting. The cessation of grazing also revealed a population on Green Fell nearby.

The silky cylindrical flowerheads give Alpine Foxtail a very handsome appearance. It also has a remarkable worldwide range.

In 2007, the species' range was extended another 26km further south when a population was discovered on Great Shunner Fell in the Yorkshire Dales, interestingly with both Sheathed Sedge and Marsh Saxifrage nearby. Within its overall range, other new sites have since been discovered, including two flushes on Ben Buck in the Ochil Hills. It is recorded from 600m in the Ochils to 1,220m on Braeriach in the Cairngorms. I have a feeling that, like Marsh Saxifrage, Alpine Foxtail might be more abundant than we realise. Its world distribution is somewhat obscured by uncertainties over its taxonomy, but within Europe it appears only to be recorded from Britain and Svalbard (where I have found it quite commonly). It is also found in North America, Greenland and arctic Russia, and recent work has concluded that it is the same species as plants from the southern Andes, Falkland Islands and South Georgia, by which token it has a truly remarkable world range.

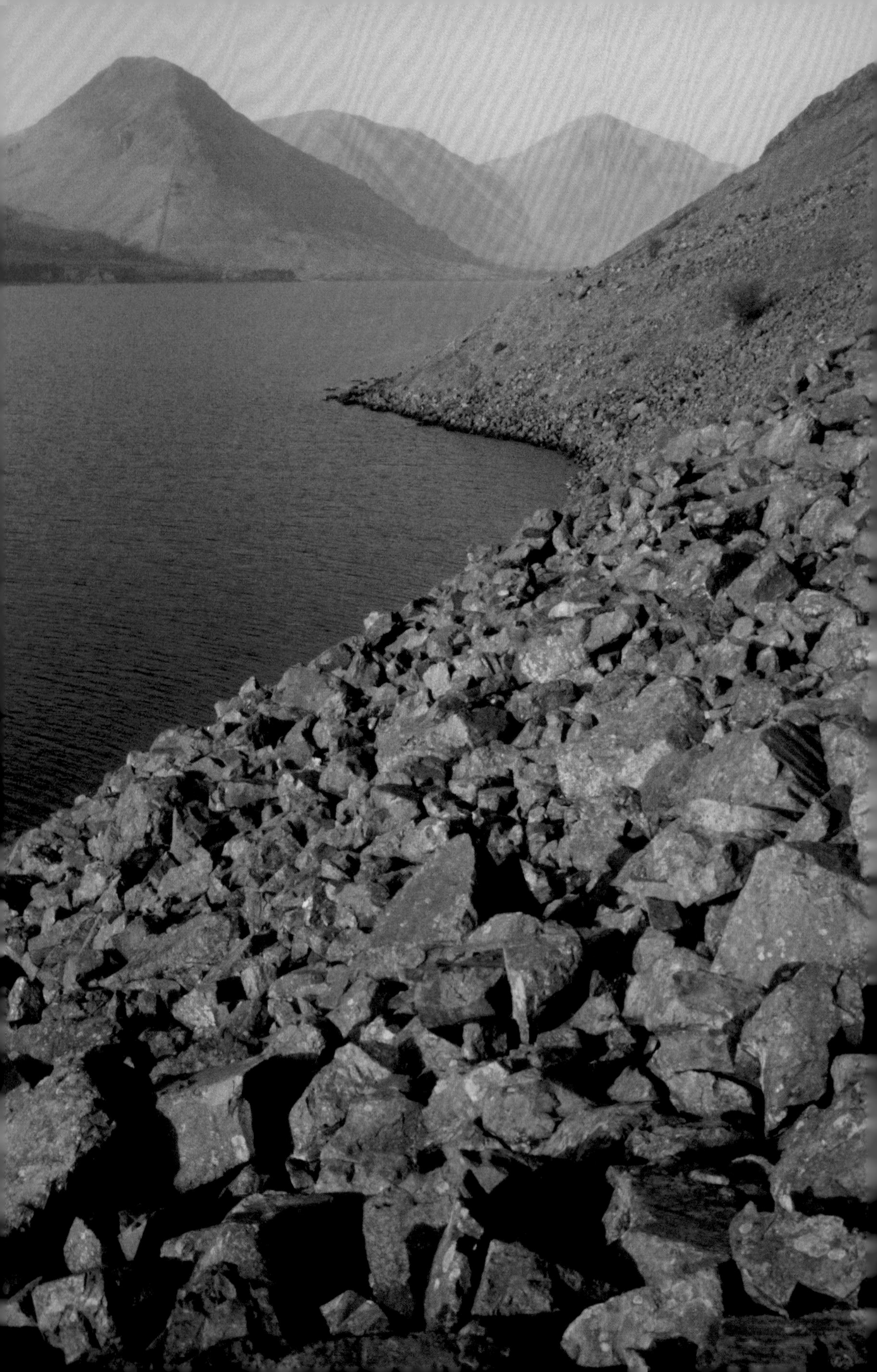

The Lake District and Northumberland

chapter nine

The Lake District offers some of the finest hillwalking in Britain, on mountains that, for the most part, are greener, gentler and more welcoming than those in many other parts of Britain, interspersed with more rugged peaks and occasional dramatic crags. The hills rise to 978m on Scafell Pike, England's highest mountain. Nowhere here is quite as species-rich as the Teesdale fells, but that is part of the botanical charm of the Lake District. It takes a little more searching to find the most interesting plants, but you are always guaranteed a wonderful walk as you seek them out. An added advantage for me, as a Scottish botanist, is that the season comes rather earlier to the Lakes; there is good botanising to be had in April and May, when mountain plants have scarcely begun to appear further north.

Fells and gills

The main rocks south of Ambleside and along the shores of Windermere and Coniston Water are a complex mix of slates, shales, grits and flags from the Silurian period. These produce an undulating landscape of relatively low, sometimes rocky hills and ridges, separated by valleys and hollows. The fells here have rounded summits and steep but relatively smooth sides, with occasional incisions where rushing water has eroded characteristic steep-sided valleys, called gills.

North of this, the main central mass of the Lake District is formed of hard Borrowdale volcanic rock, originating in the late Ordovician period. This has been eroded into rocky summits and irregular, ruggedly undulating slopes. These volcanic rocks are very variable, from ashes to lava flows. They mostly produce poor, relatively acid soils but, here and there, localised calcareous outcrops support a richer

OPPOSITE PAGE: Wasdale Screes: this is the rather tricky route where I picked my way across the screes in April 1982, before walkers had stabilised the path after winter rockfalls.

A typical Lake District view, looking down the narrow valley of Fisher Gill, north of Helvellyn on the slopes above Thirlmere.

flora. The mountains have been heavily glaciated, producing steep U-shaped valleys, often with long, linear lakes at their base, and some of the highest inland cliffs in England. In places, hanging valleys are stranded high above the main valley below; streams that emerge from these plunge into ravines down the steep valley wall. Glaciers have carved deep corries into the rocks, some of which are filled with dark-watered tarns.

The oldest rocks of the Lake District are in the northernmost block of fells, including the summits of Skiddaw (931m) and Blencathra (868m). These Skiddaw Slates date from rather earlier in the Ordovician period and are relatively soft, so they have been eroded by ice and water into rounded or conical summits, with steep slopes below which are often covered in screes of shattered slate and cut into by deep gills.

Equably wet

Because of its closeness to the sea, the Lake District has a relatively equable climate but is notoriously rainy as its mountains catch the prevailing, humid south-westerly winds. The rainfall varies greatly with location. Keswick, on the edge of the mountains at 85m, typically gets around 1,475mm of rain per year, but localities in the heart of the fells can get three times that amount. However, the area is less continuously wet than the west Highlands, for example, and dry spells of up to 30 days are not uncommon.

At Keswick, the average monthly minimum temperature drops to 1.4°C in February, but the average maximum in July is 19.7°C. Allowing for altitude, this suggests that daily average temperatures on the highest fells only exceed 5°C between May and October, so the growing season there is short. Helvellyn typically has 67 days of falling snow per year, but this drops to 20 days in the valleys. Hill fog is common at any time of year, and depresses the average sunshine on the fells to just two and a half hours per day. This climate helps encourage a montane flora on the fells, but the relatively poor soils produced by the underlying rocks explain why this flora is rather less rich than that of Upper Teesdale.

Fell flora

The mountain flora of the Lake District fells reveals itself only slowly, amongst grassland dominated by Common Bent, Viviparous Fescue and Sweet Vernal-grass, with Mat-grass and Bilberry higher on the fells. One exception is Parsley Fern, which seems almost ubiquitous in screes and old walls, and even on roadside banks in Langstrath, for example, or in the middle of Glenridding village below Helvellyn. I remember being amazed when I first visited the Lakes in the 1980s at how easy it was to see this distinctive fern, compared with the hard work needed to find it in the Highlands.

Walking the hill paths, another plant that soon makes its appearance, typically above about 500m, is Alpine Lady's-mantle. It is recorded right up to the highest tops, but also down to 135m beside Ennerdale Water. It is most frequent on the steep slopes below scree, and sometimes grows there mixed with Parsley Fern. It even grows on stone walls. Fir and Alpine Clubmosses are also quite common on exposed banks where grasses cannot grow tall. Find a spring or a mountain flush, or explore a rushing stream in one of the gills, and you will soon come across another conspicuous and common species, Yellow Mountain Saxifrage.

The hills on the Skiddaw Slate are generally less interesting botanically than those of the Borrowdale Volcanics. Parsley Fern is

still common here, but Alpine Lady's-mantle is much less so. Dwarf Willow, Stiff Sedge, Fir Clubmoss and Alpine Clubmoss grow on some of the tops. Acid bogs on the mountain slopes have Cloudberry, Bog Rosemary and Few-flowered Sedge, with Lesser Twayblade lurking beneath occasional Heather plants. Yellow Mountain Saxifrage occurs here only occasionally.

However, the area does have one important botanical site at Hobcarton Crag, above the Whinlatter Pass. Famously, this is the only English site for Alpine Catchfly. It grows on two quartz-veined ledges at between 610m and 700m on the steep, largely inaccessible eastern face. The curious two-centre distribution of this tough little plant, here and in the Angus Glens, makes it another of our three-star mountain enigmas. Were it not for the catchfly, the crag would hardly be worth a botanical visit, with only commonplace associates like Parsley Fern, Alpine Lady's-mantle and Viviparous Fescue.

Hobcarton Crag is well known to botanists as the only site in England for Alpine Catchfly, growing here on the inaccessible east face of the crag, where it is said to be more accessible to butterflies than to humans.

★★★ Alpine Catchfly *Silene suecica*

In some ways, Alpine Catchfly (which I knew for most of my botanic life by the old name of *Lychnis alpina*) is an enigma heaped upon an enigma, because it is extremely localised at just two sites: a hilltop near Glen Clova in Angus to which we will return in Chapter 11, and here on Hobcarton Crag above the Whinlatter Pass in the Lake District, where it was first discovered in 1844. Remains of seeds excavated from Weichselian sediments show that it was much more widespread in that period, with records from Northamptonshire, Huntingdonshire and even the Isle of Man. Why therefore do these two sites provide its last remaining refuges in Britain? The answer seems to lie in its taste for heavy metal (and I don't mean loud rock music!).

Alpine Catchfly is a perennial which produces tufted rosettes of rather blue-green, spear-shaped leaves and clusters of rich carmine-pink flowers. Unlike Sticky Catchfly (Chapter 10), its stems are not in the least sticky; they are sometimes sparsely hairy and sometimes hairless, but definitely could not catch flies. Despite that, the species was once placed in the genus *Viscaria*, named from *viscum*, the Latin for sticky birdlime. That leads to an intriguing connection. In northern Sweden, a copper mine was named the Viscaria Mine because of its association with Alpine Catchfly. The species seems to have a strong preference for soils rich in heavy metals, and it was the prevalence of these plants in the area that led to the discovery of copper deposits there.

Alpine Catchfly on Little Kilrannoch, Angus, where it was discovered in 1795 by the Forfar nurseryman George Don. It grows there (inset) amongst frost-shattered fragments of serpentine rock.

That ecological association is also evident at its Scottish site, where it grows in a clitter of small serpentine rock fragments at an altitude of around 870m on a hill called Little Kilrannoch. Geologists use the term *ultramafic* for serpentine and other rocks that have a very low silica content but high levels of metals such as magnesium and iron. According to Nagy (2013), the soil at Little Kilrannoch has unusually high concentrations of magnesium and nickel. These levels would appear to be toxic to many other plants, because large areas of the hill there are almost devoid of life, with less than five per cent plant cover. This lack of competition, along with prolonged snow cover (around 95 days per winter), is probably what allows Alpine Catchfly to thrive here: over 60,000 individual plants were counted in an area no bigger than three football pitches in 1993. A few dozen more plants are found on a second, flatter rock outcrop about a kilometre to the south, although it is not clear why the species is so much less abundant there.

The soil at the English site is very different. Nagy shows that it is much more acid than at the Scottish site, with low concentrations of calcium but high levels of manganese and iron. Plants from either site have been shown to grow poorly in soil from the other site, suggesting they have evolved into separate races in response to the soil. The plants on Hobcarton Crag are also generally paler pink than those on Little Kilrannoch, with occasional white flowers recorded; similar pale plants are found in Iceland, Greenland and Labrador.

Ratcliffe counted 133 plants on Hobcarton Crag in 1958, but Halliday (1997) reported only 55 plants, and Ratcliffe blamed this decline on the depredation of collectors. At least the steep rock face of the crag is inaccessible to grazing sheep and deer.

Outside Britain, Alpine Catchfly is recorded from the Pyrenees to the Alps, in northern Europe and in subarctic Asia, North America and Greenland. I have seen it in flower close to a mountain summit in southern Norway, and close to the coast in Greenland. Nothing at these sites suggested anything exceptional about the soil, and it also grows reasonably well in our garden, provided we weed it regularly. I suspect the main role of the metal-rich soils at its British sites may be to discourage competition, while the severe climate alone is enough to ensure this at its subarctic sites.

Helvellyn

Helvellyn, which rises to 950m and includes the largest continuous area above 760m in the Lakes, is a magnificent hill to climb. Glaciation excavated deep corries on its northern and eastern slopes, leaving the dramatic, sharp Striding Edge above Red Tarn which offers an especially scenic walk from Glenridding to the east. The area is heavily grazed and dominated by mixed grassland of Common Bent and Viviparous Fescue, with Bilberry abundant in places and occasional patches of Heather and Mountain Crowberry that have escaped the hungry sheep. The Red Screes at the head of Glenridding Beck have lots of Parsley Fern and Alpine Lady's-mantle, with Fir Clubmoss, Yellow Mountain Saxifrage in flushes, and Purple Saxifrage. The summit ridge has plentiful Stiff Sedge and Dwarf Willow. Occasional solifluction features point to the relative severity of the climate. However, the richest flora is to be found on the steep faces of the eastern corries, beyond the reach of sheep, where calcareous rocks outcrop, as listed in the table below.

As well as the plants listed in the table, a number of other, much more particular species also hang on here in small populations which have probably been in steady decline since the post-glacial period. Fewer than six plants of Alpine Saxifrage grow in one gully at around 855m (Halliday, 1997). Downy Willow survives on rock ledges between 810m and 870m on Helvellyn's eastern face, but is close to extinction, with only female plants present and no males to pollinate them.

Shrubby Cinquefoil was formerly recorded at around 700m on Helvellyn but has not been seen here since before 1963. Alpine Cat's-tail is also thought to be extinct. Oblong Woodsia was almost certainly exterminated on Helvellyn until 60 cultivated specimens were planted there in 2011, in a reintroduction project that we will return to in the next chapter. In 2009, as part of the same project, Natural England restored plants to a site in the High Street range, west of the Haweswater Reservoir.

Plants of the eastern corries of Helvellyn (local rarities marked *)

Holly Fern*	Stone Bramble	Moss Campion
Globeflower	Alpine Cinquefoil*	Northern Bedstraw
Alpine Meadow-rue	Wood Cranesbill	Alpine Saw-wort
Starry Saxifrage	Hoary Whitlow-grass*	Wild Angelica
Yellow Mountain Saxifrage	Mountain Sorrel	Three-flowered Rush
Mossy Saxifrage	Spring Sandwort	Black Alpine-sedge
Roseroot	Alpine Mouse-ear*	Alpine Meadow-grass*
Mountain Avens*	Red Campion	Glaucous Meadow-grass*

OPPOSITE PAGE:
The Red Screes, below Helvellyn at the head of Glenridding Beck, are a rich botanical site.

Scafell and the Wasdale Screes

There is, however, one surviving native population of Oblong Woodsia. It has been known since 1847 at a site in the Scafell area, and this is now the largest surviving British population. It grows at around 600m on two rocky ribs in a north-facing gully of a crumbling crag, approachable only up a fearsome, highly mobile scree slope. The population here seems stable, with a minimum count of 68 plants in 2012. In 1999, Derek Ratcliffe noted one particularly fine tuft there with over 100 fronds.

The Scafell range has a broadly similar flora to Helvellyn. Fir and Alpine Clubmosses seem especially abundant, and Interrupted Clubmoss grows to the east of here at about 300m on Bowfell and Crickle Crags in the volcanic rock of upper Langdale, its only surviving site south of the Highlands. A small population of about 100 plants of Dwarf Cornel was discovered in a rather unpromising-looking gully towards the east of the Scafell range in 2005, proof yet again that there are still plants lurking undiscovered in the British mountains.

A view across Wast Water to the rather treacherous Wasdale Screes on its far shore. The screes, and the crags above, are a rich habitat for montane plants.

The richest places around Scafell are where sheer cliffs were formed along fault lines, as at Piers Gill and most famously at Wasdale Screes, another famous 'hotspot' for mountain flowers in the Lake District. I have botanised at Wasdale only once, about 30 years ago. It was mid-April, too early in the year for many walkers to have created a route across the boulder scree and stabilised the winter's erosion, so it was a hard slog which necessitated eyes on the path rather than the surrounding flora. I had already found plenty of the widespread Lakeland arctic-alpines as I walked down Piers Gill, including the leaves of Starry Saxifrage. Picking my way along the scree on the south side of Wast Water, I found masses of Parsley Fern, Alpine Lady's-mantle, Alpine Clubmoss, Mountain Sorrel and Yellow Mountain Saxifrage at only 70m or so above sea level. I somehow missed Purple Saxifrage, which might still have been in flower then, and Roseroot, although I did find the leaves of Mossy Saxifrage.

I had no time to climb up to the crumbling terrace of crags, 460m above the lake, so I failed to find Shrubby Cinquefoil, which grows here in two areas of damp, calcareous rock. In the Lake District, it now only survives here, on rock ledges and in crevices at Pillar in Ennerdale at altitudes to 650m, and at a third site at Fairfield, south of Helvellyn, not discovered until 1975. Other rarities on the crags and slopes above Wast Water include Northern Bedstraw, Mountain Everlasting, Bearberry, Mountain Melick and a single inaccessible patch of Mountain Avens. Twenty-two species of ferns are recorded in the screes, including Green Spleenwort and a few plants of Forked Spleenwort.

Beyond the sites already mentioned, the other montane localities in the Lake District tend to be more limited and more localised. Ill Bell near Kentmere, for example, is one of only two sites for Pyramidal Bugle south of the Highlands, but its population there had been reduced by 1997 to just two small plants. We have therefore met four new species in the Lake District that will become much commoner further north and which merit description here.

Alpine Lady's-mantle *Alchemilla alpina*

If I were to choose a plant as the best indicator of a rich montane flora, it would be this one. In the Highlands, encountering it on grassy banks from around 600m upwards – or even washed down to river gravels at much lower altitudes – is always an encouraging sign that much more interest is likely to lie at higher elevations. It helps that

its fingered, grey-edged leaves and clusters of yellow-green flowers are easily recognisable. It is found throughout the Scottish Highlands and the more mountainous islands, including Unst in Shetland. However, it fails as the perfect indicator for rich sites because it is absent from Wales, the Pennines and the Southern Uplands, making the Lake District its southernmost British site.

Alpine Lady's-mantle has grey-edged leaves, shaped like the spreading fingers of a hand, and delicate clusters of small yellow-green flowers.

It does not seem choosy with regard to soil type, provided the site is reasonably well drained, so it grows in mountain grassland, rocky streamsides, crevices, cliff ledges and screes, at altitudes up to 1,270m on Ben Macdui. It seems to prefer rather extreme conditions on wind-blasted grassy slopes, in hollows where the snow lies late, on relatively mobile screes like Wasdale, or where active solifluction maintains open ground. The species is also common in the Alps, down the mountain spine of Scandinavia, and in Iceland and southern Greenland.

Yellow Mountain Saxifrage grows in stony flushes or alongside mountain streams. I regularly admire its shining yellow flowers on dripping roadside cuttings near where I live in the Highlands.

Yellow Mountain Saxifrage *Saxifraga aizoides*

Although this species grows at a few sites in Upper Teesdale, as we saw in the last chapter, it is relatively uncommon there. The Lake District is the first site on our northward journey where it is anything like as frequent as it is in the Scottish hills, and Cumbria is the heart of its range outside of the Highlands. It is recorded here from 75m on the shores of Wast Water to 855m on Helvellyn (and elsewhere it reaches 1,175m in the Breadalbane hills of Perthshire), but it is absent from Wales, the Peak District and most of the Pennines. This always puzzles me, because it is such a widespread plant in the right mountain habitats in Scotland,

even growing at 50m on the sheep-grazed hillside beside my home in Wester Ross.

It is a widespread species throughout the Scottish Highlands and the Inner Hebrides, but is not found on the Outer Hebrides and only on Hoy in the Northern Isles. It is also absent from the Southern Uplands, but there is one odd record on a low cliff by a small waterfall, barely 2m above the shoreline at the Heads of Ayr in Ayrshire, and it may also lurk in some of the hills nearby. It is most common in stony flushes or by the side of mountain streams. It does not seem to be strongly lime-loving, although it is commonest amongst calcareous rocks and absent from sites that are very base-poor. Beyond Britain, it is a classic arctic-alpine, common throughout the Alps, Pyrenees and Carpathian mountains, and in arctic Scandinavia, Svalbard, Iceland, Greenland and Canada.

Bearberry *Arctostaphylos uva-ursi*

Although I scrambled down to see Bearberry beside Cauldron Snout in Upper Teesdale, it does not become a significant feature in the mountain flora until we reach the Lake District, and even here it is rare. It is a low-growing undershrub with leathery dark green leaves. Its clusters of nodding, globular, pinkish-white flowers ripen into rather dry red berries. These are eaten by Ptarmigan and Red Grouse, which spread its seed. In Britain its name is somewhat academic, but elsewhere the berries are an important summer food for Brown Bears and Polar Bears, showing yet again how observant Linnaeus was in many of the scientific names he coined. In fact, that scientific name is somewhat repetitive, meaning 'grape of the bear', first in Greek then in Latin.

The species has declined greatly since the 1930s in the south of its range in the Pennines, Lake District, Cheviots and Southern Uplands, as heavy sheep grazing and muirburning has turned montane dwarf shrub heath into acid grassland. In the Lakes, it is known from just four sites, three on steep cliffs and the fourth site, where it is most abundant, amongst open scree that has protected it from fires (Ratcliffe, 2002). Yet in the eastern Highlands it seems able to cope with fires, and I think of it most typically as a plant of open, upland moors in Strathspey

The long runners of Bearberry spread into open ground to form dense mats of leathery, glossy, dark green leaves, enlivened by its delicate pink flowers.

on the edge of the Cairngorms, where its long runners creep amongst the heather or cascade down the side of cut banks. It is widespread but scattered in the Highlands, mainly on well-drained upland heaths and on gravelly and stony banks, from close to sea level on the Moidart Peninsula in Argyll to 760m in Glen Clova in Angus, but never onto the highest tops. It also grows on the mountainous islands of the Hebrides, Orkney and Shetland. Elsewhere, it is found from Iceland south to the mountains of southern Europe and east to the Himalayas, and as a rare species in Greenland and northern North America.

The spear-shaped fruits (close up) of Few-flowered Sedge (main image) are all attached closely together at the same point of the stem, like the barbs on a particularly vicious arrowhead.

Few-flowered Sedge *Carex pauciflora*

It is always satisfying to come across this easily overlooked but distinctive little sedge, most typically as you slog across a moor en route to some choice botanical crag. With experience you get to know its typical ecological niches, around the edges of bog-moss hummocks or in slightly flushed gravelly areas, and its discovery is a welcome respite from the botanical monotony of the moor. It is easily confused with the much commoner Flea Sedge or the very rare Bristle Sedge that we will meet in Chapter 13, but, with practice, it can be identified by its 2–5 spreading, spear-shaped, pale yellow fruits with a beak-like tip.

The species is known from only two sites in Wales, where it is critically rare with perhaps just ten plants. It is a good deal commoner in western areas of the Lake District and the north Pennines, quite scattered in the Galloway hills, then widespread, but very localised, in the Highlands and Hebrides. It typically grows with Cross-leaved Heath and Bog Asphodel, from near sea level in the far north to around 820m. It is a circumpolar species, found south to the Alps. It is widespread in Scandinavia and northern North America, but absent from Iceland and Greenland, suggesting it cannot cope with the coldest temperatures.

The Cheviot Hills

The Cheviot Hills of Northumberland bear some resemblance to the northern Pennines, but are very different geologically. Botanically, they are more similar to the hills of the Southern Uplands, which are also managed predominantly as sheep-walk, as we will see in the next chapter.

The Cheviot Hills are the eroded remains of an ancient volcano, into which granite was intruded from below, producing soils that are generally acidic and infertile. A few isolated tors of granite or metamorphosed lava are somewhat reminiscent of Dartmoor.

A winter view of the Bizzle. One online dictionary states that 'bizzle' means to say goodbye with a peace V sign, which might relate to the V-shape of this deep valley in the Cheviots.

Allowing for altitude, the mean January temperature at the highest point, the Cheviot (815m), is around –1°C, rising to a July mean of about 11°C. The annual rainfall is relatively low because of the eastern location, at around 1,145mm (Lunn, 2004), and snow can lie for 100 days on the Cheviot.

This combination of soil and climate produces a limited but interesting flora. The predominant vegetation is acid grassland with Bilberry in places. Blanket bog takes over on upland plateaux. Cloudberry flowers abundantly on ungrazed bogs above about 500m, both here and in Kielder Forest. Lesser Twayblade hides below heather on some of the bogs. Alpine Clubmoss and Stiff Sedge occur on a few summits. There are several colonies of Dwarf Cornel, at one of its few English sites, growing amongst Bilberry on north-facing slopes where snow lies late, with Bog Bilberry in areas of deep peat. Mossy runnels and flushes are home to Starry Saxifrage, Alpine Willowherb and Chickweed Willowherb. Pale Forget-me-not turns up in a few springs and streamsides and Hairy Stonecrop is as common here as anywhere in Britain.

The only significant outcrops of basic rocks are at the Bizzle and Hen Hole, two wonderfully named sites which are respectively a corrie on the northern side and a glaciated valley on the western side of the Cheviot. These provide a home for Green Spleenwort, Mossy Saxifrage and Globeflower, with Roseroot and Alpine Saw-wort on a single calcareous outcrop. There are two localities for Jacob's-ladder, at its northernmost native site in Britain, in a tall-herb community amongst volcanic rocks in upper Coquetdale. Elsewhere in Northumberland, Spignel grows on a low hummock of Whin Sill near Thockrington. Six of these species find their first stronghold here on our northward journey and are considered below.

Cloudberry *Rubus chamaemorus*

Cloudberry is the most widespread of the 'peat alpines' that grow in mountain and northern peat bogs. It is also the most distinctive, with its crinkle-cut, rather shiny, green leaves and big white bramble flowers. As we have seen, it grows as far south as Lake Vyrnwy in the Berwyn Mountains, with a very small number of other sites in north Wales, coming down to an altitude of 90m on the Fenn's Moss National Nature Reserve, close to the Welsh–English border near Wrexham. It is also found from the Dales northwards through the Pennines and Lake District. However, peat bogs are relatively scattered in these areas and

so Cloudberry is only occasional. In contrast, Cloudberry is one of the true delights of the Cheviots and the Southern Uplands; in places here it spreads by far-creeping rhizomes to form flowery drifts across otherwise barren moors.

Further north it is widespread in the Highlands, most typically in bogs on high valley slopes above about 600m, although it is recorded as high as 1,160m on Beinn a' Bhuird in the Cairngorms. Oddly it is absent from the islands, except for Hoy in Orkney. Although its flowers are fairly common in all these areas, its orange, bramble-like fruits seem much more sporadic. That is partly because it is dioecious, and so whole patches may have only male flowers which cannot fruit. Fruit production also seems quite marginal. If the season is late, there may not be enough time to ripen fruit within the shortened growing season. On top of that, its fruits are sought out by Ring Ouzels and other thrushes, Snow Buntings, Capercaillie and Ptarmigan, small mammals and probably Mountain Hares. Scattered fruits are quickly consumed, so we may only find them when there is a glut. Cloudberry seems to fruit more abundantly in the Scandinavian mountains, where it also grows in damp woodlands. Cloudberries are enthusiastically harvested in late summer by Norwegians, Swedes and

Cloudberry (top) is a distinctive plant on banks of deep peat in the mountains, with glossy leaves and big white flowers that can be up to 3cm in diameter. Its fruits (above) are red at first, but turn orange when they are fully ripe.

Finns, in a way that gives them a far stronger connection to their local hills than most Britons feel. The berries are used to make jam and a delicious liqueur called *Lakka* (after the Finnish name for the species). It is an arctic-subarctic plant, widespread in northern Europe, Asia and North America, south to where I have seen it in a peat bog high in the Krkonoše Mountains of the Czech Republic.

Dwarf Cornel *Cornus suecica*

In the Cheviots and throughout its range, this relative of the shrubby Dogwood is a much less common plant than Cloudberry, with which it often grows. Its flower-like heads are actually clusters of 8–25 tiny, blackish-brown true flowers surrounded by four white bracts (floral leaves). It is evident that these are leaves if you find the developing flowers in late June, when the opening bracts are still green and leafy. The flowers ripen into a cluster of tasteless red fruits in August.

Its southernmost British site was at Turton Moor, north of Bolton in south Lancashire, where it died out by 1977 following a devastating fire. Today, its southernmost surviving sites are between 135m and 230m in the North York Moors, where it grows with Chickweed Wintergreen and Pale Forget-me-not in a valley called the Hole of Horcum, north of Pickering. Bearberry and Pale Forget-me-not are also recorded nearby. As well as its Lake District site and two Cheviot sites, it also occurs in the Selkirkshire hills, to which we will come shortly, then is scattered through the Highlands, usually intermixed with Heather or Bilberry, at altitudes up to 915m in east Perthshire. It also grows on Hoy in

Dwarf Cornel is often quite shy about flowering, but occasionally it produces stunning displays, like this group in a snow hollow in Coire an t-Sneachda in the Cairngorms.

Orkney, and on Yell and Foula in Shetland, coming down virtually to sea level in the former, but not on any of the Western Isles. It is another arctic-subarctic species, found quite widely in northern Europe, south to Poland, and in Greenland, northern Asia and North America.

Bog Bilberry *Vaccinium uliginosum*

Bog Bilberry often grows alongside Cloudberry and Dwarf Cornel in banks of deep peat in upland dwarf shrub communities and in blanket bogs. It has distinctive blue-green leaves and delicate, nodding, bell-shaped flowers, which are white but tinged with pink. Its dark blue berries have a distinctive blue waxy bloom.

It is a very localised and uncommon plant in the Cheviots, Lake District, northern Pennines and Southern Uplands, but much commoner in the Highlands, especially in the west. It is quite widespread in Orkney and Shetland, where it reaches down to 8m beside Scapa Flow, but absent from the Western Isles (although there are old records on Jura). It is recorded to 1,130m in the Cairngorms. In 1994, Bog Bilberry was discovered growing with Bog-myrtle on Haddon Hill in Somerset, nearly 400km from its nearest site in northern England. However, the presence nearby of Highbush Blueberry *V. corymbosum*, a native of North America, suggests that it might be an introduction at this Exmoor site. That is probably also true for a site in the high moors of Bleaklow in Derbyshire, where it was discovered in 2004. Outside Britain, it is found around arctic Europe and Asia, in the mountains of southern Europe, in Greenland and in North America south to New York State.

Bog Bilberry often grows alongside Bilberry, but in rather wetter ground. It can be distinguished from its relative by its blue-green leaves and smooth, rather than ridged, stems. Its flowers are also paler pink.

TOP: Alpine Willowherb spreads through mossy mountain springs and flushes by short creeping stems (stolons) that run above the ground.

ABOVE: The leaves of Chickweed Wintergreen are broader and more distinctly toothed than those of Alpine Willowherb. Its creeping runners spread below the surface, rather than above ground.

Alpine Willowherb
Epilobium anagallidifolium

This and the next species are two rather similar plants growing in very similar habitats, although this one is marginally the commoner of the duo in Scotland. Both have long-stalked, four-petalled pink flowers, and I always have to remind myself which species is which. The clue is in the scientific name: *anagallidifolium* means that it has leaves like *Anagallis* – Scarlet Pimpernel and its relatives. So this species has narrower, lance-shaped leaves than Chickweed Willowherb. It also has smaller flowers, 4–5mm across, compared to 8–9mm in the other species.

It is most typically a plant of mossy springs and flushes on mountain slopes. It also grows in the splash zone of fast-flowing mountain streams and sometimes on steep, wet slopes that perhaps are kept open by solifluction. It is found at just a few sites in the north Pennines, Cheviot Hills and Southern Uplands, and then is fairly widespread in the Scottish Highlands with a rather western tendency. It still grows in the Trotternish area of Skye and on the Isle of Eigg, but it seems to have been lost from several other Hebridean islands. I have seen it at an altitude barely above 150m in Inchnadamph in Sutherland, and it is recorded to 1,190m in the Breadalbane hills of Perthshire. It sometimes establishes briefly where it is washed down to the flood gravel of streams and rivers at lower altitudes. Its world range covers northern Europe, the mountains of central Europe, Iceland, Greenland, northern North America and Asia.

Chickweed Willowherb *Epilobium alsinifolium*

This broader-leaved and more lushly growing species is more widespread than Alpine Willowherb in the south of its range, in Snowdonia, the northern Pennines, Lake District, Northumberland hills and Southern Uplands. It is much more scattered and difficult to find in the Highlands, especially in the far north and west. It grows on the Isles of Mull, Skye and Eigg, where it is recorded down to 120m, although it grows at altitudes up to 1,140m on Bidean nam

Bian in Argyll. It has similar habitats to the previous species, although it seems to prefer slightly wetter conditions in mountain springs and streams, spreading there by long, creeping underground stolons. I have also occasionally seen it on damp rock ledges, usually amongst a carpet of mosses. It is found throughout the mountains of Europe and at lower altitudes in arctic Europe, including Iceland, but not on Svalbard, Greenland or beyond. Beware that other small willowherbs, including Marsh Willowherb and Short-fruited Willowherb, can also grow in damp situations to quite high altitudes, and the introduced New Zealand Willowherb is also widely established in montane habitats. First recorded in the wild in 1908, this garden escape has become remarkably widespread in damp stony ground, at altitudes up to 1,100m on Aonach Mor beside Ben Nevis, without conflicting with any of our native species.

Lesser Twayblade *Neottia cordata*

The Cheviots are probably as good a place as any to introduce this rather shy and reclusive little orchid, which rarely grows more than 10cm tall. Its two small opposite leaves ('twa blades') and inflorescence of tiny greenish-brown flowers are easy to overlook, even when it grows on open patches of bog-moss. More typically it hides under Heather, so an active search is needed to find it, but it is always satisfying to part a leggy clump of Heather and find this little jewel hidden beneath. It can survive here because a mycorrhizal fungus in its roots supplies most of the nourishment it needs for growth, reducing its reliance on sunlight for photosynthesis.

It is recorded from Exmoor to the very north of Shetland, but has been lost from many lowland sites, and is now mainly confined to the uplands of north Wales, northern England, the Southern Uplands and throughout the Highlands and Islands of Scotland. It turns up occasionally in Scottish pinewoods, but more typically on upland moors at altitudes to 1,065m on Stob Coire Easain, east of Ben Nevis. In Europe it is found from Iceland and northern Scandinavia to the Pyrenees, as well as in northern Asia and North America.

Lesser Twayblade: the two paired leaves and short greenish-brown flowerhead look distinctive on this patch of bog-moss, but the little orchid is a challenge to find when it hides beneath Heather.

The Southern Uplands

chapter ten

As a proud Scot, I am pleased that our journey now takes us across Hadrian's Wall and into Scotland. The Southern Uplands is an area of rounded hills and mainly fertile valleys, bounded to the north by the Southern Uplands Fault where the land falls away to the Central Lowlands of Scotland. I have also included the Ochil Hills in this chapter, despite the fact that they lie on the northern edge of the Lowlands, because their flora seems to fit more neatly with the Southern Uplands than with the Highlands to their north.

Because of their height and exposure, the hills of Dumfriesshire and Galloway are the richest botanically within the area, featuring a number of species that are not found south of the border. There is plenty of interest also in the hills of the Scottish Borders and a few tantalising remnants of past botanical glories in the Pentland Hills, south of Edinburgh. As in the Lake District, the most special plants in all these areas are localised and elusive. That is partly because most of these hills have been grazed heavily over the last 500 years and burnt regularly to produce a spring bite for sheep or young heather for grouse. In recent decades, water acidification as a result of long-distance airborne pollution has also impacted on the flora, although this damage is reducing with recent improvements in air quality.

OPPOSITE PAGE: Downy Willow is a rare inhabitant of a few Galloway hills. Its lance-shaped leaves are covered with silky hairs on their upper surface and are densely grey-silky on the underside. The catkins are also downy, with short white hairs.

Where continents collided

The southern edge of the Southern Uplands marks a point where, some 425 million years ago, two continents collided. Around 500 million years ago, there was an expanse of ocean here, more than 1,000km wide, called the Iapetus Ocean. This separated the continent of Laurentia, to the north, which contained most of Scotland, the north of Ireland, Greenland and North America, from Eastern Avalonia, the continental landmass to the south that included England, Wales and southern Ireland.

Over the next 80 million years the ocean narrowed, as the Earth's tectonic plates drifted together. This movement scraped sandy and muddy sediments from the ocean floor and piled these up against the continental margin of Laurentia. Eventually the two landmasses came together, and the sediments were compressed during the Ordovician and Silurian periods to form the greywacke (a kind of coarse sandstone) and shale rocks that form the foundations of the Southern Uplands. Glaciation eroded these soft rocks into the gentle, rolling moorlands that we see today. Harder intrusions of granite in the Galloway hills and metamorphic rocks in the Tweedsmuir hills were more resistant to erosion, producing a steeper, higher and more rugged terrain which rises to 843m on the Merrick, the highest hill in southern Scotland.

The Galloway hills

Starting in the south-west corner, Cairnsmore of Fleet is an area of granite rising to the ridge of Cairnsmore itself at 710m. The areas of Woolly Fringe-moss that once dominated its summit have mostly disappeared because of heavy grazing and pollution, to be replaced by short, impoverished, acid grassland. Dwarf Willow and Stiff Sedge survive here and there, especially where a rock gives shelter from the wind. Fir and Alpine Clubmosses are commoner on the tops, and Parsley Fern is a feature of screes and drystone walls. Limited outcrops of lime-rich rock support Green Spleenwort and Mossy Saxifrage.

A little further north, the hills of the Merrick and the Kells range are a bit higher and more exposed, again with extensive summit plateaux. Stiff Sedge and Dwarf Willow grow amongst Woolly Fringe-moss heath here. There are some base-rich patches on the expanse of north-facing crags, and these provide refuge for small populations of Starry Saxifrage, Mossy Saxifrage, Alpine Bistort, Roseroot and Alpine Saw-wort. Purple Saxifrage was found at one spot in 1973. Alpine Meadow-rue is quite common on high-level grasslands, and Few-flowered Sedge is more occasional on the lower slopes. Mountain Sorrel, first reported here by John Raven, was refound in 2007.

Cairnsmore of Fleet, on the edge of the Galloway Forest: the view from the east towards the 711m summit, showing the cliffs called the Clints of Spout and the pools of How Pot in the corrie below.

In 1961, Derek Ratcliffe discovered Downy Willow on the Black Gairy crags, north of the Merrick summit ridge. He described this as a 'pitiful fragment' of the mountain willow scrub that once clad slopes at the treeline. There are also some remnants of juniper scrub on these cliffs. More recently, surveys by Forestry Commission Scotland and the Action for Mountain Woodland project have found more than 250 large, vigorous plants of Downy Willow across the Merrick, with plants of both sexes flowering well and regenerating abundantly. A further small population was also found on Kirriereoch Hill nearby. This recovery probably began when grazing sheep were removed from these hills within the Galloway Forest Park.

Although these are the most dramatic hills of the area, Galloway is worth searching for other species from our montane list. Wood Cranesbill and Globeflower grow in a few meadows and roadsides. Bog Rosemary is locally frequent in the Silver Flowe and other peat-bog areas (locally called mosses). On the coast of Kirkcudbrightshire, Sticky Catchfly is found on crags at Port o' Warren Bay and on Lot's Wife in the Scottish Wildlife Trust's Southwick reserve near Auchencairn. At the latter site only three plants remained in 1995, but the population was reinforced with more than 120 seedlings cultivated from local seed.

A vigorous plant of Downy Willow growing on the Merrick, the highest mountain in the Southern Uplands.

Downy Willow *Salix lapponum*

The Merrick population of this handsome willow is now one of the healthiest in Britain. Its compact bushes are usually less than a metre high, and from a distance they look greyish, because their leaves are covered in silky grey hairs (see photo p.194). It is a scarce species of damp, relatively base-rich sites in mountains and a significant component of the montane scrub communities discussed in Chapter 4. It is found at scattered sites across the central and western Highlands, with a few sites further north including a puzzling single record on the north Mainland of Shetland (see Chapter 17). South of the Highlands, it is known only from here, White Coomb in Dumfriesshire and Helvellyn in the Lake District. At almost all these sites it is declining as grazing animals (especially sheep and Red Deer, but also Mountain Hares) force it back to cliffs and rocky sites beyond their reach. It is recorded from 210m in the Ochil Hills (where it is now extinct) to 1,125m on the crags of Lochnagar.

It is a dioecious species (with separate male and female plants), and males need to be within about 50m of females for successful pollination by insects or wind. Isolated plants on crags may therefore contribute nothing to breeding populations and be doomed to extinction. Furthermore, its seedlings require open areas of soil and freedom from competition to establish, and this restricts it to areas of naturally disturbed ground on mountain slopes. It is a Eurasian species, widely distributed from northern Scandinavia south to the Pyrenees and Balkans, but is replaced by a closely related species, *S. helvetica*, in the Alps.

The Moffat hills

The hills north-east of the Dumfriesshire town of Moffat have long been known as a prime locality for mountain flowers. The Silurian greywackes and shales here have been highly impacted by glaciation, producing a rugged terrain. Many of the cliffs are unstable, with occasional seams of calcareous rocks, and the climate is relatively severe with long periods of snow-lie, all of which ensure a rich flora.

The area is most famous for one montane plant. In 1848 – significantly, the year when the opening of the Caledonian railway improved access to Moffat – Oblong Woodsia was discovered in a rocky cleft near White Coomb in the Moffat hills. Other sites were soon discovered nearby, most famously in the natural hill amphitheatre of the Devil's Beeftub – the site that Sir Walter Scott described in *Redgauntlet*, with characteristic romantic hyperbole, as 'a damned deep, black, blackguard-looking abyss of a hole'. Tourists were soon flocking to Moffat to collect the fern for their herbaria or to take it into cultivation in what were called Wardian cases. By 1891, just a single plant was said to be left in hills that had once held hundreds. While this decline is all too easy to explain, the general rarity of Oblong Woodsia in Britain is puzzling, and it qualifies as another of our three-star enigmas.

The plant-rich crags above Loch Skeen in the Moffat hills.

To my eye, Oblong Woodsia is one of the most beautiful of our ferns. Its feathery fronds are densely covered in pale hairs, giving them a greyish-green colour when they first expand. It is also mysterious. I find it difficult to understand why it is quite so rare in its British localities when it is widespread elsewhere in its range, although its fate around Moffat clearly shows that human depredations are part of the explanation.

Oblong Woodsia is found widely in Scandinavia, northern Asia, northern North America and southern Greenland, on both calcareous and non-calcareous soils. It also has outlying sites in the Alps and other central European mountains. In its Scandinavian heartland, it is a plant of cliffs and stable screes. It even grows in open, sunny sites within the boreal forest, often very lushly – as the photo on the opposite page from Flåm in Norway shows.

Yet in Britain today fewer than 100 aboriginal clumps (it is not always clear what constitutes a discrete plant) survive at sites in Snowdonia, the Lake District, the Moffat hills, Angus and the Cairngorms (with lost sites also on Cadair Idris and in Upper Teesdale). Even these last survivors appear to be in decline. At Black Hope near Moffat, for example, 25 clumps were discovered at one site in the 1950s, but just three plants survived by 2012.

Why is this? There does not appear to be anything notably different about its surviving sites; other nearby areas seem equally suitable. We also know that spores from wild plants can be successfully germinated and grown in cultivation. Indeed we have two cherished plants in our garden grown from spores gathered by my fern enthusiast father-in-law. Studies have shown that genetic variation is limited in surviving plants, but not excessively so. However, ferns have a complex lifecycle. Perhaps the tiny, liverwort-like gametophyte stage of Oblong Woodsia's lifecycle requires particularly demanding conditions before these can develop into fern plants. As a result, it may only regenerate at infrequent intervals; for example, it has been suggested that young plants might establish only in particularly wet years.

Oblong Woodsia: one of the small plants that clings to survival in crevices below large bluffs of rock in Coire Fee in Angus (see Chapter 11).

All its British sites have relatively low summer maximum temperatures, but this probably oversimplifies the interaction of several factors. In particular, the species seems very susceptible to drought, which may limit its distribution. Page (1997) suggests that it survives best where surrounding rock provides shelter from severe winds and driving rain, and thinks that plants may need air movement around their fronds to keep their woolly surfaces dry. Whatever the influence of these factors, past over-collection has had the biggest impact on its range and may have resulted in isolated, inbred populations that reproduce poorly. Grazing sheep, goats and deer also eat plants and damage populations by dislodging unstable rocks.

There are probably more fronds in this magnificent clump of Oblong Woodsia in a birchwood clearing, barely 300m above the village of Flåm in southern Norway, than in the whole of Britain.

Fortunately, the amenability of the species to cultivation from spores has offered the opportunity to address its decline. In 1998, a Biodiversity Action Plan for the species proposed experimental action to reverse declines at three sites threatened with extinction and restoration to three 'lost' sites. The Royal Botanic Garden Edinburgh was appointed 'lead partner' for this work, which was undertaken initially by Stuart Lindsay and Phil Lusby and subsequently by Heather McHaffie, a real fern champion who was awarded an MBE in 2014 'for services to the conservation of plants in Scotland'.

Plants cultivated from locally collected spores have since been planted out, as we have seen, near three existing sites in the Moffat hills and two in the Lake District. As there were no surviving plants in Upper Teesdale, plants propagated from several British sites were used to maximise the genetic diversity of introductions to two former sites here (see photo on p.146). A small threatened population on unstable scree in Glen Feshie in the Cairngorms has been supplemented with plants cultivated from local stock. Plants have also been put on display in demonstration gardens at the Grey Mare's Tail and near the Cairngorm funicular railway so that visitors can see this delicate fern near key sites without risking damage to wild colonies.

Sixteen years is too short a time to say whether these reintroductions have succeeded. Reasonable numbers of plants are surviving, but, unless they produce sporelings to maintain populations, this work will merely have slowed the species' decline towards extinction. However, it has shown one important lesson. At several reintroduction sites, plants in screes survived much better than those on cliff ledges, which were previously thought to be its optimal habitat. Woodsia may have survived on these ledges because they were inaccessible to plant hunters and browsing animals, but it might grow much better amongst scree, if only we could protect it there.

Today, the best-known botanical site in the Moffat area is Grey Mare's Tail, a reserve of the National Trust for Scotland named after the imposing waterfall that plunges 60m into the valley below. Above the waterfall, a dramatic hanging valley reaches back to the glacial lake of Loch Skeen, surrounded by a horseshoe of crags around its north-west slopes (see photo on p.199). A short path from the car park leads to a waterfall viewpoint, where Roseroot, Alpine Scurvy-grass and Purple Saxifrage can be spotted. The saxifrage is surprisingly rare in the Moffat hills, given its abundance at the Falls of Clyde, just a little further north. A steeper path climbs up the slopes to the east of the waterfall. Straying off onto the mobile scree here is ill-advised, but plenty of plants can be seen from the path, including Parsley Fern, Alpine Lady's-mantle and Starry Saxifrage.

Other plants require much more searching on steep and inaccessible cliffs. Base-rich springs and flushes between White Coomb and Loch

The 60m waterfall at Grey Mare's Tail near Moffat is a popular tourist attraction. The path that climbs behind it towards Loch Skeen offers an interesting array of montane plants.

Skeen provide a habitat for several species we have seen further south: Alpine Willowherb, Chickweed Willowherb, Mossy Saxifrage, Alpine Scurvy-grass, Hairy Stonecrop and Pale Forget-me-not. Alpine Foxtail was discovered here in 1956. The cliffs have further plants whose names emphasise the severity of the local climate: Alpine Saw-wort, Alpine Cinquefoil, Alpine Meadow-rue, Alpine Mouse-ear and Black Alpine-sedge, plus the equally alpine Serrated Wintergreen, Whortle-leaved Willow and Sheathed Sedge.

A tiny population of Alpine Saxifrage is also recorded nearby on one small area of mossy rock. White Coomb holds a small population of Downy Willow, now protected from grazing within an exclosure. Sixty Oblong Woodsia ferns were planted into a scree area within this exclosure in 2008 as part of a conservation project begun elsewhere in the reserve in 1999. In 2012, 58 of these plants were surviving in the exclosure, but only 24 out of an original 124 transplants survived at the other, grazed site.

Cliff ledges beyond the reach of sheep support a fine tall-herb community with Roseroot, Globeflower, Wood Cranesbill and Mountain Sorrel. Small patches of Bearberry grow on acid rocks, Lesser Twayblade lurks beneath Heather, and Cloudberry is abundant in peaty areas, along with Dwarf Cornel. Holly Fern may still cling on in remote sites around here, where Victorian collectors did not reach it.

Other valleys east from Moffat are also worth exploring. Many of the species already mentioned can be found overlooking the Blackhope and Carrifran Burns, including small colonies of Alpine Foxtail, with Northern Bedstraw, Mountain Pansy and Alpine Cinquefoil. Parsley Fern and Mountain Male-fern are common on steep slopes, and Stiff Sedge, Fir Clubmoss and Dwarf Willow grow on the summit area of Carrifran Gans. Pyramidal Bugle is recorded nearby, but Spignel has apparently been reduced to a single plant in the Moffat hills and may not last there much longer.

The Carrifran area is especially exciting as the site of one of the largest 'rewilding' projects in Scotland. 660ha of land was purchased here by the Borders Forest Trust in 2000, and since then the area has been left ungrazed. Nearly 600,000 native trees from seed of local origin have been planted on the lower slopes of the valley. Most of the higher land is being left to regenerate naturally with the aim of establishing one of the most extensive areas of treeline woodland in Britain. Additional work is also underway to kick-start the restoration of montane scrub, concentrated in two of the corries where over

20,000 shrubs have been planted, including around a thousand plants of Downy Willow. With the removal of grazing, Roseroot and Mountain Sorrel have been able to spread from their refuges on the crags and Globeflower is forming mountain meadows alongside one burn at around 650m. Oblong Woodsia has also been restored, and at least 12 plants were recorded near the top of a waterfall here in 2010.

The Carrifran Wildwood Project is making tremendous progress restoring native woodland to overgrazed and treeless valleys in the Moffat hills. This photo from August 2015 shows encouraging growth of native trees planted just 11 years previously.

The Border hills

The hills of the Scottish Borders are generally lower, less exposed and heavily sheep-grazed. As a result they are less rich than the Moffat and Galloway hills, but they still have botanical gems in hidden corners. As in the Cheviots, Hairy Stonecrop appears wherever there are suitable springs and flushes, although it is declining throughout the area due to drainage and changing land management. Parsley Fern is relatively common in screes, sometimes also with Mountain Male-fern. Lesser Twayblade is easily overlooked in its typical habitats, and Northern Bedstraw is occasional through the area. The usual grouping of Stiff Sedge, Fir Clubmoss and Dwarf Willow are found on exposed tops.

Mountain Pansy is sporadic, but surprisingly common, throughout the area, mostly in the yellow-flowered form with occasional records of purple flowers. In the past, Melancholy Thistle was a frequent feature of wet meadows, sometimes growing with Globeflower, but both have greatly declined during my lifetime, again mainly because of agricultural 'improvement' and drainage. Cloudberry occurs in many upland areas of deep peat but also seems to be in decline.

In Roxburghshire, the hills around Newcastleton are probably the richest, with Stone Bramble, Green Spleenwort, Mossy Saxifrage and some Mountain Everlasting. There is one site for Bog Bilberry at 120–180m on the Newcastleton Fells near the Cumbrian border. Bog Rosemary and Alpine Rush are recorded in some of the local mosses.

Perhaps the most interesting sites are isolated crags of Carboniferous basalt rock, one of which near Minto is home to Sticky Catchfly and

Forked Spleenwort, two species to which we will return shortly. In Selkirkshire, the Ettrick Valley is amongst the richest sites. Calcareous flushes here support Northern Bedstraw, Alpine Bistort, Alpine Saw-wort, Alpine Meadow-rue, Starry Saxifrage and Sheathed Sedge, although these may decline as the surrounding forest matures.

Berwickshire hosts a few colonies of Chickweed Wintergreen, and Parsley Fern is found on scree at Black Hill beside Earlston (Braithwaite, 2013). Wood Bitter-vetch grows on the banks of one of the burns that feed the Dye Water, west of Longformacus. Roseroot appears on sea-cliffs in the St Abb's Head National Nature Reserve, where Spring Sandwort survives on steep cliffy slopes inland.

In Peeblesshire, montane species are mainly found only in small quantity in the Tweedsmuir hills, including Alpine Willowherb, Chickweed Willowherb, Alpine Meadow-rue, Alpine Bistort, Dwarf Cornel and Alpine Saw-wort (McCosh, 2012). Starry Saxifrage and Mossy Saxifrage are rather more common. Alpine Foxtail is rare in flushes above about 600m, and Sheathed Sedge is found at a couple of sites. Pale Forget-me-not grows in a few wet runnels and flushes, close to its northernmost British limit. Mountain Sorrel is locally frequent on rocks near the Talla Reservoir. Wood Bitter-vetch again occurs as a rare species of rocks and banks, with just three known surviving stations.

The Lammermuir Hills, between Berwickshire and East Lothian, reach their highest summit at Meikle Says Law (535m). Dominated by Heather and Bell Heather, they are not high enough for a diverse montane flora and several species have disappeared, probably as a result of changing climate and agricultural practices. Cloudberry survives with Crowberry and Cowberry in just three main colonies. Hairy Stonecrop is fairly frequent although declining, and Alpine Clubmoss grows on a few hillsides. I probably know the Moorfoot Hills in Midlothian best of these hills, as a favourite walk when I lived in Edinburgh. Cloudberry is the most characteristic species here, and Hairy Stonecrop occurs much more rarely. Wood Cranesbill and Stone Bramble grow in the base-rich soil of deep valleys, locally known as 'cleughs'.

Three species from the Moffat and Border hills merit further attention before we move onwards towards Edinburgh.

Chickweed Wintergreen *Trientalis europaeus*

The joke is that Chickweed Wintergreen is so named because it is neither a Chickweed nor a Wintergreen, but a member of the primrose

family. It usually has a single, delicate flower with 6–7 white petals, often tinged with pink. Its stems reach a height of 25cm with a distinctive ruff of 5–6 leaves two-thirds of the way up. It is a submontane species of heaths, moorland, and birch, oak and pine woods, restricted to the Pennines, North York Moors and Northumberland hills in England and a few sites in the Southern Uplands. In the Scottish Highlands, it shows a distinct eastern tendency and is probably most abundant around Speyside. It is rare in Orkney, with a few sites in Shetland and on Arran, Mull and South Uist in the Western Isles.

Chickweed Wintergreen has a distinctive whorl of 5–6 leaves part-way up its stem. The stem is topped by a solitary pinkish-white flower that seems to quiver in the slightest breeze.

I think of it as a plant of middle hill slopes, although it is recorded to 1,100m on Cairn Gorm and down almost to sea level in Aberdeenshire. It is also found throughout northern Europe, south to Corsica, in northern Asia, Greenland and in western North America south to California.

Where it is allowed to flourish beyond the reach of grazing animals, Wood Bitter-vetch can be a handsome plant, with ladder-like lobed leaves and showy clusters of white flowers etched with purple veins.

Wood Bitter-vetch *Vicia orobus*

I cannot say that I have ever come across this upright-growing vetch whilst botanising in the mountains, although I have found it in a hill valley in mid Wales. It does hang on at a few sites in the Southern Uplands, despite recent declines there. It typically grows on grassy banks where boulders or thorny bushes protect it from grazing animals, at altitudes up to 560m in the Moffat hills and down to sea level near Lochinver in Sutherland. It is most widespread in hill pastures in Wales, with a few sites in the north Pennines. North of the sites in this chapter, it is mostly confined to the far north-west of Scotland and the Inner Hebrides, including Mull, Rum and Skye. Britain holds a substantial proportion of the population of this western European species, which is found from Norway south to Spain.

Sheathed Sedge *Carex vaginata*

The slopes of Black Hope in the Moffat hills were long thought to be the southernmost site in Britain for this shy-flowering sedge, which is recognised by the loose sheath that its leaves form around its stem. Then in 1976 Rod Corner, the botanical recorder for Selkirkshire and Roxburghshire, discovered it at two sites further south in the upper Ettrick Valley of Selkirkshire. However, it took the removal of sheep after the foot-and-mouth epidemic of 2001 to reveal that its range continued considerably further south. In June 2002, Rod found a large colony on Dufton Fell, 3km south of the old Moor House field station in the northern Pennines, as a species new to England. Soon after, two other colonies were found nearby, including one on Green Fell.

Sheathed Sedge has a single spike of male flowers at the tip of its stem, and one or two clusters of female flowers below. The base of its leaves form an inflated sheath around the stem.

Once local botanists had been alerted to its occurrence and began to recognise the intermittently flushed sloping grassland it seems to prefer, many more colonies were found at altitudes between 670m and 800m, over a stretch of some 41km from Yad Moss in the watershed of the River South Tyne in Cumberland to Great Shunner Fell in north-west Yorkshire (Roberts, 2014). DNA studies have confirmed that these are long-standing populations that were probably repressed previously by grazing. In 2009, the species was also discovered in a rather different habitat in dry turf over and between limestone pavements at around 610m on Long Fell, above Brough in Westmorland. It seems possible therefore that more sites may still be found for this species.

However, the heart of its range is in the central Highlands, particularly the Breadalbane and Cairngorm mountains. As in the English sites, it usually grows here above 700m to a highest recorded site of 1,150m on Cairn Toul, but it also comes down to 370m near Blair Atholl in Perthshire. It is typically found in mountain grassland that is no more than slightly acid or slightly basic, in wet flushes and streamsides, and on rock ledges. Elsewhere it is found from northern Europe south to the Alps and Pyrenees, then east to Japan.

Edinburgh and the Pentlands

I walked regularly in the Pentland Hills when I lived in Edinburgh in the seventies and eighties, though access was severely restricted in

The Pentland Hills are covered mostly in rather heavily grazed acid grassland, but they do still have some impressively wild areas for a site so close to a capital city. This view is looking towards the hills of East and West Kip.

those days because of tensions between local farmers and the multitude of walkers. Establishment of a Regional Park in 1984 helped reduce these tensions and led to improved access. This was then reinforced by the right to responsible access under the Scottish Land Reform Act of 2003. However, the flora remains restricted because of high grazing pressure from sheep.

When I knew the area best, dwarf shrub heath with Cowberry and Crowberry was very limited and I was only aware of a few patches of Cloudberry. There were three known sites for Mossy Saxifrage, and Globeflower grew at one place amongst willow scrub. Some scree slopes on Mendick Hill and Dunsyre Hill had Parsley Fern, and Fir Clubmoss occurred on exposed sandstone near the Crosswood Burn. A cleugh in the upper reaches of the Medwin Burn was a remaining site for Hairy Stonecrop and Marsh Saxifrage. I believe the saxifrage at least is still there, but I cannot vouch for the other species I have listed, which were always under extreme pressure. Bird's-eye Primrose was known from 1715 in a small marshy area between Dolphinton and West Linton, but was last seen there in 1920.

The other unlikely site for montane species with which I was much engaged was Holyrood Park in the middle of Edinburgh (my late wife Sonia was involved in the management of the park for Historic Scotland, and I helped design and run a visitor centre there for the

Scottish Wildlife Trust). In 1668, Thomas Willisel, a plant collector for the Royal Society (of London), discovered Sticky Catchfly as a species new to Britain on a bluff of columnar basalt rock within the park. By 1993 it had been reduced to just four plants, as a result of sheep grazing, accidental fires and unscrupulous collection. It had disappeared by then from its other Edinburgh sites, on the rock below Edinburgh Castle because of rock stabilisation work and from Blackford Hill because of quarrying and over-collection.

In 1993, the Royal Botanic Garden Edinburgh began work to protect the species as part of the Scottish Rare Plants Project. Seeds were collected from surviving plants and used to propagate a supply of plants to reinforce the population. In 1994 and 1996, these were transplanted onto rock ledges at low risk from fires. Seedlings from these have spread, although they suffer from rabbit grazing. Sticky Catchfly was also reintroduced to the Castle Rock and Blackford Hill, but it has struggled there because of its demanding requirements and grazing pressure from rabbits.

A small population of another basalt-loving species, Forked Spleenwort, grows at the foot of the same crag in Holyrood Park. Spring Sandwort is also found on the South Rocks of the park, at an altitude of barely 100m.

Sticky Catchfly *Silene viscaria*

Sticky Catchfly is at best only marginally submontane, with sites down to virtually sea level in Kirkcudbrightshire, as we saw earlier in this chapter. However, most of its sites are above 300m, and it is found at

Sticky Catchfly in June 1983 in Holyrood Park, within sight of the ridge of Salisbury Crags. Sadly, this fine, flowery specimen was destroyed in a wild fire less than two months later.

475m on Beinn a' Chuallaich in Perthshire. Its flowers remind me of Red Campion, but they grow in a much tighter inflorescence and its stems are made characteristically sticky by glands at the joints where its narrow leaves are attached. This stickiness stops ground-living insects from crawling up the stem to steal pollen from the flowers.

It is a plant of hard, usually igneous, rocks that are somewhere between mildly acidic and moderately basic, usually with a southerly aspect (Wilson *et al.*, 1995b). Beyond the sites I mentioned earlier in this chapter and in Chapter 6, it is commonest in the Ochil Hills, with a scattering of other sites in Perthshire. Its apparent requirement for sunshine means it is highly susceptible to shading. At one site in Glen Farg in Perthshire it had ceased flowering until trees were removed in 1994 to open up its habitat, allowing 260 plants to flower there by 2012. When I worked for Plantlife Scotland, I was pleased in 1996 to persuade the Forestry Commission to fell large trees that were shading another crag where it grows, above Pitlochry in Perthshire.

I have always been puzzled about the scarcity of this species, even more so when I spotted it flowering abundantly on a motorway cutting on the outskirts of Stockholm, but the explanation lies in its biology. It does not seem to spread vegetatively, but instead relies on copious seed production to colonise newly opened sites on eroding rock faces. Any grazing of its flowerheads stops it seeding and blocks its spread. In our garden, I have found that Sticky Catchfly flowers well but its foliage soon gets smothered by invading grasses. It clearly requires external events, such as landslips, to open up niches in which it can grow – something that may not always appeal to land managers, who prefer stability to precariousness! Outside Britain, it is found from northern Scandinavia south to the Alps and east to Russia, mostly in dry meadows, stony grassland and open woodland, rather than montane sites.

Forked Spleenwort *Asplenium septentrionale*

Recognisable by its distinctively forked fronds, this fern is recorded to 715m on Llyn y Cwm and, exceptionally, to 1,060m on Carnedd Llewelyn in the Welsh mountains, although other sites are much less montane. The *New Atlas* (Preston *et al.*, 2002) reports it in just 28 grid squares across Britain, from its single site on the eastern edge of Dartmoor (see Chapter 5) to small populations on epidiorite crags in Assynt in north-west Sutherland. It is typically a plant of exposed, sunny, usually acidic rock faces, but it also invades the spoil heaps of metalliferous mines and occasionally even old mortared walls.

Forked Spleenwort is a neat little clump-forming fern, recognisable by its distinctively forked fronds. It grows on sunny rock faces, as here on the South Rocks of Holyrood Park in Edinburgh.

The species is more at home in the continental climates of Europe, where it is widespread through the mountains of Scandinavia and central and southern Europe. It appears to be at the limits of its oceanic tolerance in Britain. That may explain its disappearance from at least half its former British sites. Page (1997) notes that it is particularly susceptible to slug attacks and suggests that is relative success in metalliferous soils may be because these exclude slugs. Scrub encroachment and afforestation also cause losses by shading its preferred sunny, south-facing sites.

The Ochil Hills

The Ochils are a 45km stretch of andesite and basalt lava from Devonian volcanoes, extending from near Stirling east to the Tay Estuary. They have a number of peaks exceeding 500m and a rugged southern face. Their name comes from the Celtic word *uchel* for high ground. They are the main British stronghold for Sticky Catchfly, with a distribution stretching over about 8km from Alva to the hills above Blairlogie. There are several thousand plants in total in this stretch, although mostly in concealed and inaccessible locations because of past depredation by plant collectors. The catchfly also survives precariously on Abbey Craig, beneath the Wallace Monument, a little west of the Ochils.

Hairy Stonecrop is one of the commoner plants of the Ochils, in mossy flushes on the higher slopes, and Mossy Saxifrage is also surprisingly common. Cloudberry appears to be in decline; in 1976 an

These botanists are exploring an open flushed area below Ben Buck in the Ochil Hills. Plants they found here included Hairy Stonecrop and Alpine Foxtail.

'exceptionally large colony of nearly 2 square kilometres' was recorded in an area of blanket bog above 500m in the west of the range, but the local botanical recorder Liz Lavery tells me that only a single small patch has been recorded there since 2000. Mountain Pansy and Alpine Bistort occur occasionally. Least Willow is found on the highest summit of Ben Cleuch (721m), with some Stiff Sedge and Cowberry, and Wood Bitter-vetch is recorded on Craig Leith above Alva. In 1992, Rod Corner discovered two flush communities with Alpine Foxtail on the north-west flank of Ben Buck, north of Ben Cleuch, growing with Hairy Stonecrop, Alpine Willowherb, Chickweed Willowherb, Mossy Saxifrage and Starry Saxifrage. This might also have been the lost site for Marsh Saxifrage, recorded in the mid-19th century in the Ochils.

At the eastern end of the Ochils, Spignel is a conspicuous feature of old sheep pasture and is responding notably well to the removal of grazing from some sites. One of the most remarkable sites, discovered by Liz Lavery, is in Geordie's Wood. Since the wood was purchased in 2000 by the Woodland Trust and fenced to encourage regeneration, at least 50,000 Spignel plants have appeared on two hillocks at the entrance to the site, and Liz has found other fine colonies nearby, although the extraordinary lushness at these sites may just be a short-lived phase following the removal of grazing.

Spignel *Meum athamanticum*

I have always suspected that Spignel is much repressed by grazing animals, and the amazing population behind the fence at Geordie's Wood in Glen Devon is eloquent proof of this. On the annual mountain flowers course I used to run in Perthshire, we always stopped to admire several magnificent plants protected by a fence from grazing animals on a bank beside the A93 road, south of Spittal of Glenshee. In contrast, I have only ever found small, straggly shoots of Spignel (also known as Baldmoney or Meu) in grazed meadows – for example, in Keltneyburn in Perthshire or on the lower slopes of Ben Lawers.

It is a plant of dry, unimproved pastures, hay meadows and roadside banks, and has declined greatly because of intensive grassland management. It is sometimes eradicated deliberately to prevent its aniseed-like taste from tainting the milk of grazing cows. It may be native at Cadair Idris in Wales, has a few sites in north-west Yorkshire and the Lake District, a single site in Northumberland, then is scattered through the Southern Uplands and southern Highlands as far north as Inverness-shire and the Cairngorms National Park (a single clump recorded on Dunnet Head in Caithness is probably not native). It is usually found below 300m, although it reaches 610m on Fealar in east Perthshire. It is found from southern Norway to the north of Spain, then east to the Balkans, so its Inverness-shire sites probably represent the northernmost point of its world range.

A spectacular display of Spignel has developed at Geordie's Wood in the Ochil Hills since 2000, when an area was fenced off to encourage tree regeneration. Without grazing, the Spignel has flourished.

The Glens of Angus and Aberdeenshire

chapter eleven

With this chapter, we reach the vast area of rugged and mountainous land universally known as the Scottish Highlands, world-famous as a magnet for tourists. It is the largest area of high land in Britain. The exact boundaries of the Highlands are poorly defined, especially to the east, but they lie north of the Highland Boundary Fault – the major geological fault line that runs from the Isle of Arran, through Loch Lomond, and past the towns of Aberfoyle and Crieff to just north of Stonehaven on the Aberdeenshire coast. All of the 282 Scottish hills above 3,000 feet (914m) that hillwalkers and climbers classify as Munros lie within the Highlands and Islands.

As you would expect, this area is also the richest in Britain for its mountain flora – a wonderful treasury of plants to which I will need to dedicate not just this but also the next four chapters. Indeed, there is so much diversity here that in this one somewhat extravagant chapter I am able to introduce no fewer than 34 enticing new species on our northward journey.

Building the Highlands

The mountains of the Highlands were formed during, or shortly after, the mountain-building event called the Caledonian Orogeny (McKirdy *et al.*, 2007). This began around 475 million years ago when an arc of islands north of the ancient continent of Avalonia began to collide with the landmass of Laurentia on which sat northern Scotland (see Chapter 10). The collision caused massive folding and buckling of rocks and threw up the Caledonian mountain chain. This chain

OPPOSITE PAGE: The flowers of Alpine Sowthistle, a tall and showy species, which enigmatically survives on only a few inaccessible rock ledges in the glens of Angus and Aberdeenshire.

'Dark Lochnagar', as Lord Byron immortalised it, is a massif of granite, rising to 1,155m, in the royal estate of Balmoral. Its north face forms a fine corrie around the loch of the same name, and is home to several rare montane species.

originally stretched from the Appalachians through Scotland to Norway, although it was later split by the rise of the North Atlantic.

The Highlands can be divided into three broad zones. The southern and western Highlands (Chapters 11, 12, 13 and 15) are formed mainly of Moine Schists, with rugged topography eroded by ice action into angular peaks and ridges. This zone also includes the mountainous islands of Mull, Rum and Skye on the western seaboard. The north-east Highlands are dominated by the mountain massifs of the Cairngorms and Monadhliath Hills (Chapter 14) and are composed mainly of red granites, surrounded by predominantly Dalradian crystalline rocks. The north-west Highlands (Chapter 16) lie north of the Great Glen – the broad fault-line that runs from the Moray Firth via Loch Ness to Fort William and Loch Linnhe. The rugged peaks here are mainly of Torridonian sandstone, sometimes capped with Cambrian quartzite, rising from an undulating base of Lewisian Gneiss. I will return to the botanical significance of these rock types as we visit each area. The overall area of high land here is so large that it creates its own climate, more continental than anywhere else in Britain, and this also influences the lower land of the glens – the valleys that lie between the mountains.

Climate and vegetation

Braemar in the west of Aberdeenshire provides a good example of this climatic influence. Surrounded by mountains, it lies only 339m above sea level yet it has one of the most severe climates in the UK with an annual average temperature of just 6.8°C. The lowest ever UK temperature of –27.2°C was recorded here in January 1982 (a record shared with Altnaharra in Sutherland), and air frost is recorded in every month of the year except July.

This climate is severe enough to restrict the growth of many lowland species, and allows montane species to flourish at unusually low altitudes. In Morrone Birkwood, a woodland of Downy Birch on the outskirts of Braemar, Globeflower, Wood Cranesbill, Intermediate Wintergreen, Northern Bedstraw, Alpine Bistort, Mountain Pansy and Melancholy Thistle flourish amongst the trees. Scottish Asphodel, Yellow Mountain Saxifrage, Three-flowered Rush and Alpine Rush grow in open, flushed areas on the edge of the wood – all at an altitude below 450m. Serrated Wintergreen and Holly Fern cling to the crags above, along with Twinflower, a delicate, scrambling woodland species with paired pink, nodding flowers.

Because of this climatic impact, the Highlands are the area of Britain with the largest range of montane species. They are also distinctive culturally and economically, corresponding broadly with the *Ghàidhealtachd*, the land of the Gaels. Land has always been managed differently in the Highlands than in the Lowlands and Southern Uplands, and the practices of land management also impact on the flora.

The Cairnwell

On the boundary where Aberdeenshire meets Perthshire, the Cairnwell towers to 933m above the Glenshee ski area. This is one of the easiest places in Britain to see a wide range of our mountain flora. The A93 road from Blairgowrie to Braemar rises to 670m, so montane species are immediately accessible by the roadside. Deep peat overlies the hillside on both sides of the road. Cloudberry is as abundant here as anywhere in Scotland. Dwarf Cornel and Chickweed Wintergreen are less common but widespread. They grow with Bilberry, Bog Bilberry, Crowberry and Heather, beneath which hide occasional plants of Lesser Twayblade.

The most interesting area lies to the west of the ski-area car park, where two wicker fences funnel down the hillside on a steep ski slope called the Tiger Run. Gravelly flushes here are mildly calcareous, enriched by a band of limestone higher on the hill, but their flora also reflects the influence that the ski development has on snow lie. The fences are designed to capture and retain snow, so that skiing can continue as long as possible through the season. Compacted by pisting machines and skiers, the accumulated snow between the fences is slow to melt. This restricts the growing season even more than the local climate would dictate, encouraging the montane specialists. The resulting erosion also helps maintain an open habitat. Management for skiing therefore benefits biodiversity on the ski runs, but this is more than counterbalanced by erosion and track building, which has damaged large areas of natural habitat on the hillside.

The gravelly flushes low on the Tiger Run are sites for Starry Saxifrage, Yellow Mountain Saxifrage, Alpine Meadow-rue, Alpine Lady's-mantle, occasional clusters of Scottish Asphodel and Three-flowered Rush and a few plants of Least Clubmoss. Another fairly common plant of the flushes is the alpine subspecies *humifusa* of Thyme-leaved Speedwell. In Scotland, this looks very different from the lowland subspecies *serpyllifolia*, with weak, trailing stems that root along their length. It also has fewer flowers with larger and bluer petals. The upland subspecies is a regular inhabitant of open gravel, wet flushes and damp rock ledges in the Scottish mountains, and might merit inclusion in our montane list were it not for the fact that plants in Wales, the Pennines and Lake District are much less distinctive and often intermediate with lowland forms.

The mountain subspecies of Thyme-leaved Speedwell, here growing with Alpine Willowherb on Glas Maol, looks very different from the common subspecies of the lowlands.

A little higher on the hill, Frog Orchid is surprisingly common in some years amongst wet grassland. Banks beside springs are home to both Alpine and Chickweed Willowherbs. The heathery slopes to the north of the chairlift support a few plants of Interrupted Clubmoss spreading across peat beneath the heather. Climbing up the steep slope of the Tiger Run, mountain zonation is well displayed, as the vegetation changes with altitude. First the Bilberry dies out, then the Heather becomes shorter and eventually disappears. Mountain Crowberry becomes dominant in the vegetation, and patches of Trailing Azalea start to appear. On the windswept summit ridge, Trailing Azalea is one of the commoner plants, along with Dwarf Willow, Stiff Sedge, Three-leaved Rush and lots of the characteristic mountaintop moss, Woolly Fringe-moss. There are a few plants of Alpine Clubmoss, and Dwarf Cudweed and Spiked Wood-rush grow on eroded banks nearby.

ABOVE: Trailing Azalea growing on the windswept ridge that runs northwards from the 933m summit of the Cairnwell.

Limestone hotspots

That species list is impressive enough, but the plateau north of the Cairnwell summit is further enhanced by three small outcrops of limestone. These are fairly conspicuous, but very fragile. I urge readers who visit them to avoid walking on open areas of limestone gravel, but to remain on the closed vegetation around the outcrops, from which all the species can be seen.

The first patch that you come across is home to a distinctive group of lime-loving species, including Mountain Avens, the shining yellow flowers of Alpine Cinquefoil, small patches of Purple Saxifrage, Alpine Meadow-rue and spikes of Alpine Bistort. Tiny little plants of Hair Sedge grow here, along with Scottish Asphodel. It took me a long time to realise that the large, purple-green, toothed leaves on the limestone belong to Alpine Saw-wort. Most special of all, the open limestone slope is one of the few sites I know for Mountain Sandwort. Alpine Speedwell grows in the grass below the limestone and in a little gully just south of it.

Above the open limestone here, a conspicuous patch of yellower grassland indicates limestone just beneath the surface. This is often scattered with Mountain Pansies, more Alpine Bistort, and a few plants of Rock Sedge. The feathery, yellow-green moss that helps colour the turf here is Wrinkle-leaved

BELOW: The limestone outcrops below the Cairnwell are reminiscent of the 'sugar limestones' of Upper Teesdale. They cover less than a quarter of a hectare in total, but support a rich flora including little plants of Mountain Sandwort.

Feather-moss *Rhytidium rugosum*, an uncommon species of mountain limestones which also occurs close to sea level in the Breckland of East Anglia. Not far below this limestone outcrop, a stream wells up from a spring, and this supports Mossy Saxifrage, Alpine Scurvy-grass and the small-flowered mountain form of Marsh Marigold.

The second limestone outcrop is easily missed, but has a few of the same species, including Alpine Speedwell. The third outcrop is an even better place to see Mountain Sandwort, alongside the white flowers and twisted pods of Hoary Whitlow-grass. In some years, the limestone is surrounded by Moonwort fern in remarkable abundance. Mountain Pansy and Northern Bedstraw grow in the grassland above. Alpine Milk-vetch, which we will meet next chapter, is a rare occurrence on a slope below the limestone.

The upland birchwood at Morrone and the mountain slopes of the Cairnwell are therefore home to no fewer than eleven species of montane plants that we have not featured previously.

Interrupted Clubmoss *Lycopodium annotinum*

The Cairngorms, east as far as the Cairnwell, are the real heartland of this fern relative, whose sprawling stems spread like green tendrils amongst the surrounding vegetation. The stems are densely covered in bristly leaves. At the end of each growing season, the plant produces a ring of shorter leaves, pressed tightly against the stem, and these form the 'interruptions' after which the plant is named. Apart from a few sites at the head of Langdale in the Lake District, it is confined these days to the Scottish Highlands, northwards to Ward Hill on Hoy in Orkney. It is recorded from altitudes of 45m at a former site at Laggan on the Isle of Mull to 1,145m on Cairn Gorm. It is mainly found on hillsides above about 450m in moist, peaty hollows, perhaps where snow lies late. Surprisingly, it is also recorded at an altitude of 240m on a coal-mine spoil heap (called a bing in Scotland) north of Shotts in Lanarkshire, and it might survive at other sites of industrial dereliction in central Scotland. It is also found throughout northern Europe, south to the Apennines and east to the Caucasus, and scattered through the mountain forests of North America.

Interrupted Clubmoss: 'pinch points' of shorter leaves on the stem, produced at the end of each growing season, explain its common name.

Interrupted Clubmoss is a very long-lived species. Its creeping branches slowly spread under the Heather, rooting at intervals, until, after a century or more, it can form patches as large as $20m^2$ (Page, 1997). Sometimes its horizontal branches vanish into the leaf litter to reappear elsewhere on the hillside, but these remain part of the same ancient, spreading plant. It somewhat resembles the much commoner but more lowland Stag's-horn Clubmoss, but it produces only solitary cones at the tip of each shoot, rather than the paired, stalked cones after which Stag's-horn Clubmoss is named.

Mountain Sandwort *Minuartia rubella*

The Cairnwell limestone and one crag on Ben Lawers are the only places where I have seen this rather undistinguished, cushion-forming plant (see photo on p.219), although admittedly it is very easy to dismiss it as a moss when its tiny white flowers (just 5–9mm across) are not in evidence. It was also discovered in the Ben Alder range in 1990, and there is a very small colony on Ben Hope in Sutherland, but that is its entire known British range. It formerly grew on the serpentine of Unst in Shetland, but was over-collected by botanists there and has not been seen since the 1950s. At both its Cairnwell and Lawers sites it is highly sensitive to trampling, although a certain amount of erosion may help maintain open habitat for it.

Seeds which might belong to this species have been found in glacial deposits from the Weichselian period, suggesting that it was more widespread at the end of the Ice Age and then retreated to a few mountain sites with suitable fine, base-rich gravel on which it could survive. That corresponds with its present-day circumpolar distribution in arctic Russia, Asia and North America, northern Scandinavia, Iceland and Greenland. The Lawers plants are probably therefore the southernmost in the world.

Trailing Azalea *Kalmia procumbens*

It is always nice to come across patches of this dwarf, trailing heath when slogging up a mountain like the Cairnwell, because it shows that an exposed summit or ridge – its typical habitat – cannot be far above. It is easiest to recognise between May and July when it flowers, although the duration of flowering at any one site is very short and the small flowers are nothing like as showy as those of garden azaleas in the same family. Its dense clusters of oval, evergreen leaves are also distinctive on it mountaintop habitats, which are otherwise largely bare of vegetation apart from patches of its typical associates – Stiff Sedge, Three-leaved Rush, Dwarf Cudweed and Dwarf Willow.

It only grows on dry, stony, windswept mountain summits, shoulders and plateaux (see photo on p.219), usually between about 500m and 900m. Its leathery leaves help it survive winter exposure in these habitats, where the wind soon strips off any protective blanket of snow. It is recorded at altitudes up to 1,100m on Ben Macdui in the eastern Cairngorms, justifying its alternative name of Mountain Azalea. In Britain, it is found only in the Highlands and Islands, with a tendency towards the windier west, including Hoy in Orkney and Ronas Hill in Shetland. In the more arctic environment of the latter, it descends to 240m. There are also old records from the Cuillin hills of Skye. It is found throughout arctic Europe and Asia, the Alps and Pyrenees, Greenland, and North America south to New Hampshire.

Intermediate Wintergreen *Pyrola media*

It is appropriate that the first mention in the book of this submontane species was in the context of Morrone Birkwood, because I regard it much more as a species of upland woods that just happens to persist in submontane heaths from which the trees have been removed. Its flowering stems arise from the centre of a rosette of bright green, roundish leaves and can be 30cm tall. They are topped by an open cluster of waxy, white flowers, shaped like an open bell, with a long style projecting from their centre. Intermediate Wintergreen is not easy to tell from other *Pyrola* species, and there is a good reason for that. It originated as a hybrid between Common and Round-leaved Wintergreen and became fertile through subsequent chromosome doubling in its cell nuclei. Its characteristics are therefore truly intermediate between its two parents. Distinguishing between the three with certainty relies on minute points of detail which I have summarised elsewhere (Scott, 2011) but lack the space to cover here.

Intermediate Wintergreen can be identified by its relatively open flowers in which the pollen-collecting style projects a little way beyond the petals. It is not always easy to tell apart from the more widespread Common Wintergreen.

It is recorded no higher than 550m in Coire Garbhlach in the Cairngorms, and is most typically a species of pinewoods (whereas Common Wintergreen, which does not qualify as montane, is found at much higher altitudes, up to 1,130m in the Breadalbanes). It has almost disappeared from northern England and the Southern Uplands because of intensive woodland management and increased moorland grazing, but a few sites may still persist in the North York Moors and Northumberland hills. It is most common in the south-east Highlands, with a few sites westwards to the Inner Hebrides, including Skye and Islay. It is rather more montane in its distribution in central Europe and Asia, and reaches well north of the Arctic Circle in Scandinavia.

Serrated Wintergreen *Orthilia secunda*

Although still submontane in its distribution, I regard this as a more true mountain plant than the previous species, from which it is distinguished by its toothed leaves and its flowers which all nod to one side of a crowded inflorescence. It grows on damp ledges, gullies and rocky streambanks in the hills, as well as in pine and birch woods, at altitudes no higher than 730m at a site in Ross-shire and down to 30m near Beauly in Inverness-shire. It also grows at a solitary site on Rousay in Orkney, in at least two glens in the Moffat hills, and on a few acidic cliffs and ravines in the Lake District. It seems to have died out recently from some of these sites and from Wales, perhaps as a result of overgrazing. Elsewhere, it is found in northern Asia and Europe, south to Sicily, and in northern North America.

The leaves of Serrated Wintergreen are finely toothed along their edges. Its greenish-white flowers characteristically droop to one side of the rather crowded inflorescence.

Alpine Speedwell *Veronica alpina*

This is another diminutive plant of the Cairnwell limestone. It is usually around 5cm tall with toothed, oval leaves and little clusters of deep blue flowers, hardly more than 5mm across. On the Cairnwell, it grows on grassland a short distance from the limestone outcrops, so the soil is enriched but not too strongly calcareous. Both spots where I know it there are in little hollows, and I think this is critical. It almost always occurs in rather damp but well-drained sites where snow lies late, and I suspect it relies on the shortened growing season after the snow melts to keep more competitive species at bay.

It is only found in the central Highlands, from Aberdeenshire and Inverness-shire west to Argyll, but is easily overlooked and nowhere common. Perhaps because of its reliance on snow-lie, it is only recorded above 710m and up to 1,190m, with both extremes occurring on the one hill: Aonach Beag beside Ben Nevis. It also grows in arctic Europe, Siberia and North America, and the high mountains of Europe, North America and even Korea.

Alpine Saw-wort *Saussurea alpina*

Alpine Saw-wort is typically a plant of damp, base-rich cliff ledges, screes and the banks of mountain streams. It grows up to 45cm tall, with purple flowerheads like a rather starved thistle. The Cairnwell limestone is a very unusual habitat, and the plant shows an atypical form to match, being little more than a rosette of a few ground-hugging leaves. I have never found a flower stem on the Cairnwell. Perhaps they never reproduce there, but constantly reinvade as seeds from some hidden refuge elsewhere in the region.

ABOVE: The flowers of Alpine Speedwell look startlingly blue, yet the plant is surprisingly difficult to spot, not least because it is rarely more than 5cm tall.
BELOW: Alpine Saw-wort has toothed leaves, and their underside is covered with a dense fuzz of greyish-white hairs. Its purple flowerheads appear in August or September.

Beyond the Cairnwell, Alpine Saw-wort is a local and uncommon species in north Wales, the Ingleborough area and the Lake District, with scattered sites also in the Southern Uplands. It is much more widespread, but with a western tendency, in the Highlands and in the hills of the Western and Northern Isles. It is recorded to 1,175m in the Breadalbane hills, but comes down virtually to sea level in Ardnamurchan and on clifftops east of Thurso in Caithness. Beyond our shores, it is found in northern Europe and Asia and the mountains of central Europe and Asia.

Dwarf Cudweed *Gnaphalium supinum*

This low-growing plant, with its stubby flowers and white-woolly leaves and stems, is only found in the Highlands, from Argyll to Sutherland. Skye is its only island home. The exposed, windswept fellfield on the ridge of the Cairnwell is very typical habitat, where it grows with Stiff Sedge, Three-leaved Rush, Dwarf Willow and Trailing Azalea. It also turns up on cliff ledges and moraines, usually in stony, well-drained sites where snow lies late. It is mainly found above 500m, ascending to the summit cairn of Ben Macdui at 1,305m, but it is very occasionally

The narrow, woolly leaves of Dwarf Cudweed form tufts along sprawling side branches. The little button-like flowerheads of these plants in the rain are just going over in late summer.

washed down to river gravels at lower altitudes. It is also found in the mountains and arctic areas of Europe, Asia, Greenland and North America.

Spiked Wood-rush *Luzula spicata*

The characteristic nodding, spike-like inflorescences of this short-growing relative of rushes are most likely to be found on exposed mountaintops, where it sometimes grows alongside the previous species. It seems to prefer open, stony, non-calcareous ground, especially where this is regularly on the move because of erosion or frost-heave (the movement caused by the expansion and contraction of ice as it freezes and melts). It is only found in the central and western Highlands, and the islands of Mull and Skye, with old records also from Harris. It also grows on bare granite debris on Ronas Hill in the north Mainland of Shetland. It is found around northern Europe and in the mountains of southern Europe, the Atlas Mountains, Himalayas and North America.

Spiked Wood-rush spreads by short creeping stems to form little tufted patches. The flowers in its spike-like inflorescence always seem too heavy for the stem, so they droop to one side.

Three-leaved Rush *Juncus trifidus*

Three-leaved Rush forms straggly tufts of leaves and stems that are rarely more than 10cm high. Its tiny grain-like flowers are tucked into the angle of two long, narrow, upcurving leaves at the stem tip. I always think it looks like a skinny ballerina *en pointe* with her arms upraised, but that analogy is often spoiled by a third stem leaf which also reaches up above the flowers. It is normally found above around 900m in the mountains. It is a characteristic feature on the bare, windswept tops

of high plateaux in the Highlands, where snow is quickly stripped off by the incessant winds, but it also grows on plateau-edges where snow accumulates for months on end. In the block-scree slopes of the Northern Corries of the Cairngorms it forms unusually lush tussocks, standing up to 40cm tall.

A typical patch of Three-leaved Rush, growing on a windswept summit plateau. Its upcurving leaves rise well above its little dark flowerheads.

Its southernmost British site is on Goatfell on the Isle of Arran, and it is then found in suitable habitats throughout the Highlands northwards to the Foinaven area in Sutherland. It is also recorded amongst the granite debris on the upper slopes of Ronas Hill in Shetland, descending there to its lowest altitude at 240m. At the other extreme, it grows within a few metres of the summit of Ben Macdui in the Cairngorms. It can be found around Askival on Rum, and uncommonly in the Cuillin hills and near the Storr summit on Skye. Perhaps its absence from Snowdonia and the Lake District can be explained by the lack of extreme winter freezing there. In Europe, it is recorded in high mountains from Spain to Siberia, and throughout arctic and subarctic areas of Scandinavia, Greenland and North America.

Rock Sedge *Carex rupestris*

A delighted cry of 'the pig' from Grant Roger used to greet discovery of this elusive sedge on the mountain flower courses we ran together. The nickname celebrated its twisted leaves, which curl like pig's tails. In the shallow, skeletal limestone grassland above the first Cairnwell limestone outcrop, its leaves are unusually frequent in the turf, but only a few plants there show their spike-like inflorescence at any one time. Elsewhere, it is more typically a plant of crumbly limestone cliff ledges.

It has a very narrow distribution in the central Highlands from Glen Doll and the Cairngorms west to the Breadalbanes, where it is recorded to 935m. It is then also found at a few sites on the limestones of north-west Scotland, often with Mountain Avens nearby. In 1981, it was also discovered on rock ledges in the limestone of Suardal on Skye. In the exposed, near-arctic conditions of coastal sites in Sutherland, it grows only a few metres above sea level. Outside Britain, it is a plant

Unusually, Rock Sedge forms a continuous turf over a small area of the Cairnwell limestone, with its characteristically curly leaves. The spike-like inflorescences grow at the tip of stiff three-sided stems.

of northern Europe, mountains from the Pyrenees to the Himalayas, Greenland and arctic North America.

Glas Maol

An even more enthralling botanical walk is to follow the rough track eastwards and upwards from the southern end of the Glenshee car park. This passes some of the commoner Cairnwell species on the climb to the peaty shoulder of Meall Odhar, where there is an interesting range of sedges including Stiff Sedge. Ahead is a magnificent amphitheatre of craggy slopes called Glas Choire, beneath the 1,068m summit of Glas Maol (which unflatteringly means 'Green Lump'). This corrie is often topped with a cornice of snow that lasts well into late summer, but sadly its wild landscape is despoiled these days by an untidy scramble of snow fences at its far end. The melting snow descends in a series of runnels of ice-cold water, and I suspect this summer chill helps encourage a number of arctic-alpine species there. On the route across to these runnels, Sibbaldia grows in its typical habitat in a snow hollow, with Dwarf Cudweed on eroded banks.

The runnels are best known as one of the few sites that support the delightful duo of Alpine Cat's-tail and Alpine Foxtail grasses, along with Three-flowered Rush, Starry and Mossy Saxifrages, Alpine and Chickweed Willowherbs, the small mountain form of Marsh Marigold and the mountain subspecies of Thyme-leaved Speedwell. The grassy slopes between the runnels are home to Fir Clubmoss, Alpine Scurvy-grass, Alpine Bistort, Alpine Speedwell, Spiked Wood-rush and Sheathed Sedge. Very rare and difficult to find here is Chestnut Rush, which we will return to in Chapter 13. Alpine Cat's-tail is also quite frequent beside streams on the south side of the dome of Glas Maol, but Alpine Foxtail is much rarer there.

Avoiding the snow fences, and continuing eastwards, the route climbs over a rounded ridge then drops to a flat, boggy shoulder whose most special inhabitant is the rare Mountain Bog-sedge. It grows here with

Grant Roger and some of the students on our mountain flowers course in 1989, searching for Alpine Cat's-tail and Chestnut Rush in the runnels below Glas Maol.

Alpine Willowherb, Starry Saxifrage, Bog Bilberry and a few plants of Alpine Foxtail and Alpine Cat's-tail. From there, it is a demanding scramble down to the precipitous crags of Caenlochan Glen, but first we must reflect on three more species.

Sibbaldia has small, greyish, three-fingered leaves that typically grow half-hidden in the surrounding turf. Its clusters of tiny greenish flowers are rather similar to those of Lady's-mantle.

Sibbaldia *Sibbaldia procumbens*

I always delight in finding this delicate little member of the rose family. It is named after Robert Sibbald, founder of the botanic garden in Edinburgh, who first recorded the species in Britain in 1684. It is nowhere common, but not too difficult to find once you know its habitat. It likes hollows where snow lies into early summer or the zone where snow cornices hang around the head wall of corries. It also grows, less commonly, on heavily weathered, open, stony, windswept mountain ridges and plateaux, irrespective of whether the rocks are calcareous or not (Coker, 1966). I suspect it is another species repressed in the Scottish mountains by the grazing of sheep, Red Deer and Mountain Hares.

It is confined to the southern, central and north-west Highlands, with a distinct western tendency. Amongst the islands, it is only found on the Trotternish and Cuillin hills of Skye, including its lowest extant site at 425m on Sgurr na Coinnich. At the other extreme, it is found up to 1,310m on Ben Nevis. An 1874 record on High Cup Nick in the Lake District probably resulted from misidentification, and it has never been refound on Ronas Hill in Shetland since Thomas Edmonston recorded it there in 1845. Its world range extends from the Alps north to Scandinavia, Svalbard, Iceland and Greenland.

Alpine Cat's-tail *Phleum alpinum*

I always regard this species in a duo with Alpine Foxtail (Chapter 8), because these two handsome grasses grow side-by-side in the Glas Choire, where the Cat's-tail is marginally the commoner. I can never remember which common name belongs to which grass, because their association with foxes and cats seems tenuous. However, Alpine Cat's-tail is distinguished in flower or fruit by the paired red bristles (awns) that project from its oblong inflorescence.

It is a plant of wet slopes, mountain runnels and damp rock ledges where the soil is base-rich or there is some mineral flushing from higher on the hill. It is a scarce species, restricted by grazing and confined to the central Highlands and a few sites in the west Highlands, from altitudes of 610m on Braeriach to 1,220m on Cairn Toul, both in the Cairngorms. It also survives at sites around Cross Fell in the northern Pennines, with an old record on Helvellyn in the Lakes. Like Alpine Foxtail, it has a remarkably wide world range, throughout the arctic regions and high mountains of Europe, Asia and North America, but including also the Andes of South America and even the sub-Antarctic island of South Georgia.

Alpine Cat's-tail: the paired red awns that project from the showy, oblong inflorescence always remind me of miniature scorpion tails.

Mountain Bog-sedge *Carex rariflora*

This rare, low-growing sedge forms carpets of shoots in a few acidic, flushed bogs at the eastern end of the central Highlands, particularly around the Caenlochan area and the Drumochter Hills. Its range extends westwards into the Breadalbane hills, but it is very rare there. The extensive population I have described below Glas Maol grows on a flat expanse of peat, with open pools in places, but it seems very shy about flowering there in some years. In the Drumochter Hills, its small populations grow in peaty soil on flat terraces beside burns. It is recorded from 790m in Drumochter to 1,125m on Ben Macdui.

It is very similar to two other species of bog-sedge, with tufts of narrow leaves, three-angled stems and hanging heads of a few, oval, pale brown flower spikes. However, it is shorter, with fewer flowers than the two other species, and these can generally also be distinguished by their range since Bog-sedge is not recorded above 830m nor Tall Bog-sedge above 685m. Mountain Bog-sedge has a circumpolar range across northern Asia and Europe through Greenland to the north of North America. Scotland is therefore the southernmost extreme of its world range.

A boggy shoulder set back from the top of the Caenlochan cliffs is one of the few sites in Britain for Mountain Bog-sedge.

Caenlochan Glen

With the corrie at the head of Caenlochan Glen, we reach another classic British montane site. Indeed, Ratcliffe (1977) asserts that it holds more montane vascular plants

The Caenlochan cliffs drop steeply below the boggy terrace in the foreground here. The only safe route down is alongside a mountain stream. The line of cliffs in the mid-distance is Druim Mor, another interesting plant site.

(67 species) than any other single corrie in Britain. The top of the Caenlochan cliff is just a short walk from the boggy shoulder of Glas Maol previously described. Some plants of Downy Willow can be seen on the clifftop here, but the approach is steep and vertiginous and should only be attempted with care. There is just one feasible route to the foot of the crags, following the side of a burn down into the glen, but that is a demanding scramble only suited to the experienced hillwalker.

At one point beside this burn, a deep gully below a waterfall holds an accumulation of snow, often well into summer. As it melts a cluster of lush, green crowns of Alpine Lady-fern enlivens the eroded grey gravel. Directly opposite, the line of cliffs to the north of the glen at Druim Mor was formerly a site for Highland Cudweed, but sadly this has not been seen here since 2001. Although those northern cliffs have an interesting flora, the better botanical route is to cross the burn and then pick a careful route across the steep hillside towards the cliffs to the south. There are no tracks here, only a few indistinct sheep and deer paths. The route scrambles across a couple of steep chutes of fine scree, where Parsley Fern hints at interesting plants to come. A low cliff beside a burn has Roseroot and Mossy Saxifrage, but the target is the sheer V-shaped bluff of crags that towers some 200m above the valley here (see photo on p.27). Outcropping bands of calcareous rock at altitudes up to 945m explain this cliff's particular richness.

Frequent species on the Caenlochan cliffs

Fir Clubmoss	Mossy Saxifrage	Alpine Bistort
Least Clubmoss	Alpine Cinquefoil	Mountain Sorrel
Green Spleenwort	Alpine Lady's-mantle	Moss Campion
Holly Fern	Grass of Parnassus	Northern Bedstraw
Moonwort	Mountain Pansy (yellow- and purple-flowered)	Yellow-rattle (subspecies *borealis*)
Alpine Meadow-rue	Alpine Willowherb	Mountain Everlasting
Purple Saxifrage	Chickweed Willowherb	Frog Orchid
Yellow Mountain Saxifrage	Hoary Whitlow-grass	Hair Sedge

Moving carefully round the foot of the cliff, it is easy to find many of the commoner montane species we have already met, as listed above. With sharp eyes or binoculars, Downy Willow can be spotted high on the crag, but Net-leaved Willow is easier to find at eye level on ledges low on the cliff, along with the nodding heads of Black Alpine-sedge. Alpine Meadow-grass turns up, unusually in its non-viviparous form, along with Alpine Hair-grass. Alpine Mouse-ear points to the calcareous nature of the rocks. Rock Speedwell is easy to spot only during the brief period when it flowers, but the flowers of Boreal Fleabane and Alpine Gentian are longer-lived and somewhat easier to find. A few plants of Alpine Woodsia grow on narrow, mossy ledges on the sheer rock faces. I have only ever found small, young Woodsia plants here, and I suspect these soon disappear because of erosion or theft, and are then replaced by spores from plants on the inaccessible higher reaches of the cliff.

Lush, ungrazed ledges on the cliff have Roseroot, Wood Cranesbill, Globeflower, Wild Angelica and Great Wood-rush, with some nice displays of Early-purple Orchid, but since I first visited the site in 1981 I have noticed changes here. The tall-herb community has declined greatly, I suspect as a result of the impact of sheep and deer, which I will return to in Chapter 19.

Continuing beyond the cliff, there is another fearsome stone chute with some plants of Mountain Male-fern, then a stretch of cliff with more conspicuous green ledges. Perhaps this is slightly limier, because this is where Mountain Avens appears, along with Stone Bramble, Mountain Melick and colourful patches of Red Campion. Beyond this, a spreading, reddish gully marks the best ascent up from the crags. Lots more Alpine Lady-fern grows near the base of this gully, and on one inaccessible ledge on the granite above it is possible to make out the big green leaves of Alpine Sowthistle – one of our rarest mountain flowers whose extraordinarily limited distribution qualifies it as another three-star enigma.

★★★ ALPINE SOWTHISTLE *Cicerbita alpina*

Alpine Sowthistle (sometimes called Alpine Blue-sowthistle) is incredibly rare in Britain, confined to the Angus and Aberdeenshire glens, and officially listed as 'vulnerable' in conservation terms. I only know it at its Caenlochan site, where a patch of incongruously luxuriant foliage fills an inaccessible rock ledge no bigger than a billiard table. Its big, green, lobed leaves are conspicuous from quite some distance away, although its tightly clustered heads of mid-blue flowers are surprisingly difficult to spot. A maximum of 45 flowerheads have been counted at Caenlochan in past years, and sometimes as few as three. It is possible to scramble up to a couple of metres below the ledge, but I would urge visitors not to try to access the ledge itself. Aside from the considerable risk to life and limb, any erosion here could open up the ledge to deer and sheep and lead to the sowthistle's rapid demise.

Beyond Caenlochan, it grows at three other sites discussed in this chapter (although beware that two non-native species of sowthistle grow at lower elevations beside a few Scottish roadsides). In Coire Fee, six colonies were once known, but it was thought to have become extinct there until a population was discovered in 1979 in an inaccessible north-facing gully, blocked at its base by a huge boulder. In 1999, 239 flowering stems were counted at this site.

In Coire Kander in Glen Callater, it survives on two rock ledges on a steep and very slippery north-facing rock face that cannot safely be reached without using ropes. Totals of 176 and 66 flowering spikes were recorded on these two ledges in 1999. Its final surviving site is on Lochnagar, where George Don first discovered it in 1801. On the cliff there, at least three patches are known in damp, shady gullies or on broad ledges where snow often lies well into summer. One of these ledges is known to climbers as the 'Potato Patch' after the sowthistle's verdant foliage. Two of these colonies in 1999 held 110 and 239 flowering stems. Interestingly, Alpine Lady-fern also grows near to all three sites.

I have been concerned for the conservation of this species ever since I first visited Caenlochan in 1981, because it is so obviously vulnerable there. It is a lush and edible species; the Swedes

Alpine Sowthistle: Pamela Clarke studying a fine plant in a gully high above Coire Fee, during a survey of the species in 1994.

call it Lapp Lettuce, because it was eaten by the Lappish people as a vegetable, and in Swedish it is *Torta*, which certainly sounds delectable! There is no doubt that it also offers a tasty feast for grazing animals. In 1994, when I was working as Scottish Officer for Plantlife, I persuaded Scottish Natural Heritage (SNH) to sponsor a full survey of the species. This was undertaken by two enthusiastic naturalists, John and Pamela Clarke, who confirmed its presence at all its remaining sites and added more counts to the species records.

John and Pam also talked to the experts who best knew the species, and their consensus was that its remaining refuges were in less than optimal habitat at atypical elevations. As evidence, they noted that seed is very rarely set at Scottish sites and is often not viable. This may be because the distance between surviving populations prevents pollen transfer and forces inbreeding. They also pointed to one former site in Canness Glen, 3km or so east of Caenlochan, where Alpine Sowthistle was known since 1885 growing beneath larch trees from a 19th-century planting. In 1934, the Scottish landscape photographer Robert Moyes Adam visited this site and took the photograph, reproduced here, which shows a large clump of sowthistle in a deep, rocky valley with several larch trees in the background. This partly wooded site, at around 535m, was protected from grazing sheep and deer by the steep sides of the gorge and a deep pool at its foot. Records by two keen mountain botanists, Claire Geddes and Sandy Payne, show that a declining population persisted here until the 1970s. However, the hot dry summer of 1976 may have emptied the pool and let deer into the gorge, and the species has not been seen there since 1977.

The occurrence of Alpine Sowthistle in this well-shaded, tree-clad site supports the theory of the experts to whom John and Pam Clarke talked. They suggested that the original habitat for the species in Scotland might have been high-altitude birch or even pine woodland. As these woods disappeared, it seems likely that the sowthistle was driven back to broad ledges, beyond the reach of grazing animals, where the soil was deep enough to support the plant and the damp, shady conditions mimicked its former woodland habitats. The scarcity of such ledges explains its rarity.

Since 1981, I have seen the species in the Alps, in arctic Sweden and in the Krkonoše Mountains of the Czech Republic, but in every case this has been under an open cover of trees. On one of my favourite walks in the

A historic image: R M Adam photographed Alpine Sowthistle in 1934 in Canness Glen, east of Caenlochan. His photo adds greatly to our understanding of the plant's ecology.

An amazing patch of Alpine Sowthistle grows in birch woodland at 800m near Vatnahalsen in southern Norway. Perhaps this is more like the habitat where it once grew in Scotland.

mountains of Norway, I know a patch of Alpine Sowthistle beneath birch woodland at an altitude of 800m which probably has more flowerheads than the entire Scottish population. Every time I see it I realise what we are missing in Scotland.

The problem is that most high-level Scottish birchwoods have been felled or destroyed by heavy grazing and occasional burning. Those that are left are regarded as valuable shelter for sheep and deer, and grazed with such intensity that they support virtually no ground flora. To test this theory, the Clarkes proposed establishing an experimental population of Alpine Sowthistle in a large grazing exclosure in the Morrone Birkwood beside Braemar. In a later report on the species, another naturalist, Leonie Alexander, suggested a second option in a wooded gully on the Balmoral Estate.

However, Leonie also reported strong resistance in principle from many in the botanical community to introducing the plant into sites in which there was no recorded evidence of its past presence. In any case, the Morrone option is no longer feasible. SNH removed its status as a National Nature Reserve in 2005 because it could not achieve a high enough standard of conservation management on land that is owned by Mar Estate and run as a shooting estate. As a result, the grazing exclosure is no longer maintained.

Alpine Sowthistle of Scottish origin has been maintained in cultivation for many years, and we now have fine plants in our garden in Wester Ross.

At least an attempt is now underway at Caenlochan to reduce the deer population there. I will return to this in Chapter 19, but I will be extremely surprised if this can reduce deer numbers even to the relatively high levels that were already threatening the plant in the 1980s. So, more than two decades on from the 1994 Plantlife survey, there has been no progress in addressing the fundamental issues that make Alpine Sowthistle one of our most threatened montane species.

Scrambling up the gully, it is easy to find Hoary Whitlow-grass, Alpine Mouse-ear, masses of Mountain Sorrel, some patches of Mossy Saxifrage and a few plants of Alpine Saxifrage clinging precariously onto rock bluffs. This is also one of the best places to spot Glaucous Meadow-grass. Within less than a kilometre, this remarkable line of cliffs has presented us with a formidable list of new species that we must now consider.

Alpine Lady-fern *Athyrium distentifolium*

The snow-filled gully beside the burn into Caenlochan Glen is typical habitat for this elegant mountain fern with its neat crowns of lacy, feather-shaped fronds. In Britain, the species is entirely restricted to the Highlands, especially towards the wetter west, but on none of the islands. It grows on rock ledges and in stable, relatively acidic block scree, usually in north- or east-facing sites where late-lying snow limits competitors and provides irrigation as it melts. The snow also protects the plants, because in years when early melting of the snow allows the fronds to emerge prematurely they can suffer severely from early summer frosts (McHaffie, 2005).

The species is recorded from 455m in the Breadalbanes to 1,220m on Ben Macdui. It is also found throughout the arctic and mountain regions of Europe, Asia and southern Greenland, with a different

The luxuriant bank of Alpine Lady-fern is growing here beside the waterfall on the route down into Caenlochan Glen. This is a typical habitat in a hollow where snow often lies well into summer.

subspecies in North American mountains. In Scotland, a form whose stems have a characteristic kink so that the fronds spread out almost horizontally was once thought to be a separate species, Newman's Lady-fern, but it is now generally accepted that this is a variety of Alpine Lady-fern adapted to nutrient-deficient sites.

Net-leaved Willow *Salix reticulata*

Net-leaved (or Reticulate) Willow is one of our most distinctive willows. It is a low-growing, mat-forming shrub, recognised by the conspicuous network of veins on the upper surface of its dark green leaves. It is found mainly in the southern Highlands on ledges of limestone, calcareous schist or other lime-rich mountain rocks, with Caenlochan at the eastern end of its range. Its stronghold is in the Breadalbane hills of Perthshire, where it is recorded to 1,125m, with discontinuous records also from the Ben Hope area of Sutherland, where it occurs down to 520m. Stewart *et al.* (1994) suggest that it is usually confined to larger outcrops of rocks where there are enough plants nearby to repopulate areas denuded by rock falls, drought or grazing. It occurs throughout arctic and subarctic Europe, Asia and North America and in the mountains of southern Europe, but is missing from Iceland and Greenland.

Net-leaved Willow: the network of veins on the rather fleshy dark green leaves make the plant instantly recognisable.

Alpine Mouse-ear *Cerastium alpinum*

It is difficult to refer to this species without mentioning Arctic Mouse-ear, its rarer 'alter ego' on hard, acid rocks (Chapter 14). The leaves and stems of what I prefer to call Alpine Chickweed are densely covered in long white hairs, whereas Arctic Mouse-ear has narrower leaves covered in shorter, stubbly white hairs. However, Alpine Mouse-ear is always found on relatively crumbly, base-rich rocks, such as limestones and mica schists, or on more acidic rocks which get at least some basic flushing from nearby. It also grows on serpentine rocks, in which the main basic constituent is usually magnesium rather than calcium.

Oddly, the Alpine species is even rarer in Snowdonia than Arctic Mouse-ear, and is known just from Carnedd Llewelyn. In the Lake District, it is one of the glacial remnants that clings on to corries on the east side of Helvellyn between 760m and 870m, and it was recently confirmed at a single site at Blackhope in the Moffat hills. It is then found at scattered sites across the southern Highlands, especially in the Breadalbanes, with a few sites also in the north-west Highlands, north to Foinavon in Sutherland, but not on any of the islands. It is recorded from 300m on Seana Bhraigh, north of Beinn Dearg in Wester Ross, to 1,214m in the Breadalbanes. It is also found throughout arctic regions of Europe, Asia and North America, and in mountains south to the Balkans.

The hairy grey leaves of Alpine Mouse-ear are somewhat reminiscent of garden Snow-in-Summer *Cerastium tomentosum*, and its big white flowers are just as showy.

Alpine Gentian *Gentiana nivalis*

This elusive plant is confined to just this stretch of crag at Caenlochan and some of the crags of Ben Lawers in Perthshire, between 730m and

Alpine Gentian has intense blue flowers which look very conspicuous in close-up, but the slender plants are rarely more than 6cm tall and surprisingly difficult to spot.

1,095m. It is easily overlooked, because it is rarely more than 6cm tall – although a few lush specimens can be twice that. Its neat blue flowers are less than 1cm across and seem to open only in sunshine – and then for only part of the day. At both its British sites, it grows on rock ledges and steep grassy slopes on calcareous rock. It appears to require natural erosion and low levels of grazing and trampling by sheep to maintain an open habitat, particularly for the establishment of its seeds, although too high a level of grazing can deplete its populations. That may explain why its numbers vary significantly from year to year, with counts on Lawers typically recording between 500 and 1,000 plants, while numbers between 4 and 200 have been recorded at its main Caenlochan site (Wigginton, 1999). It is also damaged readily by trampling, and as a result it is classified as vulnerable.

Why then is it confined to just these two sites? Its pollen cannot be identified from the fossil record, but if we assume it was more widespread at the end of the last glaciation, it may be that only these two sites provide exactly the right combination of soil type, climate and naturally maintained open vegetation for its seedlings to establish. It seems no coincidence that they are also the two crags with the highest diversity of montane species anywhere in Britain.

Alpine Gentian is one of the very few arctic-alpine species that is mainly annual or occasionally biennial (that is to say it either completes its whole lifecycle within one year or else it germinates in the first year, then flowers, sets seed and dies in the second year). The need to constantly regrow from seed would have made it highly vulnerable to past periods of climatic pressure, destroying its population and quickly exhausting its seedbank at all but highly favoured sites. It is also found in the mountains of southern Europe, Asia Minor, northern Scandinavia, Greenland and the Labrador coast of North America.

Rock Speedwell *Veronica fruticans*

The rich blue flowers of this scarce and localised species are easily identified by the red-rimmed white eye at their centre. They are deeply divided into four petal lobes with a tubular base, and are very short-lived. I suspect that plants at any one site remain in flower for little more than two weeks, and the entire petal tube falls off readily in wind or rain or at the lightest touch. Out of flower, it is much more difficult to spot and may be overlooked at some sites.

It is confined to ledges on calcareous crags, and steep, open slopes beneath them, almost always on south-facing sites that are inaccessible

The rich blue flowers of Rock Speedwell have a white centre ringed with red. It grows on the same crags as Alpine Gentian at Caenlochan and below Ben Lawers, where this photograph was taken.

to grazing animals. It is only found in the southern and central Highlands, from Beinn an Dothaidh, east of Bridge of Orchy in Argyll, eastwards to the Cairngorms and the Angus Glens. Its main centre and largest populations are in the Breadalbane hills. It is recorded from 540m at Meall an Fhiodhain, west of Loch Earn in Stirlingshire, to 1,100m in the Breadalbanes. Only around 55 sites are known for it, and it has been lost from at least ten of these (Wigginton, 1999). Many populations are small, and the total British population has been estimated at a little over 2,000 plants, so finding it anywhere is always a special treat. It has an arctic-alpine range in Europe, Greenland and North America and in most of the mountain ranges of western Europe.

The woolly stems of Highland Cudweed grow to 20cm tall. It has paddle-shaped grey leaves and clusters of dark brown flowerheads.

Highland Cudweed
Gnaphalium norvegicum

Back in 1984, I looked for, but failed to find, Highland Cudweed on Druim Mor at the head of Caenlochan Glen. It was probably already on its way out there by then, and has not been seen in the area since 2001. Indeed, I have never found the species in Scotland, although – appropriately enough, given its scientific name – I have seen it in flower high in the Norwegian mountains. Wigginton (1999) describes its typical habitat as being well-drained, enriched but acidic soils, with little other plant cover, on slopes and ledges in gullies and stream gorges. These usually face between east and south, perhaps suggesting the need for some summer sun before flowering.

The species is nationally scarce, with some 30 colonies on about 12 mountains. As well as Caenlochan and Lochnagar, it is (or was) found at a few sites in the Cairngorms, at Creag Meagaidh in Inverness-shire, and at a scattering of sites in the north-west Highlands, as far north as Beinn Dearg in Wester Ross. It is recorded from 600m at Aonach air Chrith, south of Glen Cluanie in Wester Ross, to 980m on Sgurr na Lapaich in Glen Affric, Inverness-shire. At many of its gully sites it is susceptible to avalanches and landslides, and it may have been over-collected in the past from some sites such as Lochnagar. However, the main damage at Caenlochan probably comes from the rocketing Red Deer population, which forces the animals to seek out even the most inaccessible of gullies and ledges to graze. Outwith Scotland, it is widespread in arctic and subarctic Europe, Asia, Greenland and north-east Canada, and mountains from Scandinavia south to the Alps and Caucasus.

The flowerhead of Boreal Fleabane is typical of the daisy family, with a yellow disc in the centre and upright, pinky-purple, petal-like 'ray florets'.

Boreal Fleabane *Erigeron borealis*

This is another of the mountain rarities that makes the Caenlochan cliffs so special, although its numbers are very small here. It is somewhat commoner on Craig Maud in Glen Doll and in the Breadalbane hills, as we will see in Chapter 13, where it is found from Carn Gorm, north of Glen Lyon, west to Meall na Samhna and Beinn Heasgarnach. It is recorded at altitudes between 640m at Craig Maud and 1,100m on Ben Lawers. It is long gone from the Cairngorms, where there are old records from Beinn a' Bhuird and elsewhere. Throughout this range, it is found on cliff ledges on predominantly basic rocks and in herb-rich grassland below these cliffs, provided these are largely ungrazed.

This species was a favourite of John Raven's father, Charles. When he first found it in the

Breadalbanes, he wrote 'my specimen, large, upstanding, exquisitely fluffy in the involucre, exquisitely fringed in the flower, seemed to me one of the most delightful [plants] that I had ever seen' (Raven & Raven, 2012). It stands perhaps 15cm tall, with a hairy stem, hairy oval leaves and a neat pinky-purple flowerhead. It is also found in arctic Russia, northern Scandinavia, Greenland, Labrador and Newfoundland. That makes a site near Meall na Samhna potentially its southernmost site in the world. It is not found in the Alps, so its 'official' English name of Alpine Fleabane is a misnomer, and I prefer to use the more accurate name of Boreal Fleabane.

Black Alpine-sedge *Carex atrata*

Sedges are not always distinctive, but this one definitely is, with its cluster of oval, reddish-black flowering or fruiting heads which are so hefty that the plant typically nods over to one side. In the mountains, it can only really be confused with Scorched Alpine-sedge (Chapter 13). It is rare in Snowdonia but recorded in small numbers on Cwm Glas Mawr and on Clogwyn Du below Glyder Fawr. It is also rare in Cumbria, on Helvellyn and the High Street range, and in the Moffat hills of Dumfriesshire. It is then scattered, but nowhere common, through the east and west Highlands from 550m near Beinn Udlaidh in Argyll to 1,095m in the Breadalbanes. It has a few sites also in the north-west Highlands, north to Beinn Dearg in Wester Ross. In all

Black Alpine-sedge is growing here against the distinctive backdrop of the slopes of Caenlochan Glen. It is one of the more distinctive sedges, with big, oval, reddish-black fruiting heads.

these sites, it is found clinging to rock faces and on ungrazed ledges on cliffs that are calcareous or have at least some calcareous veining in the rock. It also grows in arctic Europe and Asia, on higher mountains in southern Europe, in Greenland and in North America south to Utah.

Glaucous Meadow-grass *Poa glauca* and Alpine Meadow-grass *Poa alpina*

I will deal with these two species together because they share a very similar distribution on damp mountain rock faces, open ledges, screes and rocky slopes on calcareous substrates. Indeed they often grow together, as they do at Caenlochan. Glaucous Meadow-grass is easily distinguished by its bluish-grey leaves with a covering of whitish wax. Alpine Meadow-grass has brighter green leaves and is most often viviparous – meaning that, instead of flowers, it produces little plantlets which begin growing and sprout little tufts of leaves while still attached to the inflorescence. These make the grass head so heavy that it bends over until the plantlets touch the ground and begin rooting, if they have not already fallen off and started growing. Unusually, the plants at Caenlochan are mostly non-viviparous, flowering and setting seed in a more typical grass-like way. As a result, it is more difficult to tell the two species apart there.

This plant of Alpine Meadow-grass is very evidently viviparous, with lots of little plantlets sprouting new leaves from its inflorescence.

Both the Glaucous and Alpine species are recorded in Snowdonia and both are very rare on Helvellyn in the Lake District. Alpine Meadow-grass is also recorded in its non-viviparous form on High Cup Nick and Ingleborough in the northern Pennines. Neither species occurs in the Southern Uplands, and both are scattered in suitable habitats throughout the Highlands. Both are rare in the Cuillin of Skye, but rather more common along the Trotternish ridge, particularly the glaucous species, and both also grow on Fionchra on Rum. Indeed the remarkable confluence in the distribution of these two species strikes me as thoroughly odd.

Glaucous Meadow-grass is recorded from 300m on Fionchra to 1,110m on Lochnagar in Aberdeenshire, and Alpine Meadow-grass from 430m on Fionchra to 1,240m on Ben

Nevis. Both are species of arctic Europe, Asia and North America and at least some of the mountains of southern Europe. Alpine Meadow-grass is recorded as far south as North Africa, while Glaucous Meadow-grass even reaches Patagonia in South America.

Alpine Hair-grass *Deschampsia cespitosa* subspecies *alpina*

This was thought to be a separate species *D. alpina* when it was included in Derek Ratcliffe's list of montane species, but has now been reduced to a subspecies of Tufted Hair-grass, and furthermore one which is easily confused with the much commoner subspecies *cespitosa*. Both are relatively tall, tussock-forming species with delicate, spreading, rather ethereal-looking inflorescences. The problem is that, although the spikelets of subspecies *alpina* are normally viviparous (like Alpine Meadow-grass, above), the spikelets of subspecies *cespitosa* can sometimes also be viviparous. Indeed viviparous plants in Snowdonia and the Lake District are now believed to belong to the commoner subspecies. Given that confusion, the distribution of the alpine plant is somewhat uncertain, but it is thought to be confined to the Scottish Highlands and a few islands, including Arran, Mull and Skye. It reaches 1,305m near the summit of Aonach Beag, but is recorded down to 395m on the island of Rum. Viviparous reproduction is a useful safeguard to ensure that it can spread itself even in the short growing season of the arctic and subarctic regions in which it is found, from Canada, Greenland and Scandinavia to eastern Asia.

Alpine Hair-grass is not easy to photograph, but this shot beautifully captures the viviparous spikelets of its offspring, still attached to the parent plant.

PREVIOUS SPREAD:
Coire Fee: a view from the top of the waterfall towards Glen Doll. The Woodsia and Oxytropis crags are on the left, and Coire Sharroch is out of sight on the right.

Coire Fee

In theory, a hillwalker could continue eastwards from Caenlochan to Coire Fee (or more correctly *Coire Fiadh*, meaning the 'corrie of the deer' in Gaelic, rather ironically given the damage caused in the corrie by deer grazing). However, that would be a major day's walking with no time for botanising. The more sensible approach is from the car park at the end of Glen Clova, north of Forfar. A forestry track leads from here up towards Coire Fee – which, as we saw on page 106, is one of the finest examples of a corrie anywhere in Britain.

Mountain Pansy is immediately apparent beside the car park, and Melancholy Thistle grows by the forestry track. At one point by the White Water, there is a patch of Silver Lady's-mantle *Alchemilla conjuncta*, an introduction from the Alps, known here since 1837, which is also found in Glen Sannox on Arran. As the path leads up through the forest towards the corrie, some of the commoner montane species begin to appear, including Alpine Lady's-mantle, Mountain Sorrel, Starry Saxifrage and Yellow Mountain Saxifrage, and it is worth searching for Lesser Twayblade beneath the heather. Many of the commoner Caenlochan species are also found around the bowl of the corrie itself, but no part of the cliffs has any particular concentration of these plants. Instead, the botanical explorer needs to spend time searching every stretch of the amphitheatre of crags.

An obvious starting point is a streak of lighter rock on the north side of the corrie, which encompasses the entire population in the area of Yellow Oxytropis. The oddly discontinuous distribution of this species intrigues me, making it another enigma. It grows here with Wood Vetch, Mountain Everlasting and Alpine Bistort. Gullies in the rocks below are home to both Holly Fern and a few plants of Oblong Woodsia.

The distinction between the two woodsia species is not always clear-cut. One group of plants here was identified as Oblong Woodsia when I first visited the site in the company of such distinguished botanists as Peter Sell and Richard Pankhurst in July 1977. I returned six weeks later with fern expert Chris Page and he was convinced they were Alpine Woodsia, with just a single plant of Oblong Woodsia above. When a BSBI field meeting visited the site a couple of years later, some heated discussion ensued about the plants' identification without reaching any definitive conclusion, although I think the plants at this spot are now generally regarded as Oblong Woodsia. Continuing round the corrie anticlockwise, there is a cliff to the right of the waterfall which hosts

★★★ Yellow Oxytropis *Oxytropis campestris*

Yellow Oxytropis was discovered, new to Britain, 'on a high rock ... at the head of Clova' in 1812 by George Don, the botanist and explorer whom we will meet again later in this chapter. The plant is a very typical member of the pea family with hairy, grey-green, ladder-like leaves and a cluster of creamy-white flowers marked with faint blue lines and a distinctive, creamy-yellow blotch towards the base of the upper petal.

Today, around 400 plants still grow on that one short stretch of unusually pale calcareous schist that I described in Coire Fee, at an altitude between 500m and 640m. They also continue a little way down the scree beneath. In Raven & Walters (1956), John Raven quoted reports suggesting there was nothing peculiar about this rock, but he felt that visual evidence suggested otherwise and called for chemical analysis of this rock. I can find no record of any such analysis, but I am sure I would have heard if one had taken place and shown anything peculiar about the chemistry of the pale rock.

When I first visited the Oxytropis site in 1977 with the distinguished botanist Peter Sell, amongst others, I can remember speculating whether another factor might be at work. Yellow Oxytropis is mainly a species of central and southern Europe, where it is quite common in mountain meadows and pastures, found northwards into southern Sweden, with a separate subspecies in northern Scandinavia and arctic Russia. It is also found across northern Asia and in the mountains of North America. At most of these sites the climate is strongly continental, characterised by summer temperatures considerably warmer than we have in the Scottish mountains. I wondered therefore whether the light rock was simply reflecting more heat and creating conditions more conducive to its growth. Perhaps this added warmth might also help attract pollinating bees, encouraged by the flowers' sweet smell.

Although such speculation is unprovable, there was one test I could apply. In 1888, Yellow Oxytropis was found at a second site, on crags overlooking Loch Loch in Perthshire, which we will consider in the next chapter. When I first visited Glen Loch with Grant Roger in 1981, I asked him not to tell me where the plant grew on the crags. Instead I selected the palest stretch of crag and headed straight there; it turned out to be the centre of the limited range of Yellow Oxytropis on the crags. That proved nothing, of course, but it was at least faintly satisfying!

Yellow Oxytropis has a curious distribution: in Coire Fee, on crags above Loch Loch in Perthshire (where I took this photograph), and on a sea-cliff on the west coast of the Mull of Kintyre in Argyll.

At Loch Loch, I have sometimes come across deep pink flowers of so-called Yellow Oxytropis. A similar colour range in Argyll may explain why there was confusion as to whether they were this species or Purple Oxytropis.

As well as these two very limited sites, an Oxytropis was discovered in 1961 by Alf Slack, a botanist we will meet again in Chapter 15, on a cliff at Largybaan on the west coast of the Mull of Kintyre, within an altitude range of just 25–180m. At various times, these plants have been recorded as either Purple or Yellow Oxytropis, despite the former having rich purple flowers, as we will see in the next chapter, very different from the flowers of Yellow Oxytropis. The Largybaan plants are now confirmed as Yellow Oxytropis. However, at both Coire Fee and Glen Loch, some plants have flowers that are distinctly suffused with pale mauve and a few are definitely pale purple; that colour range might explain the confusion at Largybaan.

incontrovertible Alpine Woodsia, growing on a mossy ledge usually with Alpine Saxifrage at its side.

On the other side of the valley, Coire Sharroch has the finest surviving remnant of montane willow scrub anywhere in Britain. The best patch extends to no more than the size of a tennis court but holds around 180 bushes of Downy Willow and 120 bushes of Woolly Willow, with many additional plants of the two species on crags nearby (Mardon, 1990). These two species may also hybridise here, and Dark-leaved and Whortle-leaved Willow are also present. Back in 1991, many of the willow bushes were large and well-established but there was little sign of new plants establishing beyond the crags. It was thought that grazing by deer and sheep was responsible, so it was decided to enclose a large part of the corrie within a deer fence.

Eighteen years later, there was still no significant regeneration and the decision was taken to reinforce the population by planting (Marriot, 2014). One suggestion was that Mountain Hares might have been stopping seedlings from becoming established, so transplant sites were chosen where late snow would offer some protection from these grazers. In total over 600 Woolly, 800 Downy and 900 Dark-leaved Willows were planted at six sites in the corrie in 2009 and 2012, and monitoring in 2013 suggested that at least the Woolly and Downy Willows were surviving reasonably well.

Alpine Lady-fern and Sheathed Sedge also occur in Coire Sharroch, and the damp, open soil in one gully is home to Close-headed Alpine-sedge. Another crag, nearer the main corrie, is one of the few sites of the puzzling sedge known as Mountain Bladder-sedge. Not far from there, a rather undistinguished ledge is home to a small population of perhaps the most enigmatic of all our three-star mountain plants, Purple Coltsfoot, which occurs nowhere else in Britain. Interrupted Clubmoss and Alpine Saw-wort grow nearby.

An inaccessible north-facing gully elsewhere in the wide sweep of Coire Fee is home, as we have seen, to a remnant population of Alpine Sowthistle. Round the corner in the upper reaches of Glen Doll, the cliffs of the Dounalt and Craig Maud, overlooking a traditional route for cattle drovers called Jock's Road, have a richer concentration of species, somewhat resembling the crags of Caenlochan. Plants recorded here include Mountain Avens, Moss Campion, Rock Speedwell, Boreal Fleabane, Hair Sedge and a species we will meet in the next chapter, Alpine Milk-vetch. Coire Fee has therefore introduced us to a further five species, which I can now briefly profile.

Alpine Woodsia *Woodsia alpina*

There is no enigma about the rarity of this tufted little fern with its narrow, fragile-looking fronds. It probably always had a restricted range but suffered hugely in the past from over-collection (and perhaps still does today). I was once shown a venerable herbarium sheet on which, because of its small size, six tufts had been collected, all from the same site, just so the whole page could be filled. I believe it still clings to survival on the crags below Snowdon and perhaps in Cwm

★★★ Purple Coltsfoot *Homogyne alpina*

Part of the colony of Purple Coltsfoot on the single grassy ledge above Coire Fee, where it has been known since 1951.

The year after George Don found Yellow Oxytropis in Coire Fee, he discovered Purple Coltsfoot 'on rocks by the sides of rivulets in the high mountains of Clova, as on a rock called Garry-barns'. Its leaves resemble small versions of Coltsfoot, a common lowland plant, but its solitary flowerheads have purple florets. The colony in Coire Fee was then lost and its identity disputed until August 1951, when a 'chance search on a showery day' led botanist Alf Slack to discover a small population on a rock ledge high on the corrie wall. That ledge is still the only known native site for the species.

I have visited the ledge, which is not much bigger than a writing table, and it bothers me. Firstly, it is not by the side of a rivulet, which suggests it may not be Don's original site. Secondly, I cannot see why that ledge is different from many other ledges nearby, yet, like many botanists, I have searched neighbouring ledges and not found it. In August 1980, when I first visited, I counted 40 seedheads there; subsequent counts have recorded anything between 154 seedheads in 1987 and 10 in 1991. However, the species has not spread from its single, undistinguished ledge and there are suggestions that its seed is not viable. The population is also, by a very considerable distance, the northernmost site for the species, which is elsewhere found only in the mountains of central Europe from the Pyrenees to the Balkans.

It is possible, I suppose, that Purple Coltsfoot is an Ice Age survivor, although the fossil record does not confirm whether it occurred in Britain. Chance events may have eliminated it from other sites, so that it clings on vegetatively to this last refuge in suboptimal conditions that do not allow it to disperse its seeds. That seems unlikely to me, especially as nobody has been able to identify anything remotely special about its ledge.

George Don was a very dedicated explorer, who contributed greatly to our knowledge of the Scottish mountain flora in the late 18th and early 19th centuries, but he was also a collector of living plants, and from 1795 he ran a wild flower nursery in Forfar. This has led to suggestions that maybe he planted Purple Coltsfoot in Coire Fee, although I cannot think of any reason why he might do this. To me, it seems more likely, as the Oxford botanist George Claridge Druce suggested (Ribbons, 1952), that Don misidentified leaves of the lowland Coltsfoot in their dwarfed, mountain form in Coire Fee. Some later confusion in his nursery may explain his herbarium specimens, which are definitely Purple Coltsfoot. Subsequently, whether with good or malicious intentions, perhaps someone else planted out specimens onto that ledge, where they survived vegetatively until their discovery in 1951 (there are records of this also being attempted on South Uist in 1955). I share the view of Sell & Murrell (2006) that this species was 'probably always planted' in Scotland.

Nevertheless, whatever the species' true status, there are fewer than 200 individual plants on its solitary ledge, and there is a great risk that trampling by botanists beneath the ledge could lead to a landslip destroying most or all of the colony (which is why I have resisted a return visit). Accordingly, in 1988–1989 six plants were transplanted to a new site nearby and two to a small outlying colony, well removed from any risk of trampling. Monitoring these transplants may give us further clues as to the status of this attractive species in Scotland.

Idwal. It has a small population in these Angus glens, although it may have gone from Lochnagar. The Breadalbane hills are its main centre, from Ben Chonzie in Perthshire to the hills south-west of Ben Lui in Argyll, at altitudes up to 975m. An outlying population also grew in hills north of Loch Lochy in Inverness-shire, at least until as recently as 1995.

Most remarkably, in 2001 mountain botanist Gordon Rothero discovered it at a site on the Trotternish ridge of Skye at the remarkably low altitude of 430m (see photo on p.393), and the following year the local botanical recorder, Stephen Bungard, found another site nearby, both considerably south of an old 1884 record from Skye. Even in the

The diminutive fronds of Alpine Woodsia have distinctive triangular lobes and form a spreading, tufted rosette. This is probably a group of four newly developing young plants on a rock ledge.

Breadalbanes, Wigginton (1999) notes that 'it is unaccountably scarce and absent from many suitable-looking cliffs – a true relict from a much colder age'. Recent monitoring suggests that there are no more than 700 individual plants in Scotland and perhaps 50 in Wales, so its official conservation status is 'vulnerable'.

At all these sites, Alpine Woodsia grows on narrow ledges or in crevices with only slight accumulations of soil on steep, bare crags of strongly calcareous rocks. This habitat makes it very susceptible to desiccation. When I first visited the Coire Fee site in July 1977, I found only a single shrivelled plant on a mossy ledge, near a plant of Alpine Saxifrage. When I returned just over six weeks later, the Woodsia had revived with healthy fronds and we estimated a further ten plants higher on the cliff. Yet I was puzzled by the absence of the fern on very similar stretches of cliff nearby. Then by chance I returned to Coire Fee for a winter walk in February 1979 and discovered the stretch of Woodsia cliff encased in a mass of blue ice. Perhaps this winter deep-freeze is part of what allows this 'relict from a much colder age' to survive at this site, protecting it through the winter and excluding competitors.

When I visited Coire Fee in February 1979, the crag with Alpine Woodsia was deeply encased in a mass of ice. That might be key to the fern's survival on that short stretch of cliff.

Variation in winter conditions may partly explain fluctuations in the population here. In 2008, no living plants were found at the Coire Fee site (McHaffie, 2010), although there were dead remains on one wet ledge. By September of the following year, small fronds were sprouting once more from the apparently dead plant, confirming the resilience of the species' rhizomes, as I had witnessed in 1977. Elsewhere it is quite widespread in arctic Europe and Asia, Greenland, north-eastern North America and mountains from the Pyrenees to the Himalayas.

Woolly Willow *Salix lanata*

The most handsome of montane willows is a low-growing shrub with big, oval leaves. These are grey with a fluff of hairs of the top surface, at least when young, and persistently woolly on their underside. In Britain, the species is entirely confined to ungrazed ledges and crags on schist or other basic rocks in a few north-facing corries in the central Highlands, usually where the bushes are protected by late-lying snow. It is found westwards from Coire Sharroch and Glen Callater in Angus to Meall na Samhna in the Breadalbane hills, with its northernmost British site on a hill south of Glen Affric in Inverness-shire, at its lowest recorded altitude of 610m. It is rarely found above 900m, although it does reach 1,035m on Geal Charn, north of Ben Alder in Inverness-shire. It also grows in the Drumochter Hills and in Coire Garbhlach on the edge of the Cairngorms, as we will see in Chapter 14.

In 1994 a survey suggested that only five out of its 14 known sites held viable populations (Wigginton, 1999). Three sites had populations of fewer than 30 plants and three had just single female plants, although restoration projects have since been instigated at some of these sites. Grazing is the main threat to the species, but bees are unlikely to transfer pollen between isolated male and female plants, so these become unable to reproduce and spread. It is a subarctic species, found from Iceland eastwards to Siberia, so Meall na Samhna is probably its southernmost native site in the world.

Coire Sharroch holds one of the best surviving populations of Woolly Willow in Britain. Its big, oval, grey, hairy leaves are very conspicuous on the slope here.

Whortle-leaved Willow, with its characteristic bright green shiny leaves, on the limestone of Inchnadamph in Sutherland (see Chapter 16).

Whortle-leaved Willow *Salix myrsinites*

Beyond Coire Sharroch, I know this low, spreading dwarf shrub with bright green, shiny leaves best from the decidedly montane habitat of Coire Garbhlach in the Cairngorms and from the subarctic conditions of a limestone hill at Inchnadamph in Sutherland, where it is recorded down to 180m. It is a plant of scattered sites, mainly in the southern and western Highlands, south at least to the Ben More area of Argyll with old records also from Dumbartonshire. It may cling to a single site in the Moffat hills. It is also found on Ward Hill on Hoy in Orkney, although a plant recorded from Trotternish on Skye has not been refound in recent years. It is confined to moist, base-rich sites in the mountains, at altitudes up to 1,000m on Ben Alder. It is a subarctic species, occurring widely from Scandinavia east to the Urals and Siberia.

Mountain Bladder-sedge *Carex × grahamii*

When Derek Ratcliffe included this plant in his montane list it was thought to be a true species, *C. stenolepis*, but British plants are now believed to be a hybrid between Bladder Sedge and Russet Sedge. The hybrid was originally described from the single small population in Coire Sharroch, although Russet Sedge is rare in the Clova Hills and Bladder Sedge does not grow anywhere nearby (another possible parent is Bottle Sedge, which does grow in the vicinity). The hybrid is found more regularly in the Breadalbane hills, where Russet Sedge is somewhat more common. The hybrid is intermediate in character between its parents. Being infertile, it is most easily told by its empty fruits, which are squishy between the fingers.

Close-headed Alpine-sedge
Carex norvegica

First discovered, new to Britain, in Coire Kander (see overleaf) in 1830, this neat little sedge is rare and vulnerable on wet rock ledges, rocky slopes and grassy turf at only a few sites in the mountains of Angus, Aberdeenshire and Perthshire. It is recorded from 700m in Coire Fee to 975m on Meall Garbh in the Breadalbanes. It grows on mica schist or other basic rocks, always in north- or east-facing localities where snow lies late. Almost all its sites are small (one population in the Breadalbanes, for example, occupies an area of just 60m by 2m), and the total British population in any year may not exceed 650 flowering stems. Elsewhere it is a plant of the Alps, northern Europe, arctic Siberia and North America.

ABOVE: Mountain Bladder-sedge: I would struggle to get excited about this hybrid sedge, were it not for its dramatic location, high on the sides of Coire Fee.

Close-headed Alpine-sedge is a very rare, but not hugely distinctive, sedge, just 20cm tall with a tight cluster of greenish-brown fruits.

Other Angus and Aberdeenshire sites

From the shelter at the top of Jock's Road at the head of Glen Doll, it is possible to pick a path south-westwards towards the head of Canness Glen, round the side of Meikle Kilrannoch to a low hillock called Little Kilrannoch. Getting there is a tedious slog over an expanse of eroded peat, but the hill itself stands out as a rather bare dome shape, covered in a loose clitter of serpentine rock. This is well known as the second British site for Alpine Catchfly, which we previously met in the Lake District. When I visited the site in early August 1980, the catchfly had just finished flowering, but on a return visit in early July 1983 it was still tightly in bud. The associated flora at this site is limited, but includes Alpine Clubmoss, Thrift, Water Avens, Mossy Cyphel, Mountain Azalea and Stiff Sedge.

To the north of Glas Maol, calcareous cliffs at the head of Glen Callater, and especially those around Coire Kander, have many of the Caenlochan specialities, including Mountain Bladder-fern, Net-leaved Willow, Alpine Sowthistle, Close-headed Alpine-sedge and Rock Sedge. To the east of Glen Callater, ledges on the great cliffs of Lochnagar – the confusingly named mountain overlooking the loch of the same name – are another site for Alpine Sowthistle, growing in a tall-herb community with Roseroot, Globeflower and Wood Cranesbill. Other species on moderately acidic ground here

The cliffs of the corrie overlooking Loch Kander, at the head of Glen Callater in Aberdeenshire, are another site for many of the species described in this chapter, including Alpine Sowthistle.

include Interrupted Clubmoss, Alpine Speedwell, Alpine Mouse-ear, Downy Willow, Mountain Bog-sedge, Wavy Meadow-grass, Alpine Foxtail, Alpine Cat's-tail, as well as species we will meet later in the Cairngorms, including Dwarf Birch, Highland Saxifrage and Hare's-foot Sedge. The serpentine of the Coyles of Muick, north-east from here, is a site for Alpine Cinquefoil, Alpine Mouse-ear and Northern Rock-cress.

I lack the space to do justice to other Aberdeenshire sites, including the stretch from the Ladder Hills to the Hill of Towanreef and the Buck, whose specialities include Marsh Saxifrage and Hairy Stonecrop. I must however mention Creag an Dail Bheag, a lowish hill (863m) north of Braemar, which has another population of Alpine Milk-vetch, along with Interrupted Clubmoss, Alpine Clubmoss, Whortle-leaved Willow, Alpine Cinquefoil, Trailing Azalea, Black Alpine-sedge, Rock Sedge and Hair Sedge.

Wavy Meadow-grass *Poa flexuosa*

I hesitate to include this species here, because the only records I can trace for it at Lochnagar are pre-1969. Indeed, the only two records from this century on the BSBI online database at the time of writing are from Carn Dearg below Ben Nevis in 2002 and from a corrie beneath Beinn Mheadhoin, south of Loch Avon in the Cairngorms, in 2006. There are 1990s records elsewhere in the Cairngorms, including Coire an Lochain, and on Liathach, Beinn Tarsuinn and Beinn Alligin in Wester Ross. Since 1970 it has been recorded from only about a dozen sites, most of which support only very small populations (Preston *et al.*, 2002). The largest by far is in scree slopes below Ben Nevis, where between 200 and 300 plants have been counted (Cope & Gray, 2009).

Wavy Meadow-grass seems to be confined to acidic screes, rock ledges and fellfields at altitudes between 760m and 1,100m. There is no doubt it is a rare plant, but I wonder if it is under-recorded, because it is easily overlooked and difficult to identify with certainty (which is perhaps why none of the photographers contacted for this book could supply a photograph of it). It rarely stands more than 15cm tall, and the supposed waviness of its stems is never obvious. It is distinguished from Alpine and Glaucous Meadow-grasses (which, as we saw earlier in this chapter, are themselves tricky species to identify) by having somewhat narrower leaves which are green rather than blue-green in colour and gradually taper to a pointed tip. The species is only known from the mountains of north-west Europe.

Hills of the southern Highlands

chapter twelve

The hard rocks of the southern Highlands – formed in the Dalradian period, 800–550 million years ago – were more resistant to erosion than the rocks south of the Highland Boundary Fault. As a result, they remain tall and rugged with fine scenery that ensures their popularity with hillwalkers from the urban lowlands. Their slopes are mainly covered in rough hill grassland and extensively sheep-grazed. However, more botanically exciting areas occur wherever there are outcrops of the same band of calcareous schist that supports the flora of Caenlochan and Coire Fee.

The richest of these hills, by far, are the Breadalbanes, but they offer so much variety that I will leave them to a chapter of their own. However, the hills south and east of the Breadalbanes should not be underestimated. They offer fine walking and a rich montane flora.

Glen Loch

Having mentioned them in the last chapter, it makes sense to begin this chapter in the east of Perthshire with the crags overlooking Loch Loch – the rather daft name that I suspect was invented by mapmakers for a nameless loch in Glen Loch! Getting there requires a long walk from near the village of Straloch, east of Pitlochry. The route leads along an 8km private estate road through Gleann Fearnach to an isolated cottage at Daldhu, then a similar distance along a rough track. Alpine Lady's-mantle and Chickweed Wintergreen can be seen occasionally beside this track.

A little way beyond Daldhu, I usually abandon this track and contour across an area of flat moorland towards a conspicuous green

OPPOSITE PAGE: Purple Oxytropis is a handsome but elusive plant of the southern Highlands that grows on at least two of the hills we will meet in this chapter.

hillside that marks a small limestone outcrop. On the way across, the low wall of a ruined shieling (hut) provides a refuge for Parsley Fern, and Few-flowered Sedge grows in flushes close to the limestone. The limestone crag is home to Green Spleenwort, Common Rock-rose, Yellow Mountain Saxifrage, Purple Saxifrage, Stone Bramble, Hoary Whitlow-grass and Hair Sedge.

A narrow track then leads round the corner to a breath-taking view of the magnificent U-shaped valley of Glen Loch. A few peaty hags on the left mark the watershed of this loch, and gravelly flushes here have remarkably flowery inland patches of Thrift. Further along the east side of the loch, a steep boulder scree slope climbs up to a line of crags. Holly Fern, Green Spleenwort and Stone Bramble grow amongst the scree. The crags are another site for Yellow Oxytropis, growing here with Rock Speedwell, Northern Bedstraw, Purple Saxifrage and Hoary Whitlow-grass. Rock Sedge occurs at one point on the crags, with a plant or two nearby of a new species on our journey, Mountain Willow.

Steep boulder screes on the other side of the loch lead up towards the multiple, rugged summits of Beinn a' Ghlo. I have explored some of these slopes and found saxifrages and ferns in the gullies, but, like many other botanists who have searched here, I have failed to find the most famous historical denizen of these slopes, Arctic Bramble.

Looking towards Loch Loch from the south: the plant-rich crags are on the right of the loch in the mid-distance.

Mountain Willow *Salix arbuscula*

Mountain Willow is a shrubby willow with glossy dark brown twigs and egg-shaped leaves that are shining green on their top surface but covered in downy hairs underneath, at least when young. The species is largely confined to the Breadalbane hills, where it was first recorded, new to Britain, in 1777 by the Reverend John Lightfoot, author of the ground-breaking *Flora Scotica* published the following year. It is quite widespread but scattered in the Breadalbanes, west as far as Beinn Donachain in Glen Orchy. It grows in damp conditions on calcareous rock ledges and gravelly streamsides, from 460m on Ben Lui to 870m on Carn Gorm in Glen Lyon. It seems moderately tolerant of grazing, but landslips and rock falls may be necessary to open up suitable areas in which its seedlings can establish.

At the east of its range, it is recorded from a couple of sites in Angus, at Loch Loch and on the cliffs of Ben Vrackie, which we will visit next. It is also found north to Creag Meagaidh in Inverness-shire, but an old record from the Moffat hills has not been refound since 1934. It is a subarctic species, occurring from Scotland and Scandinavia through Siberia to central Asia.

Mountain Willow, growing here on an isolated crag near Ben Lui in Argyll, is a much-branched, shrubby willow which generally stands less than 70cm high.

Arctic Bramble *Rubus arcticus*

James Sowerby, author of *English Botany* (1813), had a herbarium specimen of Arctic Bramble which had been supplied to him as 'a dry wild specimen from the high regions of Ben-y-glo' (or Beinn a' Ghlo as we would now spell it). Ever since then, botanists have been trying without success to refind this plant, which resembles Stone Bramble but with bright red flowers. There are other old records elsewhere in Scotland, even on a moor in Yorkshire, but most floras now record the species as extinct.

Arctic Bramble is otherwise found in the north of Scandinavia, northern Russia and northern Asia. Perhaps it did cling on until the

Arctic Bramble is a common moorland and upland species in Finland and northern Sweden, but the few old records of it in Scotland are puzzling.

early 19th century around Beinn a' Ghlo as a relict from post-glacial times, but Harley (1956) offers a more likely explanation. He suggests that bramble seeds are carried from Scandinavia by Fieldfares. These birds from northern Scandinavia migrate south-westwards through Britain in autumn and are regular winter visitors to upland areas in the Highlands. They arrive in Scotland from mid-August onwards, when Arctic Bramble fruits are ripe in Scandinavia, and they might well not void seeds from fruits they have eaten until they reach Scotland. Very few seeds would ever germinate successfully here, and none would be able to set seed this far south. Arctic Bramble is therefore best regarded as a short-lived, sporadic invader in Scotland.

Ben Vrackie

Continuing eastwards, the next stop on our exploration of Perthshire might be Ben Vrackie, which can be approached by a pleasant walk from Moulin, above the town of Pitlochry. The crags beneath the summit of this relatively low hill (841m) are a mixture of acidic and strongly calcareous Dalradian schists. The calcareous influence is also evident in flushes below the crags.

From the Moulin car park, the path leads initially through woodland, then out on open moorland where Alpine Bistort, Mountain Everlasting and Lesser Twayblade might be spotted. The most interesting area on the moor is a small calcareous flush beside the track which is home to Yellow Mountain Saxifrage, Scottish Asphodel, Broad-leaved Cottongrass and Few-flowered Sedge. It also holds a colony with an interesting history of Brown Bog-rush, the next of our mountain enigmas, a puzzling plant whose true story has only recently been recognised.

★★★ Brown Bog-rush *Schoenus ferrugineus*

This rather unremarkable plant has a remarkable history in Scotland. My well-worn copy of the standard flora that I grew up with (Clapham, Tutin & Warburg, 1962) records it growing 'at the wet, peaty margin of Loch Tummel, mid-Perth, in base-rich flushes, very local (?extinct)'. It was discovered there in 1884 by James Brebner, the first rector of Harris Academy in Dundee, on a stretch of shore that was flooded in winter but where the plants could grow and flower when the water level fell in summer. A photograph by Robert Moyes Adam, reproduced here, shows it growing there in 1934, but it always seemed odd to me that it should have such a highly restricted distribution.

The history of Brown Bog-rush in Scotland in three images. **ABOVE LEFT**: R M Adam (see Chapter 11) took this photograph of a tussock of bog-rush on the shore of Loch Tummel in 1936. At the time, this was the only known habitat for the species.

ABOVE RIGHT: In April 1950 John Berry, the first Scottish Director of the Nature Conservancy, photographed the site created for the bog-rush at the level Loch Tummel was expected to reach, once dammed. He was showing it to a royal visitor, the Maharajkumar of Bhutan (in hat).

RIGHT: Dr Rosalind Smith of the Nature Conservancy Council in 1981 monitoring one of the large populations of Brown Bog-rush she discovered in calcareous flushes near Blair Atholl in Perthshire.

In 1945, the North of Scotland Hydro-Electric Board announced plans to dam the loch and raise its water level by over 5m to form the reservoir for a power station. Alerted to the threat, members of the BSBI made plans to move some of the bog-rush plants to safe sites (Brookes, 1981). A new habitat, 8m by 3m in extent, was prepared behind a rough stone bund at the planned new loch level, as shown in the second photograph reproduced above. Transplants were made into the site in early 1950 as the dam was closed. The water reached its new level in October 1950, inundating the site as planned, but during the subsequent winter the retaining wall was destroyed by the increased wave action on the enlarged loch and the plants soon vanished.

Other 'rescue transplants' were made to similar habitats nearby, but none survived. The only survivor of the official transplant programme was in the University Botanic Garden in Cambridge. In 1975, Brian Brookes, warden of the Kindrogan Field Centre, moved 29 offspring of the Cambridge plant into three sites on the north shore of Loch Tummel. All the transplants at one site died within the first year but some survived at another site until at least 1995. At the third site, beside a broad forestry track near the loch, plants protected within a small exclosure were swiftly smothered by grass, but one unprotected plant survived on an open, stony, calcareous flush and was looking healthy when I visited it in 1982 (I believe it has since died).

Another transplant was made 'unofficially' in 1945 by a Liverpool botanist called J A Whellans, who was concerned at the plant's extreme rarity. He moved single plants to two calcareous flushes on the slopes below Ben Vrackie. Some botanists criticised him for daring to move the plant a few kilometres out of the botanical vice-county of Mid Perth into East Perth, but his plants survived and increased in numbers throughout the time I knew them, until by 1993 there were 13 and 20 plants in the two colonies.

The problem was that most of these early transplants were into gravelly flushes resembling the bog-rush's habitat beside Loch Tummel, without reference to its range elsewhere in Europe, where it is known around two centres in the Alpine foothills of central Europe and around the Baltic Sea and Norway. It grows there on open peaty moorland and base-rich flushes, quite unlike the gravelly site beside Loch Tummel. It seems that only Whellans may have taken this into account with his criticised but successful transplantation.

The final irony came in 1979, when Dr Rosalind Smith, a dedicated Perthshire botanist who worked for the (then) Nature Conservancy Council, discovered two populations of Brown Bog-rush as part of a routine survey of two Sites of Special Scientific Interest on either side of

Brown Bog-rush: one of the surviving plants that were transplanted to the slopes of Ben Vrackie in 1945.

the River Tummel near Blair Atholl, at altitudes between 190m and 390m (which scarcely even qualifies them as submontane; see third photo on p.263). Even more ironically, one of these was in East Perth vice-county, only about 5km from Whellan's transplant site on Ben Vrackie. Ten populations are now known at six locations in these two areas, the largest of which holds over 9,000 plants. The typical habitat is grazed flushes within calcareous grassland, often in association with montane species like Yellow Mountain Saxifrage and Alpine Rush. There is nothing otherwise unusual about the vegetation at these sites, suggesting that the bog-rush may be hanging on there as a relict of a much wider distribution in the past (Wheeler *et al.*, 1983). It seems unlikely that seeds could have been carried from either of these two localities to Loch Tummel, so I suspect the plants there must have come from some other population that may or may not still survive elsewhere in the Tummel catchment.

The path continues onwards, past crags that hold a few plants of Stone Bramble, then crosses the Loch a' Choire dam. The crags above the dam are a site, in particular, for two species considered further below: Purple Oxytropis grows on ledges on the crags at about 650m, while Alpine Milk-vetch is more likely to be found on the steep, grassy slope beneath, along with Alpine Lady's-mantle and Alpine Mouse-ear. Other species on the crags include Green Spleenwort, Holly Fern, Whortle-leaved Willow, Globeflower, Mountain Pansy, Hoary Whitlow-grass, Alpine Cinquefoil, Alpine Saw-wort and Rock Sedge. A flush beside the main summit track is home to Alpine Willowherb and Three-flowered Rush. The exposed summit area offers spectacular views in all directions, with the usual species of windswept summits. Sibbaldia grows in a few snow hollows nearby, and Cloudberry on deeper areas of peat.

There are further interesting sites nearby. Sticky Catchfly grows on a relatively inaccessible crag in the forest near Moulin. Tullach Hill, near Blair Atholl, is an area of limestone in places reminiscent of the Teesdale sugar limestone, with Green Spleenwort, Alpine Bistort and Yellow Mountain Saxifrage. Glen Tilt is not an easy area to explore, but craggy ground at the head of Gleann Mhairc is a site for Downy Willow, along with Alpine Cinquefoil, Alpine Saw-wort and Sheathed Sedge. Alpine Lady-fern and Hair Sedge are recorded below Beinn Mheadhonach, and Whortle-leaved Willow, Mountain Avens, Rock Speedwell and Hair Sedge are amongst species recorded from the calcareous crags of Creag Mhor, further into the glen. Alpine Milk-vetch was reported here in 1978 but has not been seen since.

OPPOSITE PAGE: Alpine Milk-vetch grows in just the small area of grassy slope in the foreground, below the summit of Ben Vrackie. The crags behind are the site for an interesting range of montane plants.

Alpine Milk-vetch *Astragalus alpinus*

This rare species of lime-flushed mountain grassland is a delicate member of the pea family. Its silky leaves have 8–12 pairs of small oblong leaflets with a single, unpaired leaflet at the tip. Its short flower stalks are topped with a cluster of delicate flowers that are pale blue, tipped with purple. It is known only from the four sites where we have met it already: Glen Doll, Creag an Dail Bheag, where it reaches its highest altitude of 770m, a slope near the limestone of Cairnwell, and here on Ben Vrackie and its immediate neighbour Meall an Daimh. There are about 20 discrete colonies in these areas, most of which are small, but one contains more than 10,000 plants (Wigginton, 1999).

At many of its sites, plants are heavily grazed by sheep and deer, and few flowerheads survive to produce seeds. The best-known population, on Ben Vrackie, is on a well-used botanical path. I worry that plants here are vulnerable to trampling and would urge visitors to keep off the open grassy slope on which it grows. Outside Scotland, it is a plant of northern Europe, mountains from the Pyrenees to the Carpathians, Asia, Greenland and North America.

Purple Oxytropis *Oxytropis halleri*

Although its appearance shows its close relationship to the previous species, this is a much more robust plant, with a stout, hairy stem and clusters of 5–20 bright purple flowers. Its leaves are divided into 10–15 pairs of oval leaflets, with an unpaired leaflet at the tip. They are

A fine plant of Purple Oxytropis on the crags of Ben Vrackie. The dammed reservoir of Loch a' Choire is visible below.

covered in silky grey hairs which help to reduce water loss and protect the plant from drought.

Purple Oxytropis (see additional photo p.258) has an intriguingly discontinuous range in Scotland. As well as the cliffs of Ben Vrackie, at altitudes up to 760m, it is recorded on Ben Chonzie in Perthshire. There are old records also for the hills above Glen Garry in Perthshire and east of Loch Creran in Argyll. But I first met it in a very different habitat from these submontane sites, just a few metres above sea level on a gravelly platform at the mouth of the River Naver in Sutherland (see p.366). As we will see in Chapter 17, it also grows on a hillside overlooking Strathy Bay, a little further east along the north coast (probably its northernmost site in the world). It is likely to have disappeared from cliffs on the Black Isle in Easter Ross after a long decline there, but still grows on the other side of the Cromarty Firth on a cliff a little way north of the North Sutor. In southern Scotland, it is found on the Mull of Galloway at no more than 35m above sea level. Construction of the railway line north of the Forth Rail Bridge destroyed the site in Fife where it was first discovered by the Reverend John Lightfoot in 1777.

Most of these sites are on calcareous limestone, schist or sandstone cliffs, or are enriched by shell sand blowing inland, but on Ben Chonzie it grows on an acidic rock intrusion. Its coastal sites in Scotland are somewhat surprising, perhaps reflecting the wind exposure there, because in the rest of Europe it is definitely a montane species in the Pyrenees, Alps and Carpathians.

Schiehallion and Glen Lyon

The 1,083m summit of Schiehallion is rather dull and heavily eroded, but outcrops of limestone low on the hill host Green Spleenwort, Yellow Mountain Saxifrage and Scottish Asphodel. Bearberry and Chickweed Wintergreen grow on the open hillside. Below Schiehallion, one of the few Scottish limestone pavements in Scotland is home to Lily-of-the-Valley and masses of Scottish Asphodel, but Limestone Fern, still present in 1980, may have died out. Hair Sedge and Alpine Rush grow in a wet flush nearby.

North of Kinloch Rannoch, limestone outcrops on the southern slopes of Beinn a' Chuallaich have Alpine Cinquefoil, Alpine Penny-cress and Rock Sedge in small numbers, with Dwarf Birch on the moorland nearby. Species recorded from Cam Chreag on the north

The area of limestone at around 350m is the most interesting area botanically below Schiehallion. The distant view here looks past Dunalastair Reservoir to Loch Rannoch.

side of Glen Lyon include Alpine Woodsia, Net-leaved Willow, Alpine Saxifrage, Mountain Avens, Rock Speedwell and Alpine Meadow-grass. Even more exclusively, Alpine Forget-me-not was discovered there by a botanical society trip in 2003 (matching an old record from Carn Gorm nearby). A little further west, crags low on Stuchd an Lochain are home to Moss Campion and Purple Saxifrage. Gullies below the summit have good quantities of Mossy Cyphel, and Alpine Bartsia and Black Alpine-sedge grow on the higher cliffs. Russet Sedge is recorded from the slopes below the ridge of Creag an Fheadain.

Across the southern Highlands

If we move south and east from here, Ben Chonzie, north of Comrie, can be regarded as a southern outlier of the Breadalbane hills. The east-facing calcareous cliffs at the head of Glen Turret have a lot in common with the richest Breadalbane sites. Hoary Whitlow-grass, Mountain

Pansy and Alpine Cinquefoil are notably abundant, while rarer species include Alpine Woodsia, Downy Willow, Mountain Willow, Two-flowered Rush, Black Alpine-sedge, the non-viviparous form of Alpine Meadow-grass and, as already noted, a flourishing colony of Purple Oxytropis on a rather pale-coloured igneous rock intrusion.

Moving south-westwards, the corries of Ben Vorlich, south of Loch Earn in Perthshire, are home to Holly Fern, Alpine Cinquefoil, Alpine Saw-wort and the rare Scottish Pearlwort. Alpine Mouse-ear and Hair Sedge are recorded on its drier slopes. Ben Ledi near Callander is a pleasantly accessible hill with a nice range of commoner montane species including Holly Fern, Alpine Willowherb, Roseroot and Sibbaldia.

North of Ben Ledi, the road along the Braes of Balquhidder past Loch Voil leads to Inverlochlarig, the best access point for Stob Binnean, a delightfully rich and varied hill. The best approach is to climb from Inverlochlarig onto Stob Invercarnaig, then follow the shoulder north to the Stob Binnean summit at 1,165m. This ridge has some of the best solifluction terracing I have seen anywhere in Scotland, where ice thaw allows wedges of vegetation to slither down the hillside leaving bare, gravelly platforms behind them. These terraces support the typical species of windswept shoulders including

Mossy Cyphel is an attractive, cushion-forming plant with yellow-green flowers. It grows on Stuchd an Lochain in Glen Lyon and Stob Coire an Lochain below Stob Binnean.

Dwarf Willow, Dwarf Cudweed and Stiff Sedge. Flushed areas have the commoner saxifrages, Moss Campion and Three-flowered Rush. Sibbaldia and Mossy Cyphel grow in open areas below Stob Coire an Lochain. Alpine Saxifrage is recorded from more acidic rocks, along with Arctic Mouse-ear, which we will meet in the next chapter. The neighbouring hill of Ben More is less interesting botanically, despite its slightly greater elevation (1,174m).

To the east of Stob Binnean, the rocky summit of Meall na Dige is even richer, with Downy Willow and Alpine Saw-wort near its summit and Alpine Mouse-ear and Three-flowered Rush on its slopes, along with two more species we have not previously encountered: Rock Whitlow-grass and Two-flowered Rush. On the west side of Inverlochlarig Glen, the steep rocky area of Creagan Dubha below Stob Garbh is a site for Mountain Willow and Alpine Saw-wort, with Two-flowered Rush nearby.

South from here, Ben Lomond on the east shore of Loch Lomond is the most southerly Munro at 974m. As well as many of the common montane species, Spring Sandwort, Alpine Cinquefoil, Alpine Saw-wort, Black Alpine-sedge and Alpine Meadow-grass are recorded from its crags. Sibbaldia and Dwarf Cudweed grow on its summit slopes. On the west shore of Loch Lomond, Alpine Saxifrage and Interrupted Clubmoss grow on the 'other' Ben Vorlich in Dumbartonshire. Alpine Saxifrage, Sibbaldia, Scottish Asphodel and Glaucous Meadow-grass are recorded near its summit, and Russet Sedge grows in several wet flushes. Trailing Azalea, long gone from Ben Lomond, is recorded here down to the unusually low altitude of 460m. Four of these species merit further consideration before we move on.

Rock Whitlow-grass is told from its rather commoner relative, Hoary Whitlow-grass, by its short, usually leafless stems, and its seedpods, shown here, which are flattened but never twisted.

Rock Whitlow-grass *Draba norvegica*

Rock Whitlow-grass is much rarer than its close relative, Hoary Whitlow-grass. It is a weak competitor, confined to ledges and crevices on steep crags or amongst boulders, particularly where late-lying snow maintains an open habitat. Because it is usually self-pollinating, it can produce copious seed to help its spread in base-rich habitats, although, without the benefits of cross-pollination, all these offspring are genetically identical to the parent.

It is confined to the Scottish Highlands, mainly on schist or sandstone rocks. It has a rather western distribution, including rock ledges in the Cuillin hills of Skye. It is known from a remarkably low altitude of around 320m near Kylescu in West Sutherland to just a few metres below the summit of Ben Lawers. It is an arctic-subarctic species, found widely in Scandinavia and Iceland, west to Canada and east to northern Russia. Meall na Dige beside Stob Binnean might therefore be the southernmost point of its world range, unless it can be confirmed from old sites in Dumbartonshire.

Mossy Cyphel *Minuartia sedoides*

This attractive plant has yellow-green, petal-less flowers that barely rise above a dense, pale green cushion of leaves (see photos on p.44 and p.270). Its distribution in Scotland is broadly similar to that of the previous species, but its world range is totally different. In fact, the Scottish mountains are the only place where these two species coincide, because Mossy Cyphel is one of the few British montane plants that is found in the Alps and Pyrenees, and one or two mountains further east, but not in the Arctic. Sites around Ben Hope in Sutherland are therefore the northernmost site for the species in the world. It is a plant of exposed mountain grasslands, heaths and rock ledges, usually on calcareous schists in the southern Highlands but sometimes on more acidic rocks further north. It is recorded from altitudes of just 165m in the hills of Rum to 1,213m in the Breadalbanes. It is also found in the mountains of Mull and on the Trotternish ridge of Skye.

Two-flowered Rush: the two flowers (or later fruits) are 'terraced' on the inflorescence so that one lies slightly above the other. They are usually overtopped by a curved, leafy bract.

Two-flowered Rush *Juncus biglumis*

This neatly tufted little rush is reminiscent of Three-flowered Rush, which we met in Chapter 8, but is much rarer. It usually has just a single, short, slightly curved stem with a few leaves at its base which half wrap around the stem. As the name suggests, the stem is topped by a pair of flowers (followed later by fruits), usually with a leafy bract that reaches above them.

Two-flowered Rush is restricted to gravelly mountain flushes, mostly in the south-west Highlands. It has some sites on the eastern edge of the Cairngorms and in the Drumochter Hills and a few more in the north-west Highlands as far north as Ben More Assynt (although it may have died out there). It also grows in the mountains of Rum and on the Trotternish peninsula of Skye, with an altitude range from 370m on Rum to 1,137m in the Breadalbanes. Elsewhere it is a widespread arctic species, also found in the mountains of North America and with a single, odd discontinuous record in the central Austrian Alps.

Russet Sedge *Carex saxatilis*

Of all the sedges, this comes nearest to being truly attractive. Its rather curved fruiting stems appear at intervals along a far-creeping underground stem, so it grows in scattered patches. Its three-sided stems are up to 40 cm tall, surrounded by a tuft of narrow leaves, and its egg-shaped spikes of female flowers give rise to fruits that are the colour of burnished chestnuts. In Britain, the species is entirely confined to the Scottish Highlands, with its main distribution towards the western end of the Breadalbanes. It is rare in the Angus hills, including sites in Coire Sharroch (along with its hybrid, Mountain Bladder-sedge, as we saw in the last chapter) and below Glas Maol. It grows at a number of sites in the Cairngorms, including the northern slopes of Ben Macdui, and is scattered across the north-west Highlands as far north as Foinaven, but not on any of the islands.

It typically grows in calcareous flush communities, often where the water is draining from melting snow-beds higher in a corrie, and is regularly found with Two-flowered, Three-flowered and Chestnut Rush. It is recorded at altitudes from 460m in Glen Clunie in Lochalsh to 1,164m in the Breadalbanes. It is a circumpolar arctic and subarctic species, on which basis a record from Beinn Ime in Argyll would qualify as its southernmost site.

Russet Sedge is a very handsome sedge. Its inflorescence has a single male spike at the tip, with one or two egg-shaped female inflorescences below. These develop into rich russet-brown fruits.

The Breadalbane hills

chapter thirteen

As the map in Chapter 2 (p.28) convincingly showed, the part of Britain with the densest concentration of montane species is the wonderful area we have now reached: the Breadalbane hills of Perthshire (pronounced roughly 'bred-all-bin', and meaning 'the upper part of Alba', the former kingdom of the Picts and Scots). In these hills, a band of crumbly rocks outcrop at just the right altitudes in just the right climatic conditions to allow a remarkable range of arctic-alpine plants to survive and flourish. The riches of these hills were first recognised by botanical explorers and plant collectors in the 1770s. Since then, they have been more visited and better studied than most other Scottish hills. As we will see, one hill in particular has long been regarded as something of a botanical Mecca, but montane species are spread widely throughout the entire range.

Mountains of schist

The Breadalbane hills are formed from the same band of calcareous schist that produced the rich flora we saw in Chapter 11 at Caenlochan and Coire Fee. These schists were folded and deformed during the early stages of the great land movement called the Caledonian Orogeny. This folding weakened them so that they erode more readily, releasing basic minerals into the soil. The mica schists in the Breadalbanes seem to be particularly intensely folded. This, together with steepness of the cliffs and the action of frost at such high altitudes, makes them especially friable, so they erode into fine, silvery flakes and produce strongly base-rich soils. I have stood beneath a rich Breadalbane cliff on a still day and actually heard erosion at work, as tiny slivers of rock broke off and pattered down the cliff face like raindrops. Schist occurs as outcrops on steep, crumbling crags at high elevations almost to the

OPPOSITE PAGE: The heavily folded and crumbly schist on crags below the summit of Ben Lawers erodes to produce a rich soil which supports a remarkable array of montane species.

Looking towards the summit of Ben Lawers from the south. The flushes below Beinn Ghlas, in the foreground here, support a particularly interesting flora.

summit of Ben Lawers, the tallest mountain in the range at 1,214m, but drops to slightly lower altitudes on Ben Lui. Altitude, exposure and the rich soils produced by friable rocks on steep, inaccessible crags combine to provide perfect conditions for montane species.

Ben Lawers and Meall nan Tarmachan to its west are the richest of the hills here. They have long been known as a prime botanical site, but sadly they have suffered as a result. In the past, I have taken small groups of botanists to explore the most famous crags here and, as we left, I looked back to see our route recorded as a fresh erosion scar on the gravelly slope beneath the crags. Even worse, rare plants still occasionally disappear into the collecting bags of unscrupulous (and criminal) individuals. I could not possibly omit Ben Lawers from this book, but in this chapter I want to encourage readers to explore the Breadalbane range more widely and so reduce the pressure on Lawers itself. I will therefore begin in the west with Ben Lui and progress eastwards, revealing more of the special plants of the Breadalbanes at each step of the journey.

Ben Lui and the Argyll hills

Because of its rich flora, Ben Lui (more correctly spelt Beinn Laoigh, meaning the 'hill of the calf' from the shape of its summit) is protected

as a National Nature Reserve. It marks the western end of the band of mica schist that runs through the Breadalbanes, but here it occurs at a much lower elevation, between 460m and 600m. It is therefore the mid-slopes, rather than the summit at 1,130m, that are of most botanical interest. Almost all the species that are common in the Breadalbanes and many of the rarities grow here, but they are scattered across small crags and scree slopes, so exploring Ben Lui is like a botanical Easter-egg hunt!

Each group of crags below the summit of Ben Lui has a slightly different flora, so it is best to take time to explore them all.

The usual approach to Ben Lui is along the track beside the River Cononish, now developed for the gold mine at Eas Anie. The east-facing cliffs on the Perthshire side of the summit are the most visited and best known. Mossy Saxifrage, Moss Campion, Alpine Bistort and Scottish Asphodel on the lower slopes point to the riches above. In places the cliffs have a rich tall-herb community with banks of Globeflower, Roseroot, Wood Cranesbill, Melancholy Thistle and Wild Angelica. Green Spleenwort, Holly Fern and Northern Bedstraw are common on the cliffs, but Mountain Avens is more localised. Scattered plants of Alpine Bartsia are a particular feature on the cliffs, and Northern Rock-cress (a new species on our journey) grows at several spots here, but nowhere else in the Breadalbanes.

A north-facing cliff on the border with Argyll is even richer, with masses of Mountain Avens and scattered plants of Alpine Bartsia. This is a site for an even wider range of species including Mountain Bladder-fern, Mountain Willow, Rock Whitlow-grass, Alpine Scurvy-grass, Northern Rock-cress, Alpine Saw-wort, Black Alpine-

A group of botanists exploring the rich crags of Beinn Udlaidh, south of Glen Orchy, on a field meeting organised by the BSBI and Botanic Society of Scotland.

sedge, Hair Sedge and Alpine Meadow-grass. Alpine Woodsia, Net-leaved Willow and Whortle-leaved Willow also grow hereabouts, although I have never found them. The summit area is more acidic, with Parsley Fern in the screes and Alpine Lady-fern and Sibbaldia in late snow-beds.

A little south-west of Ben Lui, Meall nan Tighearn shares many of the same species, including Alpine Woodsia, Alpine Bartsia, Whortle-leaved Willow and abundant Mountain Willow. On the other side of Glen Lochy, the crags of Coire Ghamhnain below Beinn Udlaidh are somewhat less rich but have some classic Breadalbane species, including Mountain Male-fern, Alpine Saxifrage, Downy Willow, Alpine Saw-wort and Black Alpine-sedge. Alpine Woodsia seems to be particularly prolific here: in 1985 a group of us counted 22 plants, some with as many as 30 fronds.

A little further north, the crags below Beinn an Dothaidh also have a rich flora. The east-facing crags of Coire a' Ghabhalach have good numbers of Alpine Woodsia, as well as Downy Willow, Rock Speedwell, Glaucous Meadow-grass and many of the commoner Breadalbane species. The north-facing crags of Coire Achaladair, above about 610m, are another site for Alpine Woodsia and Alpine Bartsia, with Mountain Bladder-fern, Downy Willow, Mountain Willow, Alpine Mouse-ear, Russet Sedge and Black Alpine-sedge.

Mountain Bladder-fern
Cystopteris montana

Mountain Bladder-fern always forms spreading patches amongst mountain rocks, compared to the neat 'shuttlecocks' of its commoner relative Brittle Bladder-fern.

This delicate lacy fern is restricted to unstable gravelly slopes and ungrazed mossy ledges on cool, moist, north-facing cliffs always with some calcareous seepage. Its more lowland relative Brittle Bladder-fern also occurs in mountains, at altitudes up to 1,192m on Ben Lawers, but it always forms an upright crown of fronds, whereas Mountain Bladder-fern spreads by creeping rhizomes from which single fronds arise at intervals. Its main stronghold is the Breadalbanes (although it is rare even there) with a few other sites from mid-Perthshire to Argyll and west Inverness-shire. It is recorded from 490m on Ben Lui to 1,070m on Aonach Beag. There are outlying populations in Caenlochan Glen and Coire Fee in Angus (although it may have died out from the latter site), in Coire Garbhlach in the Cairngorms and on a shoulder of Ben Vrackie in Perthshire. It is long-gone from its single recorded site on Helvellyn in the Lake District. Outside Scotland it is found in northern Europe, the Pyrenees, Alps and Caucasus, Asia and the mountains of North America.

Northern Rock-cress *Arabidopsis petraea*

The flowering stems of Northern Rock-cress rarely exceed 15cm in height, topped by a cluster of white or pale mauve four-petalled flowers.

Northern Rock-cress has gone through a whole series of scientific names in my years of botanising, as taxonomic ideas have changed over its relationship with other species. It is a distinctive plant with a rosette of paddle-shaped, lobed leaves on long stalks, and clustered inflorescences of white or pinkish four-petalled flowers. It grows most typically on mountain rock ledges and in crevices, usually with little other vegetation, and sometimes spreads into scree slopes beneath the cliffs. It seems to prefer hard, bluffy rocks, irrespective of whether these are acidic or basic.

Its scattered distribution is probably best explained as chance survivals from a wider post-glacial range. It still hangs on in some of the corries of Snowdon, but is then absent northwards until the hills on the Cowal Peninsula in Argyll. It grows on Ben Lui and its neighbours Ben Oss and Beinn Dubhchraig, but nowhere else in the Breadalbanes. I think of the Cairngorms as its real heartland, and from there it is readily washed down onto shingles beside the Rivers Dee and Avon, and even at the mouth of the River Spey. It also occurs at scattered sites in the west Highlands, as far north as Ben Hope in Sutherland, on the Ardnamurchan Peninsula in Argyll, on Mull and in the hills of Rum. On Skye it is found in the Cuillin hills, on the Trotternish ridge and on Raasay, and in Shetland it is a rare species of the serpentine rocks of Fetlar and Unst. As a result, its altitude range is remarkable, from almost sea level on Shetland cliffs to 1,220m on Braeriach in the Cairngorms. In northern and central Europe it is also confined to open habitats amongst rocks, mainly in the mountains but also down to nearly sea level. It is common species in Icelandic fellfields and occurs also in Siberia and North America.

Glen Lochay

The hills around Glen Lochay, west from Killin, are some of the richest in the Breadalbanes. It is much more satisfying to discover some of the area's specialities here than on the well-worn paths to more famous sites. On the north side of the glen, calcareous schists on the north face of Meall Ghaordaidh have fine tall-herb ledges and a profusion of the commoner lime-loving montane species. More restricted species include Net-leaved Willow, Mountain Willow, Alpine Saxifrage, Black Alpine-sedge and Mountain Bladder-fern. Russet Sedge flowers quite abundantly in some boggy areas, with another new species, Chestnut Rush, as a rarer associate.

Continuing anticlockwise around the glen, Meall nan Subh has base-rich flushes on its lower slopes with Scottish Asphodel, Three-flowered Rush and Hair Sedge. Peaty areas near the summit have abundant Cloudberry with patches of Dwarf Cornel and Bog Bilberry. Dwarf Willow and Trailing Azalea are frequent on the summit ridge, and this is also the southernmost location in Britain for Arctic Bearberry, which we will meet in Chapter 15.

Beinn Heasgarnich (Sheasgarnaich) has spectacular summit heath vegetation and late snow-bed communities with Sibbaldia. Moss Campion and Mossy Cyphel are abundant on its exposed slopes, along with Alpine Saw-wort, Scottish Asphodel and Hair Sedge. One east-facing crag has a fine relict scrub zone, mainly of Downy and Dark-

Roseroot and Downy Willow on a rich crag below Meall na Samhna in Glen Lochay. The neighbouring Meall Ghaordaidh can be seen in the background.

leaved Willow. At the western end of Glen Lochay, Creag Mhor (1,047m) is worth exploring (its name simply means 'big crag' so perhaps it is not surprising that the map shows two of them in this one glen!). The broken, south-facing cliffs and the grassy slopes beneath have abundant displays of Mountain Avens, Alpine Cinquefoil, Bog Bilberry and Net-leaved Willow. Alpine Saxifrage, Mountain Willow, Whortle-leaved Willow, Alpine Bartsia, Alpine Meadow-grass and several sites for Alpine Woodsia are also recorded on these cliffs. Chestnut Rush and second new species, False Sedge, grow in damp flushes below the cliffs. Downy Willow is found on the nearby ridge of Cam Chreag.

On the south side of the glen, Meall na Samhna is probably the most visited hill, because its riches are well known to botanists and access is relatively easy along the Allt Innischoarach or Allt Dhubhchlair burns. The richest site is the east-facing crags overlooking Coire Dhubhchlair. Species there include Alpine Cinquefoil, Alpine Bartsia, Two-flowered Rush, Russet Sedge, Black Alpine-sedge and the viviparous form of Alpine Meadow-grass. Downy Willow and a good population of Woolly Willow also grow here, although some plants seem confusingly intermediate between them. Alpine Woodsia is found on nearby crags, along with a few patches of Mountain Bladder-fern. In 2003, Boreal Fleabane was discovered below the summit of Meall Eoghainn, west of Meall na Samhna, at what is almost certainly its southernmost site in the world. Two new species therefore merit attention before we continue eastwards.

Chestnut Rush *Juncus castaneus*

I have only ever found this handsome rush, with its dense heads of dark, chestnut-brown fruits, after a lot of searching. Its populations are always small, and I suspect its stems are quickly nibbled off by sheep or deer. It grows in base-rich, boggy sites, usually beside small

runnels, and on damp rock ledges. I only know it from the corries of Coire Sharroch and Glas Maol in Angus and below the summit of Beinn Ghlas in the Ben Lawers NNR. It is also recorded from Coire Kander in Angus, at scattered sites through the Breadalbanes west to Ben Lui, then northwards to the slopes of Beinn Dearg and Ben Wyvis in Ross-shire. It is very much a plant of the higher mountains, from 610m on Sgurr na Lapaich in Glen Cannich, Inverness-shire, to 1,030m on Beinn Heasgarnich in Glen Lochay. It is found throughout arctic regions of the world, and south to the Alps and Urals and to New Mexico in North America.

False Sedge *Kobresia simpliciuscula*

I suspect this plant is often overlooked, because it usually stands less than 10cm tall, with narrow, inconspicuous heads of spike-like flowers. I have found it beside Cow Green Reservoir in Upper Teesdale at around 360m and I have seen it high on the slopes of Meall Garbh, beside Ben Lawers, where it reaches its highest altitude of 1,065m. It grows in sedge-rich, calcareous turf and amongst hummocks of vegetation in highly calcareous, open flushes. It is fairly common on the limestone of Widdybank Fell, but its main centre of distribution is in the south Highlands, from the slopes around Beinn a' Ghlo in Perthshire west to Ben Lui and Glen Orchy in Argyll, but nowhere north of this. Elsewhere it is recorded in mountains from the Pyrenees to the Caucasus, in northern Europe, Greenland and North America.

TOP: Chestnut Rush grows up to 30cm tall, and is recognised by its dense heads of dark chestnut-brown fruits.

ABOVE: False Sedge is a rather undistinguished plant to non-botanical eyes. In a few choice sites in the Breadalbanes it forms an extensive turf, as here, with tens of thousands of plants.

Ben Lawers and its neighbours

As we have seen over the previous pages, most of the best 'Breadalbane species', including some notable concentrations of them, can be seen elsewhere, without adding to the pressure that already impacts on Ben Lawers, partly because of the large number of hillwalkers attracted to Scotland's tenth highest hill (1,214m). Furthermore, some of these species are missing from Lawers: there is only a very old record for Mountain Avens here, and Alpine Bartsia seems to have disappeared from the meadows below Ben Lawers because of overgrazing. However there is no denying that the steep grassy slopes and crags of Ben Lawers and its neighbours are especially rich because the mica schist outcrops at its highest altitude here, almost to the summit. For a few species, the Ben Lawers area is the only Breadalbane site.

The National Trust for Scotland (NTS) owns and manages the NNR here, which encompasses Ben Lawers and parts of eight other mountaintops. In recent years, the NTS has been trying to reduce people pressure on the fragile plant communities. It removed a high-altitude visitor centre and a large car park which were attracting too many casual walkers to the hill, but continues to welcome visitors with a special interest. Sadly, progress has stalled on buying out grazing rights on the hill held by local farmers, so the area continues to be heavily grazed by sheep and deer despite its international importance and its status as an NNR and a European protected site.

Meall nan Tarmachan, to the west of Lawers, is a magnificent hill. In 1996, the NTS bought a substantial area of land south and east of the summit, and began an imaginative project to recreate an expanse of montane scrub there. This was masterminded by David Mardon, the enthusiastic property manager for the reserve until 2008 and a driving force behind the Montane Scrub Action Group. Three large grazing exclosures were erected, the largest of which covers 190ha at an altitude between 520m and 920m. The land here is probably already the best site in Britain for Mountain Willow, with small populations also of Downy Willow and high-altitude Dark-leaved Willow. More plants of the latter two species have been planted out in the exclosures, along with Juniper and other montane tree species. Additionally, over 24,000 Downy Willows had been transplanted by 2007, plus 60 Woolly Willows, which are much rarer locally. The project was expanded again in 2011–2012 to include an area of submontane woodland, bringing the total fenced area to 350ha without restricting access for human visitors. The restored scrub is providing an ideal habitat for the montane community of tall herbs, and the project clearly illustrates just how unnaturally denuded many of our mountain slopes have become.

One of the grazing exclosures protects the crags that overlook the hydroelectric reservoir of Lochan na Lairige. These crags are worth exploring as a site for Holly Fern, Hoary Whitlow-grass, Alpine Mouse-ear, Alpine Cinquefoil, Mountain Avens, Downy Willow, Mountain Willow, Hair Sedge, Black Alpine-sedge, Alpine Meadow-grass and a few plants of Alpine Woodsia.

On the other side of Lawers, the flora around the summit of Meall Garbh is somewhat more acidic in nature, with Alpine Lady-fern, Parsley Fern and Three-flowered Rush. Steep calcareous outcrops below the summit are the home for Alpine Woodsia, Mountain Willow, Hair Sedge and Rock Sedge, along with many of the commoner arctic-alpines. One approach to Meall Garbh and its neighbouring peaks of An Stuc and Ben Lawers begins from the Ben Lawers Hotel overlooking Loch Tay. The route then follows the Lawers Burn to Lochan nan Cat. Scottish Asphodel grows beside the burn, and the moor below the lochan has a good range of peat alpines. Even relatively low-altitude crags have plants like Moss Campion, Mossy Cyphel, Alpine Mouse-ear and Roseroot. Some calcareous flushes on the slopes below Meall Garbh are particularly rich, with an assemblage to delight rush and sedge enthusiasts, including Two-flowered Rush, False Sedge, Russet Sedge, Close-headed Alpine-sedge and two even rarer Lawers specialities that we have not yet met: Scorched Alpine-sedge and Bristle Sedge.

These flushes are also famed as the site for another plant that was long regarded as special to the area, and indeed endemic to Britain. The plant was called Mountain Scurvy-grass and given the scientific name *Cochlearia micacea*. Rich & Dalby (1996) suggested that its range also included sites in Angus, Ben Nevis and possibly Beinn Dearg in Wester Ross. I admit that the sturdy little plants that grow on the calcareous flushes below Meall Garbh look different, but I have never been confident that I could tell them conclusively from similar plants in mountain springs and flushes elsewhere.

Now work by Estelle Gill, a PhD researcher at Edinburgh University, has confirmed my doubts (Gill, 2007). She investigated genetic and morphological variation within scurvy-grass populations, and found that there was no clear-cut way to distinguish the plants called Mountain Scurvy-grass from other upland populations. She concluded that these plants are best regarded as a form of the scurvy-grass 'species complex' adapted to higher altitudes,

Stony, base-rich flushes around Meall Garbh, like this one, are the only site in Britain for a spiky little sedge called Bristle Sedge.

rather than a distinct species in their own right. Even Tim Rich, co-author of the 1996 paper, tells me that he 'doesn't believe in it any more', so I have removed Mountain Scurvy-grass from my montane list. Nevertheless, I think the scurvy-grasses on Meall Garbh remain interesting as an extreme adaptation of a highly variable plant.

Ben Lawers – the main approach

The route onto Ben Lawers that is most often used by Munro-baggers and botanists leaves from a small car park off the minor road to Lochan na Lairige. The path follows the Edramucky Burn, then climbs over Beinn Ghlas towards the summit of Lawers itself. The route passes through another exclosure planted in the late 1990s with Mountain, Downy and Dark-leaved Willows, Juniper and various broadleaved trees. These are thriving, along with a rich display of herbaceous plants, free from the grazing of sheep and deer. The steep path up to the summit of Ben Ghlas is crossed at right angles by the conspicuous track of an old drove road. This offers an alternative botanical route towards the summit via Coire Odhar, with masses of Moss Campion, Mossy Cyphel and other common montane species beside the track.

Beyond the top of Coire Odhar, the path picks its way round another broad corrie with runnels fed by melting snow from below the summit of Beinn Ghlas. This is another classic site, with Hairy Stonecrop, Two-flowered Rush, Chestnut Rush and Russet Sedge. The low crags above these flushes were once a site for Mountain Avens, and still host two rare montane species – Snow Pearlwort and Alpine Pearlwort – with Scottish Pearlwort in grassland below the crags.

Various crags around Ben Lawers and its neighbours hold combinations of the most special Breadalbane species, including Net-leaved Willow, Alpine Saxifrage, Boreal Fleabane, Rock Speedwell, Alpine Gentian, Alpine Pearlwort and Alpine Meadow-grass. Some of them have Alpine Woodsia (around 200 clumps of this fern are regularly recorded in the reserve), and a few have an even more special plant and another of our three-star enigmas, Alpine Forget-me-not, at its only Scottish locality. A few rock ledges and loose, gravelly scree slopes support the largest British population of Mountain Sandwort at its southernmost European locality. Some unexpected species also occur here, such as Moschatel. This is normally a woodland species but finds similar conditions in the damp shade beneath large boulders here (see photo on p.22).

★★★ ALPINE FORGET-ME-NOT *Myosotis alpestris*

The British distribution of this attractive perennial perplexes me. It is a distinctive plant with hairy stems and showy flowers which open pink then turn sky-blue. In mainland Europe it is found quite commonly in the Pyrenees, Alps, Apennines, Tatra and Carpathian Mountains in species-rich grassland and stabilised scree slopes at altitudes between 1,600m and 2,900m. In Britain, as we saw in Chapter 8, it grows in heavily grazed limestone grassland on base-rich soils on Mickle Fell, Little Fell and Great Dun Fell in Upper Teesdale at altitudes between 685m and 740m. One site there is estimated to hold up to 100,000 plants (Wigginton, 1999). Within the Ben Lawers NNR it grows on several crags at altitudes up to 1,180m. It has disappeared from three of the ten locations from which it was previously known in the Lawers area, although a new site was recently discovered on the north side of Glen Lyon. So why is the species confined to just these two areas?

As we have seen, Ben Lawers represents the highest altitude at which friable, strongly calcareous rocks occur in Scotland. It makes sense therefore that ledges on the Lawers crags, and the grassy slopes beneath, might provide the right combination of base-rich soils and relatively extreme mountain climate to offer a refuge for Alpine Forget-me-not at its northernmost site in the world.

Alpine Forget-me-not is a showy plant with clusters of flowers, 8mm across, which open pink then turn sky blue. It is confined to two areas of Britain, around Ben Lawers and here in the limestone grassland of Little Fell in Cumbria.

Where it grows on grassy calcareous ledges on cliffs around Ben Lawers, Alpine Forget-me-not is never quite as showy as it is in Cumbria.

The Teesdale sites are undoubtedly special, but they are not as rich in montane species as the Lawers crags. One explanation may be that the extreme exposure of these Teesdale sites makes up for their comparatively low altitude. In his *Biological Flora* profile of the species, Elkington (1964) quoted figures from Dun Fell, near its Teesdale localities, showing that the estimated average temperature there remained below freezing for four months from December to March each winter. Based on figures for Perth, he estimated that its Perthshire sites were subjected to very similar temperatures. Both areas have freezing winter temperatures and relatively cool summers with frequent cloud and rain. However, in both Teesdale and the Breadalbanes the species generally grows on south-facing exposures, suggesting that it might need some relatively warm, sunny weather in summer, just as it would get in the Alps, to promote flowering and seed-set.

Elkington suggested that the species was frost-tolerant, at least in its Teesdale sites where its basal leaves sometimes last through the winter. However, when Teesdale plants are grown in gardens at lower altitudes, water gathers within their leaf rosettes in relatively mild damp winter weather, causing the plants to rot and die. Freezing winter temperatures may protect plants from this rotting effect, and may explain why it is confined to three relatively high-altitude fells, unlike other Teesdale rarities that grow at lower altitudes.

A combination of severe winter climate, sunny summer exposures and strongly calcareous soils may therefore explain why this species survives at just two British sites. Some accidental confirmation of this comes from Caenlochan in Angus, which otherwise supports many of the same species as the Lawers crags. In 1885, the Perthshire botanist Francis Buchanan White reported that a rather impulsive horticultural friend of his had sown seeds of Alpine Forget-me-not, derived from cultivated Ben Lawers plants, onto the Caenlochan crags. Although the introduced plants survived there until 1942, the species has since died out, I suspect because the crags are largely east-facing and so get less summer sun.

Snow Pearlwort used to grow near the summit of Lawers, but the erosion from countless hillwalkers put paid to that by 1979. Not that far from the summit, a hidden corner on the mountaintop holds a small colony of another new species, Drooping Saxifrage, which grows here with Alpine Saxifrage and Rock Whitlow-grass. Even rarer on Lawers is Highland Saxifrage, which we will meet in the next chapter. By 2004, only a single plant remained in the reserve after a decline assisted by unscrupulous collectors. Six young plants, grown from seed from plants in Glen Coe, were planted out on the hill that year to enhance the population – just in time, as it turned out, because the sole survivor perished by 2006. Six more plants were added in 2007. These transplants have begun to multiply, and by 2012 the count at two sites had reached 21 plants.

There is therefore no denying the botanical importance of Ben Lawers, which has introduced us to a further cluster of new species.

Drooping Saxifrage never grows as lushly in Scotland as these plants in the ideal conditions of the Tromsø Botanic Garden in arctic Norway. They often barely produce flowers in Scotland, and rely on their little red bulbils to spread.

Drooping Saxifrage *Saxifraga cernua*

In Britain, this rather unshowy saxifrage is found only on Ben Lawers, on the cliffs of Bidean nam Bian in Glen Coe, and high on the craggy and dangerous slopes of Ben Nevis and its outliers of Aonach Beag and Aonach Mor, at altitudes between 830m and 1,188m. It has slightly succulent, bright green, lobed leaves and a short flower stem topped by a solitary flower or sometimes no flower at all. However, it has an extra adaptation to its mountain environment where pollinators are few. In case its flowers are not pollinated, it produces up to 40 swollen crimson bulbils in the angles of small clasping leaves up its stem. These readily break off and give rise vegetatively to new plants.

It always seems to grow in crevices and hollows or beneath overhanging rocks where accumulated snow lies well into summer. In the 1980s, I saw its Lawers site under snow as late as 24 June, but, worryingly, the accumulation and longevity of snow cover has declined greatly in subsequent decades. It rarely opens fully formed flowers on Lawers, relying instead on its bulbils to spread. It flowers rather more commonly at its other sites, but is thought never to set seed in Britain because its pollen is inviable. As a result, each Scottish population probably represents a self-perpetuating clone. Even in Scandinavia, viable pollen has only been recorded north of about 66°N (a little way south of the Arctic Circle) and Svalbard is one of the few places from which viable seed has been collected.

Wigginton (1989) estimates the total British population at about 500–1,000 plants on Lawers (although only about 150 of these are mature, bulbil-producing plants), 700 in Glen Coe and around 100 in the Nevis range, but sadly some of these plants still disappear into the bags of criminal collectors. Worldwide it is found throughout the arctic regions, south to a scattering of sites in the high mountains of the Alps and Carpathians. It is also found in the Himalayas, Greenland and North America, south to the Rocky Mountains.

Alpine Pearlwort *Sagina saginoides*, Scottish Pearlwort *Sagina* × *normaniana* and Snow Pearlwort *Sagina nivalis*

It makes sense to deal with these pearlworts together. All three are inconspicuous ground-hugging plants with tiny white flowers. They are easily confused with small sandworts and with lowland species of pearlwort, which readily invade the mountains. In flower, they can be distinguished with care; when not in flower they are extremely challenging to tell apart. The best key to their identification is by Sandy Payne, who knows them well, in Rich & Jermy (1998).

Alpine Pearlwort is the least rare of the three, found in a scattering of sites in the southern and north-west Highlands, although it may be overlooked elsewhere. It is a poor competitor, so only occurs in fine gravelly soils that are mobile through frost-heave or solifluction, are highly wind-blasted, or have prolonged snow cover. I have found it near the limestone of Cairnwell in Perthshire, beside Allt Garbhlach in the Cairngorms, and below the crags of Ben Lawers. It is recorded too from Coire Sharroch and Ghlas Coire in Angus, the Northern Corries and Ben Avon in the Cairngorms, and various Breadalbane sites as far west as Ben Lui, at altitudes up to 1,213m. It also grows in the mountains of Mull and on the Trotternish ridge of Skye, where it descends to 460m at the Old Man of Storr. It may be declining or disappearing from sites in northern Scotland, an early victim of climate change. A record from Helvellyn in the Lake District is probably an error. It is a widespread

THE PERILS OF PEARLWORTS.
The three montane pearlworts are difficult to tell apart. Alpine Pearlwort, the least rare of the three, usually forms a single, spreading rosette in open ground ...

species in subarctic regions of Europe, Asia and America, and in the mountains of central Europe, Asia and western North America.

Scottish Pearlwort, previously called *Sagina normaniana* or *S. scotica*, is now regarded as a hybrid between Alpine Pearlwort and Procumbent Pearlwort *S. procumbens*, a common lowland weed which has invaded the mountains and is recorded at altitudes up to 1,150m. The hybrid occurs over much the same range as Alpine Pearlwort but at somewhat lower altitudes (to 950m on Aonach Beag) and seems to have inherited from its lowland parent an ability to invade short calcareous mountain grassland.

Scottish Pearlwort is a hybrid with the common Procumbent Pearlwort of lowlands and shares with that parent the tendency to form extensive creeping patches amongst calcareous mountain grassland ...

The last of the three mountain pearlworts, Snow Pearlwort, is by far the rarest; it forms small, dense tufts and its flowers rarely open fully.

As to Snow Pearlwort (formerly known as *S. intermedia*), I can best quote David Mardon, who is familiar with the species on Ben Lawers, from Wigginton (1999): '[It] is probably one of the least known of British montane plants and often eludes even skilled botanists, presumably because of its diminutive and inconspicuous form.' Certainly I have only seen it where it was shown to me by Sandy Payne, along with the preceding two pearlworts, on the crags below Beinn Ghlas. It is confined to the Breadalbane hills, including Beinn Heasgarnich, Stob Binnean and the area around Ben Lawers, mostly at altitudes between 900m and 1,190m but down to 640m at one site. It usually grows in open, unstable, gravelly habitats subject to frost-heave and solifluction or in mossy, calcareous flushes. Sadly, it seems to be in decline, perhaps as a result of warmer winters: 17 out of 39 known sites could not be refound in surveys in the early 2000s. It is recorded across arctic and subarctic regions, south to around 60°N in Norway, which would make Stob Binnean its southernmost world site.

Scorched Alpine-sedge *Carex atrofusca*

The shoulder below Meall Garbh in the Ben Lawers NNR is the only place where I have come across this rather elegant sedge. It grows in open, stony, calcareous flushes and more rarely on wet mountain rock ledges, between around 680m and 1,000m. It often grows alongside such equally exclusive associates as Starwort Mouse-ear, Chestnut

Scorched Alpine-sedge, growing here below Meall Garbh, is rather reminiscent of Black Alpine-sedge (Chapter 11), but is rarely more than 20cm tall and has darker female flower-spikes and fruits.

Rush, Bristle Sedge and Russet Sedge. It is confirmed from just four broad localities. In Perthshire, it is known from Meall Garbh and nearby sites; Beinn Heasgarnich in Glen Lochay; and the hills around Gleann Muillin on the north side of Glen Lyon. In Inverness-shire, it is only known from Aonach Beag (a record from Beinn an Dothaidh is now regarded as doubtful). It is also recorded from the Alps, Urals, northern and western Scandinavia and Greenland.

Bristle Sedge *Carex microglochin*

The last of our Breadalbane specialities is entirely confined to a series of gently sloping stony flushes, rich in calcium, between 610m and 975m in the corries below two peaks within the Ben Lawers NNR and on the col between them, where it was first discovered in 1923 (see photo on p.284). A few plants also turn up beside burns downstream of the

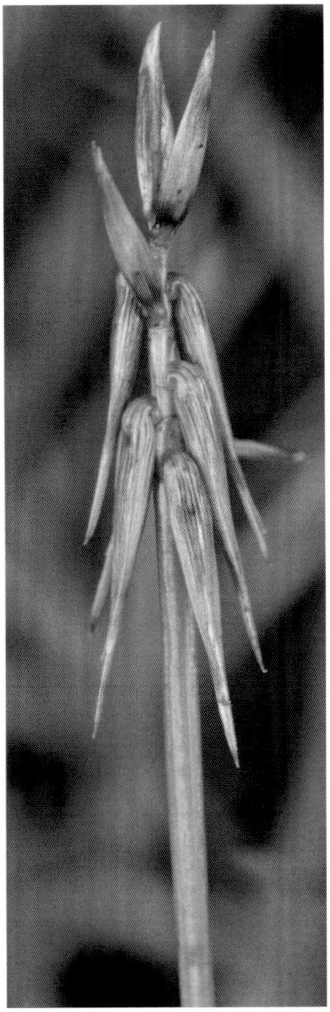

main colonies. Its slender shoots and narrow few-flowered spikes are easily overlooked except in the few areas where they grow in quantity. Stiff bristle-like hairs projecting from the fruits confirm their identity (and explain the species name). The species is widespread in arctic and subarctic Europe, Asia, Greenland and North America. I have seen it in a damp, gravelly site near Abisko in arctic Sweden, where active frost-heave maintained the open habitat, and I think this kind of process and late snow-lie explain its Breadalbane sites. It is also found in the Alps and the mountains of Asia and, like another diminutive montane species, Iceland Purslane (Chapter 15), it has somehow found its way also to Argentina, Chile and, most remarkably of all, to the Falkland Islands.

ABOVE LEFT: Bristle Sedge is a spiky little sedge. In Britain, it only grows on stony, base-rich flushes around Meall Garbh to the east of Ben Lawers.

ABOVE RIGHT: The head of Bristle Sedge can have anything between 3 and 12 narrowly conical, straw-coloured fruits, each of which has a stiff bristle projecting from its beak.

The Cairngorms and north-east Highlands

chapter fourteen

To me, the Cairngorms are the botanical high-spot of the British mountains. Ben Nevis may overtop the highest point of the Cairngorms (Ben Macdui) by 35m, but the Cairngorms are more extensive and more varied. The mountain core of the Cairngorms (often called the 'high tops') is a vast, undulating stony plateau of granite which extends over 390km^2 – roughly the size of the Isle of Wight – making it the largest area of land above 900m in Britain. Dome-like summits rise above this base, including four of the five highest British mountains (see table overleaf). This vast area is satisfyingly wild and remote, although the vegetation here is sparse and limited by severe exposure to just a few hardy montane species. The glaciers of successive ice ages have cut a few steep-sided glens into the plateau and sculpted spectacular corries around its edges. The rugged crags of these glens and corries support the richest flora, and it is these in particular that lure me back, again and again, to explore and to botanise.

The Red Hills

The Cairngorms is the informal name, derived from the best-known peak (Cairn Gorm), for the mountains that are more correctly known by the Gaelic name of *Am Monadh Ruadh* (the 'range of red hills', from the pink colour of the weathered granite). Partly because of their sheer extent and partly because they are located well clear of the warming influence of the North Atlantic Drift sea current up the west coast, they have the most arctic climate anywhere in Britain. We saw in Chapter 11 that Braemar on the edge of the Cairngorms at 339m has a severe climate, but calculations have shown that between Braemar and the top of Ben Macdui the average temperature drops by 2.2°C for every

OPPOSITE PAGE: This dramatic view from near the 1,215m summit of Cairn Lochan looks down over the two small lakes or lochans that give Coire an Lochain its name.

The heights of the Cairngorms peaks

(Ben Nevis)	1,344m (1)
Ben Macdui	1,309m (2)
Braeriach	1,296m (3)
Cairn Toul	1,291m (4)
Cairn Gorm	1,245m (5)
Beinn a' Bhuird	1,196m (10)
Ben Avon	1,171m (16)

The figure in brackets shows the place of the peaks in the list of Britain's highest mountains; Ben Nevis, the highest British peak, is included for comparison.

300m of ascent (Brown & Clapperton, 2002). This differential is even greater from April to June, when lying snow on the high plateau further chills the air. As a result, the growing season for plants drops by roughly one day for every 9m of altitude. We can therefore estimate that plants at the summit of Ben Macdui can grow for a maximum of 16 weeks between mid-May and mid-September, and even this can be cut short by late snow and frost. Only the most highly adapted of montane species can cope with such a restricted growing season.

Snow can fall in the Cairngorms in any month of the year (although it is rare in August). Blizzards are common, even in May, and it snows more regularly in June and September than on any other Scottish mountain. Snow falls on more than 100 days per year on average on the summits, and can lie for 200 days near some of the peaks. Several

The Lairig Ghru is a dramatic pass that cuts through the Cairngorms from Glen More to Braemar. The colour of the weathered granite shows why the Cairngorms are *Am Monadh Ruadh* – the 'range of red hills'.

patches of accumulated snow persist right through most years, giving the area a definite arctic feel. These snow patches have a pronounced effect on the local ecology, supporting a number of rare liverwort species as well as being preferred habitats for several scarce vascular plants. Although the survival of these snow patches is very weather-dependent, they may not be threatened by climate change, at least in the short term, because winters that are less extremely cold can actually lead to increased snowfall. The unusually mild winters of 2013/14 and 2014/15, for example, resulted in the best skiing seasons for many years on Cairn Gorm because of more regular snowfalls.

The other important difference from the mountains described in the preceding two chapters is that the prevailing rock in the Cairngorms is hard granite, which gives rise to infertile acidic soils. The predominant vegetation is therefore of calcifuge species, although there are a few small pockets of calcareous schists which add greatly to the floral diversity.

In 2003, 3,800km^2 of the wider area around the Cairngorms was designated as Scotland's second national park, and in 2010 this was extended to include contiguous areas of high land in Perthshire and Angus, bringing its area to 4,528 km^2 (amounting to six per cent of Scotland's land area). As well as the high tops, the park includes the surrounding straths (wide, flat river valleys) where 18,000 people live in towns like Aviemore, Kingussie and Grantown-on-Spey. In the National Parks (Scotland) Act 2000, the Scottish Government included the promotion of sustainable economic and social development for the local (human) communities as one of the four aims of Scotland's national parks, and, as a result, the parks are managed at least as much for the benefit of people as for wildlife. Inevitably, that has resulted in conservation conflicts and means that the Cairngorms cannot be regarded as a totally protected landscape. Time alone will tell whether this compromise in objectives is working for the benefit of the area's plants and wildlife.

Lower slopes and glens

Lower hillsides around the Cairngorms are largely covered in heather moor, with some of the most extensive and natural remnants of Scots Pine forest anywhere in Britain. Scots Pine reaches its highest altitude at 648m on Creag Fhiaclach, in an open scrub of stunted and gnarled pine and juniper shrubs, equivalent to the zone in European

OPPOSITE PAGE: The road end at Whitewell offers magnificent views to the high tops of the Cairngorms.

mountains known as *krummholz* (literally 'twisted wood': see Chapter 4). This represents the best natural pine treeline in Britain, and I am always impressed by the sheer resilience of the bonsai pines on the hillside here.

The influence of the Cairngorms to the east and the Monadhliath Hills to the west depresses winter temperatures in the valley of the River Spey that lies between them. As a result various montane and submontane species grow here at relatively low altitudes. Chickweed Wintergreen is fairly common in the woods beside Loch an Eilein. Melancholy Thistle and Alpine Bistort grow in grassland on the east side of the RSPB's Insh Marshes reserve. One of my favourite spots is Whitewell at the end of a minor road from Inverdruie. It offers superb views to the high tops of the Cairngorms, with a fine stand of Juniper in the foreground. Chickweed Wintergreen, Mountain Everlasting and Lesser Twayblade grow amongst the stands of Juniper here, as well as good numbers of Heath Fragrant-orchids, a relatively lowland species. It is one of the best places I know to see Small-white Orchids, which are much more attractive than their prosaic name suggests. This species is recorded at altitudes up to 550m, but in the past it was also found in lowland environments as far south as Sussex. Serrated Wintergreen, Intermediate Wintergreen and the unrelated Chickweed Wintergreen are quite common in the woods around Loch Garten. Bearberry grows on Tulloch Moor and by the path to Ryvoan from Glenmore. The Allt Mor burn beside the ski road, south of Glenmore, is always worth checking for montane plants, such as Starry Saxifrage, washed down from the heights by floods and melting snow.

Small-white Orchid grows amongst the Juniper in the foreground of the photograph opposite.

Cairn Gorm

In 1960, a new road was opened from Aviemore to Coire Cas on the northern slopes of Cairn Gorm to provide access for skiers to the long-lasting snow that lies there. Today the road offers an easy route to 620m, opening up access to the high tops from a massive car park. I always have mixed feelings when I visit here. I was deeply involved in the Save the Cairngorms Campaign which succeeded in stopping the ski development proposed for the area known as Lurcher's Gully, and when I look westwards from the car park I feel encouraged that this magnificent landscape is still free from development. However, when I look up the hill towards Cairn Gorm, I regret that we failed in a later campaign to block the funicular railway whose 'iron road' is now

Lurcher's Gully: still unspoilt by the ski development that was proposed here in the 1980s.

such a linear intrusion into the landscape of Coire Cas. As long as the funicular remains a 'closed' system, with no egress allowed onto the hill from the top station, it is only the landscape that is despoiled, not the precious mountain vegetation, but I worry how long this planning compromise can be maintained against economic pressure to 'open up' the high tops.

To be fair, the National Park Authority and the company that operates the funicular have made good progress in recent years in reversing past damage to the vegetation by restricting off-piste skiing and repairing erosion scars. They have also mended and improved the badly eroded path leading into the Northern Corries (see below), although that now encourages even more people to venture along its length and transmits the resulting erosion further and further into the corries.

One small element of compensation that came with the funicular is the wild plant garden that has been established behind the Coire Cas ski lodge. Dwarf Birch and several of the mountain willows have been planted here in a habitat mimicking montane scrub, together with examples of many of the local montane plants.

Thanks to the closed system on the funicular, it is a long and rather bleak slog from the wild garden to the summit, but it is one I would recommend to anyone curious about our mountain flora. Initially, the track is enlivened only by occasional plants of Fir Clubmoss and nice

The mountain garden behind the Coire Cas ski lodge is at an altitude of 650m and is probably the highest tended garden in Britain.

patches of Crowberry, but above the top station of the funicular the vegetation becomes more interesting. The high-level plateau around and beyond the summit of Cairn Gorm is not a place to find a wide diversity of species or any great rarities. It is the extent of near-natural mountain vegetation in the superb landscape that is really important. This is a place to explore widely, but tread lightly. I always feel I am experiencing the Arctic here, without any need to travel north of the Arctic Circle.

Woolly Fringe-moss is the commonest species, with a scattering of Three-leaved Rush and low tufts of the mountain form of Thrift. Dwarf Willow, Dwarf Cudweed and Spiked Wood-rush occur here and there, but Curved Wood-rush and Wavy Meadow-grass are more difficult to find. Sibbaldia grows in a few snow hollows, and there are nice patches of Parsley Fern and Alpine Lady-fern where steep slopes of block scree drop down below the plateau.

The Northern Corries

The path that heads south-westwards from the Coire Cas car park towards what are collectively called the Northern Corries offers considerably more botanical variety than the summit track. The upgraded path crosses the Allt a' Choire Chais burn and makes its way round the ridge called Fiacaill a' Choire Chais. (Seemingly unpronounceable Gaelic names are an important feature of the cultural tradition of this region, but I have neither the expertise nor the space here to explore their meanings and pronunciations. I would refer readers to several books that explain Gaelic place names, such as Drummond (1991) and Butterfield (1986)).

Almost immediately along this path, the flora becomes interesting. Cloudberry is frequent amongst the Bilberry, with Bog Bilberry in areas of deeper peat and scattered plants of Fir Clubmoss on open ground. There is impressive colonisation of the slopes here, at altitudes between 650m and 750m, by low, twisted Scots Pine trees, with occasional Juniper, Rowan and Downy Birch bushes (Scott, 2000). Some of the pines here may be 20 or more years old but they reach barely a metre in height as the bitter winds have repeatedly withered their growing tips. Forestry fencing on the lower ground has reduced access for deer, and deer are further discouraged from grazing by winter skiers and year-round walkers, allowing this *krummholz* scrub to develop.

A left-hand split in the track now leads round into Coire an t-Sneachda (the 'snow corrie'). Dwarf Cornel becomes commoner, sometimes forming large patches in snow hollows beside the path. Bearberry creeps across granite gravel and tumbles over cut banks.

A wind-pruned, low-growing, *krummholz* Scots Pine on the slopes of Fiacaill a' Choire Chais below Cairn Gorm, with the imposing bowl of Coire an Lochain in the distance.

Alpine Lady's-mantle, Alpine Bistort and Chickweed Wintergreen appear in grassy areas, and Globeflower and Alpine Saw-wort grow on the banks of the burn flowing down from the corrie. The path now climbs onto a better-drained rocky area that marks one of the terminal moraines of the glacier that once hung in the corrie here. Alpine Clubmoss, Mountain Crowberry, Spiked Wood-rush, Three-flowered Rush, Stiff Sedge and small patches of Trailing Azalea grow here. Interrupted Clubmoss creeps over areas of rather damper peat, and crowns of Alpine Lady-fern highlight hollows where snow lies late. Moss Campion and Alpine Meadow-rue suggest some calcareous influence in the soil.

The path now disappears, leaving the visitor to pick a route over large block scree. Mountain Sorrel and beautiful flowery patches of Roseroot grow in shelter between the boulders. Beyond the scree, the route skirts round a classic corrie lochan. The cliffs above are highly regarded by rock and ice climbers; just watching them clinging to the precipitous crags gives me vertigo. One of the plants that grows in a few limited spots on these crags is Highland Saxifrage. It seems to be attracted by the same features that challenge the mountaineers – massive granite rock faces with a few narrow ledges and patches of snow and ice that last well into summer. Ledges here are the only place where I have ever found Hare's-foot Sedge. Arctic Mouse-ear and Northern Rock-cress are rather more abundant and easier to spot. Alpine Meadow-grass and Alpine Hair-grass both occur here in their viviparous forms.

Beneath the crags, an obvious path, known as the Pig Track, climbs steeply up the hillside. Mountain Sorrel, Spiked Wood-rush, Mossy Saxifrage and a few plants of Alpine Speedwell grow in the unstable grassland above the track. The top of the Pig Track leads onto the Cairn Gorm plateau, with all the usual species of windswept tops including good displays of Trailing Azalea, the short, mountain forms of Thrift and Goldenrod, and occasional tufts of Curved Wood-rush. The most botanically rewarding route back from here is to contour westwards round the top of the Coire an Lochain cliffs and descend from Miadan Creag an Leth-choin down the wide slopes of Lurcher's Gully (Allt Creag an Leth-choin on the map). The streamside here hosts many of the same plants that I described in Coire an t-Sneachda but it is slightly richer, with Starry Saxifrage, both montane willowherbs, Scottish Asphodel and some fine patches of Sheathed Sedge.

The Pig Track can just be seen climbing steeply below the crags in this view, looking across the lochan at the foot of Coire an t-Sneachda.

An alternative to this route from Coire Cas is to take the right fork beyond Fiacaill a' Choire Chais. This leads into Coire an Lochain, which is even more dramatic, but a little less botanically diverse, than Coire an t-Sneachda. Interrupted Clubmoss grows on the open granite moor below the corrie, and there are the biggest tussocks I have seen anywhere of Three-flowered Rush in the scree to the west of the two lochans that give the corrie its name. The lower crags above the lochans are a site for Moss Campion, Alpine Speedwell, Spiked and Curved Wood-rush, Arctic Mouse-ear and another new species, Starwort Mouse-ear. Alpine Lady-fern is abundant in the scree, growing alongside Beech Fern, which is typically a woodland species. The higher crags should only be approached with care, but Highland Saxifrage grows here on mossy ledges irrigated by meltwater dripping from the long-lasting snow patches above, with Arctic and Starwort Mouse-ear nearby.

Almost all the most special Cairngorms plants can therefore be seen in these two magnificent corries, which I think offer the best mountain botanising anywhere in Britain. Five of these species deserve further consideration before we move on.

Highland Saxifrage *Saxifraga rivularis*

Highland Saxifrage: its rather succulent, bright green, usually five-fingered leaves are distinctive on mossy ledges and cliff faces, as here in Coire an Lochain.

I have only ever found the five-fingered leaves and unpretentious white flowers of this species growing in mossy cracks or gullies in steep mountain crags, or in mossy flushes directly beneath the crags. These sites are always difficult to reach and dripping wet with meltwater from late-lying snow just above. Presumably because of its association with summer snow, the species is restricted to north- or east-facing sites where the warming rays of the sun rarely penetrate for long and nearby snow chills the air, even on a summer's day. The resulting combination of bare rock, sparse vegetation and cold air gives the sites a distinctly arctic feel.

Highland (or Brook) Saxifrage is marginally the least rare of the delightful trio of truly montane saxifrages, found in just a few more places than Tufted Saxifrage or Drooping Saxifrage. It only grows at high altitude, from 795m above the Lairig Ghru in the Cairngorms to 1,240m on Ben Nevis. It is known from about 20 areas in the Highlands, stretching from Lochnagar in the east to Glen Coe in the west, with isolated populations around Ben Lawers in the south and on the Ross-shire mountains of Beinn Eighe, Slioch, An Teallach and Beinn Dearg in the north. The largest populations are in Glen Coe and the Cairngorms, and recent surveys have added several further populations on Ben Nevis. It is a widespread species in the Arctic, found southwards to Iceland and southern Norway, so the reintroduced plants on Ben Lawers I mentioned in Chapter 13 may be the southernmost in the world. It is also found in arctic Asia, Greenland and a few outlying stations in North America.

Arctic Mouse-ear *Cerastium nigrescens*

I always think of Arctic Mouse-ear as a sort of doppelganger on acid rocks to Alpine Mouse-ear in the base-rich hills (Chapter 11). Both are straggly, mat-forming plants with conspicuous white flowers typical of the mouse-ear genus, but whereas the leaves of Alpine Mouse-ear are covered in long white hairs, Arctic Mouse-ear leaves are bristly with short, stiff, grey hairs. That should make them easy to tell apart, but, in habitats typical of Arctic Mouse-ear, I have regularly come across

The leaves of Arctic Mouse-ear are covered in a stubbly mat of short, stiff hairs, which distinguishes it from Alpine Mouse-ear, its slightly commoner relative found on calcareous rocks.

perplexing plants that seem intermediate in their hairiness. Taxonomists say these are a variety of Arctic Mouse-ear called *alpinopilosum*, and suggest that they have undergone some inbreeding with Alpine Mouse-ear, hence this 'halfway hairiness'.

Arctic Mouse-ear is the rarer of the two species, confined to acid rocks in exposed high-altitude sites. It is recorded at altitudes up to 1,190m on Beinn Dearg in Ross-shire and rarely found below 800m, always on north-facing corrie walls and mountain crags of granite or other hard igneous rocks. It still grows in some of the corries below Snowdon, which is the southernmost site of the species in the world. Its range then jumps to an old record from Beinne Ime in Argyll. The core of its range today is from Lochnagar and the Cairngorms west to Glen Coe and the Isle of Skye. There it occurs in the Cuillin hills and around the Storr, where I have seen it on sloping, gravelly ground very different from the crags to which it is normally confined. It grows at least as far north as Ben More Assynt in Sutherland, and possibly as far as cliffs on the north coast.

Its current scientific name is more than a little confusing for anyone used to older field guides (like me!). The story behind the name is worth exploring, because it gives an insight into the methodology of taxonomy – and tells us quite a bit about the nature of our British plant. When I learnt my botany in the 1970s, Arctic Mouse-ear was *Cerastium arcticum*, which seemed pleasingly logical, and *C. nigrescens* was the name given to an endemic mouse-ear from Shetland that we will meet in Chapter 17. Then taxonomists decided that the Shetland plant was only a subspecies of the much more widespread *C. arcticum*. Unfortunately, they also found that the name *C. nigrescens* was first published for the Shetland plant in 1860, 20 years before the name *C. arcticum*. If two plants are found to belong to the same species, then, according to the rules of taxonomy, the earliest validly published name applies. Both plants therefore became *Cerastium nigrescens* and the widespread arctic form was reduced to the level of subspecies *arcticum*.

In 2008, the story became even more confusing. Based on studies of Arctic Mouse-ear throughout its range, a paper by Brysting (2008) suggested that this name in fact embraced two highly divergent populations of plants which could be separated on a range of diagnostic features. He proposed reinstating the name *C. arcticum* for plants from the high Arctic, and retaining *C. nigrescens* for plants from Britain, Scandinavia, Iceland and the Faroes. So, thanks to improved taxonomic understanding, it appears that what we call Arctic Mouse-ear in Britain is not *C. arcticum* – and not even a truly arctic plant!

Starwort Mouse-ear *Cerastium cerastoides*

After that taxonomic confusion, this is a somewhat easier species to understand. It is another creeping plant with small, white, five-petalled flowers and narrowly oblong leaves. I have come across it only rarely, usually forming a loose mat amongst mosses in damp corrie floors high in the mountains, often with late-lying snow nearby. It is often covered in sparkling droplets of spray from adjacent rushing rivulets. Its name comes from this association with wet habitats and the fanciful resemblance of its slightly translucent, bright green leaves to those of the water-starworts of lowland ponds.

Starwort Mouse-ear is told from its two commoner mountain relatives by the three styles in the centre of the flower (clearly visible in the flower left of centre), whereas the others have five styles.

It is rarely found below 750m and recorded up to 1,240m on Ben Macdui. It also establishes briefly at lower altitudes when melting snow or rainstorms wash it down rivers from the hills above. Otherwise, it is confined to high mountain sites in the Cairngorms, the Ben Nevis – Aonach Mor range (but oddly not the Glen Coe hills), hills north of Glen Affric, and a scattering of other sites in the north-west Highlands, north at least as far as Beinn Dearg in Ross-shire. It is never a conspicuous part of the vegetation, and is probably under-recorded.

Curved Wood-rush *Luzula arcuata*

I doubt anyone ever sent friends an excited text message after seeing their first Curved Wood-rush, but it is one of our rarest plants. There is also something rather pleasing about the architecture of its inflorescence, like a miniature candelabra, arising from a tuft of narrow, deeply grooved leaves. It is a real arctic survivor, growing in open, stony fellfields on ridges and plateaux below some of our highest summits, where fearsome winds whip away snow and scour the landscape. It grows amongst ice-shattered gravels of granite, quartzite

Curved Woodrush in a very typical habitat, on a big bluff of granite rock in Coire an Lochain.

and other acidic rocks where vegetation rarely covers more than a quarter of the ground. It is much rarer than the summit quartet of Three-leaved Rush, Spiked Wood-rush, Stiff Sedge and Dwarf Cudweed with which it often grows. It sometimes also spills over from plateaux onto the sides of high corries, where snow accumulates and the vegetation is rather more extensive, at altitudes from 760m on Slioch in Ross-shire to 1,290m on Cairn Toul.

The Cairngorms are the core of its British range, and the only place where I have found it. It is also recorded from a few other high mountains including Aonach Beag (probably the southernmost point of its world range), the Cannich hills north of Glen Affric, the rugged peaks south of Glen Carron in Wester Ross and Foinavon in Sutherland, almost always above 1,000m. Outside Scotland, it is found throughout arctic and subarctic Europe, Asia and Greenland, with a separate subspecies in northern North America.

Hare's-foot Sedge is named after its fluffy fruiting heads, which somewhat resemble the feet of hares.

Hare's-foot Sedge *Carex lachenalii*

I remember my excitement the first time I came across this sedge. I had just seen Highland Saxifrage on a dripping bluff of rock in a shady gully in Coire an t-Sneachda. A flat grassy shelf across the top of the gully looked beguiling, so I scrambled further up and on the ledge I found a large tuft of this delightful little sedge whose fluffy, reddish-brown fruiting heads really do look like hare's feet. It is an extremely localised plant found on wet slopes and well-irrigated ledges on acidic crags between 950m and 1,150m. Wigginton (1999) records it on 11 different hills since 1970, mainly around the Cairngorms, but with sites also in the corries of Ben Alder, Aonach Beag and on the great North Face of Ben Nevis. In 2001, it was refound in Glen Coe on Bidean nam Bian, but it has not been confirmed for many years on Lochnagar in Aberdeenshire.

It is a circumpolar species, found throughout the arctic regions, with mountain sites in Scandinavia, the Alps and Pyrenees. Extraordinarily, it is also recorded as a native species in the Southern Alps of New Zealand. It still grows in China and Mongolia, and it is suggested that it might have migrated to New Zealand via the mountains of Malaysia 1–2 million years ago – which adds a whole new perspective to its survival in the high mountains of Scotland.

Hare's-foot Sedge on a ledge at the top of a shady gully in Coire an t-Sneachda.

Glen Feshie

After a day on the Cairn Gorm plateau and another exploring the Northern Corries, I would certainly recommend at least one day in Glen Feshie, south from Aviemore. A bog in the Inshriach Forest, at the entrance to the glen, is the only place in Scotland where I remember finding Small Cranberry. I came across it in 1978 and was pleased to see that it was still growing there in 2013. The usual approach into Glen Feshie itself is by following the road south from Feshiebridge to a car park at Achlean. From there one path to the east leads steeply onto the high tops, but the track that follows the River Feshie southwards is the best botanical option, although in spring it may involve difficult crossings over a couple of rushing mountain burns.

Glen Feshie today is a heartening place. When I first knew it in the 1980s, there were a few disconsolate stands of Scots Pine in a landscape otherwise stripped bare by sheep and deer. In 2006, the Danish clothing millionaire Anders Povlsen bought the 17,400-hectare Glenfeshie Estate. He set himself the ambitious aim of more than doubling the area of native woodland, with financial support from Forestry Commission Scotland, and is doing so by significantly reducing Red Deer numbers. In 2007, I met him and his estate manager Thomas Donnell for a radio programme, and was hugely impressed by their commitment to regenerating the natural habitats of the glen. It is a delight now to see the landscape changing. Young pines are returning to the slopes, birch is regenerating everywhere and the ground flora is responding vibrantly to the reduced grazing. This revitalisation of the land further enriches what was always a delightful walk.

ABOVE: A heartening vision of ecological restoration in Glen Feshie: a fine old granny Scots Pine with a little swarm of saplings beginning to grow around it on the open moor.

BELOW: Coire Garbhlach is a deep, steep valley that opens out of granite hills on the east of Glen Feshie. Its cliffs are difficult to reach but rich in montane species.

Bearberry grows in quantity on the moor south of Achlean. Chickweed Wintergreen, Alpine Lady's-mantle, Petty Whin and Lesser Twayblade also occur by the track. Around 2km south of Achlean, a flight of steep stone steps lead down to the Allt Garbhlach. Following this burn eastwards leads up a narrow valley into Coire Garbhlach, another classic Cairngorm site. Many of commoner montane species grow on the corrie floor, and I have also found the delightful duo of Alpine Foxtail and Alpine Cat's-tail here. There are outcrops of Moine Schist on crags near the head of the corrie. This adds to the fertility of the soil and supports a calcareous flora, in marked contrast to the acid granite soils elsewhere in the Cairngorms. Indeed these crags almost match the Breadalbanes in their richness,

The montane plants of Coire Garbhlach

Fir Clubmoss	Cloudberry	Alpine Speedwell*
Alpine Clubmoss*	Alpine Cinquefoil*	Rock Speedwell*
Lesser Clubmoss	Downy Willow*	Alpine Saw-wort*
Parsley Fern*	Woolly Willow*	Dwarf Cudweed
Alpine Lady-fern	Whortle-leaved Willow*	Three-leaved Rush
Holly Fern*	Dwarf Willow*	Spiked Wood-rush*
Globeflower	Net-leaved Willow*	Hair Sedge*
Alpine Meadow-rue	Mountain Pansy	Sheathed Sedge*
Alpine Saxifrage*	Northern Rock-cress*	Black Alpine-sedge*
Starry Saxifrage	Rock Whitlow-grass*	Rock Sedge*
Purple Saxifrage	Mountain Sorrel*	Alpine Foxtail
Yellow Mountain Saxifrage	Mossy Cyphel*	Alpine Cat's-tail
Mossy Saxifrage	Alpine Mouse-ear	
Mountain Avens*	Moss Campion*	

Species marked with * are mainly confined to the higher crags; the others are more widespread.

as shown in the table above. There is no obvious focal point on the cliffs. Instead, they need to be explored methodically, as they reveal their treasures reluctantly. Beware their steepness: I once got carried away in my botanising here, getting drawn higher and higher up a steep slope by interesting plants. When I turned to make my way down, vertigo struck, and my companion lower on the hill had to spend more than an hour patiently talking me down from my precarious heights.

In 1982, I joined a Botanical Society trip that continued further south into Glen Feshie on the broad track that runs along the left bank of the River Feshie. At An Cagain, the track had been bulldozed across an open scree slope, and here, along with lots of Alpine Lady's-mantle, Yellow Mountain Saxifrage and Mountain Sorrel, I was surprised to find masses of Wood Vetch in the scree, a species that I had not previously considered to be in the least montane. Creag na Caillich on the other bank of the glen is another calcareous site for Mountain Avens and Whortle-leaved Willow.

That day we were joined by Mary McCallum-Webster, author of the *Flora of Moray, Nairn & East Inverness* (1978) – one of the best guides to a regional flora that I know because it is based on such deep personal knowledge, beautifully produced and richly illustrated. Born in 1906, Mary Mac (as she was always called, except to her face) reminded me of a much-loved but slightly feared school marm. She was one of an impressive generation of lady botanists (Elaine Bullard, Joan Clarke, Ursula Duncan, Catriona Murray and Olga Stewart were others I was privileged to meet) who tirelessly explored some of the wildest

Wood Vetch is typically a plant of open woods and scrub, but I have found it on a scree slope in Glen Feshie and on the crags above Loch Loch.

Photos of Mary McCallum-Webster are hard to find: this one shows her in casual attire, very different from her normal garb in the field.

areas of Scotland and added hugely to our plant knowledge. I only ever saw Mary in the field in a tweed skirt, but that never stopped her from venturing into the most inaccessible places. On that day, she set off alone and eventually rejoined the group, stockings torn, after a major hike on which she had discovered a new locality for Dwarf Birch. I recall that story here, partly to pay tribute to that generation of botanical explorers, but also to encourage readers to venture beyond well-trodden botanical paths and explore more widely, in the hope of returning with elusive treasure – as Mary Mac did that day.

Small Cranberry *Vaccinium microcarpum*

I never think of this as an especially montane species – but then I rarely go crawling around on my hands and knees in bogs when I am hillwalking. It is a delicate plant whose trailing stems creep through bogs of *Sphagnum* moss. It is easily overlooked there, unless its delicate pink flowers are present. It looks very similar to the much commoner Cranberry of lowland bogs. Indeed it was only relatively recently separated from that species on the basis of chromosome numbers, but field botanists have struggled to find morphological characters that will reliably distinguish the two species, and generally a combination of subtle differences is needed to tell the two apart (so this species may be under-recorded as a result).

Small Cranberry is found most widely (but never commonly) in the bogs of the east and north Highlands, north as far as isolated bogs in the Flow Country of Caithness and Sutherland. It is recorded at altitudes from close to sea level in east Sutherland to around 850m.

The small, leathery, oval leaves of Small Cranberry are well spaced along its stems. Its neat little flowers have pink petals that are folded back and a central yellow 'beak' of anthers.

Further south, it has a scattering of sites in the Southern Uplands, with three known sites in the bogs of Northumberland. Elsewhere it is found throughout northern Europe, south to the Alps and Carpathians, and in North America.

Around the Cairngorms

I enjoy exploring the Northern Corries so much that I have been remiss in visiting other botanical sites around the Cairngorms. The other peaks share many of the same species as Cairn Gorm, and are succinctly summarised by Nagy *et al.* (2006). They are somewhat more difficult to access but as a result their vegetation is rather less damaged. Heading roughly east to west, Braeriach hosts many of the Cairngorms rarities, including Downy Willow, Alpine Speedwell, Curved Wood-rush and Hare's-foot Sedge. These species also occur on Cairn Toul, along with Mountain and Whortle-leaved Willow, Alpine and Wavy Meadow-grass, Russet Sedge and Mountain Bog-sedge.

Not surprisingly, the summit region of the highest peak, Ben Macdui, provides the highest altitude record for many species of wind-swept plateaux, including Curved Wood-rush. Even Juniper turns

The vast plateau of the Cairngorms is interrupted by several wild glens, often with lochs at their base. This view looks north down Glen Einich with the summit of Braeriach off to the right.

up at 1,200m. Sibbaldia and Hare's-foot Sedge grow where snow lies late, and Russet Sedge and Mountain Bog-sedge are recorded from a few flushes. On its north-east side, the cliffs around the head of Loch Avon are home to Downy Willow, Arctic and Starwort Mouse-ear, Alpine Speedwell, Black Alpine-sedge and Glaucous Meadow-grass. Beinn a' Bhuird is one of the last sites in the area for Boreal Fleabane. Alpine Cat's-tail and Starwort Mouse-ear grow here in wet areas fed by melting snow. There is also a mysterious plant in short, wind-blasted heaths known as Issler's Clubmoss. The north-facing corrie of Ben Avon (pronounced 'Aan') is the last remaining site in the Cairngorms for Tufted Saxifrage. Nearby Mountain Avens, Alpine Cinquefoil and Two-flowered Rush indicate calcareous enrichment. Downy Willow, Arctic and Starwort Mouse-ear, Alpine Speedwell and Alpine Meadow-grass are also recorded here, but Boreal Fleabane, Rock Speedwell and Highland Saxifrage may have disappeared.

On the other side of the Spey Valley, the Monadhliath Hills (*Am Monadh Liath*, the 'range of grey hills') are less visited and less rich, but in the little time I have spent walking there I have been impressed by the extensiveness of some of the mountain vegetation. Cloudberry seems unusually common, and there are several sites for Dwarf Birch and Downy Willow. Mountain Bog-sedge grows in some of the high-altitude bogs, and the hills here provide one of the few sites for Arctic Bearberry south of the Great Glen.

Further south, Trailing Azalea is surprisingly common on the tops of the Drumochter Hills. There are occasional outcrops of calcareous schists, in Coire Chuirn for example, and the plants of these outcrops include Interrupted Clubmoss, several of the montane willows, Alpine Speedwell, Scottish Asphodel, Russet Sedge, Mountain Bog-sedge, Black Alpine-sedge and Alpine Foxtail.

Issler's Clubmoss *Diphasiastrum complanatum* subspecies *issleri* (?)

I rather hesitate to include this plant, because I have never seen it, its exact taxonomic status remains controversial, and I am sure we still have much to learn about its biology. For over a century there have been sporadic reports of odd-looking clubmosses at scattered lowland sites in southern England. They look like a larger, less compact variant of Alpine Clubmoss, with more flattened stems, spreading scale leaves and a yellow-green, rather than blue-green, colour. As lowland plants, these would not qualify for this book, and anyway they are probably

Issler's Clubmoss is recognised by its yellow-green, flattened stems, covered in spreading scale leaves. Its exact taxonomic status is still uncertain.

now extinct in lowland England as a result of burning and grazing. However, in recent years similar plants have been identified from a few upland localities including Kielder Moor in Northumberland, several sites around the Cairngorms including Abernethy Forest, and in Sutherland. They have been recorded from altitudes of 270m on Canisp in west Sutherland to 960m on Lochnagar in Aberdeenshire.

These plants have been named as Issler's Clubmoss, and the current expert consensus is that they are probably a hybrid between Alpine Clubmoss and Yellow Cypress Clubmoss *Diphasiastrum complanatum*. The latter species is widespread in European mountains, Scandinavia and the Arctic, including Greenland and North America where it has such romantic names as Northern Running-pine, Ground Cedar and Trailing Christmas-green. The hybrid is known to occur where both its parents grow in Europe and North America. The problem is that Yellow Cypress Clubmoss has never yet been recorded in Britain, raising questions as to how the hybrid could have originated. The British plants seem to reproduce readily, producing offspring identical to themselves, which hybrids would not normally do. As a result, some taxonomists suggest they are actually a distinctive form of Yellow Cypress Clubmoss which they describe as *D. complanatum* subspecies *issleri*. As this is the name used by Stace (2010) I have followed it here, although *Diphasiastrum* × *issleri* may well be the more correct name.

I rather like that there are still mysteries such as this one to be solved amongst our mountain plants. Whatever its true identity, Issler's Clubmoss is probably under-recorded in montane areas, so it is a plant that readers of this book should watch out for on their travels.

Sow of Atholl and Ben Alder

The Sow of Atholl is another site that tantalises any mountain botanist. For a long time it was regarded as the only site for Blue Heath, another species that I regard as a three-star enigma because of its perplexingly limited distribution. The Sow sits like a large hog's back to the west of the A9 road at Dalnaspidal. The usual approach is along the track from

A view towards the Sow of Atholl from the north-east; the steep rocky slope just below the summit is the habitat of Blue Heath.

the lodge there, then up the long ridge of the Sow in a climb that begins gently but gets progressively steeper. There are plenty of commoner montane species on the ridge, including Bog Bilberry on the deep peat, Alpine Willowherb and Scottish Asphodel beside gravelly runnels, and Few-flowered and Sheathed sedges in boggy patches.

Above about 700m, occasional plants of Alpine Clubmoss and Trailing Azalea begin to appear amongst the vegetation. This marks the level at which the determined botanist needs to leave the broad shoulder and pick a careful route round to the steep, east-facing flank of the Sow. It is one of these places where I feel I am clinging on by fingernails and toenails, but this sheer slope above the scree line is where Blue Heath grows amongst Bilberry and Bearberry.

We now know that Blue Heath is rather more widespread around Ben Alder, on the other side of Loch Ericht from the Sow. This is one of the most remote, roadless areas of Scotland and almost impossible to explore without camping or using the bothy (mountain hut) at Culra, south of Loch Pattack. Sadly, the bothy had to be closed in 2014 because of asbestos safety fears, although the Mountain Bothies Association hopes to replace it eventually. Starwort Mouse-ear, Alpine Speedwell, Russet Sedge and Alpine Meadow-grass grow below the summit of Ben Alder, with Trailing Azalea, Sibbaldia and Sheathed Sedge on its summit plateau. From Ben Alder, a magnificent range of hills leads westwards towards Ben Nevis, providing the focus for the next chapter.

★★★ Blue Heath *Phyllodoce caerulea*

Blue Heath is a beautiful member of the heather family, with densely leafy stems and delicate, nodding, urn-shaped, pink flowers. In recent years, I have delighted in finding it, quite abundantly, in the Arctic and grown it successfully in my garden, but I have always been intrigued by its occurrence in Britain, where it is confined to a perplexingly limited area.

I learnt my botany, back in the 1970s, from the *Flora of the British Isles* (Clapham, Tutin & Warburg, 1962), a richly informative botanical tome to which I still regularly return. I was always interested by its reference to Blue Heath growing exclusively in 'rocky moorland at *c.*2,400ft on the Sow of Atholl (Perth) in small quantity'. In 1978, I finally visited the Sow on a joint Botanical Society field meeting, and was delighted to find patches of this handsome heath in full flower on a steep, open, stony slope. Despite the plant's name, its flowers were definitely not blue. Indeed, some writers have suggested that Linnaeus, who coined its scientific name, must have been colour-blind to describe the flowers as *caerulea* ('sky blue'). However, on that glorious day in 1978, I noticed that the flowers have a bluish sheen in sunlight, which may explain the name.

The intriguing history of Blue Heath in Scotland is painstakingly reviewed by Nelson (1977). He attributes the discovery to two Perthshire nurserymen called James and Robert Brown in 1810 (the relationship between the two men is unknown, because no biographical information has been found on James). They recorded their find on 'a dry moor in the district of Moray

A hint of a bluish sheen on the flowers of Blue Heath? Perhaps that is why Linnaeus named it *caerulea*, meaning 'sky-blue'.

Blue Heath on the Sow of Atholl. When I saw the plant first in 1978, it was in full bloom – I am not sure I could tell it from Crowberry if only its leaves were present.

near Aviemore', and stated that this was within six miles (10km) of the Aviemore Inn, yet the Sow of Atholl is more like 50km from the town, well outside Morayshire, and the plant's habitat there is definitely not dry moor! Nelson comments that botanists and nurserymen were sometimes known to disguise precise localities of rare plants to put off competitors and preserve their finds, 'often for sordid motives'.

There is a tantalising earlier record from June 1771 by James Robertson in 'the mountains that lie at the head of the water of Findhorn' (which would place it somewhere in the Monadhliaths). Robertson, whom we will meet again in the next chapter, was an able young botanist who explored widely in the Highlands between 1766 and 1771 and produced first British records for Serrated Wintergreen and Trailing Azalea. Several later herbarium specimens are also labelled 'near Aviemore', and the earliest collection that Nelson records as labelled from the Sow of Atholl was in 1824.

Rapacious collectors soon descended upon known sites to gather specimens in large numbers. By 1866, Sowerby's (annoyingly mistitled) *English Botany* records Blue Heath only on the Sow of Atholl 'where it was believed to be extinct, until Professor [J H] Balfour rediscovered it in 1863'. Francis Buchanan White's *Flora of Perthshire* (1898) also records it only from the Sow (under its Gaelic name of Carn Dobrain), where he counted around 50 plants in 1875. He noted that the site was 'unfortunately too well known to others than botanists, and hence there is a danger of the species being exterminated'.

Despite those depredations, the plant survived. Around 150 plants still grow where I saw it on the Sow in 1978 over about a kilometre of hillside, at altitudes around 750m. Worryingly, these are mainly long-lived plants, with very few young plants in the population, suggesting that they are reproducing poorly and on the edge of survival. Throughout its world range, Blue Heath is confined to sites with long-lasting snow cover. Certainly, where I have found it in arctic Norway, Sweden and Greenland, it has always been in banks where snow is likely to accumulate and persist into early summer. There is evidence that its shoots are readily killed by early frosts or damaged by wind-blown ice crystals. The snow that lies near the summit of the Sow into June in most years therefore serves to protect Blue Heath from frost, while the slumping and avalanching of the snow cornice that hangs at the top of the slope excludes slower-growing competition and maintains the open, stony habitat in which the plant can flourish. Nagy *et al.* (2006) suggest it may also be unpalatable to grazing animals in summer.

Blue Heath is entirely confined to the area that is covered in snow below the summit of the Sow of Atholl. The blanket of snow protects it from frost, and avalanching of the snow cornice maintains the open habitat it needs.

Our perception of its rarity in Scotland changed a little in 1966, thanks to Ron McBeath, a keen mountain botanist who at the time was a horticultural student at the Royal Botanic Garden Edinburgh (RBGE) and later established a remarkable alpine plant nursery in Berwickshire. Ron tells me that in October 1966 he was descending from a hillwalking trip on Ben Alder. He detoured for a refreshing drink below a waterfall in a small stream called Allt a' Bhealaich Duibh at about 670m. Here, purely by chance, he found a plant that reminded him of the Blue Heath in the RBGE Peat Garden, growing amongst various heathers and Devil's-bit Scabious. Because it was not in flower, he took a small piece back to the RBGE and brought it into flower in a mist-propagation house, confirming its identity as Blue Heath. He returned in June 1967 with Grant Roger and other friends, and refound his original plant and a small colony further along the streamside. Since then, at least four other small populations have been found in a limited area around Ben Alder, numbering 150 or so plants in total.

These discoveries beyond the Sow may give some credence to the old records near Aviemore and in the Monadhliaths, although I remain sceptical that sites at these lower altitudes produce the mixture of late-lying snow and open vegetation that Blue Heath seems to require.

The western Highlands and islands

chapter fifteen

Many of the hills of the western Highlands and islands of Scotland are magnificent scenically; several offer splendidly contrasting views over nearby sea-lochs (glacially cut fjords filled with seawater). They include the highest British peak, but many of the lower hills are also home to surprising and intriguing species. Overall, they are more diverse in their character and in the species they host than the hills covered in the previous three chapters.

The hills here are under the warming influence of the North Atlantic Drift sea current, so temperatures are slightly higher than sites at equivalent altitudes in the Cairngorms, for example. That does not necessarily equate to longer growing seasons, because higher precipitation here can result in more snow lying longer into the spring. Probably the main defining factor ecologically is the windiness of the west coast, which batters and dehydrates taller plants and encourages low-growing arctic-alpines.

Ben Nevis

Ben Nevis – Britain's highest mountain at 1,344m – dominates the mountain-scape of the western Highlands. It is all the more impressive because it rises almost directly from sea level beside Loch Linnhe. It is so dominant that locally it is known simply as 'the Ben'. Ben Nevis is famously a 'difficult' hill for botanists. In Gaelic, *Beinn Nibheis* is said to mean the 'evil' or 'venomous mountain', perhaps from its treacherous ascent. Another suggestion is that it is the 'mountain with its head in the clouds' which certainly fits my experience. As a result, it is not a hill that very many botanists (myself included) know well.

OPPOSITE PAGE: Arctic Bearberry is in prime condition in late July in the Beinn Eighe National Nature Reserve. Later in the summer, the berries will ripen to black.

An aerial view of Ben Nevis and surrounding mountains. The Ben itself is on the right, with Carn Mor Dearg centre, Aonach Mor and Aonach Beag on the left, and the Grey Corries behind.

Ben Nevis is part of a string of mountains that runs more than 20km from Loch Linnhe in the west to Loch Treig in the east, including Aonach Beag (1,236m), Aonach Mor (1,220m) and the Grey Corries topped by Stob Choire Claurigh (1,177m) – the Gaelic name *Aonach* refers to a ridge-shaped mountain, while a *Stob* is a stubby top. This group of hills forms the western end of what atlases call the Grampian Mountains, a term that I have never heard used by hillwalkers, probably because it encompasses too many fine hills to be a useful description.

The first recorded ascent of Ben Nevis was by James Robertson, the same botanist who, as we saw in the last chapter, discovered Blue Heath in 1771. He was the nephew of the head gardener at the Royal Botanic Garden Edinburgh and in August 1771 he climbed the Ben as part of his exploration of the Highlands commissioned by the Garden's Keeper and Professor of Botany (although surely other unnamed individuals must have climbed the hill before him). He described how 'a third part of the hill from the summit towards the top is entirely naked, resembling a heap of stones thrown together confusedly' and he noted that the plants on the granite resembled those he had seen earlier on Ben Avon and Cairn Gorm.

Ben Nevis was formed around 425 million years ago by an extremely active volcano which erupted upwards through a complex mixture of sedimentary and metamorphic rocks dating from the Moine and Dalradian periods. The summit and northern cliffs of Ben Nevis are predominantly made of an igneous rock called andesite and basalts from volcanic lava flows. A few highly localised outcrops of calcareous rocks add diversity to the cliffs. The southern slopes are formed from an intrusion of granite. The whole landscape was extensively shaped by later glaciation, which produced dramatic crags and corries especially on the north and north-east faces of the hills. The surrounding mountains consist mainly of older schists, mica schists and slates, with outcrops of metamorphic limestones. Some outcrops are remarkably base-rich with a flora to match, notably on Aonach Beag and Beinn na Socaich. In contrast, the upper slopes and summits of the Grey Corries are made of Dalradian quartzite, which produces less rich, acid soils.

As discussed in Chapter 3, we know a great deal about the climate of Ben Nevis, thanks to a weather observatory that operated near its summit from 1884 until 1903. The annual mean temperature there was −0.3°C and there was only a very brief period in midsummer when temperatures were sufficiently high to allow plant growth. Freezing fog and strong winds are other factors depressing plant growth there. Although strong winds regularly strip snow from the high plateau, the precipitation is so great and the exposure so severe that considerable snow drifts accumulate each winter below the cliffs and in hollows on the ridges and summits. These snow-beds persist well into summer in most years, and some snow patches on the north-facing cliffs of Ben Nevis and Aonach Beag melt only in exceptional years. The plant communities of these snow-beds share several of the species that we saw in similar habitats in the Northern Corries of Cairn Gorm.

Ben Nevis: the tourist route

I am ashamed to admit that I have only once tried to climb Ben Nevis, and it was not an experience I enjoyed! I took the tourist route from the Glen Nevis visitor centre car park. This begins steeply beneath the ridge called Meall an t-Suidhe along the pony track used in the construction of the summit observatory. The day I visited, the car park was almost full and the pony track seemed more like Sauchiehall Street in Glasgow, with many people looking totally unprepared for the mountain. Several groups seemed more intent on partying than climbing, and others were clearly on some fitness challenge and not prepared to defer to anyone in following the straightest, fastest route. With such heavy usage, the path is inevitably wide and eroded, with scars and landslips where shortcuts have been taken. A lot of vegetation near the track has been stripped away, although I found a few flowery patches of Thyme, sundews and a couple of Heath Fragrant-orchids. The John Muir Trust, the wild land charity which now owns 1,761 hectares around the summit of the Ben, is trying to reverse this damage, but with so many people using the track it faces a huge challenge.

Once the track forks southwards above Lochan Meall an t-Suidhe, the vegetation became a little more interesting. Starry Saxifrage was quite common by rivulets and in ditches, with leafy patches of Mossy Saxifrage. Beside the famous zigzags that climb, muscle-sappingly, from 700m to 1,000m I found Alpine Lady's-mantle, Dwarf Willow and a couple of crowns of Parsley Fern. Then the cloud closed in and the scenery disappeared. Knowing that the path to the summit is difficult to follow, with vertiginous cliffs on either side, I aborted my trip and have never felt inclined to return.

The summit plateau, I know, has all the typical species we have already met on windswept tops. Parsley Fern, Dwarf Willow, Starry Saxifrage, Moss Campion, Sibbaldia and Viviparous Fescue grow near the summit, with Alpine Clubmoss and the mountain form of Thrift not too far below.

The path below the summit of Ben Nevis is almost completely devoid of vegetation.

The North Face of Ben Nevis

I was advised long ago that the real botanical jewels of Ben Nevis are confined to crags and gullies below the summit on the North Face, but these are so steep and impenetrable that they are best left to rock and ice climbers. They have their own names for these features: Observatory Gully and Gardyloo Gully, Tower Ridge, Castle Ridge, and, most intriguingly of all, Zero Gully, 0.5 Gully and Numbers 2, 3, 4 and 5 Gullies (whatever happened to poor old No 1 Gully, I wonder?). Years ago, I heard of one rock ledge that is the only spot in Britain where Drooping, Highland and Tufted Saxifrage grow together, but this is only accessible by ropes and so never tempted me.

I was intrigued therefore to read that a three-year project began in August 2104 to survey the North Face, using a team of climbers and botanists. The project was masterminded by the Nevis Landscape Partnership – a charitable company established to 'safeguard, manage and where appropriate enhance the environmental qualities and opportunities ... of the Nevis area'. Two of Scotland's most enthusiastic and knowledgeable hill botanists assisted with the survey, Gordon Rothero and Ian Strachan, who is also the local botanical recorder.

In the first year, the group explored a 600m stretch of crags, ledges, scree slopes and gullies between Coire Leis and the Castle Ridge that had never previously been surveyed systematically. Their results (Semple, 2014) confirmed the importance of the site. Large new populations were discovered of several species only partially recorded before on the mountain, including Highland Saxifrage, Alpine

The survey of the North Face of Ben Nevis by a team of climbers and botanists in 2014 and 2015 made many important plant discoveries. These two surveyors are looking towards the North Face from the Ledge Route used by climbers.

Abseiling on the Carn Dearg Cascades of the North Face, Ian Strachan shows the skills needed to be botanical recorder for West Inverness-shire. (Disclaimer: Readers should not attempt this without proper training!)

Speedwell, Russet Sedge and Alpine Meadow-grass. The group found two new sites for Tufted Saxifrage and two new populations of Wavy Meadow-grass, previously known from only one site locally. Alpine Saxifrage, previously unknown on Ben Nevis, was discovered at two sites, and new populations were found of Alpine Lady-fern, Arctic and Starwort Mouse-ear and Sibbaldia. Further records were added in 2015 and, with several further crags and gullies to be explored in 2016, I am sure more discoveries will be made on this impressive but daunting rock face.

The weather in 2014 did not make life easy for the survey. Only the most experienced climbers would venture onto somewhere like Comb Buttress in weather like this. Amongst many other discoveries, the survey found several large new populations of Highland Saxifrage, high on the dripping ledges of the North Face (inset).

Less widespread species found on Aonach Beag and Beinn na Socaich

Alpine Clubmoss	Alpine Willowherb	Hare's-foot Sedge
Green Spleenwort	Chickweed Willowherb	Russet Sedge
Alpine Lady-fern	Starwort Mouse-ear	Hair Sedge
Mountain Bladder-fern	Alpine Mouse-ear	Sheathed Sedge
Alpine Saxifrage	Arctic Mouse-ear	Black Alpine-sedge
Highland Saxifrage	Arctic Bearberry	Rock Sedge
Drooping Saxifrage	Alpine Speedwell	Glaucous Meadow-grass
Mountain Avens	Scottish Asphodel	Alpine Meadow-grass
Sibbaldia	Two-flowered Rush	
Downy Willow	Curved Wood-rush	

Beyond the Ben

The calcareous rock outcrops on Aonach Beag and Beinn na Socaich, to the east of Ben Nevis, are two of the richest sites for the arctic-alpines of calcareous rocks beyond the Breadalbane range and Caenlochan. Some of the more special plants of these two hills are shown in the table above. Scottish Pearlwort and Mountain Bladder-sedge are two particular rarities recorded on the crags below Stob Coire Bhealaich, a southern spur of Aonach Beag.

Aonach Mor lacks the limestone outcrops of Aonach Beag, and so is slightly less rich botanically, but Highland Saxifrage, Starwort and Arctic Mouse-ear, Arctic Bearberry, Russet Sedge and Hare's-foot Sedge are all recorded there. The massive cliffs of Stob Coire an Laoigh, south of Beinn na Socaich, support Tufted, Alpine and Highland Saxifrage, and Starwort and Arctic Mouse-ear. Russet Sedge and Alpine Lady-fern are amongst rare species recorded elsewhere in the Grey Corries, but I am sure these hills would repay further searching.

Arctic Bearberry *Arctostaphylos alpinus*

Arctic Bearberry (also known as Alpine or Mountain Bearberry) is a low-growing, mat-forming shrub with wrinkled, net-veined leaves (see additional photo p.320). Its small, white, bell-shaped flowers open before its leaves in May and June; they are mainly self-pollinated and develop into black berries. It is found most commonly north of the Great Glen – the massive glacial trench that runs for 100km from Loch Linnhe beside Fort William to the Moray Firth at Inverness – but it also grows in a number of sites south of the Great Glen in the hills of west Inverness-shire and around the Cairngorms. It is recorded in Glen Etive and was recently confirmed at its southernmost British site on Meall nan Subh in Glen Lochay (see Chapter 13). A strange record from the

By September the leaves of Arctic Bearberry turn a wonderful rich red colour – a real sign of the 'arctic' autumn.

Howden Moors above the River Derwent in South Yorkshire is probably an introduction.

North of the Great Glen, Arctic Bearberry is widespread on windswept shoulders, glacial gravels and occasionally on blanket bogs, always on acid soils, at altitudes up to 1,100m on Sgurr na Lapaich, north of Loch Affric. On the mainland, it grows as far north as the tip of Dunnet Head in Caithness, and was rediscovered on Beinn Bhuidhe above Kylerhea on the Isle of Skye in 1990. It is the county flower for Orkney, where it is found on the islands of Hoy, Rousay and Westray at altitudes as low as 90m, and it also grows on the subarctic fellfield of Ronas Hill in Shetland.

Stewart *et al.* (1994) state that the south-eastern edge of its British range is marked by the mean July isotherm for 14.5° (suggesting that it cannot thrive in warmer summer temperatures). I am sure its requirements are more complex than this, but I certainly struggled to keep it alive in the rockery of my west-coast garden. Its net-veined, toothed leaves turn a brilliant scarlet in late summer and are a colourful autumn feature in the heathlands where I have seen it near the North Cape of Norway and in Iceland. The species also occurs in the Alps and Pyrenees, arctic Asia, Greenland and arctic North America, south to the mountains of New Hampshire.

Glen Coe

Glen Coe can look just as forbidding as the north face of Nevis, but it is easier to explore and is rewarding, both botanically and scenically. My favourite walk is into the 'Lost Valley' of Coire Gabhail. This classic hanging valley was cut by an ancient glacier running to the north-east; a later glacier running east–west gouged out the glacial trough of Glen Coe, leaving the mouth of Coire Gabhail hanging high up on the south side of the glen, like a drain spout near the head wall of an ancient cathedral. A huge rock avalanche then blocked the entrance to the

corrie with a tumble of massive boulders that have to be negotiated to enter the valley. The cliffs are mainly of acidic rhyolite (a fine-grained igneous rock of volcanic origin), but a few outcrops of calcareous andesite support a richer flora. Erosion carries some of this limey influence down into the corrie floor.

Looking down into Coire Gabhail – the 'lost valley' above Glen Coe. The rock avalanche that blocks the entrance to the valley is clearly visible.

Scrambling up towards Coire Gabhail, there is plenty of Alpine Lady's-mantle, Starry Saxifrage and Mountain Sorrel. The boulders that block the entrance to the Lost Valley provide a damp, shady habitat for Wilson's Filmy-fern, and beyond them a tranquil, flat valley opens up. Yellow Mountain Saxifrage, Roseroot and Moss Campion colonise the valley floor, with Parsley Fern and Wood Cranesbill on scree slopes at its sides. Alpine and Chickweed Willowherb, Mossy Saxifrage and the mountain form of Thyme-leaved Speedwell grow in flushes below Stob Coire nan Lochan (1,115m), with Alpine and Fir Clubmoss on the grassy slopes.

The crags of Bidean nam Bian are even richer, especially those of Stob Coire nam Beith, which can be approached from Loch Achtriochtan at the west end of Glen Coe. Around 400 plants of Drooping Saxifrage have been counted here, flowering much more abundantly here than it does on Ben Lawers, perhaps because of a marginally longer growing season. Highland Saxifrage also occurs in smaller quantities, along with Alpine Saxifrage, Mountain Bladder-fern, Rock Whitlow-grass, Arctic Mouse-ear, Chestnut Rush, Russet Sedge and Black Alpine-sedge.

Unfortunately, these are crags I have never reached. My wife Sonia and I set off there one fine day in 1983. As we climbed the steep path up to the waterfall below the corrie, we suddenly realised that the sheep we thought we were hearing from the crags above was actually a lone climber calling for help. I left my pack with Sonia and hurtled down the steep slope to the mountain rescue post beside the loch. There I was fed the sweetest tea I had ever tasted to help me recuperate, as the mountain rescue team gathered and meticulously prepared. Groups of them set off two by two to reach the climber, and the rescue helicopter swooped in and hovered with extraordinary skill just a few feet from the crags, but it was too late; he had lost his hold and fallen to his death. This memory still haunts me, and I could never face returning to this magnificent site.

At the west end of Glen Coe, Meall Mor is a very different and much lower hill (676m). It has extensive, but not especially conspicuous, outcrops of limestone on which I have found Whortle-leaved Willow, Mountain Avens and Hair Sedge.

Creag Meagaidh

North-east from the Nevis range, Creag Meagaidh (1,128m) on the north shore of Loch Laggan is another rich montane site. It is mainly formed from acidic schists, enriched by a few moderately calcareous outcrops. Since the land was acquired as a National Nature Reserve in 1985, Scottish Natural Heritage and its predecessors have made tremendous progress in restoring the native woodland of birch, rowan and willows on the lower slopes by reducing deer numbers and

The magnificent gullied cliffs of Coire Ardair below Creag Meagaidh stand 300m tall, and support a rich variety of montane species.

excluding sheep. Globeflower and Wood Cranesbill are flourishing in the woodland since grazing was reduced, and I am sure this is also benefitting the flora of the crags.

The richest site is the north-east-facing Coire Ardair, which is one of the few British sites for Highland Cudweed. Arctic Mouse-ear, Alpine Speedwell, Chestnut Rush, Russet Sedge and Glaucous Meadow-grass also grow here. Records from the nearby Moy Corrie include Downy Willow, Starwort Mouse-ear, Chestnut Rush, Black Alpine-sedge, Alpine Foxtail and Alpine Cat's-tail.

Other west Highland sites

The western Highlands cover a vast area. I do not have the space to review all the mountains here in detail, but it is worth picking out three further sites, starting at Dun Ban near Largybaan on the west coast of Kintyre, which I visited way back in 1979. It is a remarkable site, because the calcareous cliffs here rise only 180m or so from the sea, yet they are home to Purple, Mossy and Yellow Mountain Saxifrage, Mountain Avens, Hoary Whitlow-grass, and, as we saw in Chapter 11,

The sea-cliffs at Dun Ban on the west coast of Kintyre – an unlikely site for montane species including Mountain Avens and Yellow Oxytropis.

Yellow Oxytropis. It nicely illustrates how exposure to winter gales can mimic arctic conditions and produce a flora to match.

Travelling northwards, I should mention the hills of Morvern, not least because Ardtornish here was the home of and inspiration for John Raven, whom I profiled in Chapter 1. The richest Morvern hills are Beinn Iadain and Beinn na h-Uamha. Neither is high (571m and 465m respectively) but both are exposed to south-westerly gales and both have cliffs formed from crumbly, base-rich basalt. They support populations of Mountain Avens, Moss Campion and both Glaucous and Alpine Meadow-grass. I failed to find Scottish Pearlwort or Arctic Sandwort when I visited Beinn Iadain, but I did spot Alpine Cinquefoil and Hairy Stonecrop there.

I will end this section with the hill near Glenfinnan where I began Chapter 1. Famously, this has long been known as the only British site for Diapensia, which grows on a windswept shoulder here at around 770m. On my visit in May 1980, I noted lots of Trailing Azalea and a single patch of Dwarf Willow growing near the Diapensia, but the only other montane species I recorded on my ascent were Fir Clubmoss, Alpine Lady's-mantle and Mountain Crowberry. Nothing else made the site seem in any way special, and that is why Diapensia is such a mountain enigma here.

The Isle of Rum

Aside from mountains, I have always been fascinated by the Scottish islands, so the mountainous islands have a special appeal. I have enjoyed exploring the hills of Arran and Mull for spectacular scenery and commoner montane species (Mull even has a site for the rare Iceland Purslane, as we will see shortly). However, I think the islands of Rum and Skye are the most rewarding botanically.

I was lucky enough to make several radio features and a television film on the Isle of Rum, and have led field courses there. This allowed me plenty of time to explore this remarkable island. When it was privately owned, Rum had the reputation as the 'forbidden island' but it was bought by the nation as a National Nature Reserve in 1957 and these days its owner, Scottish Natural Heritage, and the resurgent local community positively encourage visitors.

The main block of hills on the island, centred on Askival (812m), originated as a volcano more than 50 million years ago. The rocks here are basic or ultra-basic (meaning they are especially rich in magnesium,

★★★ Diapensia *Diapensia lapponica*

With creamy-white flowers the size of a 1p coin, and a cushion of glossy evergreen leaves, Diapensia is a distinctive plant. Admittedly, it only flowers briefly in May or June, and, when not in flower, it looks confusingly like Trailing Azalea. Even so, it surprises me that its presence was never noted at its sole British site on a windswept hill shoulder above Glenfinnan until, as we saw in Chapter 1, it was discovered there by Charles Tebbutt in 1951. On my visit in 1980 I recorded it as growing at an altitude of 770m on an outcrop of sharp rocks eroded into parallel cracks, and in gravel below the rocks. The rocks are friable and apparently quartz-rich but otherwise unremarkable. The other montane species I recorded nearby gave no clue that the site was special.

My puzzlement at its Scottish occurrence increased in 1984 when, on a botanising holiday to New Hampshire in the USA, I found it growing abundantly 1,890m up on Mount Washington – the exposed hill where the (now) second highest wind speed in the world of 231mph (372km/hour) was recorded in 1934 (see photo on p.16). I have subsequently seen it high above Abisko in arctic Sweden and on a hillside beside Nuuk in Greenland – a place with a fearsome arctic climate, even if it is south of the Arctic Circle. It also occurs in Iceland and arctic Russia, with a separate subspecies in arctic Asia and Alaska. It typically grows on exposed sites from which snow is swiftly stripped by the wind, so it must be highly adapted to cope with drought, frost and the desiccation caused by high winds. Those adaptations might explain its occurrence in Scotland if it was confined to somewhere with an especially severe climate, such as the summit of Ben Nevis. But it is much more difficult to explain why it should survive on this one, rather low but admittedly exposed, hillside near Glenfinnan, at by far its southernmost European site. I can find no records of preserved pollen or microfossils in Britain to suggest that it was here as the glaciers retreated, although fossil pollen has been found in the mountains of central Europe where the species no longer survives.

There is a further twist to this puzzle. One of the people who confirmed Tebbutt's discovery in 1952 was Alf Slack, a dedicated mountain botanist with whom I had the pleasure of spending

One of the Diapensia plants in flower on its hillside near Glenfinnan in late May 1980.

time in the hills and who has featured already in Chapter 11. A teacher by profession, Alf was botanical recorder for the area that includes Glenfinnan until his death in 1998. Alf did not return to the Diapensia site until 1979, and he told me later that he was amazed how much the plant seemed to have spread in the intervening 27 years – although he admitted that might just have been a trick of his memory.

In conversation with Alf, we began to develop a theory for its occurrence. Initially, I thought this idea was implausible, but, as I have further researched the background, the idea seems a little more feasible. Diapensia is widespread up the spine of Norway, mainly at high altitudes. In Newfoundland at least, its dry seed capsules last through the summer and can be easily dislodged (Day & Scott, 1981). Some capsules project above lying snow and disperse their seed in midwinter across the snow surface. Could dislodged capsules or seeds somehow have been transported from Norway and become established at Glenfinnan some time before 1951?

There is one potential group of carriers. During the Second World War, Norwegian soldiers formed a troop within the No. 10 Inter-allied Commandos, who went through an intensive training course based at Achnacarry near Fort William. As part of this training, commandos regularly participated in 36-hour 'yomps' through the mountains. The Glenfinnan hillside is only 27km from their base at Achnacarry – well within potential 'yomping' range. I am grateful to Nick Collins and Pete Rogers from the Commando Veterans Association for the information that some Norwegian soldiers recruited into the wartime Special Operations Executive also trained at Glenfinnan Lodge. One army captain described in his diary how his platoon 'went to Glenfinnan by train and marched past Prince Charlie's statue [beside Loch Shiel] and up into the hills', where they went 'tramping over heather'.

Norwegian commandoes trained in the hills above Glenfinnan during the Second World War, like these men from No 1 Commando in Glen Coe in 1941. It is possible the Norwegians may have accidentally introduced Diapensia to the hill where it still grows.

Is it possible that Norwegian trainees accidentally carried capsules or seeds of Diapensia in the tread of their boots, woollen socks, or trouser turn-ups? That would explain its occurrence at this otherwise unimposing site and Alf's suspicion that the population had spread between 1952 and 1979 – although Wigginton (1999) suggests that the population today is relatively stable at around 1,200 clumps.

We might have hoped that DNA analysis would allow us to estimate how long ago Scottish plants diverged from those in Norway, as was done with Mossy Cyphel plants from Scotland and the Alps (see Chapter 3). If Diapensia only arrived here last century, we would expect Scottish plants to be virtually identical to Norwegian plants genetically. Unfortunately, work in Norway suggests that the species shows very little genetic diversity, so DNA analysis is unlikely to give us any further insight into its arrival here.

The age of Diapensia plants can be estimated by counting growth rings in their stems. However, even if the species was growing here before 1945, I suspect we would be lucky now to find plants more than 70 years old in the population to prove that point. A fairly detailed study of the Scottish population was carried out in the late 1990s by Dr Alistair Headley, an ecological consultant. As part of this survey, the size of a few plants was monitored and they were shown to be growing outwards by around 3mm per year. On that basis, plants were estimated to have an average age of 40 years, with the oldest perhaps 150 years old. However, that is based on measurements of fewer than ten plants over just three years, which might have been atypical seasons, so it is far from definitive.

One thing that might disprove the commando theory would be the discovery of Diapensia at other sites, well away from commando training areas. There have been past reports of the species elsewhere in Scotland, but these most probably resulted from confusion with Trailing Azalea. I was excited therefore to hear that in 2007 Angus MacIntyre, a countryside ranger from nearby Mallaig, had found and photographed Diapensia on a hill called Sithean Mor, 16km west of the original population. Angus returned to Sithean Mor with Ian Strachan, the current botanical recorder for the area, in 2008 and, following enquiries from me, Ian searched the summit area again in June 2015, but they found no trace of Diapensia. That scenario could easily fit with a plant establishing briefly from windblown seed, or carried from Glenfinnan on a hillwalker's boot, but swiftly dying at an unsuitable site.

To be honest, I am sceptical about the commando theory. When Grant Roger, John Raven and others visited the Glenfinnan site a month after the Diapensia discovery, they observed 'several hundred specimens'. That seems unlikely if it had arrived there less than a decade before. I think it is most probably a remnant from the Ice Age whose continued existence at its last remaining site is the result of chance and the 'chequerboard theory' I outlined in Chapter 3. However, until someone can identify some special feature of the Glenfinnan site to explain its survival there, I like Nick Collins's interpretation of Diapensia in Scotland as 'a natural memorial to those brave young men who trained in the hills and who gave their lives for our freedom'.

The plant that Angus MacIntyre photographed on Sithean Mor in 2007 was definitely Diapensia, growing at a hitherto unknown site, but sadly it has not been refound subsequently.

The ultra-basic rocks of Askival on Rum support an interesting range of plants. Manx Shearwaters nest in burrows high on the mountain, and guano from these seabirds enriches the soil and explains the green 'lawns' on the slopes.

nickel, chromium and cobalt, minerals that are toxic to many species). As a result, these hills support a choice range of plants. On Askival and Hallival, I have found lovely cushions of Moss Campion and occasional patches of Mossy Cyphel, along with Fir Clubmoss, Mountain Sorrel, Stone Bramble, Alpine Lady's-mantle, Mountain Everlasting, Alpine Meadow-rue and Starry Saxifrage along streamsides. Northern Rock-cress is commoner here than anywhere else I have seen it. A large population of Arctic Sandwort (which we will meet in the next chapter) grows on the slopes of Ruinsival and the gravelly shore of a nearby loch, but is more difficult to find.

Scottish Asphodel and Two-flowered Rush are also found here, but several other dramatic records from that area, including a number of plants recorded as new to Britain, were later shown to have been introduced here in the 1940s as part of an elaborate fraud by Professor John Heslop Harrison of Newcastle University, apparently to enhance his scientific reputation (Sabbagh, 1999).

The cliffs of Fionchra, overlooking Glen Shellesder on the west of the island, are also rich. Alpine Penny-cress grows here at one of only four or five sites in Scotland, as well as three species of saxifrage, Northern Rock-cress, Hoary Whitlow-grass and Alpine Speedwell. North of the glen, Mountain Avens grows on the limestone ridge of Monadh Dubh. Forked Spleenwort is recorded from Glen Harris in the south-west of the island, and Pyramidal Bugle is a rare species on terraces above the sea-cliffs of Rum.

The adjacent island of Eigg also has an interesting flora, including Alpine Clubmoss and Dwarf Willow on the slopes of the island's highest point, An Sgurr (393m), Arctic Sandwort on screes above the cliffs of Cleadale, and Pyramidal Bugle on cliff ledges.

The Cuillin of Skye

The name Cuillin may come from the legend of the Irish hunter *Cu Chulainn*, who is said to have crossed from Ireland to Skye in two strides, or from the Old Norse word *kjölen* meaning ridges. That is already plural, so strictly we should refer to 'the Cuillin' or 'the Cuillin hills', but not 'the Cuillins'.

The Black Cuillin is a range of 23 serrated peaks of igneous gabbro and basalt rock, 12 of which are Munros. They have steep cliffs and deeply cut corries and gullies, and are mostly bare rock, although Alpine Lady's-mantle, Moss Campion and Alpine Bistort grow here and there. A few damp gullies in the corries support Alpine Saxifrage, Alpine Mouse-ear, Alpine Saw-wort, Alpine Meadow-grass and a trio of scarce members of the cabbage family: Northern Rock-cress, Rock Whitlow-grass and Alpine Rock-cress (Murray & Birks, 2005). The last of these three grows here at its only British site, qualifying it as another three-star enigma. Catriona Murray, the enthusiastic and dedicated botanical recorder for Skye from 1966 to 2006, rediscovered Trailing Azalea in the Cuillin in 1981 and in the nearby Kyleakin hills in 1986.

Glen Sligachan separates the Black Cuillin from the Red Cuillin, a range of hills with a very different character. They are composed not of gabbro and basalt but mainly of granite with a reddish tinge when weathered. This has been eroded into lower, more rounded hills that are covered in vegetation to their summits but with long scree chutes down their slopes. An unusual feature of the Red Cuillin is the large extent of Dwarf Juniper heath above about 500m. Parsley Fern is common in the screes, and Alpine Clubmoss and Sibbaldia grow on the windswept summits.

★★★ Alpine Rock-cress *Arabis alpina*

Alpine Rock-cress is a plant that would be easily dismissed, were it not so remarkably rare in Britain. To me, it looks like a typical garden weed from the cabbage family, reminiscent perhaps of Shepherd's-purse. It has a rosette of greyish, coarsely toothed, basal leaves, a few clasping stem leaves, and a cluster of small, white, four-petalled flowers that develop into long, narrow fruit pods.

My view is undoubtedly coloured by where I have found the plant. In both the Arctic and the Alps, I have seen it growing abundantly in the rubble of newly bulldozed tracks or in recently disturbed ground around chairlift stations. That is not entirely surprising. The adaptations that allow a plant to colonise glacial scree give it an advantage in invading hillsides torn up by bulldozers. I have also found it in naturally open habitats: in the rubble below a glacier in the Alps and in a gravelly scree chute kept open by regular avalanches below a mountain in arctic Sweden. These sites are united, of course, by their relatively severe climate.

So what does that tell us about Alpine Rock-cress on Skye? Its classic site lies between 820m and 850m in a corrie on the north-west corner of the Black Cuillin where it was discovered in 1887 by H C Hart, an Irish mountaineer on a mission to record the height of the nearby

The rugged and often inaccessible corries and gullies of the Black Cuillin – a classic location for Alpine Rock-cress.

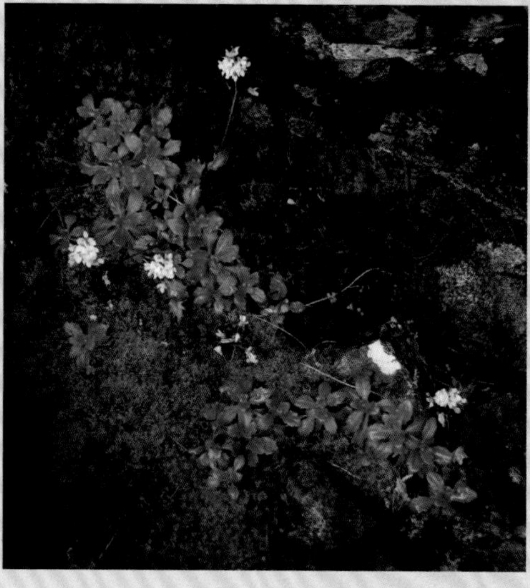

Alpine Rock-cress looked an attractive plant where I photographed it below a glacier in southern Norway (left). The rather scraggy plants that cling to survival in the Cuillin corries (right) are somewhat less appealing to the eye!

peak of Sgurr Alasdair. It grows here in two main colonies on shady rock ledges alongside Northern Rock-cress, Mountain Sorrel, Globeflower and Roseroot, with a smaller population on the slope below. Hart recorded the plant 'in three distinct places', and Catriona Murray, the local botanical recorder, methodically searched for other sites without success. Then, in 2002, two botanists discovered the plant in a second, north-facing corrie below Sgurr Alasdair, about 2km from the classic site, 'after a slow and tedious climb to the heights' (Jepson, 2004).

At both its Cuillin sites, Alpine Rock-cress grows in moist, fine gravel reminiscent of glacial moraines. This is clearly unstable: there is another record of a rock-cress site being completely buried in loose rocks washed down by snow and ice. The shadiness of the site, the instability of the scree and the severe climate create the open habitat in which the rock-cress can flourish. The relatively mild climate of Skye might allow it a longer growing season than in similar gullies further east which remain snow-filled until much later in the year.

If we assume that Alpine Rock-cress was more widespread in Britain at the end of the last Ice Age (although unfortunately the seeds of *Arabis* species cannot be told apart in fossil beds), it may have been driven back to fewer and fewer mountain sites, until eventually (in line with my chequerboard theory) only the Cuillin provided suitable conditions for its survival. I suspect it hangs on there in its two main populations, spreading seeds which briefly establish at other nearby sites until they are smothered by a landslip or grazed by deer. It clearly is a survivor species: I have found it on a wind-blasted shoulder below the summit of Pico Arieiro (1,810m) on the distinctly unarctic island of Madeira, and it also grows on the mountains of East Africa, including Mount Kenya. With only 113 plants recently counted in the Cuillin, it would only take a landslip or two, a few hungry deer or a run of unusually dry summers, and its extirpation in Britain would be complete.

Below Bla Bheinn (anglicised as Blaven), west of the head of Loch Slapin, limestone outcrops on the cliffs of Coire Uaigneich, producing magnificent tall-herb communities of Roseroot, Globeflower and Melancholy Thistle. Alpine Saw-wort is common here, along with Holly Fern, Chickweed Willowherb and Purple, Yellow Mountain and Mossy Saxifrages.

Strath Suardal, Skye

The valley of Strath Suardal, south of the Red Cuillin, is also special. Although it rises only to 283m on Ben Suardal, there are extensive outcrops of limestone, producing one of the few limestone pavements in Scotland. Green Spleenwort, Globeflower, Stone Bramble and Melancholy Thistle lurk in the grykes, along with Herb Paris and Dark-red Helleborine, two uncommon lowland species. Alpine Cinquefoil and Rock Sedge grow on open turf amidst the pavements, and Mountain Avens is common on shattered limestone rock.

The occurrence of Mountain Avens here neatly illustrates some of the factors controlling the survival of our montane flora discussed in Chapter 3. It is always suggested that the spread of trees in the post-glacial period swamped the arctic-alpine species, forcing them back to the treeless summits. Yet Mountain Avens grows abundantly in Coille Gaireallach, a delightful open wood of Downy Birch and Hazel at the western end of Strath Suardal. Closer investigation shows that it only grows where limestone is covered by soil so thin that trees cannot root there, thus ensuring the open habitat it needs. Green Spleenwort and Bearberry also grow in these thin limestone soils, but Globeflower here is very much part of the woodland flora.

Beside the bay of Camas Malag, just west of the woodland here, Mountain Avens confounds its common name by growing on limestone outcrops barely 6m above sea level (see photo on p.24), along with Roseroot, Stone Bramble and nearby Bearberry. The regular blasts of westerly winds ensure the conditions in which these montane calcicoles can flourish.

The Trotternish ridge of Skye

In the north of Skye, the Trotternish peninsula produces some of the most spectacular scenery in Scotland. It rises gently on its western slope but features lines of dramatic cliffs on its eastern exposure. The

basalt of the Trotternish ridge emerged 60 million years ago as a flow of lava, 300m thick, through fissures in the Earth's crust. It lies on top of older, sedimentary rocks which are too soft to support the weight of the basalt above. As a result, slabs of rock are slumping away from the cliff face, like fence posts collapsing in muddy soil, producing a landscape with massive landslips, tumbled rocks, collapsed basalt columns and detached pinnacles. This landscape is still actively moving, creating newly exposed rock faces due to the landslips and open gravelly soils in which arctic-alpines can flourish.

The chaotic landscape below Quiraing, with the detached pinnacle of the Prison, massive landslips and tumbled rocks. This instability helps support a rich flora.

The minor road west from Staffin gives access to one of these areas at Quiraing. A footpath leads round to a massive castellated pinnacle, descriptively called the Prison. Green Spleenwort, Stone Bramble, Alpine Lady's-mantle and flowery patches of Mossy Saxifrage grow beside the path. A typical tall-herb community of Globeflower, Roseroot and Mountain Sorrel grows on the Prison's ledges, with Purple Saxifrage, Hoary Whitlow-grass and Moss Campion on rock faces.

Even more impressive is the cliff below the Storr, 10km north of Portree. Here a phalanx of rock pinnacles stand guard over an amphitheatre called the Sanctuary, hollowed out by the collapsing rocks. The most famous of these pinnacles, the Old Man of Storr, exposed by a landslip 6,500 years ago, towers to a height of nearly 60m. Purple Saxifrage, Mossy Saxifrage and Northern Rock-cress are amongst the species growing on the rock stacks here (see also photos on p.2 and p.20). The path to the Old Man continues onwards into Coire Scamadal, where Starry and Yellow Mountain Saxifrage, Alpine and Chickweed Willowherb and Mossy Cyphel appear in wet flushes, and open gravelly areas support Fir Clubmoss, Alpine Pearlwort, Mountain Everlasting and Three-flowered Rush (although I have never found the Two-flowered Rush that is also recorded here). Most importantly, these gravelly flushes are the habitat of Iceland Purslane, another species that qualifies as a three-star enigma because of its remarkable world distribution.

Rarer plants of the Trotternish cliffs include Alpine Woodsia, Alpine Saxifrage, Whortle-leaved Willow, Alpine Saw-wort, and Alpine and Glaucous Meadow-grass. A few clumps of Arctic Mouse-ear grow in one exposed area below the Storr summit. And in June 2014 Tufted Saxifrage was found on the crags south of Ben Edra at the unusually low altitude of around 470m – an amazing discovery at such a relatively accessible site. The finder was ace botanical explorer of the Scottish hills Gordon Rothero, some of whose many contributions I have already acknowledged elsewhere in this book.

Because of the sheer variety of habitats and landscapes around Skye, it was my place of choice for botanising holidays when I lived in Edinburgh. Now that I live only an hour or so from this delightful island, writing this chapter has reminded me that I must get back there more frequently!

★★★ Iceland Purslane *Koenigia islandica*

Iceland Purslane is an unprepossessing plant but a doughty survivor. It is one of very few arctic species that are annual, so it must regrow from seed each spring despite the brevity of the summer. When I first came across it in Coire Scamadal on Skye in May 1981, I recorded 'tiny, red-stalked seedlings with rounded leaves in clumps no more than 2mm across'. They could have been seedlings of almost anything; only their distinctive habitat in wet gravelly flushes hinted that they were special. I returned in early August, and by then the plants were bigger, although a 50p coin would have covered an average specimen. Their tiny reddish-tinged, green flowers were also in evidence, with petal-like lobes barely 1mm long.

Iceland Purslane's unimpressive appearance explains the strange story of its discovery in Britain. It was first collected below the summit of the Storr in August 1934, but misidentified as the unrelated Water-purslane. The specimen lay unrecognised in the herbarium of the

Royal Botanic Gardens Kew until 1950, when B L (or Bill) Burtt, then assistant to the Garden's Director, recognised its true identity as a new record for Britain. In August of the following year, John Raven visited the Storr and found that the newly recognised species was abundant and widespread there (Raven, 1952b) – and he made the meticulous painting reproduced on page 12. Venturing more widely, he also found it commonly along the escarpment south of Ben Edra. Today, it is known along the Trotternish ridge from Ben Edra south to Ben Dearg – a stretch of some 12km – at altitudes between 314m near Loch Cuithir and 693m below the Storr summit. In 1956, it was also discovered on the Ardmeanach Peninsula on Mull, its southernmost site in Europe, where it grows on open gravelly slopes at altitudes between 380m and 520m.

In 2010, I tracked down the plant in its nominate home of Iceland, which helped me better understand its occurrence on Skye. I found it in flood gravel beside the River Öxará, where regular flooding maintains the open habitat in which it can flourish. Later I found it also in the open gravel of solifluction terraces. Clearly its habitat on Skye is torn open by the slumping of huge slabs of rock off the escarpment, but the high rainfall is also critical (the annual rainfall at nearby Prabost is 180cm, or nearly 6 feet!). Intense or prolonged rain washes scree down rock chutes on the hillside, swamping competition and creating the open, infertile gravel the species requires.

Thanks to its distinctive pollen, we know that Iceland Purslane was widespread across northern Britain after the last Ice Age. It has been found in lake sediments at Windermere in Cumbria and in glacial deposits on Tolsta Head on the Isle of Lewis, for example. Subsequently, competition must have forced it back to its refuges on Mull and Skye. It is highly sensitive to drought, which may have eliminated it from other sites, although I do wonder if it might still survive elsewhere.

In the right conditions, this unremarkable-looking plant can be a remarkable survivor. It is found throughout arctic regions, including the harsh environments of Svalbard and Jan Mayen Island, in the mountains of central Asia, in the Rocky Mountains of North America, and even, extraordinarily, in Tierra del Fuego at the southern tip of South America, where it grows in wet gravel amongst 'cushion heath' at altitudes above 800m (Moore, 1975).

Iceland Purslane is scarcely an impressive plant where it sprouts from seed each year on open gravel on the Trotternish Ridge (left). Slightly larger plants grow on river gravel in its nominate home of Iceland (right).

Hills of the far north

chapter sixteen

The hills north of the Great Glen in Scotland are some of the most rugged and remote in Britain, with sparse habitation and few roads. Each hill has its own botanical character, but all of them offer satisfying walking and spectacular scenery. Despite their botanical richness, many of these hills are visited only sporadically by botanists, and, as a result, this is the area of Britain where I suspect most strongly that interesting discoveries remain to be made. Furthermore, height alone is not a guide to the occurrence of montane plants here; many occur at much lower altitudes than further south, reflecting the increasingly subarctic nature of the climate. The main botanical 'hotspots' in the region are in the species-rich band of limestone that runs southwards from Durness on the north coast, and so it makes sense to begin this chapter there.

The Durness Limestone

Geological maps show a narrow band of limestone running south-south-west from Durness in Sutherland to Kishorn in Wester Ross. This then continues across to the Isle of Skye and the limestones we met there in Strath Suardal. This limestone formed from the shells of marine creatures living relatively deep in the sea during the Cambrian and Ordovician periods (540–440 million years ago). It only occasionally breaches the surface as stark white hummocks, like some partially buried skeleton. These scarps of limestone rock can support an interesting flora if they are not heavily grazed. Where the limestone lies just beneath the surface, it has a conspicuous impact on the landscape, producing the rolling green pastures of Durness and Elphin, north of Ullapool. To the north of Elphin, Scotland's most extensive cave systems have been cut into the limestones of Assynt.

OPPOSITE PAGE: Sgorr Ruadh, north of Achnashellach in Wester Ross: large areas of rugged, wild land in the north-west Highlands have still not been fully explored by botanists.

The main montane sites of the North Highlands.

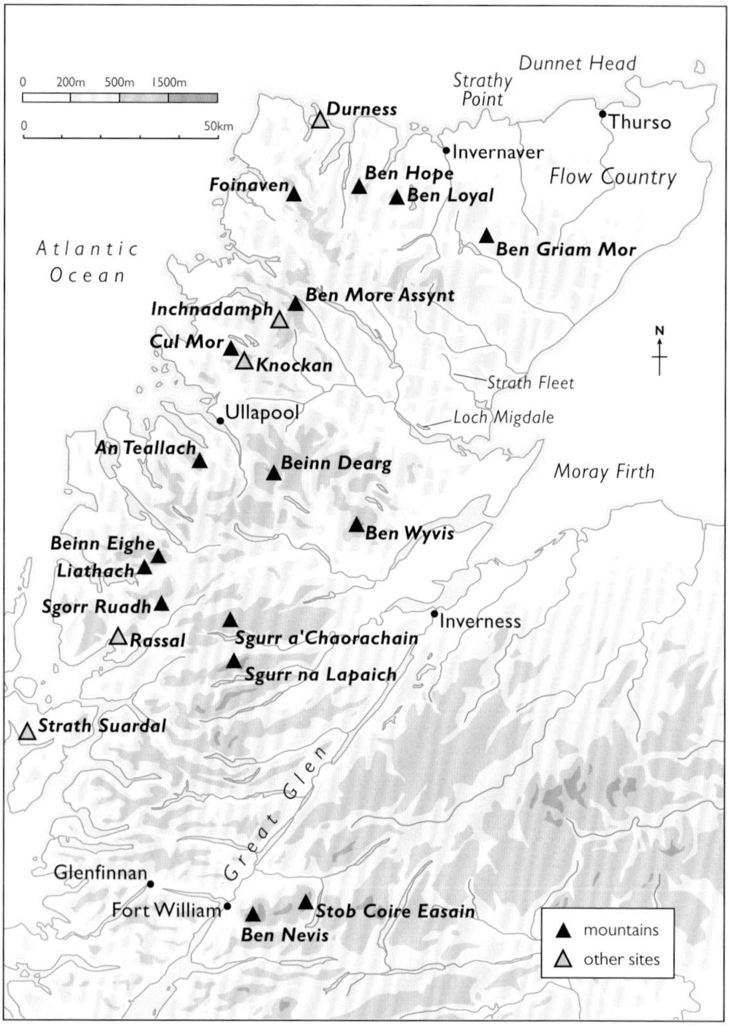

If we start our exploration at the head of Loch Kishorn, the limestone at Rassal is covered in a scattering of Ash trees. For a long time this was regarded as degraded Ash woodland, but now it is suggested that this open habitat is a cultural landscape dating back to the Viking era, which should more properly be regarded as wood pasture. Historically, this was kept open by grazing and pollarding of the trees for timber. The scarce Dark-red Helleborine orchid grows on limestone beneath the trees. The limestone scarps here are deeply fissured, with Green Spleenwort and Holly Fern in the cracks. Mountain Avens is widespread, and Rock Sedge is probably commoner here than anywhere else in Britain. Both Whortle-leaved Willow and Three-leaved Rush occur at surprisingly low altitude, along with Globeflower, Yellow Mountain Saxifrage, Mossy Saxifrage, Alpine Lady's-mantle, Mountain Sorrel and Melancholy Thistle.

Travelling north, the next prominent occurrence of the limestone is part-way down the cliffs at Knockan Crag, a National Nature Reserve. The excellent Rock Room interpretative display here shows how the rock stratification on the crag helped Victorian geologists elucidate the great Earth movements of the Moine Thrust (Scott, 2014) and leads on to a dramatic nature trail illustrating the diverse geology. It takes a bit of searching to find montane species here, but they include Mountain Avens, Hoary Whitlow-grass, Moss Campion, Rock Sedge and a few plants of Whortle-leaved Willow.

Mountain Avens on lime-rich rocks below Knockan Crag, a site of great geological significance.

Inchnadamph

Continuing northwards, the area around Inchnadamph, at the head of Loch Assynt, is the most interesting stretch of Durness Limestone botanically, partly because it reaches its highest elevation here at 520m. It is also the best karst limestone landscape in Scotland, reminiscent of the area around Malhamdale described in Chapter 7, with streams that disappear underground into caves cut through the limestone, leaving behind dry valleys which mark their previous course.

The Inchnadamph Hotel has been a base for generations of botanical explorers. The crags that tower above the hotel confused me when I first visited there as a fledgling botanist in 1979. I headed for the great wall of creamy rock that reminded me of the Malham limestone but I found this disappointingly dull. In fact this rock is mylonite, a form of limestone that was crushed and milled in the massive Earth movement of the Moine Thrust around 400 million years ago. Because the rock was compressed by this action, it erodes less readily than unmodified limestone and produces poorer soils. On the way down

Inchnadamph Cliff towers above the A837 road beside Loch Assynt. The lower, darker band of crags is more interesting botanically than the white cliff above.

Characteristic plants of the Traligill Valley, Inchnadamph

Least Clubmoss	Mountain Avens	Crowberry
Green Spleenwort	Sibbaldia	Northern Bedstraw
Holly Fern	Alpine Lady's-mantle	Alpine Saw-wort
Globeflower	Dwarf Willow	Melancholy Thistle
Yellow Mountain Saxifrage	Alpine Bistort	Mountain Everlasting

from these crags, I stopped at a lower crag of darker grey rock, and here there was much more interest: Yellow Mountain Saxifrage, Alpine Bistort, Stone Bramble, nice patches of Mountain Avens with one or two small plants of Dark-red Helleborine amongst them, and one of the specialities of the area, the grass known as Don's Couch.

Inland from the hotel, crags and slopes around the Traligill Burn support a good range of calcicoles, listed in the table above. Following the path south from here, a conspicuous limestone ridge above a large loch is even richer. It is another site for many of the species in the table, with patches also of Moss Campion and Mossy Cyphel. Arctic Sandwort grows on open limestone gravel nearby, and for some reason its flowers here often have four petals rather than the more typical five. The puzzling distribution of this species in England and Scotland qualifies it as another enigma. Towards the top of the ridge, Rock Sedge is common, and a large colony of Whortle-leaved Willow grows on a limestone cliff below the ridge. A little further south, the ground becomes more acid and is inhabited by typical peat alpines including Cloudberry, Dwarf Cornel and a few plants of Arctic Bearberry.

The serpentine rock at Nikka Vord, beside the Keen of Hamar on Unst in Shetland, is one of the few sites for Arctic Sandwort (see Chapter 17).

★★★ Arctic Sandwort *Arenaria norvegica* subspecies *norvegica*
English Sandwort *Arenaria norvegica* subspecies *anglica*

Arctic Sandwort is a double enigma, because two subspecies have been recognised in Britain, both of which are rare, extremely localised and legally protected. It is admittedly not a plant that many casual hillwalkers would divert to see, although its delicate flowers and glossy leaves have a subtle beauty. It is one of several, rather similar, tufted, white-flowered montane plants. Five petals show that it belongs in the pink family, but it could just as easily be a small mouse-ear or pearlwort. Its true interest lies in its rarity and very particular habitats.

The two subspecies vary in their features and their distribution. As we have seen, subspecies *anglica*, known as English (or Yorkshire) Sandwort, is almost entirely confined to the eastern slopes of Ingleborough in the Pennines, where it was first discovered in 1889, with a second small population on nearby Fountains Fell (see Chapter 7). That would make it a British, English and even a Yorkshire endemic. The subspecies is distinguished by its mainly upright flowering stems with lance-shaped leaves, and by growing mainly as a 'winter annual', meaning it germinates in the autumn, overwinters, then quickly flowers, sets seed and dies the next spring. In recent years, its population has ranged between 300 and 800 plants, a significant decline from an estimated 1,000–1,500 in 1981. A series of dry spring seasons and the increased use of tracks across its habitat by walkers and cyclists may explain this decline.

Subspecies *norvegica* is highly localised at a few sites already described in north-west Scotland – in Morvern, on Rum and Eigg, and here in Inchnadamph. It is also recorded at altitudes from 15m on the Keen of Hamar in Shetland (see next chapter) to 650m on hills above Glen Creran in Argyll, although its current survival at the latter site needs confirmation. All these

'Karst' limestone landscape, inland from Inchnadamph – the kind of habitat in which Arctic Sandwort grows.

In the limestone outcrops east of the Inchnadamph Cliff, Arctic Sandwort often turns up with four petals, rather than the five petals typical of the pink family.

sites have soils that are basic or ultra-basic, which partly explains its restricted distribution. The name Arctic Sandwort is appropriate, because it is found to well north of the Arctic Circle in the mountains of Norway. It also grows in base-rich soils in Iceland and Finland, and two small populations were discovered at the Burren in Ireland in 2008. It is a perennial with upright flowering shoots and several spreading non-flowering shoots. Its leaves are somewhat broader than those of subspecies *anglica*.

So how do we account for this apparent 'two-pronged' occurrence in Britain? Seeds that might belong to this species have been found in fossil deposits from the Weichselian period at several sites in southern England, but unfortunately these cannot be easily separated from seeds of Fringed Sandwort *A. ciliata*, a plant now confined to limestone cliffs in County Sligo, Ireland. As we have seen, this Weichselian occurrence is consistent with the survival of several other montane species during the Ice Age.

If English Sandwort is a separate genetic entity, it must have evolved in isolation over previous interglacial periods, then been driven south by the encroaching glaciers. At the end of the last Ice Age, it must have followed the retreating glaciers and found the conditions it needed for long-term survival only around Ingleborough. Perhaps the more widely distributed subspecies *norvegica* survived on nunataks off the west of Scotland and Scandinavia and spread from there to its present refuges on nearby base-rich montane sites.

Recent research, however, questions the subspecies status of the English plants. Similar annual plants have also been noted in disturbed habitats in Scotland, Norway and Iceland, where only subspecies *norvegica* is recorded. Studies by Conor Meade from Maynooth University in Ireland (unpublished at the time of writing) suggest that all the British populations of Arctic Sandwort are virtually identical genetically, except perhaps for plants on Rum. By that token, the Ingleborough plants may not be an endemic British subspecies after all. They may be a purely ecological adaptation for growing in hollows of the Ingleborough limestone where the accumulated thin peaty soils are subject to frequent waterlogging and occasional drought. Nevertheless, the scattered distribution of Arctic Sandwort across Britain remains a fascinating relict of post-glacial times.

The northernmost exposure of this limestone band, around the village of Durness on the north coast of Sutherland, occurs at such a low elevation that I will leave it for consideration in the next chapter.

Don's Couch *Elymus caninus* var. *donianus*

When Derek Ratcliffe included this handsome grass (sometimes referred to as Don's Twitch) in his list of montane species that I adapted for the table on pages 30–35, it was regarded as a full species *Agropyron donianum*. It was known from rock crevices and gullies on a few base-rich mountains between 670m and 910m in the Breadalbanes, where it was first recognised by George Don in 1810, and here in Inchnadamph at a mere 75–210m. As well as the crag where I mentioned it at Inchnadamph, the botanist John Raven on a visit in September 1951 recorded it 'often in profusion ... all along both banks of the Traligill Burn from 250 feet above sea level near the hotel to 600 feet near the cave where the burn disappears underground' (Raven, 1952a). It may be significant that he also found Bearded Couch along the lower stretches of the burn. Forms reminiscent of Don's Couch are also known from Iceland and Greenland.

Don's Couch is very similar to the much commoner Bearded Couch *Elymus caninus* of shaded habitats in hedges and woods. Its main distinguishing feature is its short awns (bristle-like projections at the base of the leafy bracts beneath the grass flowers). The problem is that throughout their range there are many intermediates between these two couch-grasses, making them difficult to distinguish with certainty. As a result, Don's Couch is now generally regarded as a subspecies or variety of Bearded Couch. Perhaps the two forms were more distinctive in the past. Then, as temperatures got warmer after the Ice Age and human activities increased, woodland habitats with Bearded Couch began to encroach on surviving sites of Don's Couch and the two species began to hybridise. This mixing of species characters continued until no pure Don's Couch remained, so that the plants we see today are a product of evolution in action. For all that, the large plant I saw on the crags at Inchnadamph looked distinctive to my eye.

Don's Couch: when I met another botanist below Inchnadamph Cliff in July 1979, we agreed that the grass on this ledge looked sufficiently distinctive to merit recognition as a full species.

Exploring the hills of the north

There are plenty of high hills in the north of Scotland. By my reckoning, 99 out of the 282 Munros lie north of the Great Glen. Almost all of these have some botanical interest, but none is exceptionally rich. Interesting plants can turn up almost anywhere in this region. The unexceptional hill that I look up to from the study of my home in Wester Ross rises to only 395m, yet barely 50m above sea level it has patches of Yellow Mountain Saxifrage beside small streams and ditches, and Purple Saxifrage grows on north-facing crags below the summit. Space only permits a whirlwind tour around the mountains of the north Highlands shown on the map at the head of this chapter, with a selection of the choicest species from each. As I write this, I cannot help thinking what a brilliant two-week botanical tour these sites would offer!

Inverness-shire and Wester Ross

The hills of Glens Affric and Cannich, west of Loch Ness, centred on Sgurr na Lapaich (1,150m), have already featured in preceding chapters as sites for Woolly Willow and Starwort Mouse-ear, amongst other species. They are relatively acidic with only limited outcrops of calcareous rock but carry significant accumulations of snow that lasts well into spring in many years, and so offer a home to species such as Chestnut Rush, Curved Wood-rush, Russet Sedge and Alpine Cat's-tail.

The Moine Schist hills around Sgurr a' Chaorachain, south of Strathcarron in Wester Ross, look intriguing, with some dramatic north-facing corries. They are little botanised, but Two-flowered Rush and Russet Sedge have been found there. On the other side of the valley, my local hills of Sgorr Ruadh and Fuar Tholl have some intriguing old records for species including Highland Saxifrage and Highland Cudweed, but I have explored there only briefly and failed to find these.

Continuing northwards, the hills around Kinlochewe and Torridon are deservedly popular with hillwalkers for their magnificent scenery. Beinn Eighe is amongst the most spectacular: rugged and imposing, it is topped with a cap of quartzite rock that makes its summit look snow-covered even in midsummer. It is the best-studied hill botanically, not least because of its history as the first National Nature Reserve declared in Britain in 1951. I love the Mountain Trail

here, which climbs from the shore of Loch Maree to 550m, initially through wonderfully varied open woodland with some magnificent 'granny' Scots Pine trees approaching 400 years old. Fir and Alpine Clubmosses, Dwarf Juniper, Trailing Azalea and Arctic Bearberry grow in the open moorland higher on the trail, with Dwarf Cornel in regions of deeper peat.

Further up Beinn Eighe, ledges on a few crags beyond the reach of deer have a typical tall-herb community of Globeflower, Melancholy Thistle and Wild Angelica. Pyramidal Bugle is recorded here in small quantities. Dwarf Willow, Stiff Sedge, Spiked Wood-rush and more rarely Curved Wood-rush occur on summit heaths, and occasional patches of Mossy Saxifrage highlight areas of more calcareous mudstone rock. Northern Rock-cress, Arctic Mouse-ear and Parsley Fern grow in scree slopes below the 1,010m summit, and Highland Saxifrage is also recorded.

Adjacent to Beinn Eighe, Liathach (1,053m) is mainly composed of Torridonian Sandstone, producing a sharper-topped, grey, ridged summit. Northern Rock-cress and Arctic Mouse-ear are among species on its crags. North-east from here, the mountain massif centred on Beinn Dearg (1,084m) has arisen several times in previous chapters as the northernmost site for species including Starwort Mouse-ear, Highland Cudweed and Black Alpine-sedge. After the Cairngorms and Breadalbane hills, it is one of the most important sites for montane plants in Britain, partly because it consists of both hard silica-rich rocks which produce acid soils and soft mica-schist rocks which give rise to calcareous soils. Its tantalising species include Downy Willow, Highland Saxifrage, Chestnut Rush, Russet Sedge and Alpine Cat's-tail. Norwegian Mugwort, which we will meet shortly, is also known from its outlying slopes. Its neighbour, An Teallach, whose several summits rise to 1,062m, is a mass of heavily glaciated Torridonian Sandstone, weathered to a craggy ridge of turrets and towers. It is notable as a site for Tufted Saxifrage, Highland Saxifrage, Arctic Mouse-ear and Glaucous Meadow-grass.

Cul Mor in Inverpolly is a pink sandstone mountain with a much softer, rounded profile, reaching 849m. I have climbed it a couple of times in search of one particular species. Alpine Clubmoss and Trailing Azalea are notable on the climb up its eastern slopes, but the main botanical target is on the flat shoulder running north-west from the summit. My main memory of this shoulder is the breathtaking view over a landscape of low hummocks and small lakes – known as

OPPOSITE PAGE: 'Granny' Scots Pines line the lower slopes of Beinn Eighe. Much of the hill is Torridonian sandstone, capped with quartzite, producing large areas of bare rock and scree.

Cul Mor (towards the right) is a mountain of pink sandstone, famous as a site for Norwegian Mugwort.

'knockans and lochans' – across the sea to the Outer Hebrides beyond (see photo on p.19). This shoulder is the best-known site for Norwegian Mugwort, a species so localised here and at two other sites further south that it counts as another mountain enigma. It grows here quite abundantly amongst a loose clitter of sandstone chips. Its relatively commonplace associates, such as Dwarf Willow, Alpine Lady's-mantle and Mossy Cyphel, give no clue that the site is in any way special.

★★★ NORWEGIAN MUGWORT *Artemisia norvegica*

John Raven's delightful painting of Norwegian Mugwort on Cul Mor in August 1953.

Norwegian Mugwort is an odd little plant. Its flowerhead looks a little like a failed daisy, with a yellow button of what are called disc florets in the centre but no showy, petal-like ray florets. Its finely divided silky-hairy leaves are typical of other wormwoods and mugworts. They are aromatic, with a slightly acrid smell, but as far as I know have never had any herbal uses.

The species was discovered, new to Britain, on the shoulder of Cul Mor in August 1950 by Sir Christopher Cox, whose professional career was as an educational adviser to the British government (Blakelock, 1953). This is by far the most unexpected of the quartet of new species that were first recognised in Britain during the glorious purple patch of mountain discoveries in the early 1950s. The other three – Diapensia, Iceland Purslane and Purple Coltsfoot – are all relatively widespread in Scandinavia or central Europe, but this species is extremely localised at its only other sites, in the Dovrefjell district and adjacent mountains in Norway and in the northern Ural Mountains. In 1957, a further Scottish site was discovered in stony peat on the summit ridge of a hill north of Beinn Dearg, its southernmost site in Europe, and in 1972 it was found on another hilltop just east of this. All its sites lie between 700m and 910m. Tests to interpret the gritty soil in which the Cul Mor plants grow showed that it is relatively acid, with low levels of calcium and phosphate.

Sir Christopher Cox's description of the plants he found on Cul Mor accords with what I have seen on my visits. Many clumps produce no flowers, and where flowering stems are present they often seem small or shrunken, like withered buds. I wonder if the plants' survival here is so marginal that in some years late frosts or gales kill off developing flowers, so that flowers only develop sufficiently to set and propagate the species in a few, benign seasons. The size and extent of the Cul Mor colony, and the subsequent discoveries on other mountaintops, strongly point to it being native here. Indeed our Scottish plants are sufficiently distinctive in size and leaf shape from Norwegian plants (and apparently also in the oily lipid chemicals found in their cells) that they are placed in a separate endemic subspecies *scotica*, suggesting they must have evolved here in isolation for several millennia.

Throughout its range, Norwegian Mugwort seems to be highly resistant to wind exposure. It can survive full exposure to winter frosts when winds blow off any blanket of snow. Its intricately divided leaves hug low to the ground, protecting it from the worst wind and allowing it to take advantage of whatever solar heat is available. In summer its habitat rapidly dries out, but silky hairs on its leaves trap an envelope of humid air and help reduce water loss. Its leaves have been

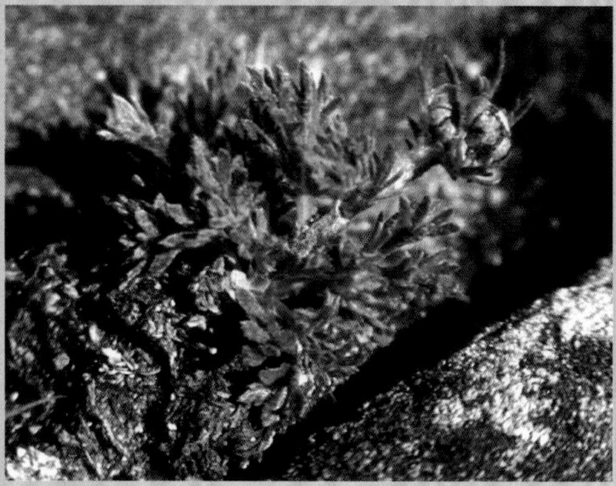

Norwegian Mugwort: many plants seem to produce only shrunken flowerheads, more like withered buds.

shown to survive summer temperatures as high as 47°C – an extreme it is unlikely to confront in Scotland!

In combination, I think that these observations explain why it survives on just these few tops in the far north-west of Scotland. Although it is adapted to winter cold, I suspect it could not survive the extreme cold of mountains further east. It may also need occasional warm summers to set seed successfully – conditions which are most likely to occur close to the warming influence of the North Atlantic Drift up the west coast. I also wonder whether, like Scots Pine (Chapter 3), it might have survived the last Ice Age on some nunataks around the Isle of Lewis and could only invade a short distance from there into the Wester Ross hills as the ice retreated.

Two other species that we have met on these hills require further consideration before we continue north into Sutherland.

Dwarf Juniper *Juniperus communis* subspecies *nana*

Typical Juniper is a shrubby conifer that can have either a neat, columnar shape or form a spreading bush. It has spiny needles and 'berries' (which strictly are fleshy cones) that begin green and ripen to blue-black. It is very susceptible to wind-pruning and often responds by growing in a prostrate form with far-creeping stems that rise to a height of no more than 50cm. If its leaves taper to a long point and are prickly to the touch, then the plant belongs to the common subspecies *communis*. The leaves of true Dwarf Juniper (subspecies *nana*) have a slightly snipped-off appearance, contracting rapidly to a short point that is scarcely prickly to the touch. The differences between the two forms are slight, which is why they are regarded only as subspecies, and intermediates are common.

I could have mentioned this subspecies earlier: it grows at scattered sites in Snowdonia and the Lake District, although oddly not in the Southern Uplands. However, I think of prostrate Juniper (whether true *nana* or not) as a plant most characteristic of windswept dwarf-shrub heaths in the far north. Indeed ecologists have identified a distinctive plant community type dominated by Dwarf Juniper and Ling Heather

Dwarf Juniper can survive to a fair age on isolated rock faces, battered by the wind and nibbled by passing grazers, as the massive twisted trunk of this specimen on Beinn Eighe suggests. The square-ended tips to its needles show that it belongs to subspecies *nana*.

(Rodwell, 1991–2000) that is only found from Beinn Eighe northwards, including sites on Skye and Harris. Subspecies *nana* also occurs on blanket bogs and on clifftops a little above sea level on the north coast and on the Western and Northern Isles. It is found to altitudes of at least 800m, although subspecies *communis* is recorded at even higher elevations, up to 1,200m on Ben Macdui. Dwarf Juniper plants readily succumb to agricultural burning and grazing, which greatly restricts the range of the subspecies. It is also recorded in the Alps and around the Arctic including Greenland.

BELOW: Pyramidal Bugle growing on the Mound, an interesting area dominated by alder woodland, south of Golspie in Sutherland.

Pyramidal Bugle *Ajuga pyramidalis*

The core range of this plant is on the Lewisian Gneiss of the north-west Highlands, where I have been shown it once but never found it for myself, perhaps because I overlook it as the much commoner Bugle. It has long purple bracts (floral leaves) that partly obscure its bluish-purple flowers so it looks less obviously flowery than Bugle. Other distinctions are more obscure: its square stems are hairy on all four sides, whereas Bugle is hairy on only two opposite sides, and, unlike Bugle, it does not spread by long creeping stems. Unfortunately it is a shy flowerer, and at many sites its flowerheads are swiftly grazed off by sheep and deer, so timing is critical to find its distinctive flowers, which I find stunningly beautiful in close-up.

It grows in small, scattered populations on grassy slopes that are free-draining and sunny with moderately rich soils, including the tops of some sea-cliffs. Presumably it was more widespread after the last Ice Age, but unfortunately there are no pollen or macrofossil remains to confirm this. It is recorded from altitudes as low as 2m, south of Lochinver in Sutherland, to 650m on rocky cliffs above Troutbeck at its only site in the Lake District. It has also been found recently at a couple of odd, isolated sites much further south in England. It grows at one site in the Moffat hills, on several of the Hebridean islands, and perhaps still on mainland Orkney. It is also found at a few sites in Easter Ross, but by far the majority of its sites are in west Sutherland and Caithness. It has disappeared from many former sites where it was smothered by scrub encroachment or eliminated by agricultural 'improvement'. Elsewhere, it is recorded from northern Norway south to northern Portugal, Italy and Bulgaria.

Sutherland and Easter Ross

Crossing into Sutherland, Ben More Assynt (998m) dominates the landscapes of Assynt, partly because its summit region is covered by bare expanses of conspicuous, light-coloured rock. The rock is Lewisian Gneiss, but in an unusually calcareous form. Corries and crags below the summit support a rich flora of lime-loving species including Rock Whitlow-grass, Two-flowered Rush and Alpine Meadow-grass. Continuing northwards, the long ridge of Foinaven (908m) and the adjoining Arkle (787m) are made mainly from quartzite and so have acidic soil. They support good examples of heathland with the two species of bearberry, Russet Sedge and Curved Wood-rush. To their east, Ben Hope – the most northerly Munro at 927m – is an isolated hogback of Moine Schist and granulite rock, standing beside the lonely road that leads from Loch Hope to Altnaharra. Calcareous outcrops support an abundance of Mountain Avens, along with Downy and Net-leaved Willow, Northern Rock-cress and Hair Sedge. Mountain Sandwort grows on west-facing crags below its summit.

The bare fellfield of Lewisian Gneiss below the summit of Ben More Assynt is typical of the rugged, wild landscapes of the Sutherland mountains.

The main thing that I remember from climbing Ben Loyal was finding scattered knee-high plants of Dwarf Birch over an open hillside beside a deep gully full of Downy Birch. At the fringe of the gully, I found a swarm of hybrids between the two species, neatly intermediate in size and leaf shape. The 765m pyramidal peak of Ben Loyal is made of syenite – an igneous, acidic rock formed at great depth in the Earth's crust – with a few outcrops of calcareous rock, but these support only the commoner calcicolous species such as Mossy Saxifrage and Alpine Mouse-ear. Further east, Ben Griam Mor (590m) is a rounded sandstone hill which is important as a refuge for montane species at relatively low elevation in the far north-east corner of Scotland. Calcareous cliffs here support a rich flora including Mountain Avens, Whortle-leaved Willow, Alpine Mouse-ear and Hair Sedge.

In the south-eastern coastal corner of Sutherland, two crags above Migdale and in Strath Fleet would be totally unremarkable were they not the only sites in Scotland for Rock Cinquefoil, a submontane species which qualifies as an enigma because of its thoroughly perplexing distribution. Finally, in Easter Ross, I have slogged on a couple of occasions over Ben Wyvis (1,046m), an impressively massive bluff of gneiss. Golden Eagles soar over its high-level plateau and the commoner peat alpines occur in notable abundance, with isolated records for Downy Willow and Rock Whitlow-grass.

★★★ Rock Cinquefoil *Potentilla rupestris*

Rock Cinquefoil is an attractive plant which stands up to 60cm tall with deeply lobed leaves, somewhat reminiscent of Meadowsweet, and delightful heads of showy white flowers. I acquired a spare plant from a Scottish conservation project and it flourished in my garden, seeding and spreading freely. That ability to spread makes its rarity in Britain all the more perplexing.

Rock Cinquefoil flowers prolifically in our garden, and seems to spread readily from its seed.

As we saw in Chapter 6, it grows in Wales at Craig Breiddin near Welshpool. It is also known from a wooded riverbank in the Wye Valley but may have been planted there. Its only other sites are here in Sutherland, where it grows between about 90m and 150m on a sheer south-facing rock face near Migdale, with a smaller group at lower altitude on a vertical south-facing crag in Strath Fleet. Derek Ratcliffe included it in his list of submontane species, which informs my list of British mountain vascular plants (Chapter 2). He is entitled to that opinion because he discovered both Scottish sites. Reading his field notes explains why: both crags were nest sites in the past for the Peregrine Falcon, the subject of Derek's most important work.

Sell & Murrell (2014) describe Rock Cinquefoil as a Mediterranean montane species in Europe. It is also found at a scattering of widely dispersed sites from southern Sweden to Russia, and in Morocco, Asia and the Rocky Mountains of North America. The Mediterranean association may explain why all its British sites have a relatively warm climate, with mean annual temperatures around 8.5°C (Wilson *et al.*, 1995a). The sites have a relatively high rainfall, but may dry out in summer (again a Mediterranean feature?).

The large population of Rock Cinquefoil on the cliff near Migdale, visited by Dr Sally Ward of Scottish Natural Heritage to monitor the condition of the plants there.

The species was discovered at Craig Breiddin in 1688 by Edward Lhuyd. Such an early date makes human introduction seem unlikely. Its habitat there is quite distinctive. It grows on open, thin-soiled ledges on a west-facing crag of calcium-rich dolerite rock at an altitude of 150–210m, along with other lime-loving species like Common Rock-rose and Bloody Cranesbill. The population here was much larger in the mid-19th century, but quarrying, afforestation and over-collection led to a drastic decline. This history hints that the species might be native here. Unfortunately there is no fossil record, but its present range in relatively mild climates suggests that it might have invaded from further south after the last glaciation.

I have never visited the Sutherland sites, but reports suggest they are rather similar to Craig Breidden, on open, dry, south-facing ledges or scree. At Migdale, the presence of Common Rock-rose confirms that the rocks are strongly calcareous. Northern Bedstraw and Pyramidal Bugle also grow there, suggesting that this could be a relict site for submontane species. The Strath Fleet crag has no strongly lime-loving species, and several of the plants that grow there are characteristic of disturbed ground. Given that the species was only discovered there in 1976, and given how freely it spreads in my garden, I wonder if this population might be garden escapes, conceivably from plants originating at the other Sutherland site. The local botanical recorder, Professor Mick Crawley, is unconvinced; he believes that both Sutherland sites have 'all the hallmarks of an intentional introduction' (Crawley, 2014). However, survival of native populations at sites as widely dispersed geographically as Craig Breidden and Migdale is consistent with its range in Europe and could be explained by the 'chequerboard theory' for chance survivors that I proposed in Chapter 3.

The arctic fringe

chapter seventeen

The far north coast of Scotland offers a dramatic landscape of wild seas, rugged cliffs and windswept hills, shared by some of the islands of Orkney and Shetland. The climate here has many features that qualify as subarctic (although Visit Scotland may never forgive me for saying so!). Whilst not exceptionally cold, the winter is characterised by short dark days and frequent gales. Temperatures are slow to rise in spring and remain depressed in summer, although there is the bonus then of almost 24-hour daylight. Wind exposure excludes tree growth from all but the most sheltered sites. The absence of trees allows montane species to survive at remarkably low-altitude sites which would not otherwise qualify as mountains. Many of these sites are delightful to explore, with intriguing combinations of montane, lowland and coastal species.

Along the north coast

I described key sites along the band of Durness Limestone in the last chapter, but at its northern end, around the village of Durness, outcrops of limestone occur at such a low elevation (generally below 60m) that they fit more appropriately into this chapter. In places these outcrops have developed into limestone pavement, although their grykes are generally too shallow to protect plants from grazing animals. Mountain Avens forms extensive dark green, leafy carpets here, in a community described by ecologists as *Dryas octopetala* heathland. This is displayed nicely, for example, on the clifftop above Smoo Cave, a magnificent limestone cavern eroded by the sea to the east of Durness. Exposure on the clifftop here creates subarctic conditions in which Yellow Mountain Saxifrage, Mountain Avens, Hoary Whitlow-grass, Alpine Bistort, Hair Sedge and Rock Sedge grow barely above sea level.

OPPOSITE PAGE: The narrow sea inlet leading into Smoo Cave, near Durness in Sutherland, was formed when the roof of a former cave collapsed. The limestone banks beside the cave are home to several montane species.

Continuing eastwards along the north coast of Sutherland, the next important site lies near the village of Bettyhill beside the mouth of the River Naver. A low ridge, rising to 100m or so, runs along the west side of the estuary at Invernaver. The hard bedrock here produces mainly acidic soils, but strong winds blow sand up the ridge slopes. Shell fragments in the sand add calcium to the soils and allow lime-loving species to flourish, while the winds have largely excluded tree growth apart from a few patches of Dwarf Birch and Hazel scrub and at least one Aspen tree. The lower slopes are dominated by Mountain Avens which slips down the unstable slopes in massive tumbling tussocks – a process of erosion that mimics the features of solifluction at more montane sites. Yellow Mountain Saxifrage, Purple Saxifrage, Moss Campion, Alpine Bistort, Bearberry and Dwarf Juniper all grow here. The deposited sand is sufficiently calcareous for a few plants of Dark-red Helleborine to establish. Even more remarkably, the shingle bank that rises just 10m or so above the mouth of the Naver is a home for Purple Oxytropis, in a very different site to its montane habitats in Perthshire described in Chapter 12. I have a special affection for the cliffs and sand dunes here, because this is where I first learnt my field botany in the early 1980s as a student at the University of Aberdeen, visiting the Botany Department's Bettyhill Field Centre.

Purple Oxytropis grows on a shingle bank, 10m or so above the estuary of the River Naver, near Bettyhill in Sutherland.

Continuing eastwards again, the steep, grassy slopes on the east side of Strathy Bay are another site for Purple Oxytropis, barely 30m above the delightful sandy bay below. The sweeping clifftop south and west of the lighthouse at Strathy Point is home to Scots Primrose, which Derek Ratcliffe included in his list of submontane species. It would be nice to digress onto this delicate Scottish endemic, because it is one of my favourite plants (I always claim it should be Scott's Primrose), but to my mind it is much more clearly a coastal species. It is confined to the grassland/heathland zone behind sea-cliffs in Sutherland, Caithness and Orkney, never more than 5km from the sea and rarely above 100m.

Scots Primrose also occurs further eastwards at Dunnet Head, the most northerly point of the British mainland, but at least here it has some montane companions. An area of acidic moorland runs back from the Old Red Sandstone cliffs at an altitude of around 120m, providing a windswept habitat for Dwarf Willow, Crowberry, Bearberry and Arctic Bearberry. Quite typically of this coast, Roseroot grows with Scots Lovage on these cliffs, but here, more unusually, it is also accompanied by Alpine Saw-wort.

Scots Primrose at Strathy Point in Sutherland. To my mind, this is definitely a coastal species. I suspect Derek Ratcliffe listed it as submontane because of its close relationship to *Primula scandinavica*, a mountain plant in Norway.

A few montane species including Fir Clubmoss, Dwarf Birch, Northern Bedstraw, Bearberry, Lesser Twayblade and Few-flowered Sedge also grow in the Flow Country of Caithness and Sutherland – the largest expanse of blanket bog in Europe, covering an area twice the size of the Lake District – although finding them can be tricky in a boggy landscape where even walking can sometimes be treacherous. I have already referred in Chapter 8 to the unexpected discovery of Marsh Saxifrage in the Munsary Peatlands reserve here.

Orkney

The island of Hoy is the most rugged of the Orkney archipelago, with towering sandstone cliffs along its western coastline. Ward Hill to the north of the island is a long ridge with steep flanks and a rounded top, rising to the

highest point in Orkney at 479m. Its summit area is conspicuously patterned with stripes of gravel and sand, eroded and kept bare by the strong winds, interspersed with parallel bands of vegetation that have established in the lee of wind-formed ripples in the gravel. During the last glaciation, movement of the ice-sheet over Ward Hill was enough to expose and scar large slabs of sandstone lying along the summit ridge.

At the eastern end of Ward Hill, the corrie called Quoyawa holds most botanical interest. Visiting there on regular holidays to Orkney, I found Stone Bramble to be quite frequent, along with Lesser Clubmoss, Yellow Mountain Saxifrage, Purple Saxifrage, Roseroot, Mountain Sorrel and Mountain Everlasting. Alpine Saw-wort and a few tussocks of Moss Campion grow in a stony gully high in the corrie wall. On the summit ridge, the usual trio of Fir Clubmoss, Dwarf Willow and Stiff Sedge are common on the vegetated terraces between bare gravel strips, along with quite abundant Arctic Bearberry and a few patches of Bog Bilberry. I missed the Hoary Whitlow-grass, Lesser Twayblade, Alpine Bistort and Viviparous Fescue that are also recorded on Ward Hill, although I did notice the perplexing absence of Alpine Lady's-mantle.

The path that leads from Rackwick to the famous rock stack called the Old Man of Hoy is a good place to see abundant Arctic Bearberry.

Most of the other Orkney islands are low-lying, although a few montane species are recorded from Rousay. Fitty Hill (169m) on the northern island of Westray is the only other place on Orkney with a notable montane flora, including Fir Clubmoss, Alpine Meadow-rue, Alpine Bistort, Moss Campion and Viviparous Fescue.

Shetland

The subarctic nature of Shetland is nicely illustrated at the Catpund Steatite Quarries, north of Sandwick on Mainland (the largest island). In Viking and early medieval times, the soft soapstone rock was excavated to make various kinds of vessels and tools. In vegetated areas of the quarry face there are clumps of Lesser Clubmoss and neat tussocks of Moss Campion, yet the site is barely 15m above sea level.

At the other end of Mainland, Ronas Hill is incontrovertibly montane – a big bluff of granite rising to 450m. Its summit area is covered in an extensive boulder field, interspersed with barely vegetated granite gravel, forming the nearest thing in Britain to the vast fellfields I have explored on Iceland. It also has some of the best solifluction terraces I know, showing the impact of regular freezing and thawing at these elevations. The wind-battered summit area has typical associates: Fir Clubmoss, Dwarf Willow, Trailing Azalea, Alpine Lady's-mantle and Three-leaved Rush. Mountain Everlasting is fairly common, but Alpine Bistort is scarce and unusually few-flowered. Goldenrod occurs here in its low montane variety *cambrica*, and there are a few plants of Juniper that approach subspecies *nana*. Where plants can find some shelter below the summit, somewhat denser vegetation develops, with Arctic Bearberry, Mountain Crowberry, Bog Bilberry and spreading runners of Alpine Clubmoss. Alpine Saw-wort grows at a few sites. A very odd record on a small island in Moosa Water, north of Ronas Hill, is Downy Willow – or perhaps a hybrid between it and another willow species (Scott *et al.*, 2002) – growing there at its only Shetland site and its lowest altitude in Britain (140m).

There is one group of Shetland specialities to which I have not yet referred. Sell & Murrell (2006) list 18 species of hawkweed as endemic to Shetland. As we will see in the next chapter, I question whether these different plants merit species status, but they are a very characteristic feature of the Shetland flora, and undoubtedly play a significant role in the ecology of the islands.

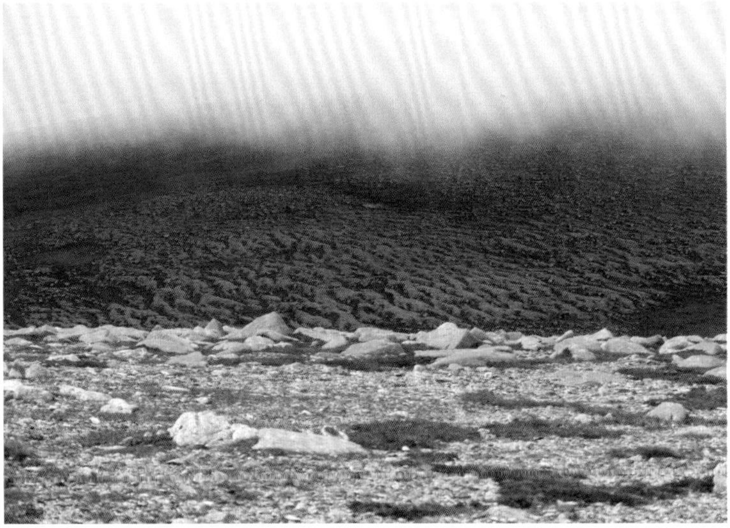

The summit of Ronas Hill is often encased in fog. The remarkable terraced pattern on its slopes is a natural phenomenon, caused by wind blasting and solifluction (see Chapter 3).

The Keen of Hamar, Unst

There is no question that the best botanical site on Shetland lies near Baltasound on the northernmost island of Unst. The extraordinary

The Keen of Hamar is the bare, rounded hill in the middle distance, in this view from another serpentine hill on Unst called Muckle Heog.

landscape of the Keen of Hamar looks more like the spoil heap from some toxic mine. Only between five and ten per cent of its stony surface has any vegetation cover, but these limited plant communities are so important that the site is protected as a National Nature Reserve.

The NNR leaflet neatly summarises the Keen as 'a mountain near sea level' (it rises as a low hill to only 89m). It is a particularly satisfying place to end this geographical tour of British montane sites because, like the Lizard where we began, it is a major exposure of serpentine rock. Here, though, the action of frost and ice has shattered the serpentine into a loose clitter of rock chips. In places the repeated freezing and thawing of the soil has rearranged these chips into conspicuous stripes of bigger and smaller stones running parallel to the contours – a feature associated much more with glaciated landscapes in the Arctic. These stone stripes are still active, moving a few centimetres down the slope each year.

Repeated freezing and thawing of the substrate in the Keen of Hamar has resulted in parallel bands of larger stones separated by smaller stones and sediment. Stone stripes like these are mainly found in the Arctic.

This soil movement makes it difficult for many plant species to establish, except for a few arctic-alpines adapted to the disturbed ground near glaciers. Even more critical is the chemical makeup of the rocks and soils. The serpentine soils here are very low in calcium, phosphorous, nitrogen and potassium, all essential minerals for plant growth, but contain high levels of chromium, magnesium and nickel – three so-called 'heavy metals' that can be toxic to plants.

I was lucky enough to first visit the Keen in 1984 with a group from the British Ecological Society, including Dr David Slingsby (now an associate lecturer at the Open University). As the then Head of Biology at Wakefield Girls' High School, David had regularly visited the reserve with his students to study the ecology of the fellfield, and he showed us something of his work. He had a series of small study plots to which he had added various quantities of nitrates, phosphates and potassium salts. His results showed that the plots with added phosphates were being revegetated quite rapidly, mostly by 'weed' species, probably because this enrichment allowed them to overcome the toxicity of the heavy metals. As it happened, this had already been illustrated on the southern half of the hill, where a field outside the reserve was ploughed up and fertilised sometime around 1970 and now has almost complete vegetation cover, in stark contrast to the National Nature Reserve area.

However, David Slingsby's work showed that the major problem for the Keen flora was shortage of water. Although Baltasound gets around 116cm of rainfall a year, this swiftly drains deep into the shattered, porous rock, especially as there is little organic matter in the soil to retain moisture. Furthermore, droughts of seven days or more are quite common there in summer. Many of the plants that cling on to survival on the Keen show adaptations to overcome this, such as succulent leaves or stems to store water, increased hairiness to reduce transpiration, or far-spreading root systems.

As a result of the instability of the substrate, the periods of water stress, the shortage of key minerals and high levels of toxic minerals, the Keen is essentially a stony desert. However, the species within that vegetation are rather special. Unsurprisingly there are coastal plants including Thrift, Sea Campion and an unusually hairy and broad-leaved variant of Sea Plantain. This was once described as a separate species but is probably just an adaptation to the dry environment. Amongst montane species, Northern Rock-cress and Mountain Everlasting are (relatively) common, and there are occasional flowery tussocks of Moss Campion. Hoary Whitlow-grass particularly grows on hummocks where Arctic Skuas (one of the special seabirds of Unst) perch and enrich the soil with their droppings. Lesser Clubmoss grows here and there, along with unusually short plants of Viviparous Fescue.

Alpine Meadow-rue on the Keen often seems to have purple leaves, perhaps an indication of mineral stress. Stone Bramble also has purple, unusually succulent leaves here. It flowers infrequently on the Keen, but I remember David Slingsby suggesting that its flowers here are pink in colour and ripen into dark red berries, reminiscent of Arctic Bramble. However, unlike that species, the Keen plants spread by stolons, so are probably a form of Stone Bramble adapted to the harsh environment.

Two rarities add greatly to the importance of the Keen and have attracted generations of botanists here. It is estimated that there may be as many as 15,000 plants of Arctic Sandwort, which we met in the last chapter, growing in scattered patches across the stony expanse and surrounding hills. Even more interesting is a neat little tufted plant called Shetland Mouse-ear. Both these plants also grow on the serpentine expanse of Nikka Vord and Muckle Heog across the main road from the Keen. The taxonomic status of the mouse-ear is the subject of much debate and qualifies it as our final three-star mountain enigma.

★★★ SHETLAND MOUSE-EAR *Cerastium nigrescens* var. *nigrescens*

This Shetland speciality from the Keen of Hamar has always provoked controversy amongst botanists, being viewed variously as a distinct species, subspecies, variety or mere form of the more widespread Arctic Mouse-ear, whose own tortured taxonomic history I described in Chapter 14. Stace (2010) decided that the Shetland plant was just a variety, although he noted that it might merit subspecies rank. However, it was treated as a full species in the *Red Data Book* that drives conservation priorities (Wigginton, 1999), and even Clive Stace originally regarded it as a species in the first edition of his flora in 1991 (I await with interest the verdict in volume 1 of Sell & Murrell, still to be published as we go to press).

It would be a shame if the Shetland plant was completely submerged into the more widespread species, because it has played a significant part in the history of Unst and because, to me, it does look quite different from the plants I know in the Cairngorms. It has almost circular, purplish leaves which, like its stems, are densely covered in stubby hairs tipped with swollen glands, whereas true Arctic Mouse-ear has much narrower, lance-shaped leaves and its stem and leaves are densely covered in short whitish hairs without glands at their tip. Admittedly, the attractive tufted appearance of the Shetland plants might be somewhat exaggerated by the harshness of their stony haunts!

Shetland Mouse-ear was discovered in 1837 on the Keen of Hamar by a young botanist from Baltasound on Unst called Thomas Edmondston. His discovery is all the more remarkable because he was just 12 at the time. By the age of 15 he had published a comprehensive plant list for the Keen, including the first British record of Arctic Sandwort. Even more remarkably, at the age of 20 he was elected Professor of Botany at Anderson's University in Glasgow (the

Shetland Mouse-ear looks distinctive, with its purplish leaves covered in a fuzz of short, gland-tipped hairs. However, this may be a purely ecological adaptation to life on the Unst serpentines.

The serpentine soil of the Keen is toxic to many plants, resulting in a sparse vegetation of just a few species – here, a small plant of Shetland Mouse-ear on the right, Sea Campion on the left, and Thrift and Sea Plantain towards the centre.

predecessor of today's Strathclyde University), but his meteoric career ended when he was accidentally shot during a botanical expedition to the Pacific coast of South America in 1846. Young Edmondston was one of the strongest advocates for the uniqueness of the plant, which at one stage was named subspecies *edmondstonii* in his honour.

There are two problems with its uniqueness. Firstly, Edmondston himself described rather different-looking plants on Muckle Heog, opposite the Keen, which he called variety *acutifolium*. I have seen plants matching this variety. They have narrower leaves, smaller flowers and a less hairy, more straggly growth form. They seem much closer to the Arctic Mouse-ear in the Cairngorms. Secondly, it is reported that seeds from the Keen cultivated in horticultural compost at sea level grow into more typical Arctic Mouse-ear plants, suggesting that plants on the Keen may represent a purely ecological adaptation to the challenges of growing on the exposed serpentine there. Whatever its status, Shetland Mouse-ear is reasonably common within its restricted range on Unst, with between 4,500 and 9,200 plants counted on the Keen and 300–800 on Muckle Heog, although numbers vary greatly from year to year depending on the weather.

There is one further consideration. It is tempting to want all plants to fit neatly into a 'box' that we call a species. However, it is easy to forget that evolution is still happening, which means there will always be confusingly intermediate specimens at the early stages of evolutionary change. The selection pressures driving adaptations in the isolated population of mouse-ears on the drought-prone, mineral-stressed serpentines of Unst must be very different from those acting on Arctic Mouse-ears high in a snowy corrie in the Scottish mountains. If evolution is allowed to run its course naturally, Unst might yet evolve its own true species of mouse-ear in a few millennia, so long as climate change does not have a devastating impact first.

Glenridding
18. viii. '53.

Mountain conundrums

chapter eighteen

Our notional journey from the Lizard to Unst has given a taste of the rich diversity of Britain's uplands and introduced all 152 of the mountain species listed in the table on pages 30–35. Keen mountain botanists, however, will have noted one rather conspicuous group of omissions.

In the preceding chapters, I discussed Alpine Lady's-mantle as a widespread montane species, but I have only briefly touched on other, more elusive species of lady's-mantle in the context of the Yorkshire limestones in Chapter 7.

Hawkweeds likewise made only a brief appearance in the last chapter on Shetland, yet these handsome plants with their showy, yellow, dandelion-like flowers are often a conspicuous feature of mountain rock ledges. Dandelions themselves also grow in the mountains, but so far I have not mentioned them either. Dandelions and hawkweeds are both important components of the tall-herb communities on mountain rock ledges, helping to stabilise the vegetation and maintain damp and shady conditions, as well as providing food for herbivores large and small, and pollen for bees, hoverflies, wasps and other visiting insects.

I have not even mentioned eyebrights, delicate little plants with spikes of two-lipped flowers that are shining white but often tinged with violet or spotted with yellow towards their centres. Yet these are often distinctive and delightful inhabitants of mountain grasslands, and the appropriately named Alpine Eyebright has been recorded to 1,190m on Aonach Beag.

The problem comes when we try to give names to these plants, because they belong to groups of what botanists call 'critical species'.

OPPOSITE PAGE: In 1953, John Raven painted this hawkweed in Glenridding in the Lake District, but similar specimens have never been seen since. It is sad to lose a fine plant like this, but I am sure other hawkweeds have taken its place.

They have particular methods of reproduction which result in a plethora of very similar-looking plants. The most recent authoritative guide to the British flora (Sell & Murrell, 1996–2014) describes no fewer than 412 species of hawkweed, as well as 232 species of dandelion, 20 species of lady's-mantle and 27 species of eyebright with multiple hybrids, many of which turn up in upland areas. Introducing that lot would have doubled the length of this book and made for a difficult read! However, I do want to say just a little about these challenging but intriguing plants, in a bid to encourage more people to engage in their study in the mountains.

A perplexity of plants

I always joke that critical plants are so called because one botanist attempts to name a plant, then everyone else criticises that conclusion. A better definition is that critical plants belong to groups in which it is difficult to recognise taxonomic differences between members. Plants in these groups are often regarded as 'microspecies', not because the plants themselves are small but because the differences between them are so small.

This complexity arises because hawkweeds, dandelions and lady's-mantles have abandoned the process of sexual reproduction which leads to genetic exchange between individuals. Instead, they are able to produce seeds without fertilisation taking place, through a process called apomixis. Because no intermixing of genetic characteristics is involved, the seedlings are genetically identical to the parent plant. Any slight changes that arise in the characteristics of one plant as a result of chance genetic mutations are perpetuated in that plant's offspring. The result is

Lady's-mantles, like this Starry Lady's-mantle *Alchemilla acutiloba* in Teesdale, seem to me to make quite convincing species, even if fine points of detail are needed to distinguish them. However, there are plenty of perplexing intermediates.

localised clones of plants which are all identical to one another, yet subtly different from any neighbouring clones.

It is even more complicated with hawkweeds. As they moved northwards after the last glacial period, it is thought that they still reproduced sexually. Hybridisation would have occurred between different species, and selection pressures would have driven change as they invaded new habitats. Then, apparently simultaneously, all the hawkweeds switched to apomixis and the variations that were then present formed the basis for the clones we see today.

My problem comes when we try to typify the clones that result from this breeding process. I am not convinced that describing 412 species of hawkweed and 232 species of dandelion in Britain adds much to our ecological understanding or conservation priorities. Furthermore, the *International Code of Botanical Nomenclature* does not recognise the concept of a microspecies. According to the code, everything that is given a binomial scientific name must be regarded as a species (Sell & Murrell, 2006). Within a species, there can be subspecies or varieties, but I do not think that hawkweeds, dandelions and lady's-mantles fit neatly into any one of these standard categories, because of their peculiar, although clearly extremely successful, breeding systems.

It pleases me that Tim Rich could name these hawkweeds on Cribyn in the Brecon Beacons as *Hieracium attenboroughianum* in honour of Sir David Attenborough. Perhaps, however, they are best regarded as handsome variants of a very variable species.

Overall, I think it makes most sense to think of these plants as the transient products of a fascinating dynamic process. Perhaps it would be better to regard hawkweeds, dandelions and lady's-mantles as three hugely successful, widespread and very variable 'superspecies'. It is fine for specialists to name distinctive forms and varieties within these superspecies and study their distribution, but we should not get unduly hung up about those in conservation policy. Instead, we should try to understand and support the processes that lead to their variability.

Mix-and-match eyebrights

The eyebrights of mountain grasslands are a different, fascinating, but equally frustrating, category of critical plants. The ovules in eyebright flowers must be pollinated before they can develop into seeds, but pollen often comes from the same flower or is transferred between flowers in the same plant. This self-pollination, like apomixis, results in clones of identical offspring around a parent plant. Furthermore, microspecies of eyebrights hybridise freely. The hybrids are also fertile, so they can interbreed with either of their parents, and their offspring can then hybridise further, producing a swarm of intermediates between the two extremes. This genetic promiscuity often makes it problematic to assign individuals to a species.

In August 1980, I joined a field course on critical plants at the Kindrogan Field Centre in Perthshire, led by Alan Silverside, an expert on eyebrights who at the time was a lecturer at Paisley College (now the University of the West of Scotland). He is still active as the botanical recorder for Wigtownshire. Alan was a patient and inspiring teacher with a fine eye for detail. We visited several rich upland sites, and Alan soon had me distinguishing confidently between Island Eyebright *Euphrasia arctica*, Purple-stemmed Eyebright *E. micrantha*, Alpine

Alpine Eyebright is a distinctive and attractive plant that can be found in mountain grasslands from the Lake District to the north of Scotland. Confusion arises because it readily hybridises with other eyebrights.

Eyebright *E. frigida* and Branched Eyebright, which has the singularly appropriate scientific name of *E. confusa*. I was even prepared to take a guess at hybrids, but I baulked when Alan described one plant as being '*Euphrasia arctica* with a touch of *micrantha*' (or something similar). If the variation between forms produces as wide a spectrum of options as a colour chart for mixing household paints, I question how useful that concept of species can be.

There are certainly distinctive forms of eyebright that represent the extremes of variation, and these may occur in isolated conditions that make them easier to identify. For example, there are two forms that are endemic to the island of Rum and another on the Isle of Lewis. We try hard to typify these as species because of our instinctive wish to categorise and label, but I suspect that, if we assessed them objectively on a global scale, we would find their apparent uniqueness is illusory.

None of that diminishes the importance of studying and understanding the transient forms of hawkweeds, dandelions, lady's-mantles and eyebrights that appear on our hills. They are significant in their own right, and they may well teach us important lessons about the transience of mountain habitats. However, we should recognise that categorising these steadily changing forms will always be just a taxonomic snapshot in time. Conservation policy should not set out to preserve individual examples, but instead aim to maintain the dynamic conditions that will allow new clones to appear and disappear.

Several hawkweed variants still grace the cliffs of Glenridding in the Lake District, even if the local clone painted by John Raven in 1953 now seems to have died out.

Looking to the future

chapter nineteen

The mountains that John Raven and Max Walters wrote about 60 years ago in their volume on *Mountain Flowers* (Raven & Walters, 1956) are still recognisable to the modern reader. Many of them are easier to reach, thanks to improved roads, faster cars, better path networks and new legal access provisions, although rarely by rural public transport, which is under threat. Rich plant communities still thrive on all the sites they described, although anecdotally many of these seem to be becoming rather less luxuriant and species-rich. We know that the grasslands of Upper Teesdale have deteriorated significantly, the meadows below Ben Lawers are no longer a site for Alpine Bartsia, and Tufted Saxifrage came perilously close to disappearing from Wales. However, no montane species have become extinct in that time (although a few 'microspecies' certainly have), and encouraging numbers of new sites have been found for some of our rarest plants. We have also seen excellent progress in restoring lost populations of a few species like Oblong Woodsia and mountain willows through determined conservation action.

I want to end this review of Britain's mountain flora by looking forward. I fear that anyone reading this book 60 years from now will be confronted by mountains that have changed profoundly, with montane plants in serious decline as lowland species invade. Beyond doubt, the biggest threat is from climate change, although, if we are to have any chance of addressing the impact of the changing climate, we will also need to tackle the mismanagement of many montane sites, particularly as a result of too many grazing animals. As I have tried to show in previous chapters, we still have much to learn about our mountain flora. This will become even more important as we face the challenges

OPPOSITE PAGE: A view towards Liathaich in Wester Ross. There are parts of the British uplands that are little visited by botanists, where I feel sure interesting plants remain to be discovered in inaccessible corners.

ahead, and I will conclude this chapter with a call for readers to play their part in the vital work that needs to be done.

Climate futures

In its definitive report in 2013, the International Panel on Climate Change (IPCC) stated unequivocally that the global climate is warming, with many of the changes observed since the 1950s being unprecedented over decades and even millennia. It concluded that human influence is 'extremely likely' to have been the dominant cause of warming since the mid-20th century, mainly through the increase in carbon dioxide and other greenhouse gases in the atmosphere.

In the UK, the most authoritative current projection is that by 2080 all regions will be warmer, with the increase greater in summer than in winter (Jenkins *et al.*, 2010). The changes in mean summer temperatures will be highest in parts of southern England (an increase of up to 4.2°C) and least in the Scottish islands (just over 2.5°C). Changes in our mountain areas are likely to lie between these extremes. Rainfall projections are more complex. Western Britain could see up to 33 per cent more precipitation in winter, although there might be a slight drop in the eastern Highlands of Scotland. Some models predict a 65–80 per cent decline in winter snowfall over mountain areas because of the combined changes to rainfall and temperature. Although summer rainfall is projected to drop greatly in southern England, there will be little change in northern Scotland. Mountains in between will probably experience at least some decline in summer rainfall. Extreme weather events, such as storms, floods and droughts, will become more common, and we may already have begun to see this occurring in recent years. Changes that we cannot yet predict to the jet stream – the fast-flowing air current in the upper atmosphere – may have particularly perverse impacts on Britain. Even if they can be achieved, the political aspirations agreed at the Paris summit in 2015 will only slow or reduce the magnitude of these impacts.

Downy Willow is now commoner in the British mountains than it was a decade ago, thanks to reintroduction projects at several sites.

Climate change and mountain plants

Fewer snow-beds, like these in the Northern Corries of Cairn Gorm, are likely to last into the summer as the climate changes, and the plants associated with them will become rarer.

What does this mean for the future of our montane flora? Simplistically, if the distribution of these plants was controlled purely by temperature, we could predict that they would be forced higher up the hillside to find the temperature regimes they require for survival. In response to a 3°C increase in average temperatures, for example, they would need to move around 450m higher. That depends, of course, on our mountains being high enough to allow for such an ascent; the Highland Saxifrage that survives 1,000m up in the Cairngorms could not find a new location at 1,450m because Scotland's highest hill is 100m too short. That also assumes that there would be suitable habitat for them at these new altitudes and that their dispersal mechanisms would allow them to spread there within such a relatively short timescale.

In practice, of course, it is much more complex than this. In Chapter 3, I questioned whether the distribution of any of our mountain plants depends solely on summer temperatures. Perhaps some species cannot survive prolonged high temperatures, but even in these cases I suggested that drought stress may be just as important as temperature. For most montane species I suspect survival depends on a complex interrelationship between summer and winter temperatures, the

occurrence of frost, the duration of snow-lie, the distribution of rainfall throughout the year, and how windy it is.

It is impossible to be sure how the interaction between all these factors will change as the climate changes. In 2009, I was commissioned to review the likely impact of climate change on the high Cairngorms, and concluded that making predictions for these mountains was fraught with difficulties: 'Despite projections of less snowfall across the country as a whole, increased winter precipitation [projected for] the Cairngorms might bring more snow in the higher mountains, at least for an interim period before temperatures rise too greatly ... Snow also tends to accumulate in the lee of slopes, so increased windiness could blow and dump more snow in these areas, which will take longer to melt even in a warmer spring. Furthermore, rainfall is one of the main factors that makes snow patches melt, so a decline in rainfall in spring or summer potentially could slow this melting' (Scott, 2009). My overall conclusion was that 'climate change will impact on the high Cairngorms, but we cannot yet say with any certainty how, and by how much.' I am sure that applies just as strongly to the other mountain areas discussed in this book.

Sibbaldia is most typically found in hollows where snow lies late into the spring, and faces an uncertain future under current predictions of climate change in the British mountains.

Very possibly the most significant impact of climate change in the mountains will be from the invasion of lowland species as temperatures rise – and there is already anecdotal evidence that this is happening. As we saw in Chapter 3, the arrival of similar lowland species at the end of the last Ice Age was the likely cause of the extirpation of arctic-alpine plants from lowland Britain. There is no reason to think that these plants would not have the same effect now if higher temperatures allowed them to invade mountain areas.

What alarms me most is that we cannot predict with any certainty what these changes will be. That makes it very difficult to decide how best to adapt our management of upland areas to give them resilience for the changes ahead. I could hazard a few guesses at the sort of changes we might see – although I would emphasise that these are no more than guesses, given how little we know about the response of mountain plants to climatic changes. It seems likely that the wonderfully rich tall-herb communities of mountain rock ledges will disappear because of rising summer temperatures and lower rainfall; indeed I suspect this may already be happening. Many of the relatively small, fast-growing montane species that are adapted to swiftly colonising newly opened habitats will be squeezed out as these habitats are invaded by ranker-growing lowland species; they will only be able to survive on a few steeper, rapidly eroding slopes. Plants that rely on the protection of winter snow cover, or that are confined to areas where patches of snow last well into summer, will have fewer areas where they can survive.

Rising summer temperatures and lower rainfall may lead to a decline in the occurrence and richness of tall-herb communities on mountain rock ledges.

Plant communities that are under stress will have even less chance of coping with climate change, and I fear that almost all our montane plant communities are already under stress. The future will be particularly bleak for the many rare montane species that rely on a particular combination of habitat type and climatic conditions, as temperatures rise at existing localities but potential new habitats are beyond their range of dispersal.

Challenges ahead

It is not all bad news for mountain plants. Since the 1980s, we have made progress in reducing levels of airborne pollution and the impact of 'acid rain'. Mosses in particular suffered in recent decades from atmospheric nitrogen pollution, which is probably the reason why Woolly Fringe-moss has disappeared from some mountaintops. Perhaps that can now be reversed. Botanical collectors are no longer the problem they once were, as responsible plant lovers are now happy to take only photographs rather than removing whole plants as herbarium specimens. At some of the most visited sites, land managers are learning how to reduce the impacts of large numbers of human visitors by careful management of paths and access (although funding for such measures is getting more difficult to find).

But we still have a fundamental problem of land use in our uplands. Many hills are grazed by herds of sheep. Low levels of grazing help maintain open habitats to the benefit of some species, but heavy grazing reduces the species diversity of hill pastures. The economics of hill sheep farming is increasingly marginal, so farmers struggle with the cost of fence maintenance and shepherding. As a result, sheep wander more widely and can access sites that are much more sensitive to grazing damage. It is uneconomic to round up sheep for shearing annually from the most outlying areas, so they are left to become virtually feral there. Feral sheep often become habituated on sites where a diverse array of plant species provides especially rich feeding – and these are often the sites where plants are most susceptible to grazing damage. The crofting system which helps maintain some plant communities in north-west Scotland is under particular threat from declining grant-aid.

Vast areas are managed as shooting estates. Some are maintained as grouse moors. In these, as we saw in Chapter 4, Heather (and the surrounding vegetation) is burnt at regular intervals to create the small-scale patchwork of differently aged Heather stands that supports the highest populations of Red Grouse. This maintains an open habitat to the benefit of some plants but greatly represses the growth of many montane species. Heather is rarely left to become old and tall enough for Lesser Twayblade to become established beneath, for example, and Bearberry is only likely to grow along the unburnt edges of tracks.

Especially in Scotland, large areas are maintained for the shooting of Red Deer. Clients pay to shoot stags. There is a financial incentive to maintain populations at high levels so the hunters can easily find the stags they want to shoot without long treks across inaccessible hillsides. Hinds are not targets and it is expensive for estates to reduce their numbers, so the sex ratio of the herds becomes imbalanced. This results in more hinds breeding and increases the population still further. Deer herds wander widely in search of food, and their impact on hill vegetation is considerable.

The impact of grazing is shown by this exclosure on Little Dun Fell in Cumbria, erected in the 1950s to keep out sheep. Grasses and Stiff Sedge grow more lushly inside, but other species may be swamped by the tall-growing vegetation.

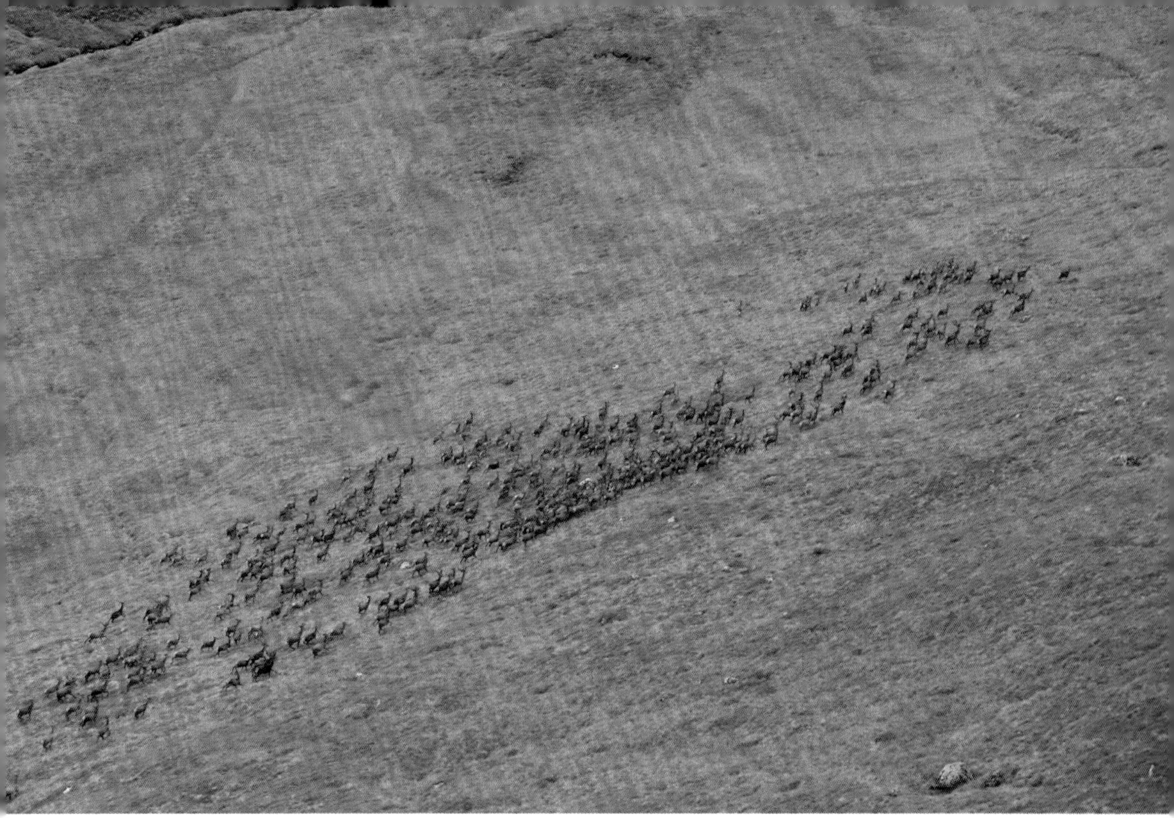

In the 1980s and 1990s, I saw a clear example of how these factors interact in my regular visits to Caenlochan Glen in Angus. I suspected that summers there were already getting drier, reducing the luxuriance I saw on some of the plant-rich ledges. At the same time, more and more Red Deer were gathering in the grasslands below the crags – so that they sometimes looked more like the Serengeti than Scotland! The deer undoubtedly reduced the plant displays on the open slopes. A few semi-feral sheep were also resident in the glen. As the deer overgrazed the lower slopes, the sheep were forced onto the cliffs in search of food, stripping off the tall herbs from some of the ledges. Without the shade of these taller plants, the cliffs were becoming even drier and, from year to year, I could see that many of the smaller montane plants were declining.

This herd of Red Deer in the glens of Angus shows how numerous the species became before measures were put in place to try to reduce their population there.

The scale of the damage was eventually recognised, and in 2005 the Deer Commission for Scotland (now subsumed within Scottish Natural Heritage) began to enforce measures to reduce the deer population there – but their aim was to reduce it to levels of the 1990s when plenty of damage was already in evidence, and even that culling target was never achieved. By 2013, there were still 20 deer per square kilometre in the area, one of the highest deer densities anywhere in Scotland. I have not been back to Caenlochan since, but I am sure it is not now the spectacular place I once knew.

A changing vision for the uplands

In recent years I have been a regular visitor to Scandinavia. The richly wooded and diverse landscapes there make me realise just how denuded and depleted most of our British uplands have become. I have one favourite walk, for example, alongside the famous Flåm Railway at the head of Sognefjord in Norway. The woodlands at around 700m there are carpeted with Alpine Sowthistle, extraordinarily lush and robust plants of Oblong Woodsia grow on a massive drystone retaining wall beside the railway, and Alpine Rock-cress is frequent and easily accessible, in stark contrast to the enigmatic rarity of all these species in Britain.

Of course, the climate and the geology are different in Scandinavia, so comparisons are not entirely fair, but the biggest difference, I think, is in the approach to land use. The Scandinavian mountains are generally regarded as wild places, owned by the state and left as a communal resource. The most fertile valleys and a few, limited mountain pastures are grazed by sheep and goats, but generally the mountain woodlands and heathlands are left to flourish with minimum human intervention. Local people delight in the autumn harvest of Bilberries and Cloudberries. Firewood and fungi are harvested from the forests. Licences are issued to local people and visitors to shoot truly wild deer in the forest, in striking contrast to the artificial shooting galleries of Scottish 'deer forests' (the most inapposite term for the open hillsides maintained for deer stalking in Scotland).

Patterns of land use and ownership in Norway seem better at sustaining both biodiversity and people, as this view near Flåm shows. I hope the Scottish Government might learn lessons from there in managing the wild land of Scotland.

The difference in Britain is that most of the uplands are owned as private estates by a few rich individuals or syndicates. It is difficult to think of any alternative to sheep grazing, grouse shooting and deer stalking that would be financially viable over such vast swathes of land. At the time of writing, the Scottish Government is in the midst of a review of land ownership in Scotland, but the changes will need to be fundamental if we want to revitalise the British uplands.

There is a lot of theoretical debate about the ecological value of 'rewilding' our uplands and a few tentative pilot projects, like the inspirational work at Carrifran in the Southern Uplands, are now in progress (see Chapter 10), but there is very little consideration of how to link this to the aspirations of human communities in these areas. Simply moving off the land is not the answer. The uplands have been denuded and depleted for so long that it will take active management to restore their functionality and vitality. That will not come cheaply, but it will provide opportunities for rural employment and it will enhance the potential for tourism. Returning to where this chapter began, restoring upland vegetation will also lock up carbon and slow the advance of climate change, and the revitalised vegetation will stand a better chance of coping with the climate impacts that lie ahead. It will improve water quality and regulate its flow, reducing the risk from floods and drought.

Mountain explorers

There is one particular lesson that I think comes from what I have discussed so far in this chapter – and indeed it has been a recurring theme throughout this book. Now, more than ever, we need to do more to understand the dynamics of our mountain flora. The constraints on public funding mean that this will need to rely increasingly on 'citizen science' by enthusiastic volunteers.

Throughout this book, I have tried to record information on the highest and lowest altitudes at which our montane species grow. I have listed southernmost and northernmost records and highlighted apparent gaps in the ranges of species. I am sure that some of what I have written is wrong – hopefully not because of my mistakes but because current records are incomplete. I would like to challenge readers to prove me wrong! Any observant hillwalker should be able to recognise our commoner montane species and contribute new records. Highest, lowest, northernmost and southernmost are not just

Hillwalking botanists need to leave the well-worn paths and explore more widely; healthy exercise and spectacular scenery – as here beside Fuar Tholl in Wester Ross – add to the rewards of potential new discoveries.

theoretical interests; these are the sites where the impact of climate change is likely to kick in first. Monitoring species at these sites will therefore offer us a valuable insight into future, more wholesale changes to our flora.

Having read this book, I hope that some hillwalking readers will be encouraged to venture off the normal walking routes to explore a nearby crag, grassy slope or expanse of mountain peatland in search of interesting plants. I hope they might be encouraged to get to know the montane plants that are trickier to identify: the 'small white flowers', the rushes, the sedges, the grasses and those troublesome hawkweeds and eyebrights, because these include many of our rarest species, and the fate of these rarities will teach us important lessons about future environmental change.

These observations are no use if they remain just a memory, a scribble in a notebook or a photo in a camera. I would encourage all

Logging your records

Gordon Rothero discovered Alpine Woodsia growing at a site on the Trotternish ridge on Skye in 2001. It is important that new discoveries of this sort are reported.

In the British Isles, we are extraordinarily lucky in having a network of dedicated volunteers who gather plant records across the country under the auspices of the Botanical Society of Britain and Ireland (BSBI). For recording purposes, Britain is divided up geographically on the basis of the old counties and shires, many of which are further divided into smaller sub-units, to produce a network of 112 vice-counties in Britain, plus a further 40 for Ireland. Each of these has an assigned vice-county recorder who collates records for that area and ensures that they are properly entered into a growing number of electronic databases and published atlases.

At the time of writing, these recorders are hard at work on surveys for *Atlas 2020*, a detailed new atlas on the distribution of the British flora, due for publication in 2019. They invariably welcome new records from their vice-county and may be happy to answer specific questions on the local flora, but they are busy people and cannot always afford the time to deal with general enquiries. Their contact details can be found on the BSBI website (bsbi.org.uk).

Many recorders have established county web pages, linked via that BSBI website, and these often include inventories of the vice-county flora and rare plant registers. You can refer to these to check whether your record is of particular interest before you submit it – but it is always better to submit a record than not. You should include at least a six-figure Ordnance Survey grid reference, together with a description of the habitat in which you found the plant; a photograph will help confirm its identification. If you are a confident botanist, full plant lists for specific sites will always be appreciated. If you are unsure about the identity of a plant, I would recommend uploading a photo of it to the wonderful 'crowd-sourced' resource of www.ispotnature.org, where knowledgeable volunteers will be happy to help identify it for you.

readers to feed their findings into the botanical recording system (see box above). Any of us can overlook the local significance of records when we visit new areas (witness, for example, my story about Hair Sedge on Papa Westray in Chapter 8). The botanical societies, the charity Plantlife and local natural history clubs provide opportunities for people to get to know our flora and contribute to genuinely valuable recording schemes. So do county ranger services, the Field Studies Council and a growing number of commercial outdoor centres.

Undetected treasures

The early 1950s, when John Raven and Max Walters wrote their *Mountain Flowers*, was a heady time for mountain botanists. In the previous few years, Iceland Purslane, Diapensia and Norwegian Mugwort had all been added to the British flora, and Purple Coltsfoot had been refound after a gap of 138 years. The potential seemed limitless. In 1953 that stimulated Nicholas Polunin, a distinguished botanist and environmentalist who had studied widely in the Arctic,

Wood Cranesbill: finding new sites for relatively common montane species is just as valuable as searching for great rarities.

to write an intriguingly speculative paper entitled 'Arctic plants not yet found in Britain' (Polunin, 1953). He described how these four recent discoveries made him wonder how many more arctic-alpines, previously unsuspected as members of the native British flora, might still remain to be found on remote Scottish mountains and isles. He listed 50 species whose continental, and especially Scandinavian, ranges suggested that they might occur in the British Isles.

As it happens, no significant new montane species have been added to the list in the intervening 60-plus years, but the challenge still remains. I remember spending several hours crawling over a montane bog in the Breadalbane hills searching for an inconspicuous little Scandinavian sedge called *Carex parallela* which someone thought they had found there. We were unsuccessful, the species is still unrecorded in Britain (although it might yet await discovery), but that did not spoil the pleasure of a day spent searching in the company of great botanical friends.

In the introduction to *Mountain Flowers*, John Raven wrote: 'Vast tracts of country, notably in the Western Highlands of Scotland, still await a thorough botanical exploration, and such an exploration can and should be undertaken by the amateur as well as the professional.' That is still true six decades on. My main motivation in writing this book is to encourage more plant explorers to venture into far-flung hills to record our mountain flora. I am sure there are still new finds to be made in the British mountains. The chance discovery in 2007 of a second site for Diapensia that I described in Chapter 15 is sure proof of that.

At the end of a visit, it is satisfying to look back at slopes that have now become familiar. Sonia Hackett, to whose memory this book is dedicated, after a wonderful day's botanising in Caenlochan Glen, Angus in July 1981.

Whether searching for new records or simply renewing acquaintance with 'familiar friends' amongst our mountain flora, there are few pastimes more enjoyable, more rewarding or more healthy than exploring Britain's mountains in the company of like-minded friends to enjoy their spectacular scenery and investigate their intriguing flora. The name of John Raven has cropped up regularly through this book, as an inspiration to my exploration of the hills. I began with words from him, so it seems fitting to end with more of his words, from Raven & Raven (2012), which beautifully encapsulate the delights of mountain botany:

> *Whatever its disadvantages, plant-hunting is not a sedentary occupation; indeed in that fact lies one of its main attractions. Rare plants grow usually in remote and lovely places, and a botanically planned holiday will take you often to places that, for other reasons, you will be grateful to have visited ... Teesdale or Ingleborough, Ben Lawers or Glen Clova – who could complain at the necessity of exploring any of these places?*

References and further reading

Balme, O E 1954 Biological flora of the British Isles: *Viola lutea*. *Journal of Ecology* **42**: 234–240

Beerling, D J 1998 Biological flora of the British Isles: *Salix herbacea*. *Journal of Ecology* **86**: 872–895

Bell, J, & Tallis, J 1973 Biological flora of the British Isles: *Empetrum nigrum*. *Journal of Ecology* **61**: 289–305

Blakelock, R A 1953 *Artemisia norvegica* in Scotland. *Kew Bulletin* **8**: 173–184

BMC 2010 *The Death of the Snowdon Lily?* British Mountaineering Council. https://www.thebmc.co.uk/the-death-of-the-snowdon-lily

Bradshaw, M E 2012 The Upper Teesdale assemblage of rare plants in decline. *British Wildlife* **23**: 392–401

Braithwaite, M E 2013 *A Botanical Tour of Berwickshire*. BSBI. http://bsbi.org.uk/A_botanical_tour_of_Berwickshire_2013.pdf

Brookes, B S 1981 The discovery, extermination, translocation and eventual survival of *Schoenus ferrugineus* in Britain. In *The Biological Aspects of Rare Plant Conservation* (ed. H Synge). Wiley, Chichester

Brown, I M, & Clapperton, C M 2002 The physical geography. In *The Ecology, Land Use and Conservation of the Cairngorms* (ed. C Gimingham). Packard Publishing, Chichester

Brysting, A 2008 The arctic mouse-ear in Scotland – and why it is not arctic. *Plant Ecology & Diversity* **1**: 321–327

Butterfield, I 1986 *The High Mountains of Britain and Ireland*. Diadem Books, London

Byfield, A 1991 Classic British wildlife sites: the Lizard Peninsula. *British Wildlife* **3**: 92–105

Clapham, A R (ed.) 1978 *Upper Teesdale: the Area and its Natural History*. Collins, London

Clapham, A R, Tutin T G, & Warburg, E F 1962 *Flora of the British Isles* (2nd edition). Cambridge University Press, Cambridge

Coker, P D 1966 Biological flora of the British Isles: *Sibbaldia procumbens*. *Journal of Ecology* **54**: 823–831

Condry, W 1981 *The Natural History of Wales*. New Naturalist 66. Collins, London

Conolly, A P, & Dahl, E 1970 Maximum summer temperatures in relation to the modern and Quaternary distributions of certain arctic-montane species in the British Isles. In *Studies in the Vegetational History of the British Isles* (ed. D A Walker & R G West). Cambridge University Press, Cambridge

Cope, T, & Gray, A 2009 *Grasses of the British Isles*. BSBI Handbook 13. BSBI, London

Crawley, M J 2013 *Plants of East Sutherland*. BSBI. http://bsbi.org.uk/vc107_flora_2013.pdf

Day, R T, & Scott, P J 1981 Autecological aspects of *Diapensia lapponica* in Newfoundland. *Rhodora* **83**: 101–109

De Groot, W J, Thomas, P A, & Wein, R W Biological flora of the British Isles: *Betula nana* and *B. glandulosa*. *Journal of Ecology* **85**: 241–264

Dixon, J M 1982 Biological flora of the British Isles: *Sesleria albicans*. *Journal of Ecology* **70**: 667–684

Drummond, P 1991 *Scottish Hill and Mountain Names*. Scottish Mountaineering Trust, Nairn

Elkington, T T 1963 Biological flora of the British Isles: *Gentiana verna*. *Journal of Ecology* **51**: 755–767

Elkington, T T 1964 Biological flora of the British Isles: *Myosotis alpestris*. *Journal of Ecology* **52**: 709–722

Elkington, T T, & Woodell, S R J 1963 Biological flora of the British Isles: *Potentilla fruticosa*. *Journal of Ecology* **51**: 769–781

Gilbert, O L 1970 Biological flora of the British Isles: *Dryopteris villarii*. *Journal of Ecology* **58**: 301–313

Gill, E 2007 Conservation genetics of the species complex *Cochlearia officinalis* in Britain. Unpublished PhD thesis, University of Edinburgh

Godwin, H 1975 *History of the British Flora* (2nd edition). Cambridge University Press, Cambridge

Halliday, G 1997 *A Flora of Cumbria*. University of Lancaster, Lancaster

Harley, R M 1956 *Rubus arcticus* in Britain. *Watsonia* **3**: 237–238

Holden, J, & Adamson, J K 2002 The Moor House long-term upland temperature record. *Weather* **57**: 119–127

IPCC 2013 Summary for policymakers. In *Climate Change 2013: the Physical Science Basis*. Contribution of Working Group I to the Fifth Assessment Report of the Intergovernmental Panel on Climate Change. Cambridge University Press, Cambridge

Jacquemart, A 1998 Biological flora of the British Isles: *Andromeda polifolia*. *Journal of Ecology* **86**: 527–541

Jenkins, G, Murphy, J, Sexton, D *et al.* 2010 *UK Climate Projections: Briefing* Report. Downloaded from http://ukclimateprojections.defra.gov.uk

Jepson, P 2004 Skye's the limit – an *Arabis* saga. *BSBI News* **97**: 31–33

Jones, B, & Radford, G 2014 Cwm Idwal. In Field Meeting Report: North West Wales, June 2013. *BSBI Yearbook* **2014**: 64–65

Kay, P, & Deacon, T 2010 UK: Is it getting too warm for the Tufted Saxifrage? http://www.plant-talk.org/uk-tufted-saxifrage-snowdonia-wales.htm

Lunn, A 2004 *Northumberland*. New Naturalist 95. Collins, London

Lusby, P, & Wright, J 1996 *Scottish Wild Plants: Their History, Ecology and Conservation*. Royal Botanic Garden, Edinburgh

Mardon, D K 1990 Conservation of montane willow scrub in Scotland. *Transactions of the Botanical Society of Edinburgh* **45**: 427–436

Marren, P 1999 *Britain's Rare Flowers*. T & A D Poyser, London

Marriot, R 2014 Monitoring planted montane willows at Coire Sharroch, Coire Fee NNR. *Scrubbers' Bulletin* **10**. Montane Scrub Action Group

Matthews, J R 1937 Geographical relationships of the British flora. *Journal of Ecology* **25**: 1–90

McCallum-Webster, M 1978 *Flora of Moray, Nairn & East Inverness*. Aberdeen University Press, Aberdeen

McClintock D, & Fitter, R 1956 *Collins Pocket Guide to Wild Flowers*. Collins, London.

McCosh, D J 2012 *Plants of Peeblesshire*. http://bsbi.org.uk/plants_of_peeblesshire.pdf

McHaffie, H 2005 Biological flora of the British Isles: *Athyrium distentifolium*. *Journal of Ecology* **93**: 839–851

McHaffie, H 2010 News from the rock face in Corrie Fee. *Pteridologist*, **5**: 180–181

McKirdy, A, Gordon J, & Crofts, R 2007 *Land of Mountain and Flood: the Geology and Landforms of Scotland*. Birlinn, Edinburgh

Moore, D M 1975 The alpine flora of Tierra del Fuego. *Anales del Instituto Botánico Cavanilles* **32**: 419–440

Mørkved, B, & Nilssen, A 1993 *Way North: Plant Life*. Tromsø Museum, Tromsø

Murray, C W, & Birks, H J B 2005 *The Botanist in Skye and Adjacent Islands*. Privately published

Nagy, L 2013 Biological flora of the British Isles: *Silene suecica*. *Journal of Ecology* **101**: 532–544

Nagy, L, Sydes, C, McKinnell, J, & Amphlett, A 2006 Vascular plants. In *The Nature of the Cairngorms: Diversity in a Changing Environment* (ed. P Shaw & D B A Thompson). TSO, Edinburgh

Nelson, E C 1977 The discovery in 1810 and subsequent history of *Phyllodoce caerulea* in Scotland. *Western Naturalist* **6**: 45–72

North, F J, Campbell, B, & Scott, R 1949 *Snowdonia: The National Park of North Wales*. New Naturalist 13. Collins, London

Page, C N 1997 *The Ferns of Britain and Ireland* (2nd edition). Cambridge University Press, Cambridge

Pearman, D A, & Corner, R W M 2004 *Altitudinal Limits of British and Irish Vascular Plants*. BSBI, London

Peterken G 2013 *Meadows*. British Wildlife Collection 2. British Wildlife Publishing, Oxford

Pigott, C D 1958 Biological flora of the British Isles: *Polemonium caeruleum*. *Journal of Ecology* **46**: 507–525

Polunin, N 1953 Arctic plants not yet found in Britain. *Watsonia* **3**: 34–35

Preston, C D 2007 Which vascular plants are found at the northern or southern edges of their European range in the British Isles? *Watsonia* **26**: 253–269

Preston, C D, Pearman, D A, & Dines T D 2002 *New Atlas of the British & Irish Flora*. Oxford University Press, Oxford

Ratcliffe, D A (ed.) 1977 *A Nature Conservation Review*. Cambridge University Press, Cambridge

Ratcliffe, D A 2002 *Lakeland*. New Naturalist 92. Collins, London

Raven, C, & Raven, J 2012 *Wild Flowers: a Sketchbook* (ed. H J Noltie). Royal Botanic Garden, Edinburgh

Raven, J 1952a *Roegneria doniana* in Britain. *Watsonia* **2**: 180–185

Raven, J 1952b *Koenigia islandica* in Scotland. *Watsonia* **2**: 188–190

Raven, J, & Walters M 1956 *Mountain Flowers*. New Naturalist 33. Collins, London

Reid, E M 1949 The Late-Glacial flora of the Lea Valley. *New Phytologist* **48**: 245–252

Rhind, P, & Jones, B 2003 The vegetational history of Snowdonia since the Late Glacial period. *Field Studies* **10**: 539–552

Ribbons, B W 1952 *Homogyne alpina* in Scotland. *Watsonia* **2**: 237–238

Rich, T C G 2003 Flowering plants – England. *British Wildlife* **14**: 290

Rich, T C G, & Dalby, D H 1996 The status and distribution of Mountain Scurvy-grass *Cochlearia micacea* in Scotland. *Botanical Journal of Scotland* **48**: 187–198

Rich, T C G, & Jermy A C 1998 *Plant Crib 1998*. BSBI, London

Ritchie, J 1956 Biological flora of the British Isles: *Vaccinium vitis-idaea*. *Journal of Ecology* **43**: 701–708

Roberts, J 2013 Identification of Teesdale Violet. *BSBI News* **122**: 29–32

Roberts, J 2014 *Carex vaginata* (Sheathed Sedge) in dry limestone pavement in Westmorland. *BSBI News* **126**: 5–7

Robinson, L 2012 Observation on the decline of *Saxifraga hirculus* in the north Pennines. *BSBI News* **121**: 53–56

Rodwell, J S (ed.) 1991–2000 *British Plant Communities*, vols 1–5. Cambridge University Press, Cambridge

Sabbagh, K 1999 *A Rum Affair*. Allen Lane / Penguin, London

Scott, M 2000 *Montane Scrub*. Natural Heritage Management series. Scottish Natural Heritage, Battleby

Scott, M 2009 Climate change and the high Cairngorms: reality and hyperbole. *British Wildlife* **20**: 389–397

Scott, M 2011 *Managing Scotland's Pinewoods for their Wild Flowers*. Plantlife Scotland, Stirling

Scott, M 2014 Reserve focus: Knockan Crag NNR. *British Wildlife* **26**: 11–17

Scott, W, Harvey, P, Riggington, R, & Fisher, M 2002 *Rare Plants of Shetland*. Shetland Amenity Trust, Lerwick

Sell, P, & Murrell, G 1996–2014 *Flora of Great Britain and Ireland*, vol 2 (2014), vol 3 (2009), vol 4 (2006), vol 5 (1996). Cambridge University Press, Cambridge

Semple, T 2014 *Ben Nevis North Face Survey: Project Report, Phase 1, 2014*. Nevis Landscape Partnership, Fort William

Stace, C 2010 *New Flora of the British Isles* (3rd edition). Cambridge University Press, Cambridge

Stewart, A, Pearman, D A, & Preston, C D 1994 *Scarce Plants in Britain*. JNCC, Peterborough

Streeter, D, Hart-Davies, C, Hardwick, A, Cole, F, & Harper, L 2009 *Collins Flower Guide*. HarperCollins, London

Stroh, P A, Leach, S J, August, T A *et al* 2014 *A Vascular Plant Red List for England*. BSBI, Bristol

Taylor, K, & Rumsey, F J 2003 Biological flora of the British Isles: *Bartsia alpina*. *Journal of Ecology* **91**: 908–921

Turner, J, Hewetson, V P, Hibbert, F A, Lowry, K H, & Chambers, C 1973 The history of the vegetation and flora of Widdybank Fell and the Cow Green Reservoir basin, Upper Teesdale. *Philosophical Transactons of the Royal Society of London, Series B* **265**: 327–408

Valtueña, F J, Dillenberger, M S, Kadereit, J W, Moore, A J, & Preston, C D 2015 What is the origin of the Scottish populations of the European endemic *Cherleria sedoides*? *New Journal of Botany* **5**: 13–25

Webb, J A, & Moore, P D 1982 The Late Devensian vegetational history of the Whitlow Mosses, Southeast Scotland. *New Phytologist* **91**: 341–398

Welch, D 2006 Performance of *Saxifraga hirculus* in north-east Scotland as measured by counts of inflorescences. *Botanical Journal of Scotland* **58**: 59–70

Wheeler, B D, Brookes, B S, & Smith, R A H 1983 An ecological study of *Schoenus ferrugineus* in Scotland. *Watsonia* **14**: 249–256

White, F B W 1898 *The Flora of Perthshire*. Perthshire Society of Natural Science, Perth

Wigginton, M J (ed.) 1999 *British Red Data Books 1: Vascular Plants* (3rd edition). Joint Nature Conservation Committee, Peterborough

Wilson, G B, Whittington, W J, & Humphries, R N 1995a Biological flora of the British Isles: *Potentilla rupestris*. *Journal of Ecology* **83**: 335–343

Wilson, G B, Wright J, Lusby P, Whittington W J, & Humphries R N 1995b Biological flora of the British Isles: *Lychnis viscaria*. *Journal of Ecology* **83**: 1039–1051

Scientific names of lowland plant species

The list below shows the scientific names from Stace (2010) for the more typically lowland species mentioned in the text. However many of these are also components of mountain vegetation, and the list quotes the highest altitude at which each vascular plant species has been recorded in Britain, according to the BSBI altitudinal database (Pearman & Corner, 2004, with updates from the BSBI website). The scientific names of montane species are shown in the table on pages 30–35.

MOSSES

Bog-moss *Sphagnum* species
Woolly Fringe-moss *Racomitrium lanuginosum*

VASCULAR PLANTS

Angular Solomon's-seal *Polygonatum odoratum* (485m)
Ash *Fraxinus excelsior* (840m)
Aspen *Populus tremula* (640m)
Autumn Gentian *Gentianella amarella* (750m)

Baneberry *Actaea spicata* (450m)
Beech Fern *Phegopteris connectilis* (1,120m)
Bell Heather *Erica cinerea* (1,210m)
Bilberry *Vaccinium myrtillus* (1,300m)
Bird's-foot Trefoil *Lotus corniculatus* (915m)
Bladder Sedge *Carex vesicaria* (455m)
Bloody Cranesbill *Geranium sanguineum* (420m)
Bog Asphodel *Narthecium ossifragum* (1,005m)
Bog-myrtle *Myrica gale* (520m)
Bog-sedge *Carex limosa* (830m)
Bottle Sedge *Carex rostrata* (1,040m)
Bracken *Pteridium aquilinum* (585m)
Brittle Bladder-fern *Cystopteris fragilis* (1,192m)
Broad-leaved Cottongrass *Eriophorum latifolium* (715m)
Brown Bent *Agrostis vinealis* (1,100m)
Bugle *Ajuga reptans* (760m)

Coltsfoot *Tussilago farfara* (1,065m)
Common Bent *Agrostis capillaris* (1,233m)
Common Butterwort *Pinguicula vulgaris* (970m)
Common Cottongrass *Eriophorum angustifolium* (1,230m)
Common Cow-wheat *Melampyrum pratense* (960m Ireland)
Common Dog-violet *Viola riviniana* (1,075m)
Common Mouse-ear *Cerastium fontanum* (1,220m)
Common Rock-rose *Helianthemum nummularium* (794m)

Common Sedge *Carex nigra* (1,050m)
Common Sorrel *Rumex acetosa* (1,235m)
Common Valerian *Valeriana officinalis* (805m Ireland)
Common Whitlow-grass *Erophila verna* (845m)
Common Wintergreen *Pyrola minor* (1,130m)
Cranberry *Vaccinium oxycoccus* (760m)
Crested Hair-grass *Koeleria macrantha* (710m)
Cross-leaved Heath *Erica tetralix* (880m)

Dark-leaved Willow *Salix myrsinifolia* (940m)
Dark-red Helleborine *Epipactis atrorubens* (610m)
Deergrass *Trichophorum germanicum* (1,190m)
Devil's-bit Scabious *Succisa pratensis* (970m)
Dioecious Sedge *Carex dioica* (1,066m)
Dog's Mercury *Mercurialis perennis* (1,005m)
Dogwood *Cornus sanguinea* (not stated)
Downy Birch *Betula pubescens* (760m)

Early-purple Orchid *Orchis mascula* (880m)
Elm *Ulmus* species (530m)

Field Maple *Acer campestre* (380m)
Field Wood-rush *Luzula campestris* (1,005m)
Flea Sedge *Carex pulicaris* (915m)
Frog Orchid *Coeloglossum viride* (915m)

Germander Speedwell *Veronica chamaedrys* (820m)
Goldenrod *Solidago virgaurea* (1,140m)
Goldilocks Buttercup *Ranunculus auricomus* (1,090m)
Grass of Parnassus *Parnassia palustris* (1,005m)
Great Wood-rush *Luzula sylvatica* (1,040m Ireland)
Green-ribbed Sedge *Carex binervis* (975m)

Hard Fern *Blechnum spicant* (1,185m)
Harebell *Campanula rotundifolia* (1,209m)
Harestail Cottongrass *Eriophorum vaginatum* (945m)
Hawthorn *Crataegus monogyna* (610m)
Hazel *Corylus avellana* (640m)
Heath Bedstraw *Galium saxatile* (1,220m)
Heath Fragrant-orchid *Gymnadenia borealis* (610m)
Heather (Ling) *Calluna vulgaris* (1,095m)
Herb Paris *Paris quadrifolia* (360m)
Hoary Rock-rose *Helianthemum oelandicum* (540m)
Horseshoe Vetch *Hippocrepis comosa* (600m)

Juniper *Juniperus communis* (975m)

Lady's Bedstraw *Galium verum* (780m)
Lily-of-the-Valley *Convallaria majalis* (470m)

Maidenhair Spleenwort *Asplenium trichomanes* (730m)
Marsh Marigold *Caltha palustris* (1,100m)
Marsh Valerian *Valeriana dioica* (780m)
Marsh (Bog) Violet *Viola palustris* (1,234m)
Marsh Willowherb *Epilobium palustre* (845m)
Mat-grass *Nardus stricta* (1,305m)
Meadow Cranesbill *Geranium pratense* (845m)
Meadowsweet *Filipendula ulmaria* (880m)
Moonwort *Botrychium lunaria* (1,155m)
Moschatel *Adoxa moschatellina* (1,065m)

New Zealand Willowherb *Epilobium brunnescens* (1,100m)

Oak Fern *Gymnocarpium dryopteris* (915m)

Pasque Flower *Pulsatilla vulgaris* (240m)
Petty Whin *Genista anglica* (730m)
Primrose *Primula vulgaris* (845m)
Procumbent Pearlwort *Sagina procumbens* (1,150m)

Ramsons *Allium ursinum* (450m)
Red Campion *Silene dioica* (1,065m)
Red Fescue *Festuca rubra* (1,080m)
Round-leaved Sundew *Drosera rotundifolia* (700m)
Round-leaved Wintergreen *Pyrola rotundifolia* (760m)
Rowan *Sorbus aucuparia* (870m)
Rue-leaved Saxifrage *Saxifraga tridactylites* (595m)

Sainfoin *Onobrychis viciifolia* (375m)
Scots Lovage *Ligusticum scoticum* (not stated)
Scots Pine *Pinus sylvestris* (1,160m)
Scots Primrose (Scottish Primrose) *Primula scotica* (not stated)
Sea Campion *Silene uniflora* (970m)
Sea Plantain *Plantago maritima* (790m)
Selfheal *Prunella vulgaris* (777m)
Sessile Oak *Quercus petraea* (475m)
Sheep's Fescue *Festuca ovina* (1,305m)
Sheep's Sorrel *Rumex acetosella* (1,050m)
Shepherd's-purse *Capsella bursa-pastoris* (780m)
Short-fruited Willowherb *Epilobium obscurum* (845m)
Small-white Orchid *Pseudorchis albida* (550m)
Smooth Lady's-mantle *Alchemilla glabra* (1,210m)
Spiked Speedwell *Veronica spicata* (400m)
Spring Cinquefoil *Potentilla tabernaemontani* (610m)
Spring Squill *Scilla verna* (415m)
Stag's-horn Clubmoss *Lycopodium clavatum* (840m)
Sweet Vernal-grass *Anthoxanthum odoratum* (1,050m)

Tall Bog-sedge *Carex magellanica* (685m)
Thrift *Armeria maritima* (1,290m)
Thyme-leaved Speedwell *Veronica serpyllifolia* (1,160m)
Tormentil *Potentilla erecta* (1,109m)
Twinflower *Linnaea borealis* (730m)

Wall Whitlow-grass *Draba muralis* (490m)
Water-purslane *Lythrum portula* (530m)
Water-starwort *Callitriche* species (890m)
Wavy Hair-grass *Deschampsia flexuosa* (1,305m)
Welsh Poppy *Meconopsis cambrica* (680m)
Wild Angelica *Angelica sylvestris* (855m)
Wild Thyme *Thymus polytrichus* (1,128m)
Wilson's Filmy-fern *Hymenophyllum wilsonii* (790m)
Wood Anemone *Anemone nemorosa* (1,190m)
Wood Sorrel *Oxalis acetosella* (1,160m)
Wood Vetch *Vicia sylvatica* (675m)

Yarrow *Achillea millefolium* (1,210m)
Yellow-rattle *Rhinanthus minor* (1,076m)
Yorkshire Fog *Holcus lanatus* (845m)

Index

Page numbers in *italic* refer to illustrations, and those in **bold** refer to the main profile of each montane plant species.

References are given for the most significant mentions of species and sites within the text. Scientific names are not included in the index, but those for montane species are shown on pages 30–35 and for lowland species on pages 399–401.

Illustration credits

All photographs are © the author, except for those listed below. Bloomsbury Publishing would like to thank those listed below for providing photographs and for permission to reproduce copyright material within this book. While every effort has been made to trace and acknowledge all copyright holders, we would like to apologise for any errors or omissions, and invite readers to inform us so that corrections can be made in any future editions.

1, 2–3 © Laurie Campbell; 6 © David Mardon; 9 © Miles King; 12 bottom by John Raven © Sarah Raven, reproduced with her permission; 20 © Laurie Campbell; 22 bottom © David Mardon; 29 © DBA Thompson; 43 © Tim Rich; 48 © Peter Llewellyn/ukwildflowers.com; 52 US Library of Congress, Prints & Photographs Division, Photochrom Collection, LC-DIG-ppmsc-07589; 66 © Lorne Gill/Scottish Natural Heritage; 69 © Laurie Campbell; 73 © David Mardon; 75 top © Lorne Gill/Scottish Natural Heritage; 76 © Laurie Campbell; 78, 79 © Bob Gibbons; 81 © Keith Bowden; 83 bottom © Laurie Campbell; 85 © Tim Rich; 87 © Simon Harrap; 88 both © Laurie Campbell; 90 © Bob Gibbons; 91 © Jeremy Roberts; 94, 96 © Tim Rich; 97 © Pearl Bucknall/Getty Images; 98 both, 99 © Peter Llewellyn/ukwildflowers.com; 100 © Simon Harrap; 101 © Laurie Campbell; 103 top © David Mardon; 103 bottom © Laurie Campbell; 104 © Lynne O'Hagan; 105 © Laurie Campbell; 106 © Lorne Gill/Scottish Natural Heritage; 107 © David Parker; 108 © Simon Harrap; 110 bottom © Jeremy Roberts; 111 both © David Parker; 113 © David Mardon; 114 © Jeremy Roberts; 116–117 © Travel Ink/Getty Images; 118 © Laurie Campbell; 120 © Heritage Images/Getty Images; 122 top © Kevin Walker/BSBI; 122 bottom © Peter Llewellyn/ukwildflowers.com; 123 © Bob Gibbons; 124 bottom © Peter Llewellyn/ukwildflowers.com; 126 © Bob Gibbons; 127 © Simon Harrap; 128 © Bob Gibbons; 129 bottom © Jeremy Roberts; 133 © Peter Llewellyn/ukwildflowers.com; 134 © Bob Gibbons; 135 both © Kevin Walker/BSBI; 137 © Jeremy Roberts; 138 © Bob Gibbons; 139 © Simon Harrap; 142 © Jeremy Roberts; 146 © Heather McHaffie; 147 © Jeremy Roberts; 148 © Heather McHaffie; 149 © Jeremy Roberts; 150 © Peter Llewellyn/ukwildflowers.com; 152 © Jeremy Roberts; 154 © Tim Waters; 156 © Jeremy Roberts; 157 © Pete Stroh/BSBI; 158 top © Jeremy Roberts; 160 top © Laurie Campbell; 161 bottom © Simon Harrap; 162 © Fred Rumsey; 163 © David Mardon; 164 bottom © Kevin Walker/BSBI; 165, 166, 167 © Jeremy Roberts; 170 © Simon Harrap; 172 © Jeremy Roberts; 173 © Fred Rumsey; 176 © Tim Rich; 178 © Jeremy Roberts; 179 inset © Pete Stroh/BSBI; 182 © Jeremy Roberts; 184 bottom © Lorne Gill; 185 © Laurie Campbell; 186 both © David Mardon; 187 © Laurie Campbell; 189 top © Ian Strachan; 189 bottom © Laurie Campbell; 192 both © Jeremy Roberts; 193, 194 © Laurie Campbell; 197 © Chris

Miles; 198 © David Mardon; 199 © Chris Miles; 204 © John Savory; 206 top © Laurie Campbell; 206 bottom © Simon Harrap; 207 © Fred Rumsey; 212, 213 © Liz Lavery; 214 © Lorne Gill/Scottish Natural Heritage; 216 © John Clarke; 218 © Jeremy Roberts; 219 top © Laurie Campbell; 220 © Simon Harrap; 222, 223 © Laurie Campbell; 224 both © Jeremy Roberts; 225 bottom © Simon Harrap; 229 top © Pete Stroh/BSBI; 229 bottom © Fred Rumsey; 230 © Jeremy Roberts; 232 © John Clarke/Plantlife; 233 courtesy of the University of St Andrews Library (image reference RMA-H-3782); 236 © Lorne Gill/Scottish Natural Heritage; 237 top © Jeremy Roberts; 237 bottom © Simon Harrap; 239 top © Jeremy Roberts; 240 © David Mardon; 241 © Fred Rumsey; 242 © Simon Harrap; 243 © Martin Robinson; 244–245 © John Clarke; 247, 251 © Lorne Gill/Scottish Natural Heritage; 253 © David Mardon; 255 bottom © Jeremy Roberts; 256 © John Clarke; 258 © Laurie Campbell; 263 top left courtesy of the University of St Andrews Library (image reference RMA-H-4971); 263 top right reproduced by permission of William Berry; 263 bottom © Lynne Farrell; 266 © Simon Harrap; 271, 272 © David Mardon; 273, 276 © Simon Harrap; 279 top © Heather McHaffie; 279 bottom © Laurie Campbell; 281 © David Mardon; 282 bottom © Fred Rumsey; 286 © Jeremy Roberts; 287 © Pete Stroh/BSBI; 290 both, 291 © David Mardon; 292 © Fred Rumsey; 293 both © David Mardon; 296 © Tim Rich; 302 © David Mardon; 307 © Ian Strachan; 311 © Jeremy Roberts; 312 top © William Gloyer; 312 bottom © David Mardon; 313 © Tim Rich; 315 © Andy Amphlett; 316 © Peter Gordon; 320 © Laurie Campbell; 322 © P & A Macdonald/ Aerographica/Scottish Natural Heritage; 324, 325 © Ian Strachan; 326 top © Alan Halewood/www.climbwhenyoureready.com; 326 bottom, inset © Ian Strachan; 329 © Lorne Gill/Scottish Natural Heritage; 330 © Ian Strachan; 334 © Imperial War Museum (catalogue no. H 15661); 335 © Angus MacIntyre; 336 © Laurie Campbell; 338, 339 right © Jeremy Roberts; 348 © Clare and Daniel Gordon; 354 © Lorne Gill/Scottish Natural Heritage; 357 by John Raven © Sarah Raven, reproduced with her permission; 359 top © Laurie Campbell; 359 bottom © Peter Llewellyn/ukwildflowers.com; 361 © Clare and Daniel Gordon; 363 © David Patterson/Scottish Natural Heritage; 366 © Laurie Campbell; 369 © John Clarke; 370–371 © Lorne Gill/Scottish Natural Heritage; 376 by John Raven © Sarah Raven, reproduced with her permission; 378 © Kevin Walker/BSBI; 379 © Tim Rich; 380 © Jeremy Roberts; 381 © Tim Rich; 385 © Lorne Gill/ Scottish Natural Heritage; 386 © David Mardon; 388 © Jeremy Roberts; 389 © Scottish Natural Heritage; 393 © Jeremy Roberts; 394 © Laurie Campbell.

Artwork on pages 10, 24, 39, 47, 72 and 346 are by Martin Brown; the diagram on page 47 is adapted from Clapham (1978) with permission from HarperCollins.

The map on page 28 was compiled from BSBI databases by Andy Amphlett and is reproduced courtesy of the Botanical Society of Britain and Ireland.

Artwork on page 61 is adapted from Fig. 1 'The distribution of *Salix herbacea* in the British Isles', in Beerling (1998), ©1998 British Ecological Society, using distribution data from the Botanical Society of Britain and Ireland, with permission from Wiley.

The jackets of *Mountain Flowers* (page 12), *Collins Flower Guide* (page 14) and *Collins Pocket Guide to Wild Flowers* (page 17) are included with kind permission of HarperCollins.

The table on pages 29–35 is partly based on information contained in *A Nature Conservation Review*, edited by Derek Ratcliffe, © NERC © NCC 1977, and is used with permission from the Joint Nature Conservation Committee and Cambridge University Press.